The
Innovative
Organization

The Innovative Organization

Productivity Programs in Action

Edited by
Robert Zager
Michael P. Rosow

Pergamon Press
New York • Oxford • Toronto • Sydney • Frankfurt • Paris

Pergamon Press Offices:

U.S.A.   Pergamon Press Inc., Maxwell House, Fairview Park,
                     Elmsford, New York 10523, U.S.A.

U.K.   Pergamon Press Ltd., Headington Hill Hall,
                     Oxford OX3 OBW, England

CANADA   Pergamon Press Canada Ltd., Suite 104, 150 Consumers Road,
                     Willowdale, Ontario M2J 1P9, Canada

AUSTRALIA   Pergamon Press (Aust.) Pty. Ltd., P.O. Box 544,
                     Potts Point, NSW 2011, Australia

FRANCE   Pergamon Press SARL, 24 rue des Ecoles,
                     75240 Paris, Cedex 05, France

FEDERAL REPUBLIC Pergamon Press GmbH, Hammerweg 6
OF GERMANY   6242 Kronberg/Taunus, Federal Republic of Germany

Library of Congress Cataloging in Publication Data
Main entry under title:

The Innovative organization.

    Includes index.
    Contents: Quality circles at Martin Marietta Corpora-
tion, Denver Aerospace / Michoud Division / Philip C.
Thompson –"Face-to-face" at Pacific Northwest Bell /
Stanley Peterfreund–The Sharonville Story / Robert H.
Guest –[etc.]
    1. Employees' representation in management–United
States–Case studies. 2. Labor-management committees–
United States–Case studies. 3. Industrial productivity
centers–United States–Case studies. I. Zager, Robert.
II. Rosow, Michael.
HD5660.U5I65   1982   658.3'14   82-5349
ISBN 0-08-029547-9 (Hard Cover) ✕   AACR2

Printed in the United States of America

Pergamon Press/Work in America Institute Series

Work in America Institute, Inc., a nonprofit, nonpartisan organization, was founded in 1975 to advance productivity and quality of working life. Through a series of policy studies, education and training programs, an extensive information resource, and a broad range of publications, the Institute has focused on the greater effectiveness of organizations through the improved use of human resources. Because of its close working relationships with unions, business, and government, the Institute is sensitive to the views and perspectives of all parties and is recognized as an objective source of information on issues of common interest.

The Pergamon Press/Work in America Institute Series is designed to explore the role of human resources in improving productivity in the workplace today and to identify the trends that will shape the workplace of the future. It will focus primarily on the issues of:

- *Quality of working life* through work innovations that encourage employee participation in decision making and offer recognition to employees for their contributions.
- *Productivity* through the more effective management of human resources.
- *Interaction between people and technology* to achieve a more satisfactory transition to the workplace of the future.
- *Labor-management cooperation* to solve mutual problems in the workplace, to achieve improved quality of product, and to make organizations work better.
- *National labor-force policy* as it relates to productivity and the quality of working life.

Contents

Preface

The Innovative Organization: Productivity Programs in Action is a product
of the fourth national policy study conducted by Work in America Institute.
The objectives of this study were to sum up what has been learned from the
past decade of experience with work innovations, that is, new ways of employing the creative abilities of employees in all occupations — and to offer
guidance to employers, unions, and others interested in following that path.
Our investigations and those of our distinguished national advisory committee leave us confident that work innovations are here to stay. Indeed, we
believe that a growth phase is now underway.

The Innovative Organization describes a dozen leading corporations and
unions which have grappled with a whole range of policy issues in regard to
work innovations and achieved meaningful answers — successfully, more
often than not. It is a companion to the policy report, *Productivity through
Work Innovations*, which defines and analyzes the policy issues encountered in the process of work innovation and recommends practical ways of
accomplishing results. Both volumes are designed to be read by laypersons
as well as by managers and union leaders.

We wish to express our thanks to the Andrew W. Mellon Foundation and
the J. Howard Pew Freedom Trust for principal support in making the study
possible, and to Phillip Morris, Inc., and Bethlehem Steel for their generous
contributions to this project. Our deep appreciation is also extended to
Robert H. Guest, who served as associate director of the study, and to
Matthew Radom, who recently took a long-deferred retirement from Work
in America Institute, for their invaluable help in organizing this book. We
are also grateful to Beatrice Walfish, editorial director, and Frances Harte,
managing editor, Work in America Institute, for their careful work in bringing this book to completion.

The statements made and views expressed in this book are those of the
contributors and editors and do not necessarily reflect the views of the organizations which have funded this book, the first of the new Pergamon
Press/Work in America Institute Series.

Robert Zager
Michael P. Rosow

Introduction and Overview

Robert Zager

The American workplace is undergoing a sea change. All over the country, in the private and the public sector, in industries of all kinds, in organizations large and small, in union and nonunion settings, employers are encouraging their employees to assume responsibilities formerly considered "managerial." In effect, employers are treating employees as full-fledged members of the organization rather than as "hired hands." Employers, employees, and unions have experienced the results and found them good. This book is designed to help those—both managers and unions—who are contemplating such innovations or who have already introduced them and want to learn from others who have been there before.

The concept of work innovation arises from the concepts of work and management. (Traditionally, it has been the duty of workers to *do* and the duty of managers to *think*.) Particularly since the triumph of Frederick Taylor's school of scientific management some 80 years ago, a huge body of engineering knowledge has grown out of the endeavor to reduce manual and clerical operations to a set of reliable motions by which the worker, the tool or machine, and the materials interact in "the one best way." To allow workers discretion of any kind is to contravene the basic purpose of this system by deflecting them from the established pattern. It is for supervisors and managers to plan, direct, coordinate, modify, measure, and evaluate.

The organization theory taught to managers during this period has held that responsibility for dealing with problems should be delegated to the lowest level of the organization competent to solve them. Rank-and-file workers, however, have not been regarded either as competent or as members of the organization, until Japanese employers proved the contrary.

While Taylor's ideas have dominated industrial practice as part of mass-production technology, a contrary approach has survived in the shadows. A few employers have always been found experimenting with methods of utilizing the ideas, experience, inventiveness, and initiative of ordinary workers. And even before World War II, there were major unions which joined employers in successful programs of this type.

Since a thinking role for workers meant letting them take part in managerial duties, the anti-Taylor approach came to be called "participation." The word was gradually stretched to include so many different degrees of consultation and decision making, and often merely the appearance of consultation, that it lost respectability. (It has also been applied to various types of sharing in ownership, profits, or cost savings.) Thus, "work innovations," a more neutral term, is now replacing "participation."

Thinking roles for workers cover a broad spectrum. At one end is the old-fashioned impersonal suggestion system, in which employees on their own write out ideas and offer them to the employer in the hope of receiving a bonus if savings are generated. At the other extreme is the producer cooperative, in which every employee holds a significant direct stake in ownership, takes a share of responsibility for managing the enterprise, and also does an operative's job.

Most of the intermediate points, which are the subject of this book, are characterized as either consultation or decision making. Management consults employees when it seeks their advice before making a decision about the production process and their part in it. But some employers also give employees the power to decide such questions for themselves, to put their decisions into effect, and to take responsibility for the outcome. What has been said about work innovations for rank-and-file employees applies equally to technical, professional, supervisory, and managerial employees, insofar as they are invited to participate in managing the work unit headed by their immediate supervisor.

During the past decade, work innovations have taken hold on a previously undreamed-of scale. Social and economic forces have converged to bring this about. The work force changed demographically and attitudinally during this period. Due to the post-World War II baby boom, the number of young people entering the work force rose rapidly in the 1960s and 1970s. By the end of the 1980s, there will be 60 million workers in the 25–44 age group, but the number of workers aged 16–24 will decline sharply. Women also entered the work force in unpredicted numbers and now constitute over 40 percent. The proportion of older workers continued to fall. The average level of education rose as workers with high school diplomas, and even college credits, became commonplace.

In addition, the youth counterculture movement of the 1960s, concern for minority rights, interest in the environment, and demands for more satisfying and challenging work—along with higher pay and benefits—made themselves felt. A few unions began to sense that, in addition to the traditional pursuit of economic gains, they must pay attention to emerging demands for more dignity and social equality in the workplace. As these changes gathered force, they invaded the workplace, but neither employers, employees, nor unions were fully prepared to deal with them. Resistance to change resulted in disruption, cynicism, and unproductive behavior—absenteeism, turnover, grievances, insubordination, and slovenly work.

Then, in the late 1960s and early 1970s, employers received the unkindest cut of all. European and Japanese competitors were ousting them from the markets for mass produced goods that had formerly been American preserves: television, automobiles, tires, cameras, calculators. For a while it was easy to attribute the losses to low wage rates in foreign countries and government subsidies. Slowly it became clear that the quality of foreign goods, and the productivity of foreign producers, had outpaced ours. At last came the recognition that the foreign competitors, particularly the Japanese, had achieved these astounding results by adapting American ideas and utilizing the minds and loyalties of their employees and managers (who, of course, are employees too) far more effectively than we did, or even now do.

The cases in this book cover the period from the late 1960s to the present. All of them are drawn from the private sector, because that is where the key experiments have taken place. They represent a wide diversity of approaches, both in old sites and in green fields, union and nonunion, blue collar and white collar. A few have been extensively publicized but not always well understood: the Gaines pet food plant in Topeka (Kansas), Rushton Mining Company, the Harman International mirror plant in Bolivar (Tennessee), the General Motors assembly plant in Tarrytown (New York). Here they are brought up to date and authoritatively interpreted.

The cases are grouped into three sections. "The Worker as Consultant" deals with instances in which employees are asked to identify problems, to offer ideas for solving them, and/or to help in implementing them. The decision to adopt a solution, however, remains with management. Various consultative mechanisms appear: quality circles at Martin Marietta Corporation's Denver Aerospace/Michoud Division, "Face-to-Face" communications at Pacific Northwest Bell, Employe Involvement groups at Ford's Sharonville (Ohio) plant, Scanlon Plan work teams at the Herman Miller Company. At GM's Tarrytown plant, workers were consulted as individuals for several years, but recently management and the union decided to introduce groups.

The second section, "Toward Self-Management," comprises cases in which workers are empowered to make and implement decisions about the work and how it is done. At Citibank, a top-to-bottom reorganization of certain major work areas has resulted in something close to self-management for the individual clerical employee. In the other cases, such as the Gaines pet food plant in Topeka, Rushton Mining Company, and a host of General Motors plants, groups of workers share responsibility for a particular product or service. The terms "semiautonomous work groups" and "self-managing teams" are used, but the range of decision making not only varies a good deal from one group to another but also evolves over time within particular groups.

The final section, "Corporate Strategy," consists of a single case, but what a case! General Motors has done a service to the economy by making public the principal strategies and activities it employs in guiding the most multitudinous and varied program of work innovations in the United States.

We asked the writers of these case histories not to concentrate on the mechanics of consultation or self-management, important as these are, but on the policy issues, the clashes of interests and views that attend the process of work innovation. Firms differ sharply as to how much participation they are willing to start with, and how far they are willing to let the process run, but certain critical issues face them all. These arise first in connection with the decision to *try* innovation, and then in launching and implementing a program, diffusing the program throughout a workplace or across a multilocation company, and ensuring that the innovative impulse evolves and survives.

One point is universal: no matter what degree of worker involvement is contemplated, the employer must be prepared for a change of organizational culture, that is, for a change in the basic assumptions that guide the assignment of tasks and responsibilities. In the most basic sense, if managers go through the motions of asking workers for advice but do not take account of what the workers tell them, it is better not to begin involving them at all. If a self-managing team is intended to manage itself, higher managers cannot second-guess. If workers are to carry greater responsibility, they need more (and different) training, information, and access to expert advice. If supervisors and junior managers are asked to delegate part of their normal duties, questions concerning job security, new job definitions, retraining, lines of promotion, and changes in the performance demands their bosses make of them will inevitably arise. If supervisors and junior managers transfer greater responsibility to their subordinates, they will expect similar behavior from their own bosses.

At every point, the forces of inertia work against innovation. When economic and time pressures intensify, managers are tempted to revert to traditional authoritarian habits. Some will have ideological or personal objections to sharing power with subordinates; they feel exposed when they drop the cloak of authority. Some will lack the talent or intellect needed for broader responsibility. Rivalries between managers will color opinions.

Since most programs are not introduced plant-wide all at once but, rather, expand step by step, there will be problems of choosing where to begin; gaining support for change; expanding fast enough to prevent frictions between units, yet slowly enough not to omit essential steps; coordinating progress; and helping workers and managers to handle their new responsibilities.

Another universal rule is that participation in work innovation must be genuinely *voluntary*. In a green-field site, new employees must know beforehand what they are getting into, and appropriate orientation and training at the time of hiring are essential. When a traditionally managed site decides to innovate, not every worker will want to take part, at least to begin with. A well-designed and well-executed program sells itself from one unit to the next by making work life better for managers and workers alike.

Where there is a union, it is of utmost importance that the union be a full partner in the program from the moment when management considers that it wants to try work innovation. The issues become: establishing trust between union and management; creating joint groups for overseeing and monitoring joint programs; involving the union in all strategic and tactical activities that affect innovation; and ensuring that appropriate roles are played by local, regional, and national officials.

All of the issues are encountered in the case histories, sometimes successfully, sometimes not. Where failures occur, the reasons should be traced with care. Last, but not least, every case in this volume, including the failures, shows that practical benefits were produced for employers and employees alike.

These cases are reviewed below in the order in which they appear in the book.

The Worker as Consultant

Martin Marietta Corporation, Denver Aerospace/Michoud Division. Philip Thompson's chapter on the Denver Aerospace/Michoud Division of Martin Marietta Corporation describes the evolution of a quality circles program from a rather mechanistic "plug-in" to an actual change in plant culture, and the subsequent elaboration of strategies and tactics to effect the change. Though the program has gone well, the reader becomes aware that the cold breath of failure is never far behind.

Michoud, which manufactures the huge external fuel tank for the space shuttle, had 3,300 (mainly salaried) employees in 1979. With management and union approval, the first quality circle was created in May 1979; by October 1981 there were 45 circles, with 450 participants. Plans call for 90 circles by October 1982, and an eventual total of 250, with 60 percent of the employees participating. Reasons for introducing circles were the common ones: low morale, excessive overtime work, high absenteeism and turnover, and the need to meet tight quality standards.

Thompson outlines the steps that go into making a system of quality circles work and keep working. The steps are of two kinds: (1) education and learning, that is, persuading managers and workers that quality, not volume, takes the first priority; and (2) political, that is, putting employees into "a limited, controlled lobbying process" that inevitably diminishes the power of middle managers.

Some nonstandard forms of circles have evolved at Michoud, for example, the "task force," consisting of volunteers from several different departments with a shared interest in a particular work process; the "joint circle," a system of telephone contacts between members of *supplier* organizations and members of Michoud who assemble their parts; and "integrated circles," in which volunteers from Michoud, the federal government, and NASA work on shared problems. Not far down the road, says Thompson, the quality circles will pave the way for self-managing work teams and new forms of incentives.

Pacific Northwest Bell. Pacific Northwest Bell's "Face-to-Face" communications program was launched as a management initiative in 1977, before AT&T and the Communications Workers of America (CWA) entered their national QWL agreement. Departments comprising some 10,000 employees — about half the hourly, craft, and clerical work force — are now involved. A local union–management QWL steering committee, set up in late 1981, has decided that Face-to-Face can coexist with future joint projects.

The program provides a mechanism for employees to identify problems affecting their work and to take part in solving them. All involvement is voluntary, for managers and workers alike. In each participating department a multilevel committee interviews a large sample of employees, submits a questionnaire to the rest, and feeds the results back to all. This leads to the election of small groups that plan and schedule remedial action, all on company time. Management gives continuing feedback and evaluation. Progress is reviewed monthly, and the process is repeated each year with some rotation of group members. At the end of the year, each department decides whether to continue or not. Thus far, only one department has dropped out.

Each department and unit is encouraged to develop its own approach. One of them, for example, spontaneously developed a joint union–management team.

As in most successful cases that begin with volunteer pilot projects, the early groups attracted the interest of adjacent units, and the chief problem has become how to limit expansion to a safely manageable pace.

Results, according to Stanley Peterfreund, include substantially improved quality, moderately improved productivity, and a growing sense among managers and workers that the organization is working more effectively. Costs of the program are relatively small.

Ford Motor Company, Sharonville, Ohio. Late in adopting the QWL approach, Ford Motor Company has been working at forced draft to make up for lost time. Gentle but unremitting pressure from United Automobile Workers (UAW) Vice-President Donald Ephlin has helped corporate management move the process forward in the face of tremendous economic obstacles.

At the transmission plant in Sharonville, Ohio, informal QWL activities were started in 1980, with assorted union–management meetings and workshops. In October 1980, a plant-wide joint coordinating committee was set up, which agreed on rules and safeguards and approved the establishment of two Employe Involvement (EI) groups, similar to quality circles. Robert Guest presents a blow-by-blow description of the subsequent program, its difficulties, its anxieties, its growth, and its accomplishments. At the end of 1981, although 450 of the plant's 2,000 hourly workers were on layoff because of the recession, union and management remained firmly committed to continuing the program.

The first two groups had to learn that they were responsible for coming up with answers, not problems. One group helped in the planning and smooth start-up of a changed assembly operation. Salaried people from several departments took the initiative and formed their own group to develop a proposal for introducing word-processing technology. Two more hourly groups were formed in March 1981, after management had at last appointed a program coordinator. In July, a union coordinator was added, and then 20 more groups were formed. Soon a new plant organization structure was adopted, to which the Employe Involvement program was tightly bound.

Many operational improvements have been made, but management deliberately refuses to assign dollar values to them, and the hourly workers have not asked for monetary rewards.

Training for the groups has departed from the norm, not so much in content as in timing. The workers are exposed to brainstorming, group dynamics, and similar techniques, not "up front," but only after they have plunged into problem solving and specific training becomes relevant.

Herman Miller Company. Herman Miller, is, as far as we know, the unique case of a company that outgrew one Scanlon Plan and constructed another to replace it. The first plan was installed by management decision (the company has never had a union) in 1950, when there were 171 employees and sales of $500,000. In 1981, there were 2,634 employees and revenues were $252,740,000.

According to Carl Frost, the need for change became urgent in the mid-1970s, as the price of success. Competition had intensified; the company had gone public; customers demanded better service; production was slipping out of control; more than 50 percent of Miller employees were now in staff or service work, rather than production; and over 60 percent had less than two years' tenure.

Top management turned the problem into an opportunity for coalescing the entire organization around the goal of improved customer service. Between 1977 and 1979, every member of the company was involved in developing and adopting a revised Scanlon Plan. Under the leadership of the executive vice-president, executives and managers wrote a detailed argument describing the need for change, which they reviewed with the entire staff, meeting in small groups. Each meeting ended with a secret ballot. Ninety percent of those attending voted in favor of the creation of an Ad Hoc Committee to work out a new plan. Representatives were elected to the committee, which drew up an "identity" statement, citing the need for more participative management.

Participation was defined as the right and responsibility to *influence* decisions, and not necessarily to make them. Every employee would be a member of a team; each department would be represented on a council to receive ideas for improvement; a corporate screening committee would have representatives from all levels; professional/technical staff would be available for advice to teams; management would be required to answer employee suggestions; and divisional performance results would be measured monthly and publicly, against explicit goals. In another round of secret balloting, 95 percent of the work force voted to adopt the plan. Company figures have shown a marked improvement in performance since that time.

General Motors Corporation, Tarrytown, New York. The General Motors car assembly plant at Tarrytown caught the public's fancy several years ago, as a rough diamond that almost everyone could identify with. If Tarrytown could turn itself from a near-disaster to a model production plant, the feeling went, anyone could do it. No one caught the spirit better than Robert H. Guest, in his *Harvard Business Review* article of July 1979. In chapter 5 he brings his report up to date.

The process of work innovation at Tarrytown actually began in 1971, when the plant manager persuaded the local union to try some joint efforts to reduce the conflicts that threatened the existence of the plant. The parties first involved workers in two major layout changes, with encouraging results. The process was formalized in 1973–74. Thirty-four workers volunteered to be trained in problem solving in a jointly managed program. By 1976, 570 volunteers had received training. In 1977, the training went plantwide, with over 3,300 workers taking part. Operating improvements multiplied, attitudes sweetened, grievances fell sharply, union–management relations entered a new era marked by toughness in collective bargaining but eager cooperation on the job. Progress was rewarded by divisional management's decision to let Tarrytown assemble General Motors' crucial new "K" model, and the changeover itself was jointly managed.

Expansion, however, brought new problems. One thousand workers were hired in 1979, and no one had time to orient them. Supervisors and managers, under severe production pressures, regressed. The union–management policy committee summoned an off-site conference of 66 managers and union officials, who concluded that supervisors needed to be more involved. All 150 supervisors then took part in a conference which put the QWL process back on track.

Early in 1981, the joint policy committee decided to create work groups, whereas previously all involvement had been individual. By the end of the year, four pilot groups had been set up, with the aid of supervisors, and the approach had been fully proved. Tarrytown's 11-year-old QWL program continues to grow and evolve.

Toward Self-Management

Citibank. Roy Walters' chapter tells us that when a survey showed Citibank to be rated low on service to its customers, even though operating costs had risen 15 percent a year for the past 11 years, a new management team with nonbanking experience was brought in to overhaul the "back office." They found all processing of transactions lumped into one big organization — with "a cast of thousands" — that served all customers. No one below the executive vice-president for operations was responsible for complete service to any customer.

The new team established independent product organizations, giving each manager start-to-finish responsibility for the quality and cost of a set of products, plus supporting staff and technology. Units were subdivided into smaller units, each focused on a small group of customers. Individual employees with minicomputer terminals were to be fully responsible for serving particular customers.

The pilot program in the letter of credit department began with a thorough analysis of the work and the workers. Interviews with 100 employees revealed that morale at all levels was low and that managers and supervisors refused to believe their clerical workers capable of performing a complete job of customer service.

Next, management set aside a special room for testing whether transaction processing could be computerized. As a result, the number of steps was cut in half and the number of processing employees reduced by 30 percent, even *before* automation. Each clerical employee was given a complete job and a new kind of work space, with front-office amenities and professional appearance. Employees cross-trained one another, eliminating the need for a large central training staff.

As a consequence of this top-to-bottom restructuring, Walters says, the letter of credit department's revenues rose almost 400 percent between 1971 and 1976, while staff size diminished by 80 percent and expenses were held constant.

General Motors Corporation's Team-Based Plants. Self-managing teams (SMTs) are currently working in about 15 General Motors locations, including Mexico, Europe, and Australia. Plans call for continual extension of this approach. Rich Cherry's chapter relates the origins of the program, from 1972 to 1975.

The first successful experiments were conducted in small, new, Southern, nonunion plants. Since 1979, local unions in new plants in the North have been involved in the design and implementation of SMT systems, although the role of union committeemen and their relation to supervisors are unclear.

The earliest experiment, at a wiring harness plant in Mississippi, stopped short of creating full-fledged teams, but did depart from GM traditions by paying great attention to communications (including employee participation in monthly departmental meetings), careful recruitment and selection of workers, and egalitarian working conditions. The plant's performance encouraged further tests elsewhere.

Shortly afterwards, for the first time in GM, a new plant (a battery plant in Canada) was designed along sociotechnical lines. However, rocky union–management relations prevented the adoption of SMTs.

The pieces came together at last in 1974–75, at a battery plant in Georgia, although not without a hitch. Because the technology of the new plant was not yet fully understood, the design team decided that SMTs would be impractical during the period of start-up. Accordingly, supervisors carried some of the more ticklish responsibilities (hiring new workers, meeting EEO requirements, discipline, assessing individual performance) while workers were building technical proficiency. Eventually, the SMTs took on these deferred duties, along with pay-for-knowledge, and supervisors gradually moved to a more facilitative role.

A Multidivisional Manufacturer. The chapter by Trist and Dwyer contrasts vividly with Rich Cherry's. Here, in a multidivisional manufacturing company, from the mid-1960s to the mid-1970s, local managers, with little help from the corporation, created semiautonomous work groups (or self-managing teams) that flickered and then faded. Some years later, a few thoughtful people at headquarters wondered whether the groups had ended because of economic forces or because of management's own actions. Research discloses that most groups had shown improved performance, that some had performed very well, and that most participating workers had liked them. Moreover, interviews with workers and managers who were involved elicited many valuable suggestions on how and how not to operate such groups. When the findings were presented to top management, one executive decided to put an organized program into motion.

The authors visited seven of the company's locations, found traces of over 60 semiautonomous work groups, and questioned over 600 employees at all levels. Some managers, they found, had started isolated projects. Others had created multiples — 19, in one case. Yet only one group had survived, and that was in a small green-field plant designed for work groups from the beginning.

Semiautonomous work groups, say Trist and Dwyer, provide an environment which many (but not all) workers find appealing. But they need more patient and careful nurturing than purely consultative groups, such as quality circles, and they make greater demands on supervisors and managers.

Harman International, Bolivar, Tennessee. As one reads Barry Macy's chapter on the well-known Harman International–UAW experiment at the company's mirror plant in Bolivar, Tennessee, it becomes clear that workers viewed it as a gain-sharing plan, with gains in the form of time off rather than additional money earned. More importantly, however, Irving Bluestone, the union vice-president, learned from it some lessons that later became part of the QWL program at GM and elsewhere. First, he assured himself that joint union–management QWL activities were feasible. Second, he learned that QWL programs succeed only if local management, unions, and workers enter them *voluntarily.* Voluntariness appears to have been absent from Bolivar, except in the persons of Bluestone and his management counterpart, Sidney Harman.

The two principals first met in April 1972. That summer they agreed to try a joint action research program at one of the Harman plants. An incident at Bolivar made it the chosen location. In October 1972, Bolivar's workers, by a bare majority, agreed to allow a program aimed at increasing worker (and manager) job satisfaction and industrial democracy. Work was to be redesigned by worker–management cooperation, under appropriate safeguards. Since the working conditions, the technology, and the content of most jobs were all rather primitive, it is uncertain how fully people understood what was being offered. Nor did they pay much attention to the feedback of the research team's thorough survey.

In April 1974, three work units began discussing work design. Almost at once they devised and inaugurated a plan for Earned Idle Time (EIT), by which individuals could finish work each day as soon as they had produced an agreed quota. Other units became envious and demanded equity, but Bluestone persuaded the local union not to expand the plan to the entire plant so soon. From that time forward, the pressure for EIT never slackened. Several other forms of job redesign were tried, but none aroused enthusiasm. In April 1975, EIT went plant-wide, with an in-plant educational program for those who had finished their daily quotas.

Efforts by the research team to turn the project back to the plant failed. When Sidney Harman sold the company and joined the Carter Administration in Washington, most of the structures vanished, leaving behind only those that had local support: the EIT program (now converted to a group basis), and a self-managing team in one department. Even so, says Macy, there were some lasting improvements in labor relations, in supervisory performance, in product quality, in housekeeping, and in reduction of absenteeism and grievances.

Rushton Mining Company. The Rushton Mining Company experiment with self-managing work groups is another well-advertised, highly promising project that died on the vine, for reasons not well understood at the time. Paul Goodman's provocative chapter shows not only what went wrong, but, surprisingly, also what went right. Essays into uncharted waters, he points out, are rarely categorical successes or failures.

The program, launched in December 1973, was the first in which an American employer and its union jointly undertook to operate self-managing work groups. The agreed primary goal was to increase safety; secondary goals were increased productivity (i.e., tons mined per day), earnings, job skills, and job satisfaction. In the experimental sections of the mine, says Goodman, safety, earnings, job skills, and job satisfaction *did* improve significantly (tonnage less so, because it was given little attention).

Success in the pilot sections aroused envy and hostility in the others. The union demanded that the program apply to all workers or to none, but the potential acceleration of wage costs ruled this solution out. The union polled its membership and withdrew from joint sponsorship.

The plant manager, determined not to give up the gains already realized, now sought to expand the program unilaterally. The union agreed to neither oppose nor help. However, drains on the research team's time, lack of active union support, and the narrow base of managerial support slowed progress to a halt. A deterioration in national union–management relations also took its toll. By 1979, practically all traces of the experiment had disappeared. Goodman concludes that this fate was not inevitable, and he traces the actions and omissions that brought it about.

Gaines Pet Food, Topeka. Few work innovations have been greeted with as much fanfare as the little Gaines pet food plant at Topeka, Kansas. Conceived in 1968 as a blend of advanced technological and organizational concepts, designed from the ground up and launched in 1970, Topeka shone brilliantly for three or four years. Then rumors of problems and decline began to surface, partly because of the overambitious hopes of its advocates, partly because of the desire of detractors to see it fail. Richard Walton, a member of the original design team, confounds the skeptics by reporting that Topeka is alive and well, its sociotechnical work system functioning substantially as it was supposed to.

Walton assesses the plant's history against the design objectives: (1) high employee commitment; (2) economic performance superior to conventionally designed General Foods plants; (3) ability to institutionalize and correct itself; (4) satisfying jobs for first-line supervisors; (5) promotional opportunities for local managers; (6) endorsement by upper-level management and diffusion to other parts of the company. The first four goals, he says, have been achieved. The other two have been disappointed. Walton offers persuasive reasons for both sets of results.

The plant has registered solid gains. Even before the current recession, applicants lined up to get jobs on the well-paid, self-managing work teams. Productivity, superior from the start, has risen every year but one. (Walton estimates that net benefits to the company have averaged $1 million a year.) And the system has kept going despite the departure of all the founding managers.

The media have blamed corporate headquarters for blocking diffusion of the Topeka model. Walton, looking back in sorrow rather than anger, blames the inexperience of the design group, himself included. They had assumed that the plant's success would sell itself and, therefore, made too little effort to gain the understanding or support of headquarters. He draws the interesting moral, however, that, while corporate support may be necessary for *establishing* a new system, the absence of corporate support (provided it doesn't turn into hostility) does not preclude *survival*.

Corporate Strategy

General Motors Corporation. The chapter by Landen and Carlson shows how effectively a giant corporation can manage the spread of work innovation when top management genuinely believes in it and then takes the lead. General Motors initiated the process of organizational change in 1968 and has stuck with it through thick and thin. Emphases may have altered, and the cast of characters has changed, but the basic impulse is the same.

Until 1972–73, the process was confined to managerial and salaried ranks, and the phrase Organizational Development (OD) prevailed. When the UAW asked to be invited in, a more neutral term was needed, and the GM–UAW National Quality of Work Life Committee came into existence. Three goals were agreed upon: a more satisfactory work life, reduction of absenteeism and turnover, and higher quality products. These goals remain in force.

Because these goals do not include the word "productivity," many people have inferred that the QWL programs at General Motors are not directly concerned with productivity improvement. This is a profound error. In the automotive industry (and in others, too), where product mix and production line speeds are preset, any improvement in product quality translates immediately into higher productivity, by any definition. Even in the crudest sense, productivity does not consist simply of more units coming off the line per worker hour; it consists, rather, of a greater number of *saleable* units per worker hour. Higher quality means a higher proportion of saleable units.

During the OD days, numerous surveys and action research programs

xxiv   Introduction and Overview

took place, aimed at identifying the operational differences between effective and ineffective managers. As the conviction grew that performance and quality of work life went hand in hand, GM's leaders took the decision to institutionalize work innovation throughout the corporation. They adopted a strategy containing these elements: a system-wide change strategy; an organizational culture that encourages and supports work innovation; a variety of mechanisms to interchange experiences from one site to another; decentralization of responsibility; and a flexible reward system that recognizes equity of responsibility, performance, and contribution.

Landen and Carlson relate the application of this strategy in detail to whet the appetite of any company contemplating change: annual national and regional conferences of executives to report and plan activities; massive training programs; pay for knowledge; publicity and promotions for those who successfully manage innovation; local freedom to determine the shape and pace of change, ranging from joint programs to reduce alcoholism, to joint design of sociotechnical systems; networks of involved managers; and joint committees with the UAW at national, regional, and local levels. Each device contributes to the success of a unified program.

I:
The Worker as Consultant

1.
Quality Circles at Martin Marietta Corporation Denver Aerospace/Michoud Division

Philip C. Thompson*

Since their introduction in the late seventies, quality circles have become the most talked about innovation in American organizations. Developed by the Japanese and then legitimized by the dramatic success of Japanese products in world markets, quality circles have been adopted by American companies at an astounding rate. No one knows exactly how many are installing circles, but the number is certainly in the thousands and rising rapidly.

Martin Marietta adopted the quality-circle concept at its Michoud Division in New Orleans, in 1979. Despite a lack of prior knowledge of how to install quality circles, it succeeded. The problems it encountered, solutions it developed, and lessons it learned parallel the experiences of those thousands of companies now installing circles and can serve as a guide for those contemplating circles in the future.

SETTING: MICHOUD

The National Aeronautics and Space Administration (NASA) administers the Michoud Assembly Facility on the intracoastal waterway in eastern New Orleans. The facility houses a number of government agencies and private contractors, but the major occupant is Denver Aerospace/Michoud Division, Martin Marietta Corporation. Martin Marietta is prime contractor for the external tank, one of the three major components of the space shuttle system.[1]

*The author acknowledges the support and assistance, in writing this paper, of Ralph J. Tortorich, Motivation Programs administrator, Martin Marietta Corporation, Denver Aerospace/Michoud Division.

The external tank is the sole product of Martin Marietta's Michoud Division. It is 154.2 feet long, by 27.5 feet in diameter, and weighs approximately 1.66 million pounds when fully loaded with its liquid oxygen and liquid hydrogen fuels. Few of the tank's components are actually produced at Michoud. Rather, subcontractors build and ship parts to Michoud for assembly and testing. The major exception to this generalization is the preparation and application of the thermal protection system (TPS), which insulates the tank's skin from extreme temperatures. Martin Marietta produces and applies both ablators and insulators at Michoud.

The assembly process involves five major processes: welding aluminum panels into subassemblies (ogives, barrels, and domes) and subassemblies into tanks (liquid hydrogen and liquid oxygen tanks); standard aircraft assembly with rivets and fasteners (the intertank connecting the liquid oxygen and liquid hydrogen tanks); final assembly (joining the hydrogen, oxygen, and intertanks, as well as installation of fuel lines, electrical wiring, etc.); application of thermal protection (both small components and the entire tank); and tests of the tank before shipment to the Kennedy Space Center.

In 1979, the employee population numbered 2,345 (628 hourly, 263 nonexempt salaried, and 1,234 salaried). In October 1981, the total population numbered approximately 3,300, with a greater proportion now in the hourly category. To date, Martin Marietta has delivered three flight tanks, with an average production, according to plan, of less than one tank per year. Projected shuttle flights require production to increase to as many as 24 tanks each year, with the employee population as a whole expected to surpass 4,000 by 1984.

ORIGIN AND GROWTH OF THE PROGRAM

During the fall of 1978 various measures, such as rates for lost time and attrition, indicated a decline in morale at Michoud. There were various causes. Driven by production deadlines for delivery of the first external tank for flight (rather than testing), employees in all departments, but especially those in manufacturing, worked extensive overtime, often seven days a week. In addition, the complexity of designing and building an entirely new vehicle, as well as the immense amount of required documentation and inspection, created frustration on the shop floor. (In the department where thermal protection is applied, workers cheered when told that they would receive a three-day suspension as a disciplinary action for poor attendance.) Among salaried employees, requests for transfer back to Denver occurred frequently among engineers and managers, originally from the Denver Division, who had relocated in New Orleans to work on the external tank project.

In November 1978, Michoud management attacked these symptoms on a number of fronts. One of them was to form a motivation office responsible for (1) expanding something called Manned Flight Awareness — a program designed to encourage employees to feel a personal role in the historic significance of the space program; (2) developing an awards program to recognize outstanding performance by employees; (3) revitalizing a moribund suggestion system to provide a means for employees to contribute their ideas for improvements; and (4) publishing a monthly bulletin to recognize publicly recipients of performance and suggestion awards.

Even before installing these programs, the motivation office — including the author — recognized that the employees needed more. Manned Flight Awareness, performance awards, recognition in bulletins, and passive submission of suggestions would provide only occasional uplift. They could not attack the fundamental items usually causing alienation among employees. Only direct action could overcome this alienation. Workers needed a means to solve, by their own actions, the daily problems that hindered the effective accomplishment of their work. They needed something new.

A search of the literature on motivation programs in U.S. industry turned up little until we discovered an article on quality circles by Harry Quong of NASA.[2] A telephone call to Mr. Quong quickly produced a list of companies experimenting with quality circles — Hughes Aircraft, Honeywell, and, surprisingly, Martin Marietta Aerospace in Denver. A member of our staff traveled to these companies to investigate and, when he returned, we proposed the quality-circle concept to Michoud management. The plant manager agreed that we could proceed with a pilot project.[3]

Looking back, it seems clear that the concept appealed to us and our management for three basic reasons. It appeared to be a simple and practical program that we could easily install in our existing organization, and it offered concrete results that we could measure. Perhaps more important, we learned of it from practical men working in organizations like ours and sharing our view of organizational life; *not* from corporate headquarters, university professors, or reformers and dreamers. In other words, the status of the messengers legitimized the message. We got it from our peers. Finally, quality circles came from Japan and, in 1979, as now, American industry had begun to awaken to the tremendous success of Japanese goods in our markets.

By design, we restricted the pilot program and subsequent expansion to a slow and steady pace. We felt that cautious, measured growth, with a constant eye toward evaluating results and learning from experience, was the only possible approach, given the dearth of published information on how to install quality circles. In May 1979, we formed and trained our first circle and followed up with three more in June. By the spring of 1980, these and younger circles had demonstrated sufficient success to warrant approval by management of a permanent quality-circle program. By October 1981, 30 months after the first circle was established, we had 45 active circles, with over 450 members, or approximately 14 percent of all employees. Thus, the number of circles grew at an average of one and a half per month.

The staff has increased in number correspondingly. Initially, an administrator and one employee investigated the quality-circle concept and presented it to management. In April 1979, we hired another person but, until February 1980, both employees spent only part of their time working with quality circles. Not until the fall of 1980, when we hired a third employee, did the quality-circle office become a full-time operation with one coordinator and two full-time facilitators, all working under the motivation program administrator. Then, in December 1980, and early in 1981, we hired three more facilitators and still another in September 1981. By October 1981, our staff included one program coordinator and five full-time facilitators who train circle leaders and members and attend all circle meetings. Although we do not commit ourselves to a specific number of circles by a specific date, we hope to double the number of circles by the end of 1982. Eventually, we expect to have at least 250 active quality circles at Michoud, with approximately 60 percent of all employees participating.

EVOLUTION OF THE CONCEPT

At the beginning, in 1979, we had only the barest information. We knew the basic concept as defined by the three major consultants,[4] the companies we had visited, and the Japanese Union of Scientists and Engineers (JUSE):

> A quality circle is a small group of employees and their supervisor, from the same work area, who voluntarily meet, on a regular basis, to study quality control and productivity improvement techniques, apply these techniques to identify and solve work-related problems, present their solutions to management for approval, and monitor the implementation of these solutions to insure that they work.

Beyond that, however, we had no information whatsoever about how to install quality circles. No published, detailed case studies existed of successful or failed quality-circle programs. We found no documentation of the kinds of problems we might encounter and how we might solve them. Most of all, nowhere could we find a statement of strategy — how to approach our task in the easiest, least costly, and most-likely-to-succeed manner. Lacking all this, our only choice was to form a circle or two and learn as we went along. We hoped to identify and overcome problems as they arose. In short, we could progress only by engaging in tactical advances, with the faith that we were moving in the right direction. We could see trees, one by one, but we could not see the forest or a path through it.

One dominant characteristic of our thinking at the time was to view quality circles as "things." That is, we focused on the formation and training of "groups" of employees, and tended to evaluate the program in terms of their internal dynamics. This was logical, given our tactical approach to installation, but it limited our understanding of what we were actually trying to accomplish.

Not until June 1981, after a year of experience with quality circles, actually solving problems and interacting with the wider organization, did we begin to see the forest — the broader picture. We came to see a quality circle not as a "thing" but as a management "process" in which the entire organization — including people outside the circles — participate, and must participate, for the program to succeed. Our subsequent efforts were aimed at developing systems to support this process.

Since recognizing quality circles as a management process, our vision has expanded further. We recognize a "countryside" beyond the "forest," relevant to the success of the quality-circle process. Specifically, the success of our quality-circle process at Michoud is affected by the kind of infrastructural support it can receive from outside the organization. Corporate-wide conferences for circle facilitators and leaders and local chapters of national associations, such as the International Association of Quality Circles to which members and leaders can belong, all provide support.

GOAL OF QUALITY-CIRCLE INSTALLATION

Although, at the beginning, we could articulate no clear long-term goal other than improving morale, during the process of expanding our vision from trees to forest to countryside, we came to understand our objective. It is, in its simplest statement, to *institutionalize* the quality-circle process within the Michoud organization. We hope that someday the organization will sustain the quality circle process as a standard part of its management practice, without our intervention. In other words, when we have fulfilled our role as a change agent, we hope to have worked ourselves out of a job. Upper-level managers, middle managers, supervisors, and employees will all feel they "own" at least part of the circle process and thus feel motivated to maintain it.

This is ambitious. It requires substantial change in the organization. And our problem, as we now see it, is to institutionalize a quality-circle process without (1) rejection by the vested powers, (2) damage to the present effectiveness of the organization, or (3) production of something we never intended — a new bureaucracy. When we first began forming quality circles, we envisioned a short time span. Today, we expect our efforts to last for at least a decade.

THE MEANING OF QUALITY CIRCLES

Our experience has taught us that the quality-circle process is really two processes. On the one hand, it is an *educational and learning process* in which employees and, in fact, all members of the organization learn to identify, analyze, and solve problems as a group. The organization as a whole learns to look for better ways to do its business. On the other hand, it is a *political process* in which employees participate directly in the decisions to implement these new and better ideas.

Of the two, the education and learning process changes the value structure of the organization from production orientation to quality orientation. It takes time and perseverance. The political process, however, changes the power relations of significant groups in the organization. It involves giving employees control of one hour each week, a room of their own in which to meet, the right to choose the topics they will discuss in that meeting, the information and guidance they need to be successful and, then, most significantly, the right of access to the relevant decision-making arenas of the organization. It involves nothing less than the creation of a limited, controlled, lobbying process where no such process previously existed. With the quality-circle process, employees do not unilaterally decide how they will do a job, but they acquire the right to enter the discussion about it. They are allowed into the political process of the organization on topics about which they have knowledge and interest.

Giving employees the machinery to lobby alters the distribution of power in the organization. Most important, it diminishes the power of middle managers. It breaks their monopoly of control over the flow of information up and down the hierarchy and allows upper management and lower-ranked employees to talk directly. Threatened by this diminution of their control, middle managers often resist quality circles, providing the major source of conflict surrounding the installation of the quality circle process.

MAJOR PROBLEMS

In the course of installing quality circles at Michoud we have encountered dozens of problems, large and small. Most of them are quite obvious — such as determining times for circle meetings that do not conflict with peak production periods — but some are major and should be emphasized.

- Misunderstanding of the concept and process by upper and middle management, creating false expectations
- Resistance by middle managers and supervisors to the concept and process, often verging on outright sabotage
- Empire building by the quality-circle office, substituting the illusion of immediate success for the long-term goal of institutionalizing the quality-circle process
- Poor and "one-shot" training for circle members, supervisor–leaders and managers
- Failure to prepare the organization to provide incentives for participation in quality circles
- Failure to prepare the organization to provide the information and support necessary for members to solve problems
- Failure of the organization to implement circle proposals
- Failure of the organization to measure the impact of quality-circle participation — on defect rates, productivity rates, attrition rates, accident rates, scrap rates, grievance rates, lost time rates, and so on
- Failure to develop and codify a set of process rules prior to forming the first circles
- Moving too fast — forming more circles than the quality-circle office or the organization can deal with adequately

INSTALLING QUALITY CIRCLES

Installing quality circles involves at least eight major steps designed to overcome the difficulties previously listed. We will consider each one in sequence, relating them to our experience at Michoud.

Winning Approval and Commitment from Upper Management and the Union

It is extremely difficult, if not impossible and foolish, to attempt to install quality circles without approval of top management in an organization. The same holds true for the union, if one exists. The quality-circle process affects the entire organization and requires a change in the way in which upper-level managers, middle managers, supervisors, support specialists, and employees deal with one another. In essence, it involves an alteration of the power relations between these various groups. If upper management does not understand this, it cannot deal with the stresses and strains that inevitably arise and will not support the effort when most needed.

At Michoud we were fortunate. Upper management supported the program at every major juncture. At every opportunity, the general manager mentioned the program and praised it. He attended all of the first management presentations by circles and continued to attend any of them when time permitted. He dropped in on circle meetings. And, when on the floor, he stopped to chat with circle members whom he had met in management presentations.

The union, a local of the United Auto Workers (UAW), offered equal support. We presented the proposed quality-circle program to them in spring 1979 and, after determining that the one-hour meeting time was indeed "paid" time, they agreed wholeheartedly with the concept. Over the last two and a half years, a union president, two members of the bargaining committee, and numerous stewards have actively participated in quality circles. When the contract was renegotiated in spring 1981, the union requested detailed information on the impact of quality circles on employee performance. We supplied all the information we had collected, and the local and national officials enthusiastically reendorsed our efforts.

Establishment of a Quality-Circle Office

The installation of a quality-circle process requires the formation of a quality-circle office, or, at the very least, a single, responsible officer. This office coordinates all activities involved in installing a circle process: forming, training, facilitating, evaluating, and policing. To achieve these things, the best location for the office is on staff to the highest office in the organization, above and unidentified with any other function or department. This location gives the office the access and clout necessary to overcome resistance. It also avoids identification with a single department or function, such as quality control or industrial relations.

At Michoud, the motivation office was originally part of the product assurance department. This caused difficulties on several occasions because employees could not distinguish the quality circle from the quality control office; and, for production workers, quality control represented an adversary, not a friend. Fortunately, recognizing the problem, the plant manager shifted the motivation office to his own staff. This gave the office a structural position superior to and unidentified with any of the major departments within the organization. It ceased to be tainted by the image of quality control and gained credible access to the highest authority. Hard-nosed middle managers who resisted the quality-circle effort could not easily dismiss it.

Determining a Strategy

Determining a strategy is probably the most important step in installing a quality-circle process. There are two basic approaches: top-down and bottom-up. Top-down implies that one first alters the style of managers, at both the upper and middle levels, as well as supervisors, before forming circles. Bottom-up suggests that one forms circles at the bottom of the hierarchy first, letting managers and supervisors learn to live with and respond to circles through actual experience, changing their management style on the job.

Though some organizations with enduring quality-circle efforts may have employed these strategies, we would recommend neither of them. A rigorously top-down approach inevitably takes too long. One assumes that upper-level management must, by some mysterious criteria, "be prepared" for quality circles. To do this, one holds discussion sessions and formal meetings and sends the managers to expensive training courses. This takes time — often years — and money and, in the end, leaves them no more prepared than they would have been with a simple set of informational discussions. Managers cannot learn how to behave in the quality-circle process in the classroom. They have to get involved. The bottom-up approach, while it takes less time to implement, invites excessive conflict. One can easily start circles and set them to problem solving. However, if supervision and middle management do not understand the process in order to support and deal with it, they will resist it. They may kill the effort, and often have, in quality-circle efforts around the country.

When we undertook our circle effort at Michoud, we had no clearly defined strategy and, as a result, began unwittingly with a bottom-up approach. We formed circles and trained members with the supervisor present but no involvement whatsoever by middle managers. Within six months we realized our error. Middle managers vigorously resisted the circle efforts. They refused to let their employees attend. They blocked meetings by manipulating manufacturing schedules. They loudly and publicly ridiculed the concept in the presence of their supervisors and their employees. When circles in their shops gave presentations, they resisted, even though logically the proposals benefited them as well as their employees.

In the face of this resistance, we quickly developed a new installation strategy. We call our strategy a "middle-down" strategy because it is aimed at middle management. Ideally, we train middle managers (though we are still in the process of developing a complete middle-manager training program) and involve them in the process of planning a quality-circle promotion in their departments. Then, with their help, we seek out interested supervisors and train them in the quality-circle process, participative leadership, and group problem solving. Once they have completed a ten-hour course, they and a facilitator from the quality-circle office promote the formation of a circle, calling for volunteers from among the supervisor's employees. This strategy, of course, involves middle managers and supervisors directly in the installation process. It gives them a stake in the process, before the circle is actually formed and trained.

Full-Time versus Part-Time Facilitators. An important decision arises when one determines an installation strategy: the choice between full-time facilitators and part-time facilitators. A full-time facilitator works solely for a quality-circle office and has no function other than facilitating (advising) circles, often as many as 15 or 20. In contrast, a part-time facilitator works for another department — planning, manufacturing, quality control — and works as a volunteer only one or two hours each week, advising a single quality circle.

There are advantages and disadvantages with each of these arrangements. Full-time facilitators offer a centralized, controllable program to a quality-circle program administrator. When a problem arises, the administrator learns of it immediately and can react. Moreover, full-time facilitators learn their role more quickly. They work with many circles and can quickly spread insights and ideas from circle to circle. One disadvantage is that full-time facilitators can create the potential for empire building by the program administrator. Furthermore, they prevent the institutionalization of the quality-circle process within the organization. They inhibit ownership among managers, supervisors, and members. Rather than institutionalizing the quality-circle process, full-time facilitators tend to institutionalize their own role.

Part-time facilitators prevent the process of empire building. Because they become instant proponents of quality circles within their own departments, they increase the possibility of rapid institutionalization and spread of ownership within the organization and ease the process of program growth. But, part-time facilitators do not provide the program administrator with centralized control and effective ability to react to problems. Since they are paid and evaluated by other managers, their major loyalty is elsewhere. And since they are volunteers, other priorities may prevent them from fulfilling their duties as facilitators.

We believe that full-time facilitators are essential in a hostile environment and/or during the early stages of a quality-circle effort, while part-time facilitators are effective in a receptive environment and/or during the later stages of a quality-circle effort. The two types are not, however, mutually exclusive; and it appears likely that, in large organizations, mixed programs will be the rule rather than the exception.

At present, the program at Michoud contains only full-time facilitators. When it started, we were aware of no other alternative. In the future, however, part-time facilitators may be utilized because of the large number of circles that we expect to form. Furthermore, the quality-circle office will be decentralized so that the administrator retains the functions of the central office — developing training materials and issuing periodic reports — while certain full-time facilitators operate within the staffs of major functional departments, such as manufacturing and engineering. These facilitators will be specialists, reporting to some degree to the directors of these departments and overseeing the activities of part-time facilitators working with circles in that department.

Parenthetically, Michoud's facilitators are all specialists with training in the social sciences and, with one exception, no prior experience in aerospace. Two have doctorates in social anthropology, one has a doctorate in psychology, and the two others have master's degrees in psychology. While we are not convinced that all facilitators should have graduate degrees in the social sciences, we have found it beneficial to our efforts. Our training allows us to visualize organizational possibilities that people who have "learned by experience" cannot see. Most of us, in addition to our formal training, have acquired practical experience in working with small groups and have a "feel" for how small groups operate. All of us, coming from outside the organization as well as outside of aerospace, are not "programmed" into the hierarchy of the organization. We work comfortably with hourly employees and plant manager alike. In other words, we cross social boundaries with relative ease. Finally, we all have the ability to motivate others to action.

Training

There are at least seven crucial roles in the quality-circle process: manager, support specialist, supervisor–leader, employee–member, program administrator, trainer, and facilitator. Of these, three require specific training programs: manager, supervisor–leader, and employee–member. Of course, if a program includes voluntary, part-time facilitators, they, too, must receive training.

In the program at Michoud, there is a ten-hour member training course, based on materials originally supplied by a consultant. Responding to the need to support supervisors in their role as circle leaders, a ten-hour leader training course was developed in addition to the regular ten-hour member course. We are writing a manager training course, which will also serve for support specialists. Since our facilitators are all full time, we do not have a facilitator training course and send our facilitators to the International Association of Quality Circles (IAQC) facilitator training courses for their initial indoctrination.

As mentioned previously, training comprises one of two major aspects of a quality-circle process. Without good, continuous training, a quality-circle effort will miss the mark and will likely fail. In this light, it is beneficial to regard the education process not as "training" but as "study." The former is passive and one-time, like programming a machine; the latter actively engages employees in the ongoing process. Quality-circle training should be regarded as a permanent study of productivity and quality improvements by circle members.

Preparation of the Organization

As a process, quality circles involve the entire organization and will fail quickly and dramatically unless one takes at least four aspects of the organization into account: incentives, technical information and support, effective and timely implementation of circle proposals, and measurement of results.

Incentives. Employees participate in quality circles primarily because they enjoy it. It gives them an opportunity to voice their opinions about how the job should and could be done better and to put these ideas into effect. Equally important, the management presentation recognizes their worth as contributors to the successful goal of the organization. Supervisors, for once, sit and listen seriously to their ideas.

But a successful quality-circle effort eventually needs more than these intrinsic rewards. At Michoud we recognize each management presentation through articles and photographs in a monthly bulletin. Many organizations also offer awards, such as pens, medallions, plaques, and periodic banquets for circle members.

Even with such recognition programs, quality circles will probably require some form of monetary incentive. Unlike their Japanese counterparts, who may earn as much as 30 percent of their annual income in bonuses tied directly to personal performance as well as to the organization's performance, American employees find no link between improved ideas and more income for themselves. As a result, the motivation to participate in quality circles lasts only as long as the novelty of having one's say and seeing one's ideas put to work. As one employee at Michoud expressed it, "We came up with an idea which will save the company thousands of dollars each year. The vice-president will receive a nice bonus because of the quality-circle program results. But what's in it for us? We get the same pay whether we participate or not."

At Michoud we have tied our circle program directly to the suggestion system. Thus, each circle proposal automatically becomes a suggestion and is eligible for a suggestion award. This resolves some of the incentive problem, but not all of it. The rewards to circles are divided among the members equally, thus diminishing their value considerably. Eventually, we will have to develop a system of rewards to circle members that sustains their active interest, but we should not fall into the obvious trap of paying directly for ideas. We have considered a proposal that would call for the suggestion system to evaluate each successful proposal and make awards substantially larger than those given for individual suggestions. These awards would then be deposited in a profit-sharing account for each individual member of the circle. Of course, this proposal calls for extension of the profit-sharing plan to hourly and nonexempt salaried employees and inevitably involves tighter control over circle membership and more detailed bookkeeping. Whatever the solution, however, it is clear that the quality circle process in the United States, as in Japan, cannot operate without incentives.

Technical Information. To produce solutions and proposals that benefit both themselves and the organization, circles need accurate and timely information. This can present problems. If the organization does not take the stance that circle members should have access to all information relevant to a specific project (with obvious exceptions such as personnel files), then it demonstrates a complete lack of trust. Circles may produce inadequate and inferior solutions that hinder the operation of the organization rather than help it. Members, with justification, will quit the circle. If, however, the organization forces information on circles, it risks stealing their initiative and sense of autonomy. Again, the members will resign and the circles will die. The problem is a delicate one.

At Michoud we sought to solve this problem in two ways. First, we stated a policy that all information relevant to a circle's project would be accessible. There has never been a serious difficulty with this issue. Second, we initially formed circles with support specialists as full-time members. Thus, for example, a welding circle had a weld engineer, a weld inspector, a weld planner, and a weld preplanner as members, as well as the welders and their supervisor. Unfortunately, this solution proved unworkable. The support specialists felt threatened by the idea that mere welders could voice opinions on technical matters and, in response, talked incessantly, defending their professional turf. The hourly employees, on the other hand, were timid, afraid to talk for fear that their lack of technical expertise would embarrass them. In circle after circle, the hourly membership dwindled while the salaried, support specialists talked and talked, accomplishing little except defense of their roles. Eventually, we solved the problem by removing the support specialists from all circles. Now, when a circle needs technical support, it invites a specialist to sit in as a guest member on a temporary basis. This leaves control of the circle clearly in the hands of the lowest ranked members, which is where it should be.

Effective and Timely Implementation of Proposals. It is relatively easy to form and train quality circles and assist them in the development of solutions that management will accept. Unfortunately, the organization can just as easily fail to implement these solutions, even though management has approved them and ordered their implementation. There are many causes for this breakdown in the process. Managers and support specialists, harried by normal production demands, pay little attention to "special" projects. They give them low priority. The projects become simply "lost" in the system, especially in large organizations. Occasionally managers and support specialists who feel that they do not want the project react even more strongly. Unwilling to speak up during the public management presentation, they may actively work to sabotage it afterwards by mobilizing a network of fellow supervisors and managers to ignore the proposal.

At Michoud, we ran into this problem. To solve it, we instituted a tracking system in which each proposal, once accepted, is recorded in a folder containing the proposal, the names of members and leaders, the facilitator's name, and the names of the manager and support specialists who agreed to the proposal. This folder goes directly to the central planning and control office, which monitors the progress of its implementation. If the project bogs down, the planning and control office has the right to bring the folder to a weekly meeting of the plant manager as a "hot item." This right to make it a high-priority issue, taking up the time and energy of the top office of the organization, gives the clout necessary to ensure that projects are implemented effectively. In addition, all circles are trained and encouraged by facilitators to keep track of their projects at all times. They call up the design engineers and ask to see drawings if the proposal requires design of a new tool. They call up the tool fabrication shop and have their friends keep tabs on their tool when it is being built.

Measurements. Most quality-circle efforts measure only one thing—estimated cost savings of projects proposed by quality circles. This is shortsighted. Cost savings are important, but utilizing them as the sole measure of the success of quality circles distorts the intent of the effort. A quality-circle effort attempts to change the entire organization, to make everyone function more effectively. Thus, it is more meaningful to measure the impact of the circle participation in as many dimensions as possible, especially indirect items such as defect rates, productivity rates, attrition rates, absenteeism rates, scrap rates, accident rates, grievance rates, and scales of employee attitudes. Only when you prepare an organization to take these results into account can you accurately assess the importance of a quality-circle effort and realistically measure its worth. More important still, circle members need and want to see measures such as these in order to know that their efforts have an impact. Members should know these results so that they can consciously take pride in their successful improvements or strive to overcome certain deficiencies.

Collecting raw data for tabulating these rates is usually the responsibility of another agency in the organization. At Michoud, we are able to utilize data on unpaid lost time hours, grievances, occupational injuries, safety incidents, and attrition.

Comparison of hourly members before and after joining circles (1980):
45 percent reduction in rate of unpaid lost time hours

58 percent reduction in rate of grievances
57 percent reduction in rate of occupational injuries
68 percent reduction in rate of safety incidents
59 percent reduction in rate of employee-attributable hardware nonconformances

Comparison of hourly nonmembers to hourly circle members (1980–81):
39 percent lower rate of lost time for circle members
33 percent lower rate of grievances for circle members
55 percent lower rate of occupational injuries for circle members
38 percent lower rate of safety incidents for circle members
69 percent lower rate of attitude-related attrition for circle members

We also administer an attitude questionnaire to all new circle members and repeat a similar questionnaire every six months as a gauge of the impact of circle participation on employees' attitudes toward themselves, their work, their supervisors, their managers, and the organization. In addition, Denver Aerospace administers a more extensive attitude questionnaire to all employees annually, and this will eventually provide us with another measure of the impact of circles on the satisfaction that employees feel toward their work.

Preparation of the Rules of the Quality-Circle Process

There are numerous rules and procedures to codify and communicate to all employees prior to forming circles: meeting times, meeting place, selection of problems and restrictions on problems, dealings with other organizations, management presentations, slipping meetings, canceling meetings, altering a project once approved, and disbanding circles. In themselves, they are not major. But, if they are not specified prior to the formation of circles, it is difficult to enforce them later.

At Michoud, quality circles meet one hour each week, paid time, at a time that least conflicts with production demands. Circles meet in special quality-circle meeting rooms away from the work area. Circles select any problems or projects they would like to discuss, provided they do not involve wages, salaries, benefits, vacations, grievances, job classifications, or personalities. Managers cannot dictate on which projects a circle must work, but they may make suggestions. If, in the course of analyzing a problem, a circle has reason to contact a supplier, contractor, or government agency, it must do so with the permission and aid of the quality-circle office. As a rule, regular meetings are not canceled, but rescheduled at a later date. If they must be canceled, however, the supervisor does so with the agreement of the circle members and the facilitator. Circles present their ideas to the lowest management level necessary for a decision on the given topic. Usually, there are preliminary presentations to even lower-level managers and support specialists as the analysis progresses. If they receive a negative decision, they always have the right to carry their request to the highest office in the organization. If a project is approved and, then, for some unforeseen reason, it must be altered, another meeting of the entire circle and relevant managers is called to review the matter. Managers and support specialists cannot unilaterally cancel or alter a proposal once it has been accepted in a management presentation. Unless a blatant violation of rules occurs, only circle members themselves may disband a circle and, even then, the circle simply becomes "inactive." Every shop or office, once it has formed a circle, has the potential of re-forming at any time, and at Michoud we have had a number of circles do just that.

Participation in Growth of the Quality-Circle Infrastructure

It is possible to build a quality-circle process within an organization without reference to similar efforts in other organizations. But it helps tremendously to put circle members, leaders, and facilitators in contact with their counterparts in other organizations. It makes them feel part of a larger, meaningful movement.

At Michoud, we originally did little of this. Though the author has participated as a member of the board of directors of the International Association of Quality Circles (IAQC), none of the circle members or leaders belong to a local chapter of the IAQC or have attended the annual IAQC conference. However, Martin Marietta corporate headquarters has helped to spread the word about quality circles, and there are quality circles at a number of other Martin Marietta facilities. The corporate headquarters plans eventually to promote conferences and develop standard training materials and uniform policies. Other major corporations have moved more rapidly. General Electric, for example, has held four annual conferences of quality-circle facilitators, leaders, and representative members and is producing a uniform set of training materials, both written and on video tape.

Slow, Steady, Documented Growth

Nothing can endanger a quality-circle effort more than too rapid growth. The objective, as stated previously, is to institutionalize the quality circle process — to make it permanent. This involves change in the relative power of key groups in an organization and, consequently, resistance and reaction by many of them. Furthermore, every organization differs. There is no single formula — only general guidelines of the kind just given. In each effort, one must learn by practical experience how the process will work in one's own organization and adapt it to the organization's special needs and traditions.

At Michoud we have made a conscious effort to develop slowly. And we have done so in a methodical manner. For each circle we keep detailed records. After every circle meeting, the facilitator writes a report and files it. Thus, for each circle we have a written record or case study of the circle's progress from its inception. This data base has served as an invaluable source of reference for "learning from our mistakes."

Innovations

While most of the quality circles at Michoud conform to the standard circle structure — a supervisor–leader and volunteers from among his or her employees — it may be useful to promote certain variant structures to meet specific needs. These include the "task force circle," the "joint, intercompany circle," and the "integrated company–customer circle."

Task Force Circle. The task force circle is composed of volunteers from various functional departments who interface in a common work process. The circle focuses on a problem or problems related to that common process. Unlike the classic circle, members do not all work under the same supervisor, and the group usually disbands once it solves the problem. At Michoud, we have formed circles of this type primarily among white-collar administrative workers involved in complex paper-flow processes.

Joint Circle. A single supplier commonly manufactures certain subsections of assemblies. Where this occurs, we promote a circle among workers who fabricate parts and put those workers in telephone contact with circle members who assemble these same parts at Michoud. Thus, when problems arise that relate to fabrication of parts, the Michoud circle can contact its counterparts at the supplier, explain the problem, and request a solution.

Integrated Circle. For major production areas, particularly those which must increase production from less than one tank per year to two tanks per month, we have found it necessary to promote a radically different kind of circle in addition to classic circles. It is composed of representatives — all volunteers — from Martin Marietta, the government auditing agency, and NASA. For example, in the major weld area, it includes two hourly welders, a welding supervisor, the welding general foreman, a welding engineer, a welding inspector, and a welding manager, as well as two representatives from NASA and two from the government auditing agency. The three groups receive regular quality-circle training and proceed to solve major management problems in the weld process that are beyond the scope of smaller, more shop-oriented quality circles and that can only be solved through a cooperative effort between company and customer.

THE IMPACT OF QUALITY CIRCLES

Quality circles are *not* the panacea that many consultants and popularizers have claimed. While they constitute a process of participative management and group problem solving that helps any hierarchical organization operate more effectively to the satisfaction of all — from top management to hourly employee — they will not bring about major technological changes. They will not cause American management suddenly to deal in five-, ten-, and twenty-year plans instead of organizationally destructive three- and six-month profit-and-loss reports. They are a small part of a larger picture.

Despite their limitations, however, we see them contributing to certain major trends in hierarchical organizations. First, they mark the first, highly restricted step towards semiautonomous work groups. Second, decades from now, as these semiautonomous work groups take on more and more responsibility, the need for middle managers will diminish. Correspondingly, the numbers of middle managers will decline. While in some industries this compression of the strata of hierarchical organizations can occur quickly, perhaps by fiat, most will see it occur slowly, over many decades. Quality circles will contribute to this trend. Third, quality circles put power, albeit limited, back in the hands of workers. Middle managers will find themselves supporting, rather than ordering, their employees. Fourth, what holds true for the organization holds true for the union. Employees who learn to participate meaningfully within the organization that pays them will demand similar participation in the organization that represents them. Finally, increased participation in decision making and increased participation in problem solving eventually will force a restructuring of the incentive system of our organizations. Employees who find themselves contributing directly — from designing better tools to better products and services — will demand, and deserve, better rewards.

NOTES

1. The space shuttle system is composed of the external tank, two solid rocket boosters, and the orbiter.

2. Harry Quong, "QC Circle — Evolution or Revolution," in Thirty-first Annual Technical Conference *Transactions*, (Milwaukee: American Society for Quality Control, 1977), pp. 258–61.

3. The program is known as Systems Refinement Teams, but to conform to common usage, the generic term quality circles is used.

4. Wayne Rieker, Jeff Beardsley, and Don Dewar were the three major consultants. Because Michoud was technically part of Denver Aerospace, and Denver had a contract with Wayne Rieker, Michoud paid for and utilized Rieker's training materials.

2.
"Face-to-Face" at Pacific Northwest Bell

Stanley Peterfreund

The "Face-to-Face" process in Pacific Northwest Bell (PNB) is not there because it is unusual. Face-to-Face is unusual because it is still there.

Though the process itself contains some singular features, what is unusual is that in a corporate culture that has spawned and supported program after program, most of which have come and gone quickly through the years, Face-to-Face is now in its fifth year and still growing.

The process, initiated in four districts employing a total of 780 persons in 1977, has now been launched in one form or another in over 35 PNB districts employing over 7,500 people, roughly a third of the company.

- It has survived major organizational changes which have disassembled units using the process and reassembled them into new operating entities, still using it.
- It has survived the constant introduction of new technology and operating systems, some of which have severely affected the definition and content of jobs.
- It has survived the frequent change of management leaders so characteristic of a large company. In some cases, units have already had three or four different managers at their head since launching the process. The company itself has had a new president, two new executive vice-presidents, and two major realignments of departmental leadership since Face-to-Face was begun.
- It has survived a major change in business emphasis, from an operations-oriented to a market-driven operating philosophy.
- It has survived, in some units, geographic and physical relocations of both people and operations.

Indeed, Face-to-Face, rather than being defeated by change, has proved in many cases to be vital as a facilitator of change.

21

WHAT IS THE FACE-TO-FACE PROCESS?

Face-to-Face is a PNB-developed process in which top management is committed to the improvement of communication within a unit, as a means of better accomplishing its organizational mission by enhancing the role and contribution of *all* employees. It is an orderly, coordinated, managed discipline within which:

- Employees define problems, needs, and priorities for improvement (diagnosis)
- Employees at all levels become involved in problem-solving action (planning, implementation)
- Continuing feedback and evaluation enable progress to be measured and effort redirected, as required.

Procedurally Face-to-Face involves a variety of approaches, but most often:

- The concept of the process is introduced and described to *all* management persons in a unit whose leader has expressed interest and volunteered.
- Acceptance and commitment are sought.
- The unit selects a coordinating committee and identifies a coordinator. Unit-wide communications describe the concept and the process to all.
- Some or all employees are interviewed by members of the coordinating committee, to begin the identification of problems, issues, needs, and opportunities for improvement.
- With the aid of in-house staff and/or an outside consultant, a questionnaire is designed to measure the breadth and intensity of concern about the key issues emerging from the interviews. *All* employees are invited to participate in the survey, administered on company premises, during working hours.
- The survey results are tabulated, reported back to the coordinating team, and fed back to all employees, who participate in the setting of problem priorities and begin suggesting solutions.
- Action is initiated by the unit's coordinating committee, as well as by subunit groups which are organized to deal with problems of local concern, and by special problem-solving teams which deal with functional or unit-wide problems.
- Teams usually lay out plans of work containing specific objectives, proposed actions, an assignment of accountability for their accomplishment, and targeted completion dates. Progress is generally reviewed in monthly meetings, which tend to average two-to-three hours each; much of the problem-solving activity (study and implementation

by individuals or small groups) takes place between meetings, but on company time.

- What takes place at the meetings (problems discussed, action launched or completed) is reported back to *all* employees, through workplace meetings of their crews or work groups, as well as through written bulletins.
- Usually at the end of a year and a half, the process is recycled: the questionnaire is readministered (modified to reflect special emphasis on priority areas and/or new issues), progress evaluated, and priorities reassessed.
- Generally, concurrent with the progress report, some or all of the team members are rotated, to bring fresh thinking and to broaden direct involvement.

About the Company

Pacific Northwest Bell is AT&T's operating company serving the states of Washington and Oregon, and a small portion of Idaho, with corporate headquarters in Seattle, Washington. It employs over 24,000 employees organized in functional departments. As in all Bell operating companies, there are three operations "segments": business, residence, and network. In addition, there are many other staff and support departments providing common services to the field. Most hourly clerical and "craft" employees are represented by the Communications Workers of America (CWA), with a smaller number in the Order of Repeatermen and Toll Testboardmen (ORTT). About a third of the company's personnel are in salaried and management positions, not in these bargaining units.

Each department is organized into divisions, districts, and subdistricts, all of which are measured against a wide variety of performance, cost, quality, and other service standards, as well as a host of personnel indexes.

BACKGROUND

PNB's top management became concerned, in 1977, that in a period of accelerating change (in the company's technology, services, structure, operating environment, and market competition), employee attitudes (as measured both in a variety of surveys and in observable behavior on the job) were in a downward trend. Especially alarming were sharp declines in the attitudes of supervisory management.

Led by the then president's commitment to "turn things around," focus was placed on the improvement of communication throughout the organization. This was identified as the essential prerequisite to improving operational effectiveness and employee satisfaction with the quality of jobs and work environment.

Having already in place an array of "award-winning" publications and other formal media, it was concluded that the principal defect in the company's employee communication system must be the quality of face-to-face communication. In response to the need to improve interpersonal communication, the entire top management team committed itself to a series of meetings throughout the company, in which teams of two executives would meet for open discussion with *all* of the company's management people throughout the entire territory (an average of 12 days' commitment per executive). Tactically, it was felt that if supervisors couldn't be "turned around" first, there would be little chance of positively affecting the craft and hourly clerical force.

Furthermore, it was also recognized that "one-shot" meetings, even if held annually and supported by periodic TV messages, would contribute only slightly to altering the company's environment. Only an ongoing process, integrated into the company's operational flow and management style, would have a chance to have enduring impact.

At this point, therefore, it was decided to undertake the development of such a process. Stanley Peterfreund was selected as the consultant, based on his long-time relationship with and knowledge of Bell System operations, and experience in researching and counseling other Bell operating companies on employee communication matters, especially those emphasizing employee involvement.

It was not until 1980 that AT&T and the Bell System unions signed an agreement to work jointly on QWL. Face-to-Face was a management-sponsored process when it was begun in 1977.

Piloting Face-to-Face

As in most such ventures, a pilot unit was chosen to model the process. Top management asked department heads to volunteer and, from those who did, one was chosen. This person, in turn, asked for a volunteer from that organization's division heads. Concurrently, the company's public relations department assigned the responsibility for support and coordination to the division head (fourth level) whose bailiwick included employee communication. An in-house staff consultant (a second level manager with field operating experience) was selected and assigned the coordinator's role, as well as responsibility for coordinating the executive field visits and other related tasks.

Meetings were held with division management, then with *all* in management. The process was explained; support was requested. At the conclusion of each meeting, a "miniquestionnaire" was distributed, asking: "How does the idea sound to you?" "Do you want to participate?" and "If so, what problems or action needs would you give highest priority?" The response was 90 percent positive, albeit with some reservations: "Does management really mean it?" "Will something really happen?"

Coordinating Committees were then organized, one for the division, one for each of the four districts (three were installation and repair districts, responsible for putting telephones and other equipment into homes and offices and then maintaining and repairing them; one was a construction district, responsible for the lines and cables linking telephone company facilities to customer premises. Each committee was organized on a "skip level" basis, that is, second-level managers sat on the division coordinating committee (with the division manager and a coordinator sitting in as ad hoc members), while first-line supervisors comprised the district teams (with the district manager sitting in ex officio, and the second-level manager representing the district on the division team also sitting on the district team). (See fig. 2.1.)

Once organized, the teams began a problem-identification process (with a general announcement about Face-to-Face first going to all employees). Each team member talked with from six to ten craft/hourly/clerical employees to get their ideas about needs and problems. The team then pooled these inputs and structured a workplace-specific questionnaire (with the consultant's help). This was administered to all who wished to fill it out voluntarily (about 85 percent did). Even while the survey was being analyzed, interim action was launched, to take care of a number of "easy-to-resolve" needs identified through the interviews. In less than eight weeks, every management person had an opportunity to become involved, almost 25 percent of the total work force had been interviewed, everyone had a chance to participate in a survey, and some action had already begun.

The completed survey forms were then processed, analyzed, and the results reported back to the Coordinating Committees (by the consultant). Discussion established some tentative priorities for action. Objectives were defined and a plan laid out for feedback to all, of all the results. Findings were reported, in Face-to-Face meetings, for the division overall, for each district separately, and for every subdistrict. This provided a blueprint for action right down to the work-group level. Feedback sessions varied in length from an hour to two days. At this point, face-to-face dialogue was beginning to open. The skeptics, who felt they'd never hear anything, were disarmed, and constructive suggestions for action began to flow.

The Coordinating Committees, after the completion of the feedback meetings, which the team members conducted, then formalized the program for action. Six priorities were set:

1. Improve the service order process (this is the flow of paper which specifies and directs the work).
2. Improve coordination with the control center within their department.

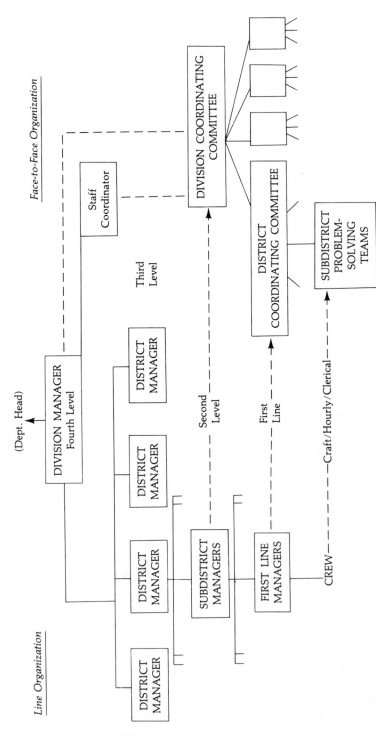

Fig. 2.1. Committee Structure—Pilot Division

Line Organization

Face-to-Face Organization

(Dept. Head)

DIVISION MANAGER
Fourth Level

DISTRICT MANAGER

DISTRICT MANAGER

DISTRICT MANAGER

DISTRICT MANAGER

SUBDISTRICT MANAGERS

FIRST LINE MANAGERS

Staff Coordinator

Third Level

Second Level

First Line

DIVISION COORDINATING COMMITTEE

DISTRICT COORDINATING COMMITTEE

SUBDISTRICT PROBLEM-SOLVING TEAMS

CREW ————Craft/Hourly/Clerical————

3. Improve coordination with the network department, which has the responsibility of having dial tone ready when installations are complete.
4. Improve supply accountability (this department is dependent on another for the supplies loaded onto its trucks and vans).
5. Improve training.
6. Improve communication.

At this time, six months had gone by since the process was first discussed. An average of three-and-a-half hours per employee had been spent in Face-to-Face activities, including the time spent by Coordinating Committee members.

Action went forward against a timetable of assignments, deadlines, and objectives. Employees at every level were involved in a wide variety of study teams, action groups, and other activities.

At the end of the year, the survey was readministered and progress evaluated in a variety of ways. The report concluded: "The process is working. . . ."

- Forty-seven percent said Face-to-Face communication has improved.
- Asked to rate progress toward 15 other goals and objectives, improvement was registered on 13.
- The improvement in managers' views was substantial; the attitudes of hourly and craft workers improved significantly, though not as much.
- Progress was made on all priorities, with considerable improvement especially on five of them.
- And, on measured results:

> Safety, service, and productivity in the Division has continued to improve during 1978, in spite of an extremely heavy work load, many new managers and craft personnel (over 30 percent) . . . a variety of organizational realignments — and a physical move of one garage. . . . The Face-to-Face process has lessened the impact of many division, department and company changes during 1978.

There were no miracles, but there was solid progress. Measured results held their own or improved during difficult times. The "testimony" about the process was enthusiastic. Both managers and crafts indicated clearly that they wanted to keep the process going after the year's piloting was completed.

The Process Spreads

At the end of the first year, the first progress report was made to the president, officers, and department heads. There had been no "fishbowling" of the pilot, no second guesses, no one hounding the division to "tell us what you did yesterday." The willingness of the department head to make himself available on request but not to press for premature accounting contributed greatly to building a sense of ownership in an environment that permitted experimentation.

The data was impressive, but of equal importance was the personal enthusiasm with which the division manager and others communicated their impressions of the process, and their commitment to continue it.

The question, then, was: Should Face-to-Face go company-wide? The position adopted: No! Instead, it was agreed that other department heads who wished to participate could volunteer to do so. And, indeed several did. To handle the expanded load, another person with line experience was added to the employee communication section of the public relations department as a staff specialist, and trained as a coordinator.

The start-up process in other units was basically similar to the "pilot." Recognizing the increased volume of survey work the process was generating, the company also assigned a research person to the Face-to-Face process and began building in-house capabilities to handle the questionnaires.

As the load grew, an additional requirement was imposed: Any unit wishing to launch Face-to-Face was asked to designate a coordinator from within its own organization. In most cases, this was a part-time assignment. In two organizations, a full-time person was dedicated to the process. The headquarters coordinators and the consultant coached and trained the unit coordinators.

The resource people soon had all they could handle. At this point, units which wanted to "start something" and were unwilling to wait, were encouraged to develop their own approaches. Thus, variations of Face-to-Face began appearing: one called "Two-Way Communication," another dubbed "The Poor Man's Face-to-Face," and even one called "The No-Name Process." Later, as publicity about quality circles and other QWL techniques began to appear in the press and journals, various units "piloted" their own versions of employee-involvement processes. For instance, when the company's many "repair bureaus" were centralized into two locations, they were designed and launched with the guidance of a joint union–management QWL committee.

In 1981, the company established a formal QWL organization in the employment and labor relations department, and transferred into it the two Face-to-Face coordinators as well as other personnel specialists, in an effort to coordinate all participative activities within a coherent strategy, and to prepare to make the transition to a full partnership with the unions on *all* QWL activities.

As of early 1982, the strategy was working. As noted, over 50 districts — scattered in all geographic and functional segments of the business — now have one form or another of Face-to-Face underway. Of the 10,000 persons employed in these units, over a thousand by now have had firsthand involvement through participation on a coordinating committee, problem-solving team, task force, or special study group.

In addition, other departments have been stimulated, by example and by objectives set at the top of the company, to develop other approaches. As noted earlier, Face-to-Face has executive endorsement, but is not being driven by directive or edict.

In common, all Face-to-Face units have employed:

- *A defined structure*, coordinating teams, linked as a communicating network, at each level of the organization.
- *A "coordinator,"* either appointed full or part time from within the unit and/or a headquarters staff consultant.
- *Widespread communication prior to launching* Face-to-Face orientation sessions, often supplemented by bulletins and/or letters from the unit's top management.
- *Systematic diagnosis*, using interviews and questionnaires to assess attitudes and define roadblocks and problems.
- *Open and full feedback* of results to *all* employees.
- *Extensive employee involvement* in both the planning and implementation of action.

But the form, the mechanics, the timing, and the flow of the process varies substantially from unit to unit.

As noted, *staff support* in some cases has come from the company's public relations department (employee communication staff consultants) or from the unit's own designated coordinator. The functions performed by these individuals include *communication* (e.g., assistance in preparing bulletins and letters, arranging for the production of TV tapes), *administrative duties* (e.g., arranging for meeting schedules, facilities, notices, invitations to other management or resource persons, arrangements for surveys) and *facilitation* (coaching the teams, counseling, training, and other guidance especially in problem solving).

The *consultant* assisted in designing the process; developing procedures and guiding the pilot activities; giving technical support on survey construction, analysis, and feedback; and, most important, working with the coordinators to transfer these skills and develop the coordinators' ability to operate self-sufficiently. Heavy participation in internal pilots and subsequent "launches" has given way to a less operational role and more emphasis on strategic planning, survey analysis, and process evaluation.

Coordinating committees, initially, were composed exclusively of management persons, generally two levels below the organization head at each level. This fairly rigid definition of structure has since been modified and much more varied team composition is now encouraged. For instance, nearly every unit launching Face-to-Face in the past two years has begun with a "vertical" committee consisting of people at various management levels *and* craft/hourly/clerical people right at the outset. Some use the quality-circle concept for problem-solving teams; while others use committees drawn from a variety of organizational entities to work on unit-wide or interunit problems.

Further, since the units are within *functional* departments, and so many of the priorities for problem solving are interdepartmental, some committees have invited groups or individuals from other departments to join their teams. Where this has happened, or where teams representing different departments within a given geographical area have met together, the benefit has usually been as great in terms of informational exchange and increased understanding of one another's problems — not incidental values — as in terms of substantive action or problem solving.

Union participation has been "natural" rather than formal until just recently. (As noted, the joint agreement signed in 1980 by AT&T and its unions at the national level, contractually calling for full "partnering," is only now being implemented.) Union officials have always been kept informed about Face-to-Face concepts and activities, but they have not been involved in an "official" capacity heretofore. Their participation has been voluntary by their constituents' choice rather than automatic by virtue of their position.

The "diagnostics" procedure — identifying the priorities — is one of the most unusual and important features of the Face-to-Face process. Rather than rely on a standard diagnostic instrument, a customized survey instrument is built by each team. The team members do the interviewing. They analyze the inputs from others (a first step toward building broad involvement in the process). They, with the help of the coordinators and/or consultant or in-house survey specialists, develop a questionnaire covering their own workplace situation with great specificity. (When the survey is administered, it gives a second opportunity for participation to all.) This creates a sense of ownership which generates great interest in the survey results and a high motivation for action. The contrast with the reception given to the typical staff instrument or company survey is marked. The results are *used* — as the basis for feedback (a third wave of total involvement), action planning, and, later, as a basis for measuring trends.

To measure trends, a relatively small number of key indicators appear in every survey. But, left to their own devices, coordinating committees ask some kinds of items frequently — in almost every survey, as a matter of fact. The most commonly asked items, as one looks across the units:

On Communication
- Openness of communication
- How well informed (about both general and very specific matters)
- Communication and management of change

On Job-Related Matters
- How effectively you feel able to perform your job, personally; how well circumstances permit you to perform; and what (specific) road-blocks keep you from performing at the top of your ability.
- Operating effectiveness of your unit
- The quality of customer service
- Control over job conditions and objectives
- (Specific) factors influencing quality of work, including practices, procedures, and work systems
- Interdepartmental problems, communications, and operating relationships

On Management Style
- Supervisory performance and relationships
- Personal treatment (as an individual, as a member of a group)
- Opportunities for involvement; degree of freedom in the job
- Feedback on job performance (including formal appraisals)
- Balance between quality and production emphasis
- The use of measurements and/or other control systems

Other
- Administration of (and needs for) overtime work
- Training
- Safety

But the real pay-off comes from being able to become specific about these items: it is not interdepartmental relations, in general, but what kind of help and cooperation do you in garage X get from the people in central office Y? It is not whether you have needs for tools and equipment, in general, but which ones? Nor is the issue whether roadblocks prevent you from working as well as you could, but what are they? And what are your ideas about getting them fixed?

About the Action

Although individual coordinating committees address their own environment from "scratch," it is useful to observe both the commonality and the differences.

Given "anything" on which to go to work, with the only limiting factor being the suggestion that they not try to change the whole world overnight, invariably the teams will come up with common, broad objectives:

- Open communication (often starting from a "closed" system)
- Remove roadblocks (there are always plenty of them)
- Improve results (the craft employees are as frustrated as management when they feel that the customer — internal or external — isn't being served as well as they feel should be the case, or when they see waste or practices that appear counterproductive)

When the teams set priorities (after securing broad-scale employee input), invariably — if they are identifying a half dozen or so major targets — four or five will be operational, one might be personnel-oriented, and the other two will be *training* and *communication*. Almost intuitively, the employee teams themselves recognize:

> If we are going to be successful at improving the business, substantively, our people must have the skills and training to do the job right. And if we are going to move decision-making processes closer to the workplace — and have reasonable and effective decisions made — we must have both the information and the climate needed to enable our constituency to make good and responsible proposals and decisions.

Significantly, because the Face-to-Face process is structured on a multilevel basis and is linked by overlapping membership (i.e., every lower-level team has at least one representative on the team at the next higher level), it becomes possible to handle specific workplace matters or issues of singular concern, locally, at the appropriate level, without having people sit in meetings where matters of broader concern to the higher-level committees are addressed.

As the process matures, the Face-to-Face teams themselves seem to develop commonsense rules about what they can decide and what they must propose. Initially, the pattern is one of bringing up matters with the expectation that: here's the problem, and here's what we want you (the management side of the table) to do. As time goes along, two things happen: employees realize there's a great deal they can do within their charter — and they start implementing as well as proposing. Later (and this is a sign of process maturation), higher management will come to the teams and say, "Here's a problem that's landed on my desk. Can you give me some help in solving it?"

The following vignettes illustrate the kinds of interaction that may take place between Face-to-Face teams and higher management.

A FACE-TO-FACE TEAM ENGINEERS A RELOCATION

In one very unusual but very clear example of interaction, a district and subdistrict learned at a very late date that they were being dispossessed (physically) from their garage and office building. Presented with the problem, the Face-to-Face team organized a "sweep" of their territory to look for a suitable new building, phoned in leads, actually did locate a new site, and helped plan the mechanics of the move which occurred soon after.

A TYPICAL MEETING

The meeting was being held in a corner room of a central office, reached through a maze of switches and frames. (The scene could be duplicated in a garage lunch room, a basement training room, or in a neatly appointed conference room.)

As the discussions begin, the eight or ten or so people around the room all present reports, discuss action underway, bring in "new issues" which their peers and/or subordinates had asked them to bring up. Conversation is businesslike, lively. The chairperson tries to maintain order. Were it not for the fact that some of the men wear ties and others do not, it would be impossible to tell from the points of view being expressed who are the managers, who are the crafts. The appearance of the women present offers no clues.

As the meeting begins, a safety problem is discussed. A proposal is presented to paint and light up a back-alley door leading to a parking lot; vagrants in the neighborhood seem to congregate there. How to provide adequate coverage of switches in multilocations on a part-time basis is detailed; the team has some firm ideas about procedure. A discussion follows of how to use and keep up-to-date a "functional" directory prepared by a Face-to-Face team, which enables employees to know what desk to call with a particular problem. Another subcommittee reports that a new "ozone" machine is helping clear cigarette smoke from a confined area, but that some are still complaining. Other items come to the table; an assignment is given to one member to contact the central training facility to develop a special course to remedy a need employees had identified in a special survey.

The top manager of the unit drops in, is filled in on the items discussed, and volunteers to intervene with another department that is felt not to be doing its part to process service orders as rapidly as they are needed. While there, he fills in the team on a few pending personnel changes and answers questions about rumors of reorganization. On two items, he doesn't know the answers but promises to investigate before the next meeting, one month later.

At the end of exactly two hours, the chairman adjourns the session, and the committee members, armed with notes, leave to feed back the "minutes" to their respective work teams. Another Face-to-Face Coordinating Team meeting is over.

HIGHER MANAGEMENT REVERSES A DECISION

For years, PNB's outside plant (construction crews) has enjoyed the privilege of starting work early, for instance at 7:00 A.M. and finishing at 3:30 P.M. They've avoided freeway rush-hour traffic, have had ease of parking at their garages, and have been through work early enough to take advantage of the Pacific Northwest's "great outdoors."

A new department head, hearing complaints from other departments that outside plant was not available late in the day to handle emergency work (most departments work 8:00–4:30 or 5:00 P.M. hours), decided to require *all* crews to work hours that conformed to the other departments with whom they interacted. (Management, by contract, can set the day's schedule.)

The complaints were fierce. Grievances showed up on many other issues, one of which resulted in a walkout. Relations were strained.

At this point, three construction districts were in the Face-to-Face process. From their survey and problem-identification work, they concluded that the no. 1 problem was work hours. One of the coordinating teams addressed itself to the issue with informational assistance from the others. They studied the actual need for interaction late in the day and then worked out ways to provide coverage of those hours by rotating the assignment or finding individuals who preferred a later schedule.

Their proposal was developed, documented, and sent up the line to the department head, apparently with enough persuasiveness to cause him to reverse his decision and return work-hour scheduling authority to local management.

The large majority of crews are now back on their former schedules. Work relationships are again more "normal." And the Face-to-Face teams are concentrating again on solving operational work problems.

MEASURES OF SUCCESS

In its four years of growth, the Face-to-Face process has resulted in *substantial attitude improvements, positive impact on operating results* (especially measures of quality), *endorsement* from participants (only one of the districts which launched the process has dropped out), and *many cases of problem resolution*. There's also evidence that the process, per se, has a benefit that transcends the results of any specific problem-solving activity. The longer a person works in a Face-to-Face district, the more positive that person's attitudes seem to be. Not surprisingly, since communication is both the focus and the "enabler" in this process, the follow-up survey results on employee communication, especially, have been consistently on an uptrend and show a cumulative impact. The views of management people seem to improve first, followed soon after by equivalent improvements from the craft, hourly, and clerical people.

Testimony

How do people feel about it? The word of mouth is good. Another kind of compelling testimony: When a unit commits to the process, it is asked to do so for at least a year. Significantly, of those units completing their original "contract" only one thus far has defected. (The district manager felt, after being in the process for three years, that he and his people were operating in a participative manner and no longer needed the formal process of questionnaires and results.) All the rest have continued the process. Local newspaper publicity in 1979 also helped; the president of the largest CWA local was quoted in the public press as endorsing Face-to-Face as a responsive way to involve PNB employees in improving their job circumstances.

Operating Results

Measured results have tended to be, at worst, no lower than before, at best, substantially improved. Though the "indexes" vary from department to department each is measured in some way on quality and production. Where Face-to-Face is in place, quality usually improves substantially, production somewhat. Little effort has been made, since some of the earlier pilots, to deliberately track indexes against process activity. For one thing, it's not possible to compare Face-to-Face units with "control" units. No one in PNB is standing still; any number of other activities and efforts underway are aimed at improving both the quality of work life and operating effectiveness. Too many other internal and external forces are involved to perform a "pure" evaluation of the program. But virtually every Face-to-Face team has *at least* a few activities to which it can point that indicate that the effort has "paid off."

Survey Indicators

To date, follow-up surveys have been conducted in over twenty units. Although items vary from one district or division to another, the pattern of improvement is consistent. Individual questionnaires have contained as few as 21 items, as many as 92. On the average, over half the items measured have shown year-to-year improvement: One district showed gains on 65 of 90 items; no district has failed to improve on fewer than 25 percent of the items it specifically tracked. Looked at in terms of "what got worse," no district lost ground on more than 25 percent of the items asked. One district recorded a significant year-to-year decline on only *one* of 92 items asked.

This becomes all the more significant because, during this same time period, craft and supervisory attitudes, at best, held their own on companywide surveys and, on a number of key issues, declined in the company as a whole. On two Bell system-wide surveys, PNB's results are encouraging. On items which Face-to-Face might be expected to affect positively, PNB is indeed above Bell System average.

Items which improved most frequently in year-to-year follow-up studies in Face-to-Face districts include:

- Emphasis on "proper balance" between quality and production
- Efficiency of one's own work group
- Clearer definition of jobs
- Attitude about adequacy of number of people in own and other support work groups, even though the actual number remained constant or was reduced
- Specific operating problems
- Openness of communication, especially with higher management
- Ratings of immediate supervisor
- Less conflict seen between different departments' objectives
- Better informed on advancement and transfer opportunities
- Employees' treatment by the company
- Helpfulness, fairness of employee performance appraisal
- Information about own work location, future plans

Further, the magnitude of improvement is as impressive as the number of positive changes (see tables 2.1, 2.2, and 2.3).

Another notable trend: the longer employees are in the process, the more improvement they see. The process seems to have a cumulative impact that supersedes the effect of any particular problem-solving efforts (see tables 2.4 and 2.5).

Actions Taken, Problems Solved

Attitudes only reflect perceptions. Here are some of the *substantive* changes and activities employees see underway or accomplished. Some examples of operational actions are listed here:

Table 2.1. Division Improvements

For a whole division, for which a year-to-year change of ±3 percent would be significant, these year-to-year improvements have been recorded:

+45%	"Doing the job right the first time"
+44%	Being able to say what you think to immediate supervisor
+22%	Balance between quality and production
+16%	Praise for job well done
+15%	Information on future plans for work group
+13%	Time spent waiting on telephone (i.e., lost time)
+12%	Openness of communication
+12%	Information about division
+12%	Fewer "chicken" rules
+10%	Management's concern for individuals

Table 2.2. District Improvements

For a district, where ±5-to-6 points would be a significant change, these improvements were recorded:

+32%	Open communication within district
+28%	Balance between quality and production quantity*
+27%	Well informed about district
+27%	Openness with manager one level above my supervisor
+27%	Record keeping is satisfactory
+21%	Performance objectives are realistic
+26%	Satisfaction with career counseling
+19%	Attitudes about Equal Employment Opportunity/Affirmative Action Plan
+19%	Openness with manager two levels above one's own supervisor
+19%	Well informed about support services

*Other districts: +22, +17, +15, +15, +12

- A "functional director" for the downtown Seattle complex (to enable those who have a particular problem to reach the "right" desk, with consequent savings in time and aggravation, and to save the time and tempers of those at such desks from misdirected calls).
- Reduced estimates of "hold" time by 10 minutes, "unnecessary" calls by 7 minutes. (People in the field calling in to "inside" bureaus or offices often are put on hold. Those inside often have to "waste" time on unnecessary calls. These time reductions, in *one* district, add up to the yearly equivalent of five full-time employees.)
- New concepts of "quality rides." (The company uses various means of observing or literally riding with outside personnel, to ensure that they do quality work, and to train and coach on an individual basis. In a garage where this responsibility was given to peers rather than supervisors, the improvement in quality was especially outstanding.)
- Between-shift coverage of garages for supplies; new emergency delivery system of supplies needed at a customer's premises.

Table 2.3. Subdistrict Improvements

In subdistricts, or single offices, improvements of this magnitude are not unusual after as little as a year:

+65%	My supervisor motivates me to sell
+48%	Communication with district manager
+48%	More control of my time to finish work
+43%	Quality of training is satisfactory
+34%	Communication (in general) is getting better
+33%	My office is more efficient

Table 2.4. Improvements for All (Management and Craft People)
in One Division

SCORES*	ALL THOSE IN SURVEYS		
	FIRST TIME	SECOND TIME	THIRD TIME
Communication, overall	40	47	53
Speed with which word gets to us	49	57	61
Information on work done in other groups	52	57	58
Management's interest in views, ideas	53	59	60
Keeping us abreast of organizational changes	54	58	61
Face-to-face communication	55	63	66
Being able to say what you think	65	66	69
Good treatment by the company	60	63	67

*0 = No Improvement At All, 50 = Some Improvement, 100 = Great Improvement

- New system of "lead numbers" on poles. (Telephone poles are numbered so that repair persons can be dispatched to a particular pole to fix a line problem. The new system enables people to locate a given pole much more quickly.)
- Interdepartmental actions.
- "Suitcase training," custom-developed. (Bringing trainers to the field to customize programs in individual offices, instead of sending everyone to a central facility for certain standard courses.)
- Lighting problem fixed in mobile repair shop.
- New referral system for customer contacts to marketing. (Installers and repair persons frequently come up with sales leads or spot customers who are potentially discontented. Locating the right person in marketing and ensuring follow-up was often a random process. One Face-to-

Table 2.5. Improvements for Management

SCORES*	MANAGEMENT ONLY, IN SURVEY		
	FIRST TIME	SECOND TIME	THIRD TIME
Communication in the district	54	54	72
Our own work schedule	55	61	64
Amount of paperwork	31	43	45
Cooperation between departments, in general	40	47	50
Face-to-face communication	67	74	76
Able to say what we really think	70	69	76
Speed with which word gets to us	60	67	71

*0 = Most negative, 50 = Neutral, 100 = Most positive

Face team came up with a system that facilitates this procedure, has
worked successfully, and has since been broadly adopted throughout
the company.)

Examples of action taken with regard to personnel are listed here. Many
of these have operational implications.

- Career workshops, career counseling.
- Video tapes on job placement related to new technology, centraliza-
  tion, and consolidation (i.e., produced by the Face-to-Face team, with
  volunteer employee–actors, and entirely scripted by them, to commu-
  nicate what each of a half dozen jobs *really* are like).
- Training councils.
- Appraisals improved (frequency and quality).
- Special programs instituted (i.e., drug and alcohol abuse).
- Smoking–no smoking issues (resolved by employees, not by manage-
  ment directives).
- Overtime policy (equality of administration, communication of need).
- Housecleaning, improvement of layout, physical working conditions.
- Stimulation of face-to-face communication, per se.

Results

Why has Face-to-Face taken root, endured, and grown?

1. All the evidence indicates that it works. As previously mentioned,
   the "word-of-mouth" press has tended to spread this word.
2. Management has gone beyond "commitment"; managers have become actively involved, perhaps because participation has been voluntary and no one has forced it down their throats.
3. Problems have been solved; management and employees have responded with action, not just words. Craft and hourly employees
   have learned they can influence and control their workplace results
   to a considerable extent and can accomplish things which previously
   (and early into the process) they automatically looked to management to do.
4. The operating results have not been adversely affected by time spent
   in the process. If anything, because the time has been expended
   against mainstream problems and the gut issues of the business, the
   things that have been accomplished as a result have contributed positively to operating results — especially improved quality.
5. Prudent risk has been encouraged; some things have been tried that
   do not literally conform to "going by the book."
6. Trust has been building as communication becomes more open.

7. Employees at all levels have been learning how to *be* managed as well as how to manage. They develop an insight into the decision-making process that makes them realize that things don't just happen overnight. They become more aware of their own responsibility to make things happen and to communicate upward.

8. The *structure* of the Face-to-Face process has been useful as a fast-track communication channel to identify problems and send them rapidly up the line when local-level authority isn't sufficient to implement desired actions. Little disappears into nonresponse; if action cannot be taken (or if management cannot authorize a proposed change), responsive explanatory communication comes down the line (in contrast to traditional brush-offs or nonresponses).

9. Ownership grows. Management's priorities coincide with the employees' priorities. Action is more likely to be taken and to *work*, because the employees have become involved in developing the solution.

10. The stifling effects of bureaucracy have been minimized. Headquarters isn't peering over the unit's shoulder (yet has been supportive and available on call). In fact, top corporate management has been given only two systematic progress reports in four years.

11. Groups have been allowed to work against their own objectives and criteria for success. In an environment notorious for "indexing" everything, Face-to-Face has not been allowed to become a competition between units. Each is out to improve its own situation in whatever ways it deems most necessary.

12. Out-of-pocket costs for Face-to-Face have been minimal. Consultants' fees, the cost of processing the workplace attitude surveys, the dedicated coordinators (the equivalent of three to four persons has supported the entire process), and occasional media activity (TV, print, etc.) are the totality of out-of-pocket expenditures. The principal investment is in time: meetings of the Coordinating Committees; study-team activities; and time spent in the interview, questionnaire, feedback, and progress report meetings (some of which would take place anyway).

13. And operationally,

- *Action is programmed, not buckshot.* With accountability, timetable, and deadlines, it is an orderly process.
- *Manageable number of objectives for improvement.* With the focus usually on no more than a half dozen major targets, people find — almost to their amazement — that problems begin to be resolved.
- *Higher management commitment and support.* The process provides a clear channel to higher manager/officers when escalation is appro-

priate and necessary; the Face-to-Face teams find that, as a group, they have clout which individuals alone, raising the same issues, do not.

- *Persistence/ingenuity.* The teams don't give up; they seek alternate solutions if the first proposals don't work.
- *Greater sensitivity to the need to communicate.* More people know what's going on. The process creates a sense that "someone cares." It stimulates more of a sense of control and responsibility in the work force, and it results in increased use of *other* media (bulletins, letters, TV, etc.) to support and reinforce Face-to-Face.
- Finally, the process isn't cast in concrete; it is continually being improved.

14. These are some other observations about the process:

- Sometimes, it's a rough road. Some groups take longer than others to coalesce. Some have expectations that a lot is going to happen fast (and, of course, there's no quick fix). Some become overly dependent on the coordinator, the consultant, or the top manager of the unit, or at least try to shift the burden. Some generate a flurry of activity and then bog down. Some "can't find time" for the meetings, studies, and other activities that are involved in the process. But almost inevitably, the groups coalesce, expectations become more realistic, roles become clarified and defined, leadership emerges from within the group, the groups learn how to manage and schedule the process for sustained activity rather than "bursts" of activity, and the time is "miraculously" found when supervisors begin to realize that effectively managed communication helps them achieve their objectives.
- While orientation to the process has been handled fairly well, the teams have probably had less training than would be desirable. The fundamental "training" strategy has been experiential; the consultant and coordinator or coordinators have coached and counseled the teams, rather than formally "trained" them. In PNB, supervisors and managers are normally exposed to substantial training opportunities. Craft and hourly clerical people generally are involved in ongoing job-skill training. But, Face-to-Face has gone forward without the kind of team building, problem solving, or other formal training generally associated with such efforts in other companies. While in many cases the lack of programmed process training does not seem to have inhibited the effort, there's little doubt that, in other units, the application of formal training might well have expedited the process.
- Managers, especially, have enjoyed the process. It has, in the turbu-

lent environment of change mentioned before, given them a new handle on their jobs, a new and meaningful role to play. They feel better about being involved, having more say in decisions which affect them, being put in a position of leading their people toward newly defined objectives which they've had a chance to develop and in which they believe, as opposed to "driving" their people toward goals and objectives dictated to them from above.

- Their priorities for action, developed in collaboration with their employees, are theirs — not just higher management's. Although theoretically they have always had a chance to develop their own goals, in actuality, they work more often in a reactive mode. This process gives them a chance to balance the longer term with today's priorities, and a vehicle to assure that the problem is being addressed. And more than anything else, the process has improved the openness of communication with those to whom they report, which, in turn, enables them to manage communication more effectively with their own subordinates.

EPILOGUE: GOING "JOINT"

In 1977, Face-to-Face started as a management-sponsored process. In August 1980, the Bell System and its unions negotiated an agreement to work toward the improvement of quality of work life *jointly* — as equal partners in efforts in which bargained-for employees would be involved in processes launched.

In April 1981, the Joint National Committees released a nine-point statement of operating principles to each of the individual Bell System companies and their respective union locals. These guidelines defined both the outcome and process qualities which any joint efforts should aim to achieve.

By mid-1981, PNB had reached an agreement with its local unions' leadership to approach all QWL efforts involving union members in a partnership mode. A Joint Union-Management QWL Steering Committee has been established, and a variety of options are being explored for launching QWL efforts.

One of the most difficult issues to resolve has been: What about the Face-to-Face process? Held up against the nine principles, both sides agreed that Face-to-Face meets most criteria. But it is a management-sponsored process. It has been lighter on training than the guidelines recommend as necessary. And the union locals, while kept fully informed and informally involved, have not been full partners and have not selected their own "authorized representatives" to serve on coordinating committees or problem-solving teams, as is suggested in one of the nine principles.

As of this writing, the company and the unions are working to develop a joint process which will include those who are already involved in the Face-to-Face process. While the particular mode of accommodation has not yet been agreed upon, some provisos will be in effect. No new units containing bargained-for employees will initiate the process unless *both* the manager and the union leadership agree to do so on a voluntary basis. Nor will the presence of an ongoing Face-to-Face activity preclude the introduction of any other QWL technique, such as quality control circles, if the Joint Steering Committee elects to use them.

In short, as Pacific Northwest Bell, with its unions, works toward this newly defined collaborative relationship, it does so with over 7,500 of its people already having had a taste of employee involvement, liking it, and ready to move on to new QWL plateaus.

3.
The Sharonville Story: Worker Involvement at a Ford Motor Company Plant

Robert H. Guest

A brief background . . .

The Sharonville plant of the Transmission and Chassis Division of the Ford Motor Company is located near Cincinnati, Ohio. It was built in 1957 and is one of eight plants in the division. It is engaged in machining and assembling parts into transmissions for certain models of Ford automobiles. In August 1980, when the Employe* Involvement (EI) process began, there were approximately 2,500 hourly and 435 salaried employees. It was critically concerned with the need to reduce costs and improve product quality. At the same time, it was looking for the opportunity to involve all employees to a greater degree in workplace problem identification and solution.

Historically, the Sharonville plant, according to observers, had enjoyed reasonably healthy employee relationships. It had its share of labor-management difficulties but nothing out of the ordinary. It was not a plant known for wildcat strikes and slowdowns.

Why the case was selected

The present case was selected for a variety of reasons. Since the inception of Employe Involvement at Sharonville, the process has been implemented successfully and shows promise of continued success despite the overall depressed condition of the economy. By May 1982, 65 percent of the production department were involved in EI, with 43 problem-solving groups meeting on a regular basis. Many plant problems of varying degrees of magnitude were solved by the employees and support personnel. The case reflects the importance of strong leadership and skilled coordination in mak-

---

*It is the custom in the automobile industry to spell the word employee with a single "e" — employe. Therefore, the names of programs and documents in chapter 3 (Ford Motor Company) and chapters 5, 7, and 12 (General Motors Corporation) will conform with industry custom. The general text will conform to the more conventional spelling — employee.

ing the effort work. Also, it illustrates many of the problems and difficulties which are common in American companies in which EI/QWL efforts are launched and sustained. Several times in the months since the inception of the EI process, there have been problems and trying situations which threatened its progress.

Launching EI with a joint national committee . . .

The origins of the Sharonville story go back to October 1979, when the United Automobile Workers (UAW) and the Ford Motor Company, during their negotiations, signed a letter of agreement to the effect that union and management would jointly cooperate in a sustained effort to increase the involvement of employees in matters affecting their work. The parties agreed to provide joint management and union leadership by establishing a National Joint Committee on Employe Involvement (NJCEI) cochaired by the director of the UAW National Ford Department (and UAW vice–president) and the vice–president of labor relations for the company. A series of joint memos were sent out by the NJCEI during the following months and into early 1980. These memos stressed the original agreement, namely:

> Inherent in our understanding was the fact that employe participation in employe involvement projects should be strictly voluntary, and that employe involvement activity should proceed outside the traditional collective bargaining process and should be based on local circumstances and needs. The parties recognized that local union and plant management participation can contribute in an essential way to the effective implementation of employe involvement activities that include the represented work force.

Later memos put forward some general guidelines for proceeding. These guidelines emphasized the importance of orienting all parties as to the purpose of EI. It recommended the establishment of local joint management–union steering committees followed by the selection of pilot groups on a small scale.

The Transmission and Chassis Division carried the message down to its various plants. During 1980 several meetings were called by the division with plant representatives to encourage the plants to proceed under the NJCEI guidelines. The division announced that it would provide budgetary support for consultant services and certain other expenses to launch the effort in the various plants.

Early informal efforts

Although Sharonville itself did not start any formal activity until the fall of 1980, a number of informal communication and orientation activities were conducted. One superintendent, for example, expanded the weekly safety meetings among his supervisors, hourly operators, and himself to include discussions for involving employees in decisions affecting operations. Problem-solving workshops were made available to first-line supervisors. A

tape was made on how to conduct group meetings with employees to increase participation in solving departmental problems. Sessions were held
by top management personnel and the union leadership on the challenges of
Japanese competition and the need to involve employees in improving product quality.

Enter a new plant manager . . .

Two important events occurred in late summer 1980, which preceded the
formal launching of EI at Sharonville and which proved crucial to its later
success. A new plant manager was brought in from another plant. He had
previously held positions at Sharonville and was widely known at the plant.
He had a reputation of being a skilled, tough but effective, and fair manager. He himself admitted that he had been cut from the traditional authoritarian mold that had been said to characterize management at Ford in the
past. He also admitted, "Those times are past and we have to take a new approach." He acknowledged to his management and union leadership that he
wholly supported EI and the joint union–management agreement to involve
employees more in decisions affecting the workplace and their jobs.

Restructuring the organization . . .

A second important event was a change in organization structure, a change
which other plants were also adopting. The change involved dividing the
manufacturing area of the plant into two separate areas. Each area would
have not only the usual production functions, but also representatives from
quality control, engineering, and other functions, assigned on a permanent
basis. We note the importance of this move because, later on, when problem-solving groups at the hourly level were formed, the groups had more
immediate and easier access to the necessary support personnel in solving
shop-floor problems. The quality control and engineering managers continued to report to the plant manager, but they assigned representatives to the
two area manufacturing managers. The other key parts of the organization
—controller, industrial relations, material control, and purchasing—remained essentially the same but did designate advisors to work with area
managers. The plant manager, subsequent to the establishment of the new
"area" concept, personally conducted a series of meetings with all plant
supervision and hourly employees to acquaint the organization with the
new concept. It was during these meetings that he took the opportunity to
describe briefly the plant's plans for more involvement of everyone through
the Employe Involvement process.

Consultants make an assessment . . .

In September 1980, the division approved the management consultants on
EI selected by the Sharonville plant.[1] The consultants proceeded to interview all members of the top management team. The essential purpose of the
interviews was to get a feel for the organization, to find out the extent to
which top managers were aware of EI, to assess their readiness to proceed,

and to get their ideas about organization and first steps. In one of the regular biweekly management meetings, the consultants also presented the larger picture of the EI/QWL movement and shared their experiences in other successful efforts.

The union reacts . . .

Early in September 1980, the plant manager called a meeting of his top managers, the consultants, and the president and unit chairman of UAW Local 863. Although the chairman had received all the communications about EI from the national union headquarters, he expressed considerable skepticism as to whether it would work out at the Sharonville plant. He did not veto the idea and would not oppose it, but he simply said he would "wait and see." He did agree to cooperate in assigning local union officials to a proposed joint union–management coordinating committee.

Considering a start-up . . .

Several further discussions followed in subsequent weeks, and interviews were held with the area managers and superintendents to get their ideas as to where some pilot projects might be started. Two departments were suggested, one from each of the two production areas. The consultants had expressed the opinion that it was important to choose areas where there was evidence of commitment on the part of supervision and union representatives and where there was a probability of initial success. They felt that a failure in the beginning could have a negative effect on future progress. On the other hand, they wanted to respect the choices of the key production managers, and so the decision was made to go along with management's recommendations.

Choosing a line manager as temporary coordinator . . .

Also, in anticipation of the future leadership of the joint committee, it was considered important to choose a member of management who could effectively organize the initial efforts. There was a shift manufacturing manager who had had previous exposure that year to a start-up EI effort at one of the other plants. He also expressed a strong commitment to having the process work at Sharonville. Inasmuch as the plant manager himself felt it was not appropriate for him to be cochairman of the joint committee, the recommendation was made that the project be coordinated by the shift manager. It was also recognized that in time there should be full-time coordinators, preferably one from management and one from the union.

Forming a committee . . .

Early in October 1980, the Employe Involvement Coordinating Committee was formed. It was agreed that wherever possible the membership should be made up of equal numbers of representatives from management and from the union. The chairman of the union bargaining committee submitted the names of three elected union representatives. He also said he would be willing to cochair the committee. At a later date the union added another union representative. The plant manager asked the manager of quality control, the manager of engineering and facilities, a supervisor in labor relations, and the shift manufacturing manager to represent management on the committee with the latter acting as cochairman. The manager of industrial relations, whose advice on the implementation of EI had been invaluable, chose not to be on the coordinating committee. He had always been one of the strongest proponents of EI but felt that he could serve the effort more effectively in an advisory role.

Laying down the guidelines . . .

The first full meeting of the EI Coordinating Committee was held on October 21. The members of this policymaking body for implementing EI agreed on certain overall responsibilities. They would oversee the process, prepare the organization through a variety of communication efforts, select pilot areas for starting up the program, and determine how and when it would expand. By mutual agreement, and according to the national guidelines, the committee reaffirmed the importance of not being a mechanism for dealing with collective bargaining issues. This latter agreement was important because, at many times in the subsequent history of the development of EI at Sharonville, there were situations bordering on contractual matters. The committee also agreed to meet biweekly and to establish a format of communication which would always include a letterhead designed locally to indicate joint union and company participation and support. The committee emphasized that all efforts should be voluntary and that problem-solving groups, when formed, would have utmost discretion in determining which issues they wished to address. Finally, the committee gave its approval to start the process in two specific departments on a small scale.

Spreading the word . . .

The month following the establishment of the Coordinating Committee was a period of broad-scale communication and orientation. A letter announcing the purpose and membership of the committee was mailed to the homes of all employees in the plant. It was signed by the president of the union, the plant manager, and the two cochairmen (the local union chairman and the management cochairman, the latter who would serve temporarily as the Employe Involvement coordinator).

A full-scale presentation was made to the Plant Operating Committee, which consisted of all members of management and supervision through the level of superintendent. Further discussions were held with the operating zone superintendents, general supervisors, and supervisors in those areas where the pilot experiments were to proceed. Names of hourly employees were also being accumulated to determine who would be interested in joining the prospective problem-solving groups.

During this period, the industrial relations manager at the plant was receiving planning guidelines from the division general office which included information on possible training programs and work force resource needs. He was also receiving a series of advisory NJCEI letters, sent throughout the division, putting forth more specific recommendations on the overall process and specifically on the functions of the local joint committees.

Reinforcement from high levels . . .

The capstone event in launching EI at Sharonville occurred on October 10, 1980, in a visit which included the top operations manager for the division, his key staff members, the plant manager, industrial relations manager, and division and corporate staff labor relations representatives. The union side included national representatives of the union (with a member of the National Joint Committee on Employe Involvement) and six local committee members including the chairman. Forceful statements were made by representatives of both sides regarding the importance of commitment to EI. Frank comments were made to the effect that involvement of everyone was necessary to improve the quality of the work environment and of the product and the effectiveness of the organization. The challenge to meet Japanese competition was emphasized. The theme of quality product cooperation was underscored throughout the discussion and, as one high-level division manager commented, "Company management will not tolerate managers who preach *quality* but operate with *quantity* as a primary objective." The plant manager concluded the meeting by assuring the group that "nothing is going to stand in the way of moving forward on the program."

But understanding and commitment was not universal . . .

In retrospect, one can be impressed with all of the efforts to communicate the commitment which the Sharonville plant had made to date. Every form and media of communication was used to orient the organization to EI. Certainly there was general awareness throughout the plant that there was a strong wind blowing for change. Yet the full impact throughout the organization was doubtful. The orientation efforts were touching only a comparatively small number of personnel. The average supervisor, for example, had yet to know and understand what the program was all about and what it would mean for him. The hourly employees and union representatives were interested to some extent, but the wait-and-see attitude was still pervasive. Except for some planning by the joint committee, very few persons had any direct involvement to date.

It should also be emphasized that, during this period and, indeed, during the many months to follow, the Sharonville plant was under enormous pressures. It had experienced large-scale reductions in personnel. By the end of the year, it was directed to bring about a substantial reduction in costs. This plant, like all the others, had been expected to implement a dozen other programs for cost and quality improvement.

There was as yet no individual designated to coordinate the program on a permanent basis. The temporary coordinator (one of the cochairman of the

EI Coordinating Committee) was the full-time manager on the night shift. He had no secretary and yet he had to make announcements, take minutes of meetings, call for meetings, and in general maintain communication among those who were launching the program. Despite these difficulties, there was now enough leadership and momentum to keep the effort on track.

The problem-solving groups get underway . . .

Concrete progress was made during the last quarter of 1980 with the formation of two problem-solving groups. They represented two departments in different areas of the plant and had been selected and approved by the EI Coordinating Committee. In addition to seven hourly production employees who had volunteered, there was an inspector, a supervisor, and a process engineer in each. Union representatives from the coordinating committee were also present as observers. The coordinator and the consultant gave a brief presentation about EI and the general ground rules that had been laid down. The groups would meet one hour each week on "company time." It was emphasized that a group could select its own problems and choose its own leader.

Each group wasted no time in choosing a supervisor as its group leader, and all of them plunged into a discussion of a variety of operating problems they thought were critical. One group selected four or five problems on which they wanted to see action and proceeded to diagnose the problems and eventually prepare recommendations. The other group focused on a single major problem, which consumed many meetings in the months to follow. It was obvious in the meetings that the groups had some deep suspicions about EI in terms of management's intention. Most of the members had high seniority and had experienced management programs in the past which never came to anything. They could not believe that if they arrived at solutions to operating problems that had plagued them for many years, management would do something about them. In these initial meetings, and many that were to follow, the coordinator emphasized that under the new system a group was not simply supposed to identify problems and then "dump" them on management; they had the authority *and* responsibility to seek whatever resources they needed to come up with concrete answers. The ball was in their court.

Gearing up for training and orientation . . .

In the weeks to follow, the temporary coordinator attended a week's training workshop on EI sponsored by corporate staff. He returned convinced that much more needed to be done in training both leaders and groups in problem-solving techniques. On this score, there was some disagreement with the consultants who, although convinced of the critical importance of stimulation and orientation, believed that problem-solving training should not be carried out in an "up front" fashion but, rather, brought in as appropriate when groups were dealing with specific operating problems of direct concern to themselves. However, both agreed that it would be extremely useful to have these newly formed groups exposed to the experience that groups in other locations had had in launching an EI effort. Late in October 1980, the EI administrator from another plant, together with a member of the union, came to Sharonville for a two and one-half hour session with both of the newly formed groups. This served as another vehicle for stimulation and encouragement.

By the end of the year, the two groups were functioning on a weekly basis while the coordinating committee laid the groundwork for the creation of additional groups in other parts of the plant. An unused set of offices in the center of the plant was renovated and set up to serve as a meeting room for the problem-solving groups. Later it was expanded to an EI Center that could accommodate four group sessions simultaneously as well as offices for the full-time coordinators of the process, one salaried and one hourly.

Participation in a change in plant operations . . .

A series of events of some significance also occurred during this period. A major change in the assembly operations was being planned. The change involved the elimination of the four original final assembly lines and the rebuilding of two new lines in their place. The traditional approach to such major changes in the past was to have the engineers draw up the blueprints, the work-standards specialists establish the appropriate job standards, and the maintenance crews install the operation. This time, with the new interest in EI, the procedure was changed in one significant way. The superintendent, general supervisor, and supervisor discussed the projected change with the hourly employees, seeking their ideas as to how the operation could be put in efficiently and effectively. During a plant shutdown of one week, the new lines were installed. The operation started up smoothly. The industrial relations manager for the plant was impressed by the fact that the operation had gone off as well as it did. He said, "In times past we have always had a flood of grievances on work standards whenever a new installation was put in under the old system."

By the end of the year, it was becoming increasingly obvious that the person who was acting as temporary coordinator and cochairman of the coordinating committee (as well as having a full-time job) was overburdened. Unless a permanent coordinator could be found, the entire EI process would probably have difficulty moving forward.

Salaried employees also get interested . . .

The other significant event at the end of 1980 was the creation of a committee to sponsor involvement activities among salaried workers. Information picked up at the time of the area management survey and during informal interviews with white-collar employees made it quite obvious that they too were stimulated by the interest in EI. The consultants also were strongly urging the plant manager to encourage activity for salaried people. A number of these employees from different departments asked that something be done. They were given further encouragement by the salaried personnel supervisor. In November, a group representing each of the major departments came together and formed the Salaried Employe Involvement Coordinating Committee. After some general orientation, they set to work planning what their mission should be, namely, to encourage the formation of problem-solving groups (they adopted the name "quality circles") in their respective departments. Each committee member took on the responsibility for "sounding out" other office personnel to determine who was interested and how groups could be formed. This committee was the salaried counterpart of the Employe Involvement Coordinating Committee.

Although the salaried employees committee still lacked direction, it was aware of the fact that it was probably among the first salaried EI groups in the entire Ford Motor Company. Soon afterwards, one group in industrial engineering began to tackle a major problem in communications. The members were organizing themselves to investigate the possibilities of installing a modern computerized word-processing system in the plant.

Within a year after the committee was formed, there were eight problem-solving groups functioning and covering most of the administrative departments.

Pressures building for more permanent coordination . . .

January 1981 was a period of marking time. The temporary coordinator was overburdened with his regular work and found it difficult to respond to some of the pressures for expanding into other areas. During the same month, he was taken off his manufacturing job and put in charge of planning for an entirely new transmission model that was to be produced at the Sharonville plant. Pressures were intensified to seek budgetary funds for a full-time salaried coordinator. The decision was made not to bring in someone from the outside but, rather, to find a person inside with the interest, enthusiasm, and willingness to do the job. The coordinating committee was anxious to push ahead. It was known that at least two other departments wanted to get started. One of the committee members, the quality control manager, launched a program plant-wide whereby employees were encouraged to send in written suggestions for the improvement of quality performance.

The plant manager emphasizes success . . .

The plant manager was especially anxious to see to it that EI move ahead as rapidly as possible. Although not a member of the coordinating committee, he would frequently sit in on the meetings and give strong support to its efforts. As he put it in one of the meetings, "We have to make sure that the guys out on the floor know that the top people here are supporting them and that we keep stressing the successes of the problem–solving groups we have going." And there were successes. In one of the groups more than ten problems had been solved which had resulted in substantial savings in production downtime and scrap. There were also marked improvements in the plant record of quality performance. These were measured by required repairs by automobile dealers as indicated by warranty claims being made. Nevertheless, the two groups were having some difficulty in getting support for their recommendations. This problem continued for a long time. The groups, it may be recalled, included not only hourly operators and a supervisor but also representatives from support departments, such as engineering and inspection. But many of the issues they were dealing with required the expertise of other support personnel and had to be followed by concrete management action. Solutions to the problems that they had diagnosed required action by persons beyond their control. Particular criticism was directed at the maintenance representatives. Their staff had been reduced in the earlier cutbacks, and they found it difficult to spend time on their regular jobs as well as take care of requests from the groups.

A full-time coordinator is appointed . . .

The most important event in February 1981 was the appointment of the first of two full-time coordinators. After screening a number of candidates, the coordinating committee chose an enthusiastic cost analyst who, although he had no special training in EI, expressed a strong desire to take on the job. He was given an office in the EI Center, where the problem-solving groups met and which was conveniently located in the center of this large plant. He immediately went to work going over all of the materials on EI which had been accumulated by the temporary coordinator and by the industrial relations manager. He was also briefed by the consultants on background issues and future perspectives. For administrative purposes he was assigned to the industrial relations manager, but it was made clear to him that his "boss" was in fact the coordinating committee. He was also made aware of the fact that there was strong pressure to appoint a co-coordinator eventually, someone from the union hourly ranks who could share jointly in coordinating the activities. He not only approved of the idea but felt it was a necessity if future groups were to be convinced that EI was a truly joint union–management effort.

Immediately after his appointment, a corporate staff training specialist was brought in to conduct a two-day workshop on problem solving. It was attended by 25 persons, including representatives from the current work groups, staff support personnel, and persons who would be involved in the future EI effort, as well as four representatives from the new Salaried EI Committee.

More stimulation for involvement . . .

In the weeks following the appointment of a full-time coordinator, a number of systematic efforts were made not only to increase the number of groups but also to provide more information and feedback throughout the plant. For example, the cochairmen of the coordinating committee sent a note to the members of the present groups thanking them for their interest and participation. The note was posted on all plant bulletin boards. Again the theme of improving quality was emphasized. As the memo stated in part, "As you know, we have too often been negligent about quality in the past — often sacrificing quality for quantity — and as a result, our company and the rest of the auto industry has been taking a beating in sales. If our joint committee can be of any help in any way, please do not hesitate to contact us." One of the groups took it upon itself to sign a "Memo to all Ford Employes" (a copy of which was sent to both corporate and national union headquarters). In simple forceful language it stated, "We care, and we know you care. In the present crisis, our personal and our company attitudes must change for the better. Many of you know where improvement can be made, and we would welcome your help. We trust in your determination to keep the Sharonville Transmission Plant in operation, and we need your help to achieve this goal."

The plant manager continued to express his commitment publicly. In his March letter, mailed to the homes of all employees, he gave a frank picture of the general business situation and of plant performance. A paragraph was devoted to underscoring his commitment to Employe Involvement. At every opportunity during the various meetings with management, he repeated the theme. For example, "We can put millions into systems and equipment, but only our people right out on the floor can save us."

A survey of all salaried personnel was taken during this period as a follow-up to the original survey on the effectiveness of the area management restructuring. This time it also included questions about awareness of, and interest in, EI. More than 80 percent of the respondents said they understood the purposes of EI. An overwhelming majority was in favor of the idea, but it was obvious from the responses that there were many members of supervision who had some reservations. Many had not yet been directly involved. The new coordinator was fully aware that there were large numbers of people, both in management and among the hourly employees, who knew little about what was going on in the plant. He acted as an informal channel of communication, taking every opportunity to talk with managers, staff personnel, superintendents, supervisors, and union representatives to explain EI and encourage them to become involved.

Activities and plans move ahead substantially . . .

By the end of March 1981, two more EI groups had been formed. In one of the production zones, approval was given to organize all six departments under its own coordinating committee and a zone coordinator. This was a significant move. It set the pattern for the future.

The balance of spring 1981 was taken up in developing a master plan for the expansion of EI throughout the plant. The coordinator drew up a program detailing how new groups would be set up. It called for a minicoordinating committee made up of hourly employees and supervisors for each of the six manufacturing zones. It highlighted the labor and training requirements. At the urging of division officials, the plan also called for a system for assessing results. The plant manager and members of the coordinating committee expressed concern about placing too much emphasis on results. As the plant manager put it, "I've told the division not to expect 'bottom line' figures. If the idea got around that we were only interested in tumbling numbers on results, it would destroy the process."

The coordinator, supported by the consultants and the plant manager himself, was urging that action be taken as soon as possible to bring in a co-coordinator for the program, someone well respected from the union membership. The union chairman (cochairman of the coordinating committee) made known his strong feelings. "Things will turn around here only when we get a union co-coordinator on board."[2] He made it clear that there were many people on the shop floor, including members of the EI groups, who were still suspicious that EI was a program dominated by management for its purposes only.

Nevertheless, substantial progress was being made in the problem-solving groups. More than 20 operating problems had been identified and solved. There continued to be a tendency for the groups to fix blame on management for not carrying through with recommendations, but they were gradually coming to recognize that they had the power (and the support of top management) to see to it that action was taken. In one instance, the area manufacturing manager was asked to attend by the group. In another case, a group made a direct appeal to the coordinating committee for action. Not every meeting was productive. One group even threatened to disband unless a supervisor out on the shop floor was disciplined by management for violating the contract by working on the line. Other similar incidents occurred and had to be handled delicately. A fundamental principle of EI was that matters of bargaining relationships were not to be brought up in the problem-solving meetings.

Union elections show significant results . . .

A number of significant events occurred during May 1981. The triennial election of union officers in the plant took place. No one opposed the reelection of the chairman of the bargaining committee who, as has been noted, was the co-chairman of the coordinating committee. All but one of the union members of that committee were reelected or newly elected. In light of the earlier suspicions on the part of the hourly work force about EI "as just another management program," the election results were seen as significant.

Sharonville makes its big EI presentation . . .

The highlight of the year to date was a visit to Sharonville by the National Joint Committee on Employe Involvement, including the vice-president for labor relations for the company and the UAW vice-president and director of the Ford Department, both cochairmen of the NJCEI. Top division representatives, together with 25 persons from the plant, were also present. The day's visit included an initial presentation by the people at Sharonville, a plant tour, and some observations by the two key visitors. The plant manager opened the meeting by affirming his conviction that "EI is vital to the organization and has been a gratifying success to date." The management cochairman of the coordinating committee outlined the progress. He was followed by the union chairman, who openly admitted that attitudes on the shop floor "had improved 90 percent." His statement was of considerable significance because, up until now, most of his public comments had been guarded. The most stimulating part of the meeting came with the introduction of two members from the problem-solving groups. Each stood up and gave a straightforward, enthusiastic endorsement of his experience in the work groups.

The plant tour that followed was conducted entirely by representatives from the four problem-solving groups. They took the visitors to specific locations in the plant where changes had been made based on the groups' own recommendations. Following the tour, the top company and national union officials gave a ringing endorsement to what they had seen and heard. The next day, the *Cincinnati Post* carried a major piece on the visit headlined "Ford Employe Involvement Pays." The importance of the meeting was not so much that a group of "big shots" came to Sharonville, but that the wide publicity connected with their visit served internally to stimulate a sense of positive reinforcement for those who were involved and for hundreds of others in supervision and the hourly work force who were still "on the outside" but curious.

During May 1981, the coordinator continued to spend many hours working with the EI groups, the group leaders, supervisors, managers, and union representatives and laying the groundwork for expansion.

Approval of an hourly co-coordinator . . .

Other developments are worth noting. One, the coordinating committee received the necessary approval for the appointment of an hourly worker as co-coordinator, based upon the unique circumstances at Sharonville. At the time, only one other plant in the entire Ford Company had filled the position of what was called an "hourly facilitator," reporting to an EI "administrator." At Sharonville, both were to report to the coordinating committee and mutually share the coordinating responsibilities.

A major manufacturing problem is solved . . .

Another development was that the one problem-solving group that had been working for months on a single difficult manufacturing problem (the problem had been in existence for many years) made a major breakthrough. The complete solution had not been fully worked out by the group itself but its efforts had stimulated management to take a new look at the problem. After some engineering effort, the now-famous "62 hole" problem was solved. The plant engineer admitted that the savings in improved tool performance and the reduction in downtime and scrap were worth many thousands of dollars.

A white-collar quality circle also comes through . . .

At the same time, one of the quality circles sponsored by the Salaried Employe Involvement Coordinating Committee was prepared to present to management its proposal for a computerized word processing system which would have substantial effects on internal plant and office communications. This group, none of whom were members of management, had called in representatives of the major computer companies for presentations on hardware capabilities. They had made a detailed analysis of the potential cost savings. After a formal presentation to top management, the plan was accepted.

The hourly co-coordinator comes on board . . .

In July 1981, a co-coordinator from the hourly ranks was appointed by the coordinating committee. He had been a member of the committee and was one of its most supportive members. The regard his fellow employees had for him was demonstrated by his having been previously elected a shop-floor district committeeman. His appointment helped to dissipate the suspicions of large numbers of workers who thought that EI might be "another management gimmick."

The two coordinators immediately went to work developing a 178-page manual dealing with every aspect of EI training, organization, and implementation. It served not only as a training guide for the 20 new groups that were formed in the following months, but it was used extensively in sessions with managerial, supervisory, and support personnel who were involved or who would become involved. Pulling together experience from Sharonville and that of outside consultants and practitioners, they worked out statements of objectives, plans, and progress.

A permanent structure is put into place . . .

The rapid growth of a number of problem-solving groups required a more permanent organizational structure. By May 1982, 43 groups, covering two-thirds of all production departments, were functioning. The two coordinators alone could not handle the time demands for orienting, training, and guiding the new groups as they formed. They knew what the structure would look like. One production zone had set the example by appointing a utility supervisor as a kind of minicoordinator for all six departments in the zone where EI groups had been formed. This person worked closely with the two EI coordinators in setting it up. It seemed reasonable to adopt this same structure for all zones in the plant.

The opportunity for adopting a plant-wide structure came in September

1981 with a decision by the plant manager, supported by the division, to reorganize the plant hierarchy. The general supervisor level was completely eliminated. Part of the reason was cost saving; part was to shorten communications channels. In its place, each zone superintendent was assigned an assistant known as a manufacturing planning specialist who, as the name implies, was to provide planning and coordinating assistance to each superintendent. The individual was not to be in a position of line authority. His position description called for another responsibility which was to have a profound effect on the future "management" and growth of the EI process. He was to act as the departmental coordinator for all present and future EI problem-solving groups, working closely with his own superintendent and the plant co-coordinators.

Training the minicoordinators and others . . .

Most of those in this new position had little direct experience with EI so a major orientation and training effort had to be launched. As a kick-off, they attended a two-day training session with the two plant coordinators, using the newly developed manual as the centerpiece (a full-day session was also given to all superintendents, production engineering and quality control supervisors, production supervisors, and, later on, to the full plant bargaining and district committees). The sessions included instructions on methods for selecting new groups; information about names of people who could provide support services; and advice on developing group leaders, maintaining meeting notes, transmitting information to superintendents and "action completed" lists to superintendents and area managers, and so on.

The training process for new groups . . .

It was understood that the two plant coordinators would handle the initial orientation and training for the new groups that were formed; this continued to be the practice well into 1982. A word about the specifics of the training: each new group went through seven introductory sessions that included orientation, group dynamics, brainstorming, cause-and-effect analysis, median charting, data gathering, and presentation techniques. There was one aspect of the training program that differed substantially from most group training programs. The customary method is to go through all of these subject areas as an "up front" process before getting on with the business at hand, which is identifying and solving operating problems. What the coordinators at Sharonville had learned from experience was that these subjects in the abstract did not make too much sense to the average participant. They might serve as a kind of intellectual stimulation, but exposure alone had no lasting effect. Rather, the formal training techniques were made secondary to the work of dealing with specific shop-floor problems. After the first orientation session and the selection of a group leader, the participants were urged to plunge right into a listing of problems that they felt were important and that needed to be solved. The groups then established their own priorities. This was followed by problem definition, data gathering, and the formulation of concrete recommendations. The coordinators, in presenting the sessions, made use of the training techniques (brainstorming, cause–and–effect analysis, etc.) only to the extent that they were helpful to the group in working on problems of importance to them. In short, "training" should not occur in a vacuum or use examples not directly related to the participants' own experience. They rejected the common notion that skill training in the abstract is automatically transferable in applying the learning later to concrete situations. In this program, the "concreteness" was right before the group itself.

More important than the group training sessions as such was the "climate of involvement" they created. With a successful experience, the employees were saying in effect, "At last, we have an opportunity to get into the act, to have our voices heard, to have some impact on what happens, both to our jobs and to the plant that we work in."

Taking stock of results

By May 1982, 21 months after the Sharonville EI effort began, the climate in the plant had changed substantially. There was greater coordination and communication between line and staff personnel in solving problems. Supervisor-worker relationships were healthier. And the union and management were actively cooperating in finding ways to improve quality and performance.

How effective was Sharonville's EI effort when measured in terms of performance indexes? The answer is difficult to quantify. It was an agreed-upon policy that there were to be no formal measurements of a group's performance. The philosophy at Sharonville was that EI's purpose was to improve the quality of work life for the employees themselves. If it were directed primarily at productivity, those involved would perceive it as just another management-controlled effort at "speed up." On the other hand, management as well as the union hoped that there would be some spin-off results which would make Sharonville a better functioning organization.

The measures of quality performance for the entire plant had reached the highest level in several years by spring of 1982. There is evidence, even if not formally recorded, to show that in those departments with EI groups many of the problems worked on resulted in operating efficiencies. One group, for example, proved to the engineering specialists that two small hydraulic cylinders could replace a larger worn out cylinder with proven savings of more than $700 per week. Another group initiated a program for having each machine in sequence in its department checked and overhauled, resulting in a dramatic reduction in downtime and scrap. Management estimated a substantial cost saving even before the project was completed. Mention was made earlier of the group which, although it did not provide the final technical answer, stimulated action to solve a coolant problem, resulting in demonstrable reductions in downtime and scrap. The one manufacturing zone to have all six of its production departments involved in EI reported a 22 percent improvement in direct labor efficiencies. When asked how much production time was taken up in EI meetings to accomplish these results, the superintendent replied, "They took 2.5 percent of their time. I'd say that for a 22 percent improvement that small amount of time was a pretty good investment."

A review of the many dozens of "completed action" reports submitted by the groups suggests other, less dramatic results which, taken cumulatively, must have led to substantial savings in costs and improved quality performance. The curious fact is that there is little evidence that any problem-solving group ever asked management for any kind of monetary reward for its efforts, nor did any file for rewards under the plant's regular suggestion program. *Just being involved in improving the operations in their own work areas was its own reward.*

The entire EI effort has been sustained even in the face of drastic cuts in personnel. By the end of 1981 more than 450 hourly employees were laid off. Also, for several weeks the entire plant was shut down because of the sharp reduction in car sales. Such events would be considered highly disruptive in sustaining any kind of involvement effort; but from the plant manager on down the commitment held firm.

The great challenge for the future

Sharonville faced a new challenge in 1982 which in considerable measure would test the effectiveness of its EI experience. The plant assumed the responsibility for producing a transmission previously machined and assembled in another plant. This meant that 365 machines were being brought in and more than 250 Sharonville machines retooled. This was probably the most important development at Sharonville since the plant was built a quarter of a century ago. Everyone involved in EI to date was convinced that the successful implementation of such a dramatic change at Sharonville would depend heavily not only on managerial skills and technical expertise but also on the problem-solving process developed through Sharonville's highly successful EI activities.

Launch teams were formed in each area where the incoming machines and equipment were to be installed. Members of these teams were turning to several of the 43 EI problem-solving groups for advice and recommendations.

In addition, to meet the burgeoning growth in activities, the EI effort underwent further restructuring in May 1982. Each of the two major production areas established EI subcommittees made up of the area manager, maintenance superintendents, quality control superintendents, the two plant EI coordinators, and two union district committeemen. As a result, virtually every level of the Sharonville organization became formally represented in the total effort. Thus, after 21 months from its inception, EI became fully institutionalized at the Sharonville plant.

Lessons learned from the Sharonville experience

- The highly visible interest and commitment of a top manager is crucial to the implementation of a QWL participation effort.

- The appointment of a co-coordinator from the hourly ranks working jointly with a salaried person on a mutual basis is further evidence of management's interest and commitment. The teamwork and enthusiasm of the coordinators is key in accelerating the process.

- The support and active participation of union representatives and especially members of a joint union-management committee is a "must."

- Knowledge that there is a joint union-management agreement and support at the national level is important in setting the stage for actions at the plant level.

- Keeping collective bargaining issues separate from the involvement process is essential.

- Starting on a small scale with pilot groups is useful in gaining experience for future growth. The "master plan" for structuring and diffusing the process comes only after the key parties involved have learned what will work and what will not work. Flexibility and voluntarism are essential.

- Although orientation to the philosophy and purpose of employee participation is necessary to stimulate group interest, the actual training in problem solving need not be considered a separate "up front" part of the process. Rather, problem-solving skills are introduced only when the group members are dealing with their own problems, which they identify for themselves.

- On the central issue of how interest in problem solving can be maintained over time without artificial stimulation, experience clearly demonstrates that there is virtually no limit to the number of shop-floor operating problems that continually crop up and cry out for solution.

- Fixing responsibility on groups to work out solutions to problems, rather than to just identify them and "dump" them on management, takes a long time to develop but is central to the success of the entire process. In this case, the process was facilitated by the composition of the groups (which often included technical support personnel) and by the fact that groups had the authority to call in the required help.

- On the other hand, tight technical or managerial resources make it difficult to provide prompt "service" for the problem-solving groups. But at least groups need to know, and they are willing to accept, honest reasons for action delays. Prompt feedback is essential.

- As in this case, substantial dollar savings can accrue from the activity, yet the problem-solving groups do not necessarily demand monetary compensation. Two explanations are suggested in this instance. One is that, given the serious downturn in business, job security is the motivating factor. Workers want to do what they can to save the plant from shutting down. But other evidence suggests a more subtle reason. Being involved, having a "say" in decisions, and demonstrating an opportunity to use their knowledge and experience is its own reward.

- EI/QWL is often mistakenly viewed as an activity authorized at the "top" and carried out at the "bottom." Middle and lower management are often forgotten. What this case proved is the necessity of simultaneous knowledge, interest, and commitment at all levels. This can be preached but not mandated. The process "takes hold" among middle managers and supervisors when they come to recognize that solutions to operating problems at the grass-roots level, with their support and involvement, make their own jobs more manageable — in short, improves the quality of their own work lives.

NOTES

1. The management consultants chosen by the Sharonville plant were Stanley Peterfreund Associates.

2. The chairman did not mean a staff person paid by the union but rather someone selected by the coordinating committee from the hourly workers.

4.
The Scanlon Plan at Herman Miller, Inc.: Managing an Organization by Innovation

Carl F. Frost

The quality of competence in executive leadership is a prerequisite to the exploration and implementation of the Scanlon Plan.[1] Until and unless executive leadership defines accurately the reality of the organization and enables most, if not all, of the employees to understand accurately what this reality is, one cannot expect employees to accept the responsibility or ownership of the daily demands for productivity and profitability.

Again, it is the quality of leadership that is critical in explaining the compelling need and rationale for change and for the setting of standards. If leaders do not set high expectations for innovation, they will not be disappointed. On the other hand, experience has demonstrated that when chief executive officers do establish high expectations, they are not often disappointed either.

Herman Miller, Inc., is an organization whose chief executive officers have increasingly assumed the responsibility of leadership. The company has utilized the Scanlon process for 30 years, but the kind of leadership that permits it to identify accurately the changing reality predates the original implementation of the Scanlon Plan in 1950. One distinctive difference between managers at Herman Miller and other companies has been their identification of the motivating forces as the demands of the end users (customers) and the employees, and not the authority and dictates of management.

As early as 1934, D.J. DePree, president and chairman emeritus of Herman Miller, Inc., exercised this leadership role. While in Detroit on a visit, he was struck by the incongruity of two reported incidents: Henry Ford was gathering antiques in New England for his Greenfield Village, while the majority of Ford Motor Company employees had been laid off as a result of the Great Depression. This behavior seemed irrational to DePree, and then he realized that his absence from his own company at that time and his unresponsiveness to the effects of the Depression were also irrational. DePree returned promptly to Zeeland, Michigan, to address the problems of Herman Miller:

diminishing demand for the company's product — highly ornate home furniture — and sharply reduced employment among the company's employees.

The necessity of finding solutions to these problems led to his pursuit of two objectives: (1) to develop functional contemporary furniture, and (2) to provide fifty weeks of work annually for Herman Miller employees. The worldwide recognition of Herman Miller for functional design is evidence of the many great innovations in concept and product that took place over the next few decades. But that is another story. This chapter focuses essentially on another innovation — Herman Miller's approach to managing its human resources.

THE SCANLON PLAN: IDENTIFICATION

Throughout the period of innovation initiated by DePree in 1934, new products were designed to meet customer needs and new marketing concepts were developed. A third innovation was also instituted: a new approach to the leadership of employees in the organization.

In 1934, when DePree returned to Zeeland, he realized that the responsibility for employing his people in a new relationship required invention and innovation. Employees as well as industrial organizations needed consistent income and operations planned on an annual basis. DePree was committed to predictable employment 50 weeks a year for his employees, and also to employment for the disabled — programs that were unique in the 1930s and 1940s.

In 1950, after a presentation on the Scanlon Plan by the author of this chapter, DePree, his son Hugh DePree, and their accountant became interested in the idea as an organization development concept. In a visit with the author, this concept and its relationship to Herman Miller were discussed and the Herman Miller organizational reality was assessed. The history and the current status of the company revealed an awareness of the need to change.

When DePree was asked repeatedly, "Why are you pursuing the Scanlon process?" he stated, with some frustration, "Because we believe we have to do a better job. Customers will not wait 26 weeks for delivery. And the quality of our product does not equal the quality of our designs."

The officers were aware of the reality of a situation that was hampering the company's growth, but awareness of the problem was not evident among manufacturing employees, who comprised 80 to 90 percent of the work force at that time. Thirty-five percent of these manufacturing people were on individual incentive rates, almost equivalent to being "in business for themselves"; they were paid primarily for quantity but not necessarily for the quality of their output.

The early version of the Scanlon Plan was introduced at Herman Miller in the spring of 1950. Even then we were advocating the process of identification as the fundamental Scanlon Plan requirement. DePree, Sr., and the author met informally with all the employees in the lumber kiln. DePree described the history of the company and its reputation for excellence in design and pointed to the consequences of customer disappointment in not receiving the product in reasonable time and to the disparity between manufactured product quality and design quality. The author discussed the larger frame of economic demands and competition. These realities suggested the necessity for change and the potential for invention and innovation implicit in company-wide cooperation to serve the customers, the employees themselves, and the investors to better advantage.

Even though the introduction of the Scanlon Plan was primarily a management decision, the employees were made aware of the need for change, for greater productivity, and for their participation in fulfilling these objectives. The employees in each department were confronted with reality and helped to commit themselves to a new format with the help of the Scanlon Production and Screening Committees. The individual piece-rate departments were confronted with their "privileged status" and asked to join in the total organization's commitment to quality and improved performance. Piece-rate earners were assured that even though they would need to abandon their individual earnings, they would earn additional money in monthly bonuses as the total number of company employees improved productivity.

Table 4.1 indicates the steadiness of employees' financial progress and their success in having their suggestions implemented. Built into this performance record is a continuous series of innovations in marketing, manufacturing, development, and financing as Herman Miller changed from a relatively modest home-furnishings manufacturer to an international organization manufacturing institutional furnishings. Physical growth is represented in numbers of employees, from 171 in 1950 to 2,634 in 1981, and in sales volume, from $500,000 in 1950 to $252,740,000 in 1981. The company now concentrates on those markets — offices, institutions, hospitals, laboratories, and factories — which executive leadership has clearly identified as the right job for the Herman Miller Company.

THE SCANLON PLAN: PARTICIPATION AND RESPONSIBILITY FOR INNOVATION

From our first encounter in 1950, Herman Miller has accepted the fact that all employees and the Herman Miller organization itself are in the process of change. More important, executive leadership has accepted the responsi-

Table 4.1. Herman Miller, Inc., Scanlon Plan Bonus and Suggestions,
1950–1975

Year	Monthly Bonus Paid	Reserve	Total Bonus Paid	Number of Part. Emp.	% of Bonus	Number of Suggestions
1950	22,330	3,941	26,271	171	8.93	131
1951	45,576	7,507	53,083	179	8.44	208
1952	54,988	6,744	61,721	192	8.69	199
1953	65,532	11,565	77,097	197	10.28	182
1954	22,380	0	22,380	168	3.21	174
1955	56,189	9,057	65,246	163	9.74	149
1956	68,136	10,000	78,136	169	10.41	130
1957	105,463	10,000	115,463	190	14.70	40
1958	91,418	10,000	101,418	195	12.20	83
1959	131,358	10,000	141,358	202	15.87	225
1960	161,613	10,000	171,613	210	17.16	217
1961	70,731	10,000	80,731	205	8.21	224
1962	100,926	10,000	110,926	225	10.14	198
1963	58,047	0	58,047	231	4.97	260
1964	71,396	0	71,396	229	5.93	213
1965	95,322	10,000	105,322	247	7.52	214
1966	127,721	10,000	137,721	300	8.65	179
1967	165,771	14,458	180,229	360	9.16	292
1968	142,262	7,924	150,186	355	6.56	304
1969	343,862	16,000	359,862	504	12.39	243
1970	201,468	0	210,468	524	5.48	347
1971	94,139	0	94,139	473	2.65	344
1972	330,112	30,000	360,112	371	8.31	412
1973	475,141	25,363	500,504	418	10.23	421
1974	1,157,662	45,000	1,202,662	565	22.82	431
1975	450,304	50,000	500,304	586	8.61	557
1976	1,139,257	60,000	1,199,257	762	16.73	
Totals	5,849,104	377,559	6,235,652		10.95%	

bility for managing this process: it is more effective in doing the right job
and more efficient in doing the job right.

Herman Miller's chief executive officers have increasingly assumed their
unique and singular responsibility for determining and defining that "right
job." The right job for Herman Miller, they believed, was no longer furnishings for homes, but for offices and other organizations. Once the right job
was determined, the executives recognized that they had a commitment to
assure the quality of competence throughout the organization to do the job
right. In fact, the implementation of the Scanlon Plan emphasized the need
for competence, not only in executive leadership, but also throughout
management.

What aspects of Herman Miller's reality have fostered invention and innovation in the workplace? Reality is, of course the workplace at Herman Miller: factories, offices, research/development, and sales and marketing — everything, in short, relating to the company. Those aspects of reality most responsible for continuing invention and innovation were clearly defined by the mandate of the chief executive officer, Hugh DePree, several years ago:

The Herman Miller Mandate

Herman Miller must be an international organization in which people define and solve problems. Problem definition, problem solving, through innovation wherever possible, must result in products and services which improve the quality of life in the working and healing environments.

At Herman Miller, people do this through having the responsibility and opportunity to contribute, to participate, to be involved, to own the problem, and, indeed, to own Herman Miller.

We are committed to quality and excellence in all that we do and the way in which we do it.

We seek to be socially responsible and we share a concern and responsibility for the quality of the environment in which we and our neighbors live and work.

Profit is an essential and enabling factor in all annual and long-range planning and operations. Specific profit goals will be set annually.

Growth is implicit but must come because of the quality of the problem solution and the potential in our people and our program.

The word mandate is not new in our general vocabulary. However, its usage in our industrial/organizational development process is recent — and it is somewhat unique in the implementation of the Scanlon Plan. Most organizations have had objectives, goals, or missions. These statements were often internally defined and personalized as well as of short duration. In contrast, the mandate, although developed by the chief executive officer, was based on the internal and external demands of the organization's reality. For example, customers or clients were unrelenting in their demand for the best return on their investment in the service or product — and competitors did not relent in their efforts to excel. That mandate defined reality and prompted invention and innovation to meet these expectations for superior quality, service, performance, deliveries, and price. When DePree stated in the mandate that Herman Miller was an international organization, he was not expressing a personal ambition. It was dictated by worldwide customers who expected dependability of quality, service, and price wherever they were located.

The mandate stated clearly that the shareholders demanded a superior equity as a return on their capital investments in facilities, equipment, and technology. Their financial portfolios could be changed with considerable flexibility. That reality was made obvious to employees, and their response was to be sufficiently innovative in the use of these facilities to maintain the interest and loyalty of the shareholders.

The mandate defined profit as a cost of doing business as required by the external corporate or lending institutions. Profit was not a reward for a personalized few. The corporate and financial worlds were continually evaluating the profit generation of an operation in order to decide if that company's earnings justified maintaining, continuing, or increasing their support and investment. This mandate represented a reality, which prompted greater invention and innovation to prevent plant closings or surrender to domestic and foreign investors.

The mandate focused on another group of investors, the employees, who often invested more heavily with their daily lives, energy, education, expertise, and commitment than the capital investors. These employee investors evaluated their investment continually by asking, "Is this my best job opportunity? Is this my most secure job opportunity?" The employees became less naive and more sophisticated in the management of such a major personal investment. This reality, mandated because of its immediate and personal consequences, evoked inventions and innovations. Reality was not hidden or disguised; it was conspicuous, convincing, and personalized.

All of these investors not only expected but insisted on superior, consistent, predictable returns on their respective investments. The mandate was the unique personal responsibility of DePree, as president and chief executive officer. It was, in fact, a tool used by the Scanlon Plan to optimize and maximize inventions and innovations throughout the organization.

Innovation in the workplace was dependent on the initial application of this mandate with the top-echelon executive committee. The chief executive officer initiated the process that we have termed the "W" process, with his immediate staff. The first step, as shown in figure 4.1, was the confrontation procedure, to assure awareness of the realities that he had identified. The second step was the open challenge to the chief executive officer by his immediate staff as to the validity and reliability of the data documenting the mandate. During the second step there was emotional exposure of entrenched positions, anxieties concerning the implications of the data, questions of the subjective and personal evaluations and judgments of the data. It was a vigorous feedback confrontation.

Once the chief executive officer had worked through the subjective as well as objective challenges to the mandate and had distilled professional staff inputs representing all of the relevant areas of customer service, marketing/sales, technology, manufacturing, quality, central systems, finance, and human resources, he was able in the third step to consolidate the mandate and articulate it for the entire organization.

The final stated mandate was the instrument used to gain the steps of con-

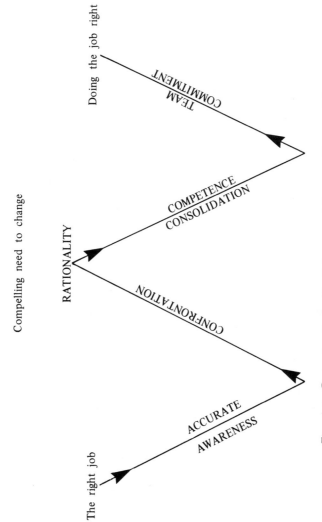

Compelling need to change

The right job

Doing the job right

RATIONALITY

ACCURATE AWARENESS

CONFRONTATION

COMPETENCE CONSOLIDATION

TEAM COMMITMENT

Fig. 4.1. Opportunity to Participate and Become Responsible

solidation and commitment which complete the "W." Referring to figure 4.1, the process began with the identification of what was the right job for the organization and ended with the identification of the competence and commitment to do the job right. The ultimate purpose of the "W" process was to make clear the compelling need to change as dictated by the mandate.

THEORY AND APPLICATION: THE SCANLON PROCESS

The application of the Scanlon process requires three specific and purposefully separated actions or steps. The first action is the studied and intensive presentation of the mandate. The documentation supporting the sales and market, the capital investments, the financial requirements, the technology and manufacturing, and human resources demands is painstakingly thorough. The mandate is written from the perspective that historical or past performance is inadequate to meet current and future changing demands. Consequently, the data and arguments must be so persuasive that they will be accepted as a compelling need to change.

After presentation of the data and supporting arguments, followed by debate by organization executives, it is necessary and appropriate for the chief executive officer to request a secret vote. The vote is not addressed to the question of whether the staff members know these facts, but whether they understand and comprehend the facts and their implications for the organization. The validity and reliability of the data must be convincingly *rational.*

The secret vote is essential after this set of vigorous challenges to inform the CEO of the degree of consensus regarding the mandate and to reduce the possibility that staff members are "obliging" the chief executive. The secret vote also gives the executive staff members an evaluation of their own peers' consensus regarding the mandate. The results of the secret vote are "hard data" which should establish the degree of confidence the chief executive officer and the executive staff can expect in managing any change.

The mandate of any one division of a multidivision corporation ought to have the unanimous understanding, approval, and support of the corporate executive committee. The staff members of the division need to have the assurance that their chief executive officer has successfully processed their mandate through the corporate executive office. This procedure gives a substantial degree of assurance to the chief executive officer and, in turn, the staff that the corporation's expectations for their division and themselves personally will be predictable and rational. This is the minimum guarantee a corporation ought to give its respective divisions.

As a second and separate step in the process, the CEO addresses the staff with the question: "Are you able and willing to accept the ownership of the mandate (problem)?" Inasmuch as this step imposes a significant change and a new set of demands upon each staff member and his or her area of responsibility, this question is a new and highly personalized challenge. It is a minimum courtesy to ask this question (at the mid-point of the "W") before proceeding toward the implementation. It is not uncommon for staff members to evaluate the new demand as being more than they want to accept, considering their other options, their health, their age, or their personal commitments. The secret vote is preceded by the opportunity to explore and clarify the perceived change demanded by the mandate both personally and professionally. Again, the chief executive officer needs this confidential data in order to make plans. Also, the staff members need to know the position of their peers. The secret process preserves the integrity of the individual. It emphasizes the appropriate amount of self-responsibility and self-accountability. It provides hard data to justify the degree of confidence in initiating any change in the organization.

The third step encompasses the consolidation and commitment stages of the "W" process. This step is taken separately from steps 1 and 2, and occurs after an interval of time. The CEO requests staff members to prepare a comprehensive statement of the personal and professional contributions they are prepared to make to fulfill the demands of their ownership of the mandate. This preparation is made with three considerations in mind: "Am I competent to do the job right?" "Is the staff competent to do the job right?" "Are the competencies of staff members of sufficient quality to permit them to do the job right?" The consultant generally plays a key role in this assessment.

Staff members must prepare privately to present to their superior and their peers a statement representing their understanding and ownership of the mandate and its commitment to change for the organization and for themselves. The statement includes the staff member's credentials for membership on the team in terms of competence and commitment. Preparing and presenting this statement is generally considered to be a unique and highly significant personal and professional experience.

The conclusion to this third step, and to the entire mandate procedure, is the final secret vote. The chief executive officer now requests the members of the executive staff to review the staff's comprehension of the mandate; their ability and willingness to own the problem of change; and their own competence, their peers' competence, and their respective contributions to effect the changes necessary to achievement of the mandate. With the benefit of these data, the chief executive officer requests the staff to vote responsibly: "Are you willing to commit yourselves to this team with confidence in its corporate competence and success in meeting the mandate?"

It should be obvious that success will depend more on the team's performance in doing the job right than on the individual team member's relationship with the chief executive officer. To commit to a team that is not totally qualified and committed is foolhardy. A vote of less than unanimous confidence suggests the need for serious additional personal and organizational development. It is the primary responsibility of the chief executive officer to take this additional step to assure the staff that it has the organizational competence to do the right job right.

In terms of the relevance of reality to invention and innovation, this process accurately identifies the reality that is critical to every member of the executive organization: the corporation officers, the chief executive officer, and executive staff members. Exhaustive opportunities and procedures are used to assure the validity, reliability, and believability of this reality data. Only when the comprehension and ownership of these respective elements of the organizational reality are assured, do we proceed to challenge the organization's competence and commitment to innovate in making the changes requisite to improvement.

The potential for organizational innovation ought to be greatest at this executive level. However, the release of that organizational innovation potential is directly dependent on the leadership of these executives in their respective areas of responsibility. That leadership is expressed in the essential but rare quality of *serving* as the best means available — not just managing — and it is the key to generating innovation throughout the organization. The organizational development process just described tends to identify and overcome self-serving behavior and to gain sincerity and uniformity of commitment.

Once the process has been completed successfully in the identification, ownership, and commitment to the company mandate at the executive management level, then there is the need to educate the entire organization by echelons. It is a formidable assignment, especially in an organization where employees number hundreds or thousands. The education process is essential, however, if every employee is going to become "accurately aware," or organizationally literate, because only then can anyone and everyone expect employees to *become* responsible.

It is incumbent upon the chief executive officer to act as both leader and educator because he or she is the most informed, knowledgeable, and proficient in regard to the operation. This assignment is contrary to the opinion of one executive who said, "Twenty years ago I decided to forgo the gentle professions of teaching, healing, and preaching to become an entrepreneur." Obviously, he had missed "his calling." It was no wonder that he had just experienced a bitter, seventeen-week strike in his company. This organizational executive or entrepreneur had delegated for too long a time his responsibilities as a teacher–leader and was now suffering the consequences — employees who did not know or understand company economics, did not accept ownership for productivity, and did not commit themselves to job and profit security. Therefore, the Scanlon process of continually educating all its employees must be the unequivocal priority and responsibility of the company chief executive.

THEORY IN PRACTICE: THE 1979 SCANLON AT HERMAN MILLER, INC.

The Herman Miller organization had had the Scanlon Plan for 25 years and had used its principles of identity, participation, equity, and competence. The company executives had managed the transformation of a small traditional furniture manufacturing company into an international organization that designs and manufactures office, institution, and hospital–laboratory–factory concepts. They had consistently identified the right job for the company and had enabled their employees to participate through the establishment of production and screening committees. Table 4.1 documented this history.

In 1976, 1977, and 1978, the Herman Miller reality was changing radically and rapidly. The decision to manage aggressively a new office concept led them to support a price reduction contrary to the strategy of all of their competitors. Cumulative innovations over several years had effected substantial cost savings. Innovative marketing strategies made this dramatic decision rational and compelling. The fact that over 50 percent of the company's employees were staff support and were employed in services rather than in production constituted a new reality for Herman Miller's investment in human resources. The enormous capital commitment to people-oriented facilities for manufacturing and staff-support administrative people represented an increasingly visible commitment to physical resources that had to pay off. The reality of accelerating investment in sophisticated facilities and systems alerted every employee to his or her personal responsibility to assure increasing returns to the company.

This investment was reinforced by the fact that Herman Miller had entered the over-the-counter equity market to gain the required capital to launch this major thrust. The reality of the financial market analysts' expectations and the shareholders' needs for substantial dividends were compelling responsibilities in terms of quarterly financial reviews and daily productivity performance reports.

The acceleration of investors' expectations; the seemingly insatiable appetite for financial resources; the extreme frustration of trying to meet schedules with available manufacturing facilities, materials, and equipment; and the frightening disarray of new and different human resources — was best summarized in a *Business Week* article as "torrid growth."[2] All of these expectations would challenge the validity and viability of the Scanlon process at Herman Miller, Inc.

The emerging reality was never more demanding. The historical answers of more orders, more equipment, more money, more people were never more obsolete or inappropriate.

However, the process of identifying accurately the current reality and asking the question, "Is there a compelling need to change?" was not an operational process of the Herman Miller program during the late sixties and early seventies. Neither the annual nor long-range plans of the company had been concerned with the gathering or submission of data to executives or employees in the vigorous educational "W" processes of awareness, confrontation, consolidation, or commitment. This 1976–1978 frantic myopic behavior is typical of most organizations that are preoccupied with momentary success or survival.

But the Herman Miller reality had changed. In many ways, the reality suggested that the perennial green light had turned to amber and, if predictions followed on course, the operational light would become red. The marketplace in which Herman Miller enjoyed dominance was now occupied by industry "giants" and other "Johnny-come-latelies." The customers were demanding better service, efficient and on-time deliveries, competitive prices, and innovative applications. The procedures of manufacturing, systems, schedules, controls, engineering, and capacity of production were almost without reason and seemingly uncontrolled. The demands for money were exceeding the historical, relatively modest predictions and requests. The lending agencies introduced and required more regular and sophisticated accounting requirements and professional surveillance. The sheer number of employees in every category exceeded all scheduled recruitment, orientation, and training programs. Over 60 percent of the employees had less than two years' tenure with Herman Miller. The percentage of "knowledge workers," or support staff, had now exceeded the 50 percent ratio of employees. The emphasis of the original Scanlon Plan was on manufacturing productivity and had consequently limited the innovations and inventions to that area. The potential of that productivity was still available. However, the complexity of factors, the sophistication and heterogeneity of personnel inputs, the timing and sources of financial resources, and the competitive advances in technology made the program and process of the original Scanlon Plan less than adequate. Questions were asked frequently by the increasing majority of staff and support personnel: "How do I participate?" "How do I contribute?"

Obviously, the perception of the Herman Miller reality had become an irrational composite of myopic personalized interests. Neither the older nor the newer employees had the benefit of past achievements to assist them in surviving and succeeding in the current demands. There were few rational experiences in their everyday work lives. Some of the turmoil of this period is typified by the amazement of the customer who received 17 packages with nothing in them. Less than 50 percent of the shipments were made on time. Inventories were in excess of the operational demands. These facts evidenced a new reality — a compelling need to change!

The irrational world of work caused most employees to search naively for simple answers, such as more materials, more inventory, more finances, more people. There was little comprehension of the reality, the cause-and-effect relationships, or approaches to remedy or control the situation. These conditions were particularly adverse to the use of invention or innovation in improving productivity.

So, it was back to fundamentals. The mandate still proved to be valid and to be a reliable tool for determining the right job and the directions and principles for doing the job right in 1977–1979.

Beginning at the executive echelon, the Scanlon Plan was central in the concept of Herman Miller Company's self-renewal.

IDENTIFICATION: HERMAN MILLER PAST, PRESENT, AND FUTURE

The first step of the Scanlon process was the identification of the current Herman Miller, Inc., organization. The realities of the past were integral to this ongoing organization and a tangible source of pride, camaraderie, and commitment. The new reality, however, was gross obsolescence. Current weaknesses and inadequacies were identified with graphic illustrations and data in every part of the organization: in the manufacturing and support-service facilities; in the financial market of investors, lenders, and vendors; and in human resources. Sixty percent of the current employees had not been identified with the Herman Miller Company two years previously.

The essence of the new reality was the demand for Herman Miller to develop and identify again a unique reason for being which could be recognized by all the investors — customers, shareholders, corporate and lending investors, and employees — as their best investment, outdistancing any competitors or alternatives. That reality maximized the mandates for invention and innovation throughout the organization.

The full impact of that realization was most apparent in June 1977 at a special coffee-time employee celebration of the monthly bonus. When Hugh DePree announced the bonus to the employees, he also reported that service to the customers had deteriorated substantially. He stated that there would be no further celebration of bonus earnings by the employees until the customers had far more to celebrate in their Herman Miller investments than

the employees. Every investor — customer, capital, and employee — must
have great and genuine cause for celebration. No one investor must celebrate at the expense of the other investors. DePree then set in motion the
renewal of the Scanlon process. Based on his own mandate, he assigned the
organization education process of the changed reality to Glenn Walters, the
executive vice-president. With 25 years of intensive and extensive experience in Herman Miller, Walters was uniquely qualified to carry out this
assignment.

The fact that DePree identified the reality but did not preempt it for himself was innovative. The recognition of the difference between his personal
leadership responsibility and his professional competence to manage the
changed and complex reality was innovative. (He knew that he personally
could no longer go back to being in charge of sales and marketing, manufacturing, and finance.) Recognition of the responsibility of the chief executive
officer to release the full potential of that reality for motivating invention
and innovation was, in itself, innovative. The process of releasing that organizational potential by assuring the employees' accurate awareness and
comprehension, by recording their ability and willingness to accept the responsibility, and by specifying the required competence and commitment
was innovative. Small-group meetings were conducted by Walters and the
consultant with all employees in a concentrated period of time.

Identity: Employee Awareness and Potential for Change

The challenge of confidential feedback votes on this mandated reality
was posed by these questions: "Is there a compelling, convincing need to
change?" and "Is there genuine potential for improvement?" This was another innovation in confronting reality. The insistence on a secret vote
when every employee was asked to "vote in your own, your family's, and
your company's best interest" proved to be a novel organizational experience for most employees. A 90 percent majority, rather than a simple or
two-thirds majority, was an innovation in establishing a recorded data base
of widespread, shared consensus for the entire organization.

Identity: Every Employee within the Company

When the organizational reality was described as primarily the expectations, involvements, and perceptions of four key investors — customers,
shareholders, corporate moneylenders, and employees — a different frame
of reference was provided in which to pose the question, "What is in it for
you?" It stated the need for the several investors, but emphasized particularly the impressive personalized investment of the employees, eight hours a
day, forty hours a week, fifty weeks a year — a lifetime. What returns did

they expect from their investment? The confidential question was a studied attempt to assure that the employees were not disappointed in their expectations and were not a disappointment in meeting the company's expectations.

Participation in Ownership, Competence, and Commitment

The greatest challenge to innovation in the Scanlon education process, however, was represented by Glenn Walters' final question: "Are you willing to elect an Ad Hoc Committee to work with management in developing a proposal for your organization?" Implementation began after an affirmative vote exceeding 90 percent, and the election of the employees' most qualified representatives to this one-time, one-purpose committee to develop innovatively their own unique proposal. There was no standard program to be copied or replicated from other companies. Management had no prepared program to submit or to sell. The realities of the criteria, understood and accepted by 90 percent of the employees, were effective service to the customers; effective use of facilities, equipment, and technology; effective use of monies; and effective use of human resources.

The process of "how" to meet the demands of the organizational reality was to be discovered by the elected committee. The Ad Hoc Committee addressed the responsibilities by dividing its functions into three subcommittees: the Education Committee, the Rules and Regulations Committee, and the Equity or Formula Committee.

Education and Communications Committee. The Education Committee had the assignment to state the historical identity of the organization, the current compelling need to change, and the rationale for more intensive personal and professional implementation of participative management. The identity statement pinpointed the current relevance of the past, but particularly the inadequacies and inappropriateness of the past in addressing the demands of the current situation. It accepted the organizational mandate statement as an authorizing document. It defined the current implications of meeting and not meeting the demands of the mandate. And it outlined the need for all employees to understand the mandate, to be able and willing to accept ownership of the mandated productivity and profitability, to make the necessary contributions to change, and to achieve the increasing imperatives of the company's changed situation.

The Education Committee had the responsibility of soliciting questions from the members of the Ad Hoc Committee, as well as from all employees. These questions revealed the major concerns or critical issues of the employees. The Education Committee then formulated clear and informative answers to the questions. These questions and answers were put into the format of a true-or-false "Quiz You Cannot Fail." This quiz gave the entire organization a review of the many issues that were relevant and addressed by the Ad Hoc Committee, assuring a high degree of consistency in the employees' information.

The Education Committee prepared a sample ballot with the appropriate instructions for confidentiality and responsibility to be included in the proposal book.

Rules and Regulations Committee. The Rules and Regulations Committee had the assignment to develop a communications system to assure that every employee would know and understand the changed reality accurately. This awareness enabled every employee to anticipate and identify problems as well as participate in influencing decisions by making and implementing suggestions. Participation was specifically defined as the right and the responsibility to *influence*, not to make, the decision. Management always had that responsibility. The structure at Herman Miller identified every employee as a member of a work team — everyone belonged and was expected to participate and to be responsible. Each peer group had an elected caucus representative to facilitate and process suggestions and concerns with its elected leader. Each department of the division had a representative on the council as the final divisional authority. Then there was a corporate screening committee or council made up of representatives of all levels of all divisions (fig. 4.2).

The committee developed a Problem/Suggestion/Action (PSA) process. Once the reality demands were clearer and the ownership accepted, the employees were alerted to the daily or periodic problems that they experienced. They had often experienced the frustration of trying to cope with these problems, often with no suggestions for resolution or access to appropriate resources to assist them. The process of problem identification brought into focus competent, available resources who emphasized the clear definition of the problem and its implications before hurrying to suggested change. Engineering and maintenance personnel had training and skills which proved to be particularly helpful in problem identification. These particular personnel were sometimes "standing members" of work teams or of departmental production committees.

The suggestion system was specifically personalized, beginning with the clear identification of the suggestor, his or her rationale for making the suggestion, the justification for its priority, and the procedure and personnel for implementation. Provision was made for action of the supervisor of the Work Team or Production Committee, and of the Screening Committee or Council, as well as the person assigned the responsibility for providing feedback or implementing the suggestion and the date for action. (The form used for making a suggestion and the procedures followed in taking action on the suggestion are shown in figure 4.3.)

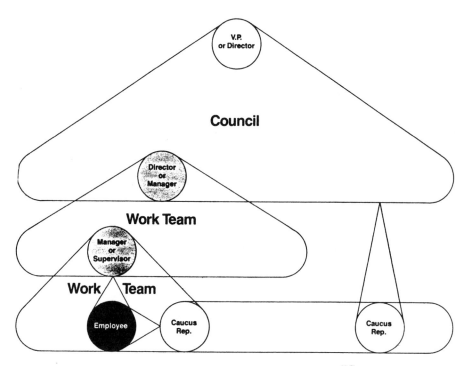

Fig. 4.2. Typical problem/suggestion/action flow. This figure shows the primary way an employee can get action — beginning with his or her manager/ supervisor, possibly involving his or her work team and/or higher-level work teams, and eventually being reviewed by the council.

The entire emphasis of the Rules and Regulations Committee was to assure communication for understanding the responsibilities, accepting the ownership, and commitment to assure attention and action. It was made very clear that management always has the responsibility to make the decision. The process was not a democracy in organizational action. It was a highly disciplined process of leadership in which followership was voluntary because of management's competence and rationality of interest, commitment, and action.

This system of communications may seem obvious for any organization, but the number of applications in organizations of such problem identification and suggestion systems is limited. The assured openness to challenge — "how come?" "why not?" — and the assured rationality of the response by all members of the organization are extraordinary at Herman Miller. Management has commonly assumed the privilege of managing with little commitment to the idea that employees should perceive the rationality of their decisions. In fact, management members have not provided themselves a

herman miller

PSA Scanlon '79   no. [   ]

submitted by	department work team	shift/ location	date __/__/__

suggestion

referred to _____ date __/__/__
      (type responding council leader's name here)

referred by _____ due date __/__/__
      (suggesting council leader's signature)

suggestion priority

☐ A — Immediate Action — written response within 30 days   ☐ C — Not Urgent —written response within 6 months

☐ B — Written Response — within 60 days   ☐ D — Information Only — no written response required

response

☐ accepted ☐ declined	cost savings
date implemented __/__/__	☐ labor $ _____
	☐ material $ _____
_____ __/__/__	☐ other $ _____
respondent's signature date	

respondent	suggesting council	Scanlon Office	responding council	suggestor's work team
white	**green**	**yellow**	**pink**	**goldenrod**

ZA99.0   906-234

Fig. 4.3. Scanlon 1979 Employee Suggestion Form

communication system that assures them of "receiving" contrary opinion — not that they must "oblige," but at least they should hear the contrary opinion. Management will be perceived as arbitrary and irrational unless a guaranteed system is established for sending and receiving communications.

The Scanlon communications process at Herman Miller established not only the *right* but also the *responsibility* for every employee to demand rationality in assuring (1) superior quality in performance, delivery, and price to the customers; (2) superior performance on the capital investors' returns on their monies; (3) superior profit advantage to the corporation in maintaining, continuing, and increasing its operational support; and (4) security, income, and satisfaction to the employees.

The Herman Miller Ad Hoc Committee proposal documented its system of communication. The proposal included long-term and annual planning of strategies and tactics. It established a communications system that assured awareness, to understand; confrontation, to assure debate of differences and similarities; consolidation of competencies; and commitment to integrity.

Equity or Formula Committee. Equity in its broadest significance for all investors was explored and defined. The importance of the Equity/Bonus Formula Committee became appropriate to fulfill the need for a regular, rigorous accountability for the responsibilities that had been defined and articulated by the Education Committee and for the ownership of the problems and commitment to participate as established by the Rules and Regulations Committee. The employee had no claim for recognition, reward, or even self-respect unless and until he or she had documented the specific performances which earned them. Therefore, the Equity Committee clearly set forth accountability to the customers who expect quality of product and service as well as price, to the capital investors who expect substantial returns on their investment, to the corporation which expects sufficient profits to justify maintaining and advancing the operation, and to the employees who expect safety, security, and success.

Consequently, Herman Miller's Ad Hoc Committee proposal included not only the definition of equity but also specific areas of responsibility and accountability. The format of the monthly report of accountability provided criteria to which every member of the organization related by calling out performance data on customer service, physical resources usage, human resources, and monies (fig. 4.4). Each division was held equally accountable for all criteria. The largest-volume division was as responsible and accountable as the smallest-volume division for the customers, capital and corporate investors, and employees.

The weightings among the four factors of customer service, human re-

Performance to Plan Score

Customer Service	O/I	H/S	IS	Operations	Corporate	Average	Total
On-time Shipments							
Correct Shipments							
Past Dues							
Rapid Response Index							
Effective Use of Labor	**O/I**	**H/S**	**IS**	**Operations**	**Corporate**	**Average**	**Total**
Orders							
Production							
Projects							
Administrative Service							
Effective Use of Material	**O/I**	**H/S**	**IS**	**Operations**	**Corporate**	**Average**	**Total**
Inventory Investment							
Scrap							
Shrinkage							
Effective Use of Money	**O/I**	**H/S**	**IS**	**Operations**	**Corporate**	**Average**	**Total**
Expense Control							
Net Revenue							
Accounts Receivable							
Material Price Variance							

Performance Score

Points

Fig. 4.4. Performance to Plan Score

sources, physical resources, and financial resources have some variance to reflect current priorities in any particular year. However, there is a high degree of visible and rational balance among these criteria.

The range or tolerance of the individual criteria may change, for example, the customer demand for quality or time delivery may be increased. The requirement that the sales organization exceed its predictions by no more than 5 percent may be loosened if the backlog of manufacturing work is being reduced and represents less than optimal capacity (fig. 4.4).

Consequently, Herman Miller developed a process that holds all employees accountable for the customer's receiving prompt and accurate delivery of the product and service as well as quality. The monthly report charges all employees with the obligation of meeting their assigned responsibilities; for example, the sales and marketing personnel are expected to meet their predicted quotas on schedules that match manufacturing capacities as well as the client's needs. The report indicated whether the sophisticated development and engineering staff people were meeting required time and budget targets. The production employees were accountable for meeting and beating sophisticated industry standards. All organization members had accountability for performance with safety, quality, and efficiency.

The process demonstrated accountability for the application and use of physical resources. Such reports as the operating time of equipment; the usage of utilities and energy; the scrap, reject, and rework experience; or inventory control were objective criteria of accountability essential to a satisfactory return on capital investments.

The process included indicators of accountability for the usage of monies. Monies reported on items of price variances in purchasing, accounts receivable, revenues, and cost of interest on borrowed funds were easily understood and available for accountability.

In all of these factors required for accountability, the need for rational employee performance was stated. The appropriate measures of accountability were applied so that all members exercised the proper responsibility. For example, sometimes "more is better," i.e., more on-time shipments give significant advantage to the customers and investors, as well as producers. Sometimes "less is better," i.e., less inventory gives greater number of inventory turns and requires less borrowed monies. Sometimes "on target is best," i.e., the accurate accomplishment of goals, such as sales projections, means all the planning, scheduling, producing, servicing, and delivery services are significantly advantaged in carrying out their functions (fig. 4.5).

The process of accountability identified clearly the leadership throughout an organization that defined the responsibilities in every area and then enabled employees to carry out their personal and professional responsibilities. The work teams and council (originally designated as the Production and Screening Committee) structures made these leaders physically visible and available to acknowledge their responsibilities and then made them accountable for their fulfillment. The chief executive officer as moderator of the Screening Committee or Council identified the key resource people for recognition of performance as well as the failure to perform. This regular public accountability process was another innovation. Public accountability inhibited any "innovative" attempts to use alibis, rationalizations, or deviousness.

When the three subcommittees had completed their respective assignments, the Education Committee prepared and collated the materials and convened the entire Ad Hoc Committee. The proposal was thoroughly reviewed, revised, and finally approved by the entire Ad Hoc Committee. Approval of the Ad Hoc Committee was sought so that the education, understanding, and acceptance of the entire organization would be assured. When each Ad Hoc Committee member signed the "authors' signature page" endorsing the proposal and recommending their peers' acceptance and activation of the process, approval was personally advocated.

Performance to Plan

On-time Shipments

Points							
70	80	90	100	110	120	130	
70%	80%	90%	92%	94%	96%	98%	100%

Plan

Performance

More is Better

Inventory Investment

Points						
70	80	90	100	110	120	130
120 Days	110	100	90%	80	70	60 Days

Plan

Performance

Less is Better

Orders

Points												
70	80	90	100	110	120	130	120	110	100	90	80	70
80%	85%	90%	95%			100			105%	110%	115%	120%

Plan Range

Performance

On Target is Best

Fig. 4.5. Three Types of Measurement Used to Measure Performance to Plan

A formal occasion was arranged for the Ad Hoc Committee to deliver the proposal to DePree. He had the responsibility for evaluating whether the proposed process would enable the entire organization to do the job right. He again had the opportunity of deciding whether he personally was able and willing to lead the organization in this process. This evaluation proved to be a sober decision point because now he had to fulfill the commitment to change and to become a leader.

Once DePree approved the Ad Hoc Committee proposal and decided he was able and willing to commit to its specifications, he had the responsibility of leading a team to make the presentation to the corporation's executive committee. His elected and selected team also had the opportunity and responsibility of hearing and knowing the corporation's acknowledgment and commitment to their mandate. Also, the corporate officers had the opportunity and responsibility of challenging the representative team in regard to their fellow employees' understanding, ownership, and commitment to achieve the mandate. The Executive Committee's official response to the Ad Hoc Committee proposal was in writing and was included in the Ad Hoc Committee proposal.

Then every employee received a personal copy of the proposal in book form. The books were assigned personally to each employee with the advice that the book was "company confidential" and would be a "great comfort" and advantage to competitors if they were to obtain a copy inadvertently. The employees were urged to study the proposal and to write questions regarding any issue in the margins provided. After a week, including a weekend, one-hour small-group meetings were scheduled to answer any questions about the proposal. During this period, Ad Hoc Committee members served as resource people to explain the rationale for the provisions of the proposal and to act as advocates for acceptance.

Several factors were pointed out by the Ad Hoc Committee. They acknowledged that their proposal was not perfect, but they believed that it was sound and they recommended adoption. There were provisions for changes that might be justified after periodic reviews and, at the least, an annual audit.

At the end of each meeting, a secret vote was taken on whether employees were willing to work under this process. On the ballot, employees were reminded of their responsibility to themselves, their families, and the company and were asked, therefore, to vote responsibly. A 90 percent majority was again required. The vote resulted in a 95.4 majority for acceptance.

The processing and acceptance of the Ad Hoc Committee proposal established a consensus on the individual employee's and the organization's reasons for working together. In contrast to traditional collective bargaining, the proposal was innovative in the cooperative spirit it generated and in the

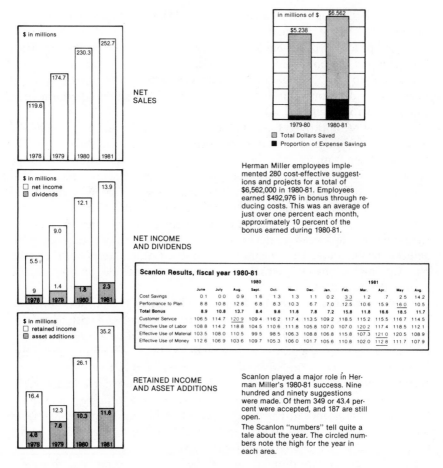

NET SALES

NET INCOME AND DIVIDENDS

RETAINED INCOME AND ASSET ADDITIONS

Herman Miller employees implemented 280 cost-effective suggestions and projects for a total of $6,562,000 in 1980-81. Employees earned $492,976 in bonus through reducing costs. This was an average of just over one percent each month, approximately 10 percent of the bonus earned during 1980-81.

Scanlon played a major role in Herman Miller's 1980-81 success. Nine hundred and ninety suggestions were made. Of them 349 or 43.4 percent were accepted, and 187 are still open.

The Scanlon "numbers" tell quite a tale about the year. The circled numbers note the high for the year in each area.

Fig. 4.6. Scanlon Plan Results

responsibility and accountability it required from every employee for *all* resources, not just human resources. The proposal was also innovative in contrast to the traditionally authoritarian "management by objectives" because it was authorized or legitimatized by the mandates of all investors, not just by financial investors, and because its success was dependent on a self-reviewing process that made employees aware of changing reality and helped them to respond appropriately. It was a process that assured organizational literacy.

The Herman Miller story documents an innovative leadership process that motivates employees' potential for innovation—a potential that is tapped consistently throughout the organization. This self-renewing process is essential in managing what the employees and organization are "becoming."

The consequences of the process are a continuing flow of innovations, dependent primarily on the compelling quality of the reality, as perceived by employees. The record of the number of suggestions made under the Scanlon process and the dollar value of the savings (fig. 4.6) document the degree of innovative activity which has taken place at Herman Miller since the acceptance of the Ad Hoc Committee proposals.

NOTES

1. C.F. Frost, J.H. Wakely, and R.H. Ruh, *The Scanlon Plan for Organization Development: Identity, Participation, and Equity* (East Lansing, Mich.: Michigan State University Press, 1974).

2. "Why Herman Miller Seems So Enticing," *Business Week*, March 6, 1978, p. 104.

5.
Tarrytown:
Quality of Work Life at a
General Motors Plant*

Robert H. Guest

This is the story of the General Motors car assembly plant at Tarrytown, New York, from 1970 to 1982. In 1970, the plant was known to have one of the poorest labor relations and production records in GM. In the decade to follow, the plant turned around to become one of the company's better run sites.

Born out of frustration and desperation, a quality-of-work-life (QWL) program developed at Tarrytown. The effort involved mutual commitment by management and the union to change old ways of dealing with work on the shop floor. "Quality of work life" is a generic phrase that covers a person's feelings about every dimension of work, including economic rewards and benefits, security, working conditions, organizational and interpersonal relationships, and its intrinsic meaning in a person's life.

For the moment, I will define QWL more specifically as a *process* by which an organization attempts to unlock the creative potential of its people by involving them in decisions affecting their work lives. A distinguishing characteristic of the process is that its goals are not simply extrinsic, focusing on the improvement of productivity and efficiency per se; they are also intrinsic, regarding what the worker sees as self-fulfilling and self-enhancing ends in themselves.

In recent years, the QWL movement has generated broad-scale interest. Since 1975, more than 850 articles and books have been written on the subject, and at least four national and international study and research centers

*Reprinted by permission of the *Harvard Business Review*. "Quality of Work Life — Learning from Tarrytown" by Robert Guest (July/August 1979). Copyright ©1979 by the President and Fellows of Harvard College; all rights reserved. New material has been added to this account by the author, bringing the Tarrytown story up to date.

focus on quality of work life as such. Scores of industrial enterprises throughout the United States are conducting experiments, usually on a small scale; and in an eight-month world study tour a few years back of more than 50 industrial plants in Japan, Australia, and Europe, I found great interest in "industrial democracy."

What is so special about the Tarrytown story? First, it has the earmarks of success. Second, it illustrates that achieving success is an unending process. External events, such as the economic condition of the automobile industry, have a disturbing influence on sustaining QWL efforts, but so do internal developments, decisions, personnel changes, and a myriad of other factors that frustrate the implementation and diffusion of QWL. Moreover, from 1979 to the present, the Tarrytown project has suffered from the glare of national press publicity, some of which has overglamourized the story. The fact is that many other plants in General Motors are in some respects more advanced in their application of QWL than is Tarrytown. Nevertheless, Tarrytown remains one of the most extensive efforts to date, involving close to 4,000 human beings in one location and training costs of well over $1.5 million. Finally, Tarrytown's successes and failures bring into sharp focus some underlying principles of successful organizational change in a variety of work environments. Tarrytown represents in microcosm the beginnings of what may become commonplace in the future — a new collaborative approach on the part of management, union, and workers to improve the quality of life at work in its broadest sense.

The Background for Change

In the late 1960s and early 1970s, the Tarrytown plant suffered from much absenteeism and labor turnover. Operating costs were high. Frustration, fear, and mistrust characterized the relationship between management and labor. At certain times, as many as 2,000 labor grievances were on the docket. As one manager puts it, "Management was always in a defensive posture. We were instructed to go by the book, and we played by the book. The way we solved problems was to use our authority and impose discipline." The plant general superintendent acknowledges in retrospect, "For reasons we thought valid, we were very secretive in letting the union and the workers know about changes to be introduced or new programs coming down the pike."

Union officers and committeemen battled constantly with management. As one union officer describes it, "We were always trying to solve yesterday's problems. There was no trust and everybody was putting out fires. The company's attitude was to employ a stupid robot with hands and no face." The union committee chairman at that time describes the situation the way he saw it: "When I walked in each morning I was out to get the per-

explode. If not solved, then you get the men riled up against everything and everybody."

Moving the two departments was carried out successfully with remarkably few grievances. The plant easily made its production schedule deadlines. The next year saw the involvement of employees in the complete rearrangement of another major area of the plant, the chassis department. The following year, a new car model was introduced at Tarrytown.

Labor–Management Agreement

In 1972, Irving Bluestone, the vice-president for the General Motors Department of the United Automobile Workers Union (UAW), made what many consider to be the kick-off speech for the future of the quality-of-work-life movement. In his statement, repeated later in different forms, he declared:

> Traditionally management has called upon labor to cooperate in increasing productivity and improving the quality of the product. My view of the other side of the coin is more appropriate; namely, that management should cooperate with the worker to find ways to enhance the dignity of labor and to tap the creative resources in each human being in developing a more satisfying work life, with emphasis on worker participation in the decision-making process.

In 1973, the UAW and GM negotiated a national agreement. In the contract was a brief "letter of agreement" signed by Bluestone and George Morris, head of industrial relations for GM. Both parties committed themselves to establishing formal mechanisms, at least at top levels, for exploring new ways of dealing with the quality of work life. *This was the first time QWL was explicitly addressed in any major U.S. labor–management contract.*

The Tarrytown union and management were aware of this new agreement. They had previously established close connections with William Horner of Bluestone's staff and with James Rae, the top corporate representative in the organization development department. It was only natural that Tarrytown should extend its ongoing efforts within the framework of the new agreement. Furthermore, Charles Katko, then vice-president and general manager of the GM Assembly Division, gave his enthusiastic endorsement to these efforts.

Local issues and grievances, however, had to be faced by both parties. In the past, it had not been uncommon for strike action to be taken during contract negotiations. The manager and the union representatives asked themselves, "Isn't there a better way to do this, to open up some two-way communication, gain some trust?" The union president was quick to recognize "that it was no good to have a 'love-in' at the top between the union and management, especially the personnel department. We had to stick with our job as union officers. But things were so bad we figured 'what the hell, we have nothing to lose.'" The union president's observation about that period is extremely significant in explaining the process of change that followed:

> We as a union knew that our primary job was to protect the worker and im-prove his economic life. But times had changed and we began to realize we had a broader obligation, which was to help the workers become more involved in decisions affecting their own jobs, to get their ideas, and to help them to im-prove the whole quality of life at work beyond the paycheck.

The negotiations were carried out against the background of another effort on management's part. Delmar L. Landen, director of organizational research and development at General Motors, had been independently pro-moting an organizational development (OD) effort for a number of years. These efforts were being carried out in many plants. Professionally trained communication facilitators had been meeting with supervisors and even some work groups to solve problems of interpersonal communication.

What General Motors was attempting to do was similar to the OD pro-grams that were starting up in many industries and businesses in the United States. But, as with many such programs, there was virtually no union in-volvement. As the training director put it, "Under the influence of our plant manager, the OD program was having some influence among our managers and supervisors, but still this OD stuff was looked upon by many as a gim-mick. It was called the 'happy people' program by those who did not understand it." And, of course, because the union was not involved, it was suspicious.

Nevertheless, a new atmosphere of trust between the union and the plant manager was beginning to emerge. Local negotiations were settled without a strike. There was at least a spark of hope that the Tarrytown mess could be cleaned up. Thus, the informal efforts at Tarrytown to improve union–management relations and to seek greater involvement of workers in prob-lem solving became "legitimatized" through the national agreement and top-level support. Other plants would follow.

The Testing Period

In April 1974, a professional consultant was brought in to involve super-visors and workers in joint training programs for problem solving. Manage-ment paid his fees. He talked at length with most of the union officers and committee members, who report that "we were skeptical at first but we came to trust him. We realized that if we were going to break through the communications barrier on a large scale, we needed a third party."

The local union officials were somewhat suspicious about "another management trick." But after talking with Solidarity House (UAW's headquarters), they agreed to go along. Both parties at the local level discussed what should be done. Both knew it would be a critical test of the previous year's preliminary attempts to communicate with one another on a different plane. Also, as one union person says, "We came to realize the experiment would not happen overnight."

Management and the union each selected a coordinator to work with the consultant and with the supervisors, the union, and the workers. The consultant, with the union and the management coordinators, proposed a series of problem-solving training sessions to be held on Saturdays, for eight hours each day. Two supervisors and the committeemen in the soft trim department talked it over with the workers, of whom 34 from two shifts volunteered for the training sessions that were to begin in late September 1974. Management agreed to pay for six hours of the training, and the workers volunteered their own time for the remaining two hours.

Top management was very impressed by the ideas being generated from the sessions and by the cooperation from the union. The regular repair people were especially helpful. Not long after the program began, the workers began developing solutions to problems of water leaks, glass breakage, and molding damage.

Layoff Crisis

In November 1974, at the height of the OPEC oil crisis, disaster struck. General Motors shut down Tarrytown's second shift, and laid off half the work force — 2,000 workers. Workers on the second shift with high seniority "bumped" hundreds of workers on the first shift. To accommodate the new schedule, management had to rearrange jobs and work loads the entire length of the two miles of main conveyors, feeder conveyors, and work stations. A shock wave reverberated throughout the plant, not just among workers but among supervisors as well. Some feared the convulsion would bring on an avalanche of '78s' — work standards grievances — and all feared that the cutback was an early signal that Tarrytown was being targeted for permanent shutdown. After all, it was one of the oldest plants in General Motors and its past record of performance was not good.

However, the newly developing trust between management and the union had an effect. As the union president puts it, "Everyone got a decent transfer and there were surprisingly few grievances. We didn't get behind. We didn't have to catch up on a huge backlog."

What did suffer was the modest and fragile quality-of-work-life experiment. It was all but abandoned. Many workers who had been part of it were laid off, and new workers "bumping in" had not been exposed to it. Also, a number of persons in the plant were not too disappointed to see it go. Some supervisors, seeing worker participation as a threat to their authority, made wisecracks such as "All they are doing is turning these jobs over to the union." Some committeemen felt threatened because the workers were going outside the regular political system and joining with representatives of management in solving problems.

In spite of the disruption of plant operations, the quality-of-work-life team, the plant manager, and the union officials were determined not to give up. Reduced to a small group of 12 people during 1975, the team continued to work on water leaks and glass breakage problems. This group's success as well as that of some others convinced both parties that quality of work life had to continue.

During this period all parties had time to reflect on past successes as well as failures. The coordinators (one from the union and one from management) had learned a lesson. They had expected too much too soon: "We were frustrated at not seeing things move fast enough. We got in the trap of expecting 'instant QWL.' We thought that all you had to do was to design a package and sell it as you would sell a product."

Also, during this period, the grapevine was carrying a powerful message around the plant that something unusual was going on. The idea of involving workers in decisions spread and, by midyear, the molding groups were redesigning and setting up their own jobs. Other departments followed later.

At this time, everyone agreed that if this program were to be expanded on a larger scale, it would require more careful planning. In 1975, a joint policy committee made up of the plant manager, the production manager, the personnel director, general superintendent, the union's top officers, and the two QWL coordinators was formed. The program was structured so that both the union and management could have an advisory group to administer the system and to evaluate the ideas coming up from the problem-solving teams. Everyone agreed that participation was to be entirely voluntary. No one was to be ordered or assigned to any group. Coordinators and others talked with all of the workers in the two departments.

A survey of interest was taken among the 600 workers in the two volunteering departments; 95 percent of these workers said they wanted to be included in the program. Because of the large number that wanted to participate, pairs of volunteers from the ranks of the union and management had to be trained as trainers. Toward the middle of the year, a modified program was set up involving 27 off-time hours of instructional work for the 570 people who were interested. Four trainers were selected and trained to conduct this program, two from the union and two from management.

A second crisis occurred when the production schedule was increased to a line speed of 60 cars per hour. Total daily output would not be enough to require a second shift to bring back all the laid-off workers. Instead, the company asked that 300 laid-off workers be brought in and that the plant operate on an overtime schedule. Ordinarily, the union would object strongly to working overtime when there were still well over 1,000 members out on the streets. "But," as the union president puts it, "we sold the membership on the idea of agreeing to overtime and the criticism was minimal. We told them the survival of the plant was at stake."

Full Capacity

Despite the upheavals at the plant, it seemed that the quality-of-work-life program would survive. Then, a third blow was delivered. Just as the first 60 workers were completing their sessions, the company announced that Tarrytown was to return to a two-shift operation. For hundreds of those recalled to work, this was good news. Internally, however, it meant the line would have to go through the same game of musical chairs it had experienced 14 months earlier when the second shift was dropped.

Workers were shuffled around according to seniority and job classification. Shift preferences were granted according to length of service. With a faster line speed than before, the average worker had fewer operations to perform, but these had to be performed at a faster pace. In short, because of possible inequities in work loads, conditions were ripe for another wave of work standards grievances. Happily, the union and management were able to work out the work-load problems with a minimum of formal grievances.

But, again, the small, partially developed QWL program had to be put on ice. The number of recalled workers and newly hired employees was too great, and turnover among the new employees was too high for the program to continue as it had been. Capitalizing on the mutual trust that had been slowly building up between them, management and the union agreed to set up an orientation program for new employees — and there were hundreds of them. Such a program was seen as an opportunity to expose them to some of the information about plant operations, management functions, the union's role, and so forth. At one point, the union even suggested that orientation take place at the union hall, but the idea was dropped.

The orientation program was successful. Some reduction in the ratio of "quits" among the "new hires" was observed. The union president did feel that "we had set a new tone for the new employee and created a better atmosphere in the plant."

The Big Commitment

Early the next year (1977) Tarrytown made the "big commitment." The QWL effort was to be launched on a plant-wide scale, involving approximately 3,800 workers and supervisors. Charles Katko, vice-president for the division, and UAW's top official, Irving Bluestone, gave strong signals of support. The plant manager retired in April and was replaced by the production manager. The transition was an easy one because the new manager not only knew every dimension of the program but also had become convinced of its importance.

The policy committee and the quality-of-work-life coordinators went to work. In the spring of 1977, all the top staff personnel, department heads, and production superintendents went through a series of orientation sessions with the coordinators. By June, all middle managers and first-line supervisors (general foremen and foremen) were involved. Thus, by the summer of 1977, more than 300 members of Tarrytown management knew about the QWL approach and about the plans for including 3,500 hourly employees. All union committeemen also went through the orientation sessions.

Also, during mid-1977, plans were underway to select and train those people who would eventually conduct the training sessions for the hourly employees. More than 250 workers expressed an interest in becoming trainers. After careful screening and interviewing, 11 were chosen. A similar process was carried out for supervisors, 11 of whom were subsequently selected as trainers, mostly from among foremen.

The two coordinators brought the 22 designated trainers together and exposed them to a variety of materials they would use in the training itself. The trainers conducted mock practice sessions which were videotaped so they could discuss their performance. The trainers also shared ideas on how to present information to the workers and on how to get workers to open up with their own ideas for changing their work environment. The latter is at the heart of the quality-of-work-life concept.

The trainers themselves found excitement and challenge in the experience. People from the shop floor worked side by side with members of supervision as equals. At the end of the sessions, the trainers were brought together in the executive dining room for a wrap-up session. The coordinators report that "they were so charged up they were ready to conquer the world!"

Plant-Wide Program

On September 13, 1977, the program was launched. Each week, 25 different workers (or 50 in all from both shifts) reported to the training rooms on Tuesdays, Wednesdays, and Thursdays, for nine hours a day. Those taking the sessions had to be replaced at their work stations by substitutes. Given an average hourly wage rate of more than $12 per attendee and per replacement (for over 3,000 persons), one can begin to get an idea of the magnitude of the costs. Also, for the extra hour above eight hours, the trainees were paid overtime wages.

What was the substance of the sessions themselves? The trainee's time was allocated to learning three things: first, about the concept of QWL; second, about the plant and the functions of management and the union; and third, about problem-solving skills important in effective involvement.

At the outset, the trainers made it clear that the employees were not to use the sessions to solve grievances or to take up labor–management issues covered by the contract itself. The presentation covered a variety of subjects presented in many forms, with heavy stress from the start on participation by the class. The work groups were given a general statement of what quality of work life was all about. The union trainer presented materials illustrating UAW Vice-President Bluestone's famous speech, and the management trainer presented a speech by GM's D.L. Landen stressing that hourly workers were experts concerning their own jobs and had much to contribute.

The trainers used printed materials, diagrams, charts, and slides to describe products and model changes, how the plant was laid out, how the production system worked, and what the organizational structures of management and the union were. Time was spent covering safety matters, methods used to measure quality performance, efficiency, and so forth. The work groups were shown how and where they could get any information they wanted about their plant. Special films showed all parts of the plant, with workers "conducting the tour" for their own parts of the operation.

To develop effective problem-solving skills, the trainers presented simulated problems and then asked employees to take part in a variety of experiential exercises. The training content enabled the workers to diagnose themselves, their own behavior, how they appeared in competitive situations, how they handled two-way communications, and how they solved problems. According to the trainers, by the final day "the groups themselves were carrying the ball, with a minimum of guidance and direction from the two trainers."

Trainers took notes on the ideas generated in the sessions and at the end handed out a questionnaire to each participant. The notes and questionnaires were systematically fed back to the union and management coordinators, who in turn brought the recommendations to the policy committee. The primary mode of feedback to their foremen and fellow workers was by the workers themselves out on the shop floor.

Major Model Change — A New Hurdle

Seven weeks after the beginning of the program in September 1977, just over 350 workers (or 10 percent of the work force) had completed the training sessions. The program continued through 1978, and by mid-December more than 3,300 workers had taken part.

When all the employees had completed their sessions, the union and management immediately agreed to keep the system going on a continuing basis. From late December 1978 through early February 1979, production operations at Tarrytown were closed down to prepare for the introduction of the all new 1980X model.

In preparation for the shift, managers and hourly personnel together evaluated hundreds of anticipated assembly processes. Workers made use of the enthusiasm and skills developed in the earlier problem sessions and talked directly with supervisors and technical people about the best ways of setting up various jobs on the line. What had been stimulated through a formal organized system of training and communication (for workers and supervisors alike) was now being "folded in" to the ongoing planning and implementation process on the floor itself.

In evaluating the formal program (September 1977 to December 1978), the trainers repeatedly emphasized the difficulties they had faced as well as the rewards. Many of the men and women from the shop floor were highly suspicious at the start of the sessions. Some old-timers harbored grudges against management going back for years. Young workers were skeptical. Some of the participants were confused at seeing a union trainer in front of the class with someone from management.

In the early period, the trainers were also nervous in their new roles. Few of them had ever had such an experience before. Many agreed that their impulse was to throw a lot of information at the worker trainee. The trainers found, however, that once the participants opened up, they "threw a lot at us." Although they understood intellectually that participation is the basic purpose of the QWL program, the trainers had to experience directly the outpouring of ideas, perceptions, and feelings of the participants to comprehend emotionally the dynamics of the involvement process.

But the trainers felt rewarded, too. They describe example after example of the workers' reactions once they let down their guard. One skeptical worker, for example, burst out after the second day, "Jesus Christ! You mean all this information about what's going on in the plant was available to us? Well, I'm going to use it." Another worker who had been scrapping with his foreman for years went directly to him after the sessions and said, "Listen, you and I have been butting our heads together for a long time. From now on I just want to be able to talk to you and have you talk to me." Another worker used his free relief time to drop in on new class sessions.

By May 1979, the Tarrytown plant, with the production of a radically new line of cars, had come through one of the most difficult times in its history. Considering all the complex technical difficulties, the changeover was successful. Production was up to projected line speed. The relationship among management, union, and the workers remained positive in spite of unusual stress conditions generated by such a change. As the production manager puts it, "Under these conditions, we used to fight the union, the workers, and the car itself. Now we've all joined together to fight the car." The hourly employees were substantially involved in working out thousands of "bugs" in the operations.

Success, Slippage, Reassessment, and Forward Movement

The sale of the new models being assembled at Tarrytown and at two other plants was a success in the marketplace and continued so through 1981 in spite of intense competition from Ford and Chrysler, and especially from the Japanese imports. Lines were running at capacity. In fact, more than a thousand new workers were hired at Tarrytown in 1979 to meet production demands. This again created the difficult problems associated with balancing the line and moving workers around. Time constraints were such that few of the new employees were exposed to the three-day training and orientation sessions.

But there were deeper concerns. The joint policy committee continued to meet on a regular basis, but it raised some serious questions as to whether the QWL philosophy had permeated all levels of the organization. Key persons in both management and the union wondered whether the intense pressures for production were beginning to cause some slippage in commitment, especially among supervisors and higher managers. Also, it was felt by the union as well as the management coordinator that they were "running" the QWL effort without enough involvement of those responsible for making it work.

The decision was made to plan for a full-day session off-site to review where Tarrytown had been and where it should be going. In preparation, the coordinators interviewed union shop committeemen and members of higher management to ascertain their present feelings about every aspect of the program. This preliminary information was fed back to the joint committee. "Surprisingly enough," states one of the coordinators, "there was substantial agreement between both the union officials and the managers as to what our present and future problems were." The committee mutually agreed that the proposed large session of 66 management and union representatives should raise a number of questions and discuss them. They felt that the definition and meaning of QWL should be reexamined and clarified. They wanted a review of current labor–management relations. They expressed the need for a more structured program for involving workers in problem solving that went beyond the stimulation provided originally in the three-day orientation and training session. Most important, both parties found themselves realizing that despite all the past efforts, highlighted by the glare of national publicity, much needed to be done to promote further understanding of, and commitment to, QWL *at all levels.*

The extensive planning resulted in the off-site meeting of these 66 people. To provide further stimulus and support, William Horner from the national UAW office was invited to attend. All of the major issues brought up in the preliminary meetings were openly and thoroughly discussed. Those present felt that the session helped measurably to give focus to the future of Tarrytown's QWL effort. All were in substantial agreement that a key to future success lay in greater involvement of the first two levels of supervision. "You have a lot of work that needs to be done with them," said a union committeeman to the top managers. "Why don't you expose them more to all the things that have concerned us today."

In meeting with his staff after the session, the plant manager said, in effect, "Before we go any further, we had better take a good look at our management organization and 'shape up the ship.'" As a result, beginning in January 1980, the entire "front line" of the organization (more than 250 supervisors and general supervisors) attended a one-day session patterned after the one held in November. That is, they were encouraged to pose questions and to suggest solutions with respect to the basic issues of QWL — how they defined it, what they thought would generate greater commitment, and where it should be going. All of them had been under pressure "to get the product out the back door" on schedule and at the highest standards of quality. The sessions, it was reported, gave them a renewed sense of perspective about QWL. More important, and perhaps for the first time as peer groups, they felt that they were being asked to chart a course of action. They, too, were becoming involved much more substantially than they had been in the orientation program two years earlier.

The degree of involvement between supervisors and their key workers, known as utility persons, picked up during 1980. Many operating problems were being addressed on the shop floor. When new installations or changes in an area were being introduced, a mock area was set up for supervisors and workers to examine the new arrangements and make suggestions. As one of the coordinators put it, "This whole business of exposing people to changes and getting their ideas may seem unusual in many industrial plants, but here it has become a normal operating procedure and is going on all the time." The union coordinator added, "It's not like it was in the old days, that's for sure."

Although common practice in other GM plants, the system of "Quality Audit" served as another vehicle of involvement and is continuing right up to the present (1982). Each day, cars are "audited" to identify defects and other quality problems. A period of time is set aside the next day to bring foremen and workers together with department superintendents to diagnose causes and propose action. More than 20 hourly workers attend, including some from the department where a particular problem originated. It is common for those attending to go back to their work sections and discuss the issues with their work colleagues. Each week approximately 125 different workers are involved. By the end of 1981, almost every worker in the plant had attended at least one quality audit session.

A New Structured Effort for Greater Involvement

In early 1981, the joint committee decided to launch a new kind of effort to involve supervisors and workers in a more structured program of shop-floor involvement. The decision was a logical outcome of the various discussions described earlier. It may also have been influenced by activities going on in other plants of the corporation. In many other locations, a network of quality circles and other forms of work group problem-solving structures had been created with considerable success. Up until now, at Tarrytown, the major effort was the massive three-day orientation and training experience for management, the union, and hourly employees. This effort resulted in a marked improvement in the climate of relations and in overall organizational effectiveness. It stimulated *individual* workers to take the initiative in suggesting job and work-system improvements. Yet, few structures had been created to systematically tap the potential problem-solving creativity of specific work *groups.*

After discussion, the joint committee gave the go-ahead to set up four pilot groups in two major departments, the body shop and chassis departments. In each department, there was to be one group for the day shift and one for the second shift. The choice of the specific areas was made jointly by the department superintendents, general supervisors, and committee persons on both shifts.

The four area supervisors that were selected underwent an intensive two-day orientation program by the two plant coordinators, one union and one management. Not only was the format of the program explained, but the supervisors were given the opportunity to help design the details. The general supervisors (general foremen) were also keyed in. Because it was difficult to shut down a whole section for meetings, it was decided that the core group would consist of the supervisor and the key people in the section, the utility repairman, and utility trainers—experienced persons who knew all the operations in the section. Each section had approximately five utility persons.

By early summer 1981, the plan was in operation and the groups were functioning. Each group developed its own system. Usually they met for a half hour once a week to identify and take action on a variety of operating problems. The members served as the link with the regular operators and sought their ideas on problems and solutions. In one group, five or six of the regular operators were brought into the meetings. Another group took a day off to go to another plant to learn about housekeeping methods and make a report to the production manager. Because many of the operating problems involved the experience and know-how of other support personnel, it was not unusual to ask material handlers or other support personnel to discuss particular issues. Individual members were delegated to seek out information, e.g., on a tooling problem, which could lead to a solution. Indeed, it was becoming accepted that any group member could take the time to go to any part of the plant in search of information.

By the end of 1981, the new experimental group structure had clearly proven its value. As one member of the joint committee put it, "Literally thousands of small but irritating shop problems have been solved. The pressure is coming from the bottom up and this is what QWL is all about." It is expected that in 1982 the program will be diffused and extended to many other parts of the plant.

By the end of 1981, the Tarrytown plant had continued its strong position with respect to performance when compared with other similar plants. Although absenteeism was high, as it was in all plants, the number of formal grievances continued at a low level. There was in 1981 a political problem in the union. The shop chairman, who was also on the joint QWL committee, was defeated. But the president of the local, who was one of the spark plugs of QWL at Tarrytown, was using his influence to urge the new shop chairman to give full support to the developing program.

Learning from Tarrytown

Although the Tarrytown story is, of course, unique, persons responsible for bringing about change in an organization might derive some useful generalizations and important messages from it.

Bringing about any kind of change is extraordinarily difficult in modern organizations. It is challenge enough to introduce new machines, computers, management information systems, new organizational structures, and all the bureaucratic paraphernalia required to support complex production systems. It is even more difficult to organize and stimulate people to accept innovations directed at greater efficiency. Perhaps most difficult of all, as one looks at the quality-of-work-life process and Tarrytown as an example, is for managers, union officials, and even workers themselves to adjust to the idea that certain kinds of changes should be directed toward making life at work more meaningful, and not necessarily toward some immediate objective measures of results.

Even when people become committed to this idea, starting the process is not easy. Witness, for example, how long it took to turn Tarrytown around. Look at the roadblocks its people had to overcome: deep-seated antagonisms between management and labor and the impact of changes at all levels, especially among hourly workers. Just when the quality-of-work-life efforts gained some momentum, an unanticipated event intervened and the program was stopped dead in its tracks — almost. Indeed, one gets the impression that the only constant was change itself.

Some observations are in order. Developing this climate for change takes extraordinary patience. It takes time. It calls for sustained commitment at all levels. In most of the efforts to change human behavior that I have observed directly, these characteristics are lacking. Managers and leaders are under pressure to change things overnight. They draw up a program, package it, press the authority button, set deadlines, then move. It all sounds so easy, so efficient, so "American."

In changing the way Americans work, we have, as the former chairman of Local 664 said in 1979, "barely scratched the surface." What went on at Tarrytown (and other plants in General Motors are even more advanced in concept and application) was only a beginning. The intrinsic nature of repetitive conveyor-paced jobs has not substantially changed. The commitment to quality of work life is strong at the local level and among some people at division and corporate levels, but it is not universal. Changes in management or new crises could threaten further developments. Nevertheless, a new atmosphere about change and the worker's role in it is clearly emerging. People feel they have some "say," some control over their work environment now and in the future.

QWL at Tarrytown may, however, reflect something more important about the quality-of-work-life efforts that are springing up in many other places in the United States. Studies show that workers in our large, rationalized industries and businesses are seeking more control over, and involvement in, the forces affecting their work lives. Due in part to the rising levels of education, changing aspirations, and shifts in values, especially among young people, I believe we are witnessing a quiet revolution in what people expect from work, an expectation that goes beyond the economic and job-security issues that led to labor unrest in an earlier day.

In parts of Europe, the response to this quiet revolution is manifest in broad-scale political efforts on the part of labor and government to gain greater control over the management of the enterprise itself. In the United States, the response is different. Workers or their unions have given no indication that they wish to take over basic management prerogatives. As Tarrytown illustrates, what they want is more pragmatic, more immediate, more localized — but no less important.

The challenge to those in positions of power is to become aware of the quiet revolution at the workplace and to find the means to respond intelligently to these forces for change. What management and the union are doing at Tarrytown is but one example of the beginnings of an intelligent response.

Some Generalizations

What generalizations or principles might one derive from the Tarrytown story? The list below combines those of the participants themselves with my own observations about quality-of-work-life experiments here and abroad. The list is not exhaustive. The first six are limited in general to organizations with collective bargaining agreements. The others have more universal applications.

1. For quality of work life to succeed, management must be wholly competent in running the business as a profit-making enterprise. When management lacks organizational competence and adequate technical expertise, no amount of good intentions to improve worker–union–management communication will succeed. Workers will not be willing to become involved if they know that management lacks the competence to do anything about their ideas.

2. The union must be strong. The members must trust their leadership, and this trust must exist within the framework of a democratic "political" process.

3. In most instances, management has to be the first party to initiate change, to "hold out the olive branch."

4. Quality of work life should never be used by either party to circumvent the labor–management agreement. The rights, privileges, and obligations of both parties should remain inviolate. Dealing with grievances and disputes can be made easier through quality-of-work-life efforts, but at no time should management give up its right to manage nor the union its right to protect its members on matters related to wages, hours, benefits, and general conditions of employment.

5. Top management and top union officials must make an explicit commitment to support quality of work life.

6. Even with agreement at high levels and a demonstrated concern on the part of rank-and-file employees, it is essential that middle management and front-line supervisors (and shop stewards) not only know what is taking place but also feel they have a say in the change process. Supervisors naturally feel threatened by any moves to give subordinates greater power in determining how work is to be performed. Union representatives can perceive unilateral work participation as a threat to their political position.

7. A quality-of-work-life program is unlikely to succeed if management's intention is to increase productivity by speeding up the individual worker's work pace or, if it uses the program *as such*, to reduce the

work force through layoffs. Workers will quickly see such actions as unfair exploitation. This is not to say that cost savings from better quality performance, lower absenteeism and turnover, and better production methods should not be an expected consequence of the effort.

8. A program should be voluntary for the participants.

9. Quality of work life should not be initiated with a detailed master plan. It should start on a limited scale focused on the solution of specific problems, however small. It should be flexible.

10. At each step in developing a program, all small bottlenecks or misunderstandings must be talked out and solved on the spot. If set aside simply to get on with the "important" plans, the little misunderstandings can later explode with enough force to destroy the entire program.

11. It is not enough to expose employees to the principles of effective interpersonal communication and problem-solving skills. There must be immediate opportunities available for them to use these skills in practical ways right in the job situation itself. Further follow-up action of some kind is necessary to serve as positive reenforcement to the employees.

12. Quality-of-work-life efforts should not be thought of as a "program" with a finite ending. There must be a built-in momentum that is dynamic, ongoing, and that can continue regardless of changes in the personnel in the organization. Once employees come to believe that they can participate and do, in fact, become involved in solving problems, the process gains a momentum of its own.

There is an implied warning here. Management may have the *formal* power to drop quality-of-work-life efforts summarily. Union officers may have the *political* power to scuttle such efforts. However, both would be acting at their peril in taking such action for, under quality of work life, the workers will have gained a unique power to influence substantially the quality of their own lives at work. For them there is no turning back.

II:
Toward Self-Management

6.
The Citibank Project: Improving Productivity through Work Redesign

Roy W. Walters

Introduction

During the 1970s, Citibank fundamentally changed the way it delivered financial services. Beginning in the early 1960s, most financial institutions had to deal with rising volumes, costs, and paperwork. In light of these events, failure to change would have been suicidal in terms of profit and loss. The principles underlying the changes made by Citibank are most noteworthy because they fly in the face of conventional wisdom.

A traditional approach to the problems these institutions faced would be the addition of staff and the creation of a functional organization in order to obtain specialization of skills. Citibank's approach was the decentralization of operations and the organization of service operations around its customers, preferably one person providing the complete front-to-back product for a single customer.

A traditional approach would be the creation of a large, centralized data processing system and organization to take advantage of the economies of scale and the technical management requirements of such a system. Citibank's approach was to decentralize data processing to minicomputers managed and operated by customer-service professionals responsible to specific customers.

A traditional approach would be the addition of a large contingent of checkers, quality controllers, and work-flow coordinators to ensure that the work got out in a timely and quality fashion. Citibank's approach was to design management and clerical jobs so that the provision of quality service would become their basic motivation.

Historical Perspective

Bank services before 1950 were in roughly the same stage that manufacturing had been in 150 years earlier. Volume was low, and production was by hand and personally tailored to individual customer needs. Like the craftsman of the eighteenth century, the banker had a one-to-one relationship with the customer and provided all services.

The Industrial Revolution helped create greater demand for manufactured goods, and machine tools and mass production methods were devised to produce more at less cost. The economic boom of the 1950s and 1960s, which led to banks' greatest period of growth, produced little immediate change in the way things were done. Growing clerical staffs generated growing piles of paper. The new computers of this period were supposed to be the back-office equivalent of industrial mass production, but they were generally misunderstood and misused. Banks saw them as a way to control the proliferation of paper — which they did not do.

Instead, more clerical-type jobs were created to feed the monsters and make sure they digested the data correctly, and there was more paper than ever before. The Citibank central computers generated enough paper every day and a half to reach the top of New York's World Trade Center. When material and labor costs threatened to start eroding industry's profit margins, manufacturers turned to the technology of automation. When large banks entered a similar period in the late sixties, the response was more of the same — more clerks, more paper, and more problems.

The Problem

In 1970, an Opinion Research Corporation survey of major banks rated Citibank very low in terms of service to the customer. This dismal finding was made intolerable by the fact that, for the period 1960 through 1970, the bank's internal operations costs had risen about 15 percent a year.

At the peak, Citibank operations starred a cast of thousands who shuffled the papers that were the basics of the "transaction processing system." These people were handling only a part of the whole, a single task over and over again. The repetitiveness of their work, and the fact that they had no sense of its completion, militated against consistently error-free performance. In fact, out of monotony or lack of attention, clerks tended to create errors in the processing flow. At one point during 1970, a backlog of some 36,000 customer-inquiry items accumulated. Proof problems and discrepancies in records were not uncommon.

The institution's top management decided to make some fundamental changes in the back office, the seat of the bank's financial transaction processing. Management made the direction for that change clear by bringing in a new management team recruited from manufacturing industries and from other distinctly nonbanking environments. The new managers, schooled in quantitative analyses and production methods, found the situation very nearly out of control.

Organization Structure

A major cause of these problems was the functional way the institution was organized. Transaction-processing activities were lumped together in a large, functional organization, as opposed to customer- or business-oriented activities. Services for all customers — both corporate and individual — were processed together. It was like a giant pipeline, with all transactions flowing in one end and out the other. Managers were responsible only for a given function that cut across this continuum. No one — except the executive vice-president in charge of operations — was responsible for any service, from customer input to delivery. It was a classic horizontal management, a structure in which each manager's ability to perform his or her job was dependent on the performance of the function that preceded in the sequence. If a break occurred anywhere in the pipeline, everything was affected. A single transaction could be routed among more than a half-dozen different departments, causing errors, lost items, and lack of control.

There was clearly a need to restructure operations — to push control over services to customers down to a level where it could be managed effectively.

The approach utilized was to establish independent, stand-alone, product organizations or channels. Where, previously, work in process was passed off to many other units, under different managers' control, for next-processing step operations, work in process now was contained in one unit under a single manager's control. Even though the work was still fragmented, it was now structured under one manager with start-to-finish responsibility.

In the international money transfer unit, all the work steps necessary to process this customer request (to move money from one location to another) were controlled by one group of workers under one manager. There were no more pass-offs to other units under different managers. The same would be true for letters of credit, lock box, stock transfer, or any of the other services.

This restructuring phase was called "channelization." In essence, the channels were like assembly lines, with as many functions as possible performed by one organizational unit, on one floor, under one head.

This structural change produced a vertical management: Managers who managed a channel now had control over the total transaction from the time it entered the bank until the customer was advised of its completion.

In conjunction with this change in organizational structure, there was an urgent need for effective planning and control of work flows and costs. Also needed were skills of effective work design, financial analysis, product development, and production management. The clerical operations needed measurements for costs, timeliness, and accuracy.

The organization established a managerial base for accountability, control of costs, and customer service. Citibank had to develop a technological base that would support and facilitate the process. Mainly, that meant automating as many functions as possible to reduce the costly and error-prone manual routines.

In order to provide customers with a quality product tailored to their needs, management decided to review the basics of management process, organizational structure, and job design. First, they recognized that the product-oriented channel structure was not tailored enough to the marketplace and that responsibility for customer service still resided solely at the top of the organization. Second, despite changes in the organization, in the management process, and in management jobs, clerical job structure still had not been affected substantively.

These perceptions led to the next two structural changes:

- Organization around market segments.
- The redesign of clerical jobs, away from a focus on function to a focus on the customer.

Organizational Design

Citibank's evolution into a structure focusing on market segments took place over several years. Creating a natural unit of work for an individual job and market segmentation are the same concept applied at different levels of the organization, and either may face constraints which require time phasing. A "natural unit of work" means designing work according to a logical group that is aligned with the unit's mission. In the letter of credit unit, natural work units were structured around market segments, i.e., by types of customers—governments, correspondent banks and branches. These segments were further divided into natural units of work by geographical location—e.g., Europe, Near East, Far East, and South America.

After "channelization," the structure provided each group head with a natural organization. A channel with all processing functions—from customer input to delivery—vertically integrated under one accountable manager had been developed. Figure 6.1 shows that separate divisions—marketing, corporate services, and EDP services—were integrated under one group head.

The next major evolution was to more fully develop natural work units

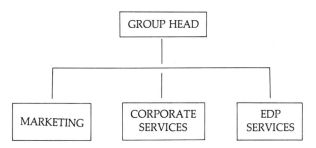

Fig. 6.1. Financial Transaction Services

by reorganizing into groups facing off against the major market segments: the International Banking Group, the World Corporate Group, and the National Banking Group. Since the marketing department had restructured according to these segments, it was necessary to structure corporate services in the same manner.

The natural work units selected split the marketing department into function processing groups aligned with the major market segments. Each of these groups offered its own services within the group, i.e., loans collections, letters of credit, money transfer, and so on (see fig. 6.2).

These groups were, in turn, broken into more clearly identified functions which, at the processing level, are held responsible for servicing certain products. As a result, the organization has created many more fully accountable units, each dedicated to filling the needs of a segmented customer set.

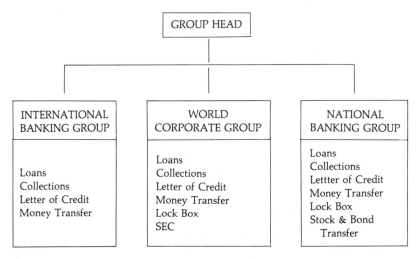

Fig. 6.2. Financial Transaction Services of the Marketing Department

Decentralization of Data Processing

In order to establish these as independent customer organizations, Citibank took advantage of the rapid technological changes in the computer industry. Simply stated, it switched from maxicomputers to minicomputers. Where there had been one centralized data center for the bank, there are now many, each meeting the specific requirements of its own market segments. The bank feels that the results over the long term will be dramatic. First, the decentralization will allow considerably more flexibility in the support of specific customer segments. Second, assuming current trends continue, it will be less expensive. Finally, it will enable full accountability by management to the customers it services.

Job Design

It was very clear what the objectives of the first-level job structure should be: service quality to the customer, high level of productivity, minimum personnel problems, and high levels of organization and individual performance. The structure designed was a logical extension of the decentralized organizational structure and envisioned giving each of the clerical staff complete processing and customer-service responsibility for a single, small group of customers. The power of the concept was exciting.

In essence, coupled with the decentralized organizational structure, it would mean that every member of the organization would have customer responsibility for at least one product. The mission of the organization was now the mission of *every* member of the organization. This restructuring held costs constant for a period of time, and the stage was set for the redesign of clerical jobs.

Motivational Work Design

Motivational Work Design is the theory on which the desired job design was based. This theory maintains that productivity, quality, and job satisfaction can be attained if the job has certain characteristics (this model is explained in fig. 6.3).

Behavioral scientists have found that three "psychological states" are critical in determining a person's motivation and satisfaction on the job.

- *Experienced meaningfulness.* Individuals must perceive their work as worthwhile or important by some system of values they accept.
- *Experienced responsibility.* They must feel personally accountable for their efforts.

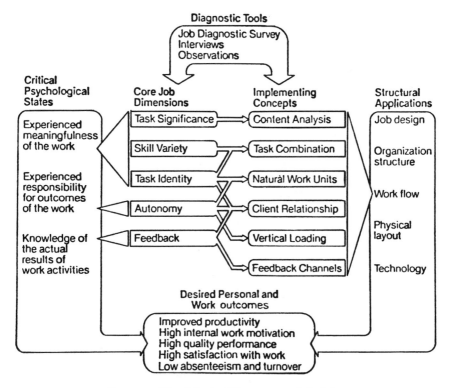

Fig. 6.3. The Work Effectiveness Model
Reprinted by permission, Roy W. Walters & Associates, Inc.

- *Knowledge of results.* They must be able to determine, on some fairly regular basis, whether or not the outcomes of their work are satisfactory.

If these three conditions are present, people tend to feel good about themselves when they perform well. And those good feelings will prompt them to try to continue to do well—so they can continue to earn these positive feelings in the future. That is what is meant by "internal motivation"—being turned on to one's work because of the positive internal feelings that are generated by doing well, rather than being dependent on external factors (such as incentive pay or compliments from the boss) for the motivation to work effectively.

Recent research has identified five "core" characteristics of jobs that elicit the psychological states described here. These five core job dimensions provide the key to objectively measuring jobs and to changing them so that they have high potential for motivating the people who do them.

Toward Meaningful Work. Three of the five core dimensions contribute to a job's meaningfulness for the worker

- *Skill variety*. The degree to which a job requires the worker to perform activities that challenge skills and abilities. When even a single skill is involved, there is at least a seed of potential meaningfulness. When several skills are involved, the job has the potential of appealing to more of the whole person, and of avoiding monotonous repetition of the same task, no matter how much skill it requires.
- *Task identity*. The degree to which the job requires completion of a "whole" and identifiable piece of work, i.e., doing a job from beginning to end with a visible outcome.
- *Task significance*. The degree to which the job has a substantial and perceivable impact on the lives of other people, whether in the immediate organization or in the world at large.

Each of these three job dimensions represents one important route to experienced meaningfulness. If the job is high in all three, the worker is quite likely to experience his or her job as very meaningful. It is not necessary, however, for a job to be very high in all three dimensions. If the job is low in any one of them, there will be a drop in overall experienced meaningfulness. Even when two dimensions are low, the worker may find the job meaningful, provided that the third is high enough.

Toward Personal Responsibility. A fourth core dimension may lead a worker to experience increased responsibility in his or her job. This is *autonomy*, the degree to which the job gives a worker freedom, independence, and discretion in scheduling work and determining how it will be carried out. People in highly autonomous jobs know that they are personally responsible for successes and failures. When autonomy is high, how work is performed will depend more on the individual's own efforts and initiatives than on detailed instructions from the boss or from a manual of job procedures.

Toward Knowledge of Results. The fifth core dimension is *feedback*. This is the degree to which a worker is informed of the effectiveness of his or her work activities. Feedback is most powerful when it comes directly from the work itself — for example, when workers have the responsibility for gauging and checking components they have just completed, and learn in the process that they have lowered the reject rate by meeting specifications more consistently.

The implementing concepts are specific action steps to improve both the quality of the working experience and the work productivity of the individual. They are:

- *Content analysis.* Examining the content of the job to make sure that irrelevant, redundant operations are not present. This determines whether or not the job is seen as significant by the person performing the work.
- *Task combination.* Combining fragmented tasks into a complete task module. This will provide additional interest, challenge, and a feeling of responsibility for a whole, clearly identified task.
- *Natural work units.* Designing the work according to a logical group that is aligned with the unit's mission. This allows the worker to experience a personal feeling of responsibility and to identify with this group.
- *Client relationship.* Forming relationships with clients representing certain sets of companies within the natural work units. Workers start to call their companies "my customers" and take on a high degree of ownership.
- *Vertical loading.* Pushing responsibilities down from higher levels and giving the workers more control and increased responsibility. This is done selectively, according to individual competence.
- *Feedback channels.* Setting up conditions for feedback from the job itself is very important in the transition from a one-task job to a partial or full-task module. Workers and supervisors must know constantly how they are doing in order to improve their work.

The Motivation Work Design model was taught to all managers and supervisors so they could actively participate and contribute to the work redesign process. The use of this model, together with the already defined organizational changes and the new computer technology, led to the development of a concept called Work Station Management. This concept gives one clerical employee total responsibility for servicing a single, small group of customers in a defined product area. The employee has a personal computer terminal tied into the division's minicomputer. Emphasis has been placed on a paperless work flow in which the terminal is the key. Filing of documents is on microfilm, and each employee has a film reader in addition to a telephone for immediate client contact.

This design benefits employees by providing better jobs, including all of the core dimensions indicated in figure 6.3, and benefits Citibank as well by allowing more control, fewer space requirements, and improved customer service.

Letter of Credit: A Case Study

At the end of the channelization phase, the letter of credit unit was organized on a functional basis, with the processes of payment examination, processing, filing, issuing/amending, customer service, and accounting each

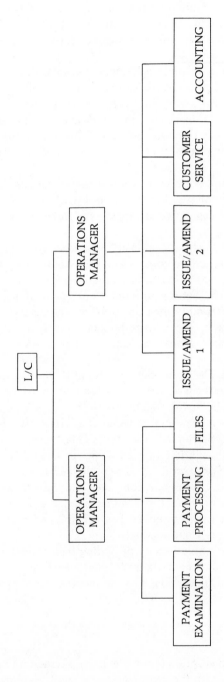

Fig. 6.4. Letter of Credit Organization: Functional

118

representing distinct organizational entities within the channel, as shown in figure 6.4.

The next step taken was the realignment of the channel around the types of customers dealt with: governments, correspondent banks, and branches. Within this organization, however, the assembly line work flow was maintained, as shown in figure 6.5.

The next step entailed a detailed process review, or content analysis, to ensure that both managers and supervisors had complete understanding and control over the manual, labor-intensive work flows prior to automation.

After this thorough analysis, the management team decided that the only way to fully understand the process was under controlled conditions, in a laboratory-like environment. The team created the "white room," a separate walled-off area in the letter of credit unit, and put in it all the equipment needed to process a letter of credit: typewriter, adding machine, forms, rubber stamps. As pieces of the assembly-line process were put together, they were thoroughly tested in the "white room." This "room" was a computer facility for testing pieces of the manual-processing function to determine whether or not they could be computerized. Software programs were written for processing functions, such as *preprocessing, encoding, amending,* and *issuing,* and trials were run to determine whether they could be eliminated as separate manual functions.

It made a splendid testing ground for measuring the difference between what was written as an existing practice and procedure and what was being done in actual processing. It was an area in which to experiment on what might be. In a short time, the managers were able to reduce the steps required in processing by half and to reduce the number of people in the processing operation by 30 percent — all before automation.

Richard Matteis and Sandra Jaffee, the two vice-presidents who guided the redesign effort, state that the "white room" concept was the most impor-

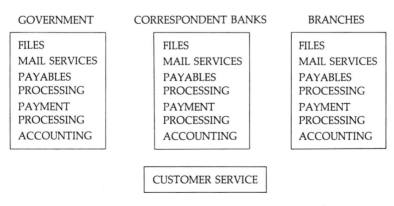

Fig. 6.5. Organizational Cut by Business Segment Preprocessing

tant step in the conversion to a more effective work system. They are convinced that this step should always be taken to permit thorough experimentation prior to any system changes, to maintain management control, and to allow for critical examination of details that might otherwise have been overlooked.

Automation was implemented piece by piece, only after the affected processes had been streamlined. Once the processes were completely automated, the training effort required to combine the assembly-line functions into the work station job was begun. This combination yielded the letter of credit work station shown in figure 6.6.

The Work Stations

To support this job redesign, a physical environment was developed in which all of the tools necessary to perform the job were at the fingertips of the work station representative: a cockpit type of furniture design, which contained a data entry CRT, a microfilm reader, and a telephone. The work stations were in a pleasant, open space and grouped in clusters by customer

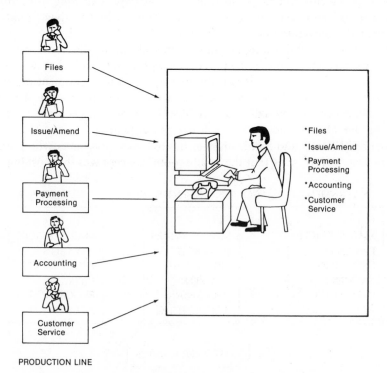

Fig. 6.6. Letter of Credit Work Station

aggregate. The "back office," in essence, had all of the amenities of the front office and was professional in nature.

In the original diagnostic work that was necessary to determine the details of the operation problems and the type of organization climate that would support the change effort, about 100 interviews with key managers, supervisors, and workers were conducted. It was necessary to get firsthand information about the employees' attitudes toward their work as well as toward change.

It was obvious that none of those interviewed liked the way the current processing flow was operating. They all felt the pressure from backlogs, unmet schedule dates, error rework, customer complaints, and so on. Managers and supervisors thought the workers were not performing well, and the workers felt they were not being utilized well. Workers also felt that system procedures were an impediment to improving the operation and did not permit them to make contributions to their work. The morale of both groups was very low.

When managers and supervisors were asked to conceptualize the type of employee qualified to operate a newly designed single job that would contain *all* the functional processing pieces, none of them believed that the current workers would be able to perform this theoretical job. They said that the job would require workers of a much higher caliber, probably from the country's top graduate business schools. However, they were willing to experiment with other models.

Their reaction was not uncommon. Managers and supervisors often fail to understand that the performance of subordinates is predicated on what they have been given to do. If their work is simple, repetitive, and narrow in scope, their performance will be just that. Thus, any effort to conceptualize employees as adequate for a more complicated, expanded job will usually result in negative reactions. Simply put, people will do better jobs when they have better jobs to do.

It was suggested that the employees train one another, so that each would become familiar with all the functions required by the new job. This proved to be successful and eliminated the need for a large central staff of skilled trainers. Employees took a great deal of pride in teaching others the details of their function and in learning the details of all the other functions. They were enthusiastic about the process as this cross-training effort got underway. In the few instances where workers could not master all the functions required in the new job, they were moved to other locations in the bank.

Managers and supervisors were all educated in work-effectiveness concepts and collectively designed the new work station. Employees who could acquire the knowledge and skills to operate the new work station were also involved in the testing process used in the "white room" and, ultimately, in the new design.

The letter of credit unit was the starting point. Since the institutionalization of this new configuration, other divisions (e.g., money transfer and lock box) have gone the same route. These changes have been made slowly and with deliberate care. Five years is not a long time for such sizeable change.

The impact of this new environment on employees has been significant. Instead of being cogs in a wheel, each is a manager of services. The jobs have variety, interest, and importance, and the people who perform them can see the results of their efforts.

The measurement of the motivating potential of this job has clearly demonstrated that the desired job characteristics of skill variety, task identity, autonomy, task significance, and feedback are present to a greater extent in

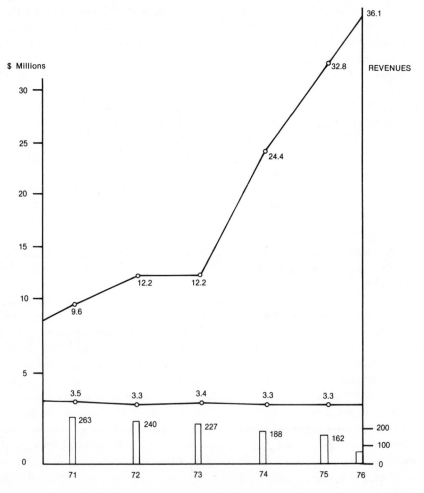

Fig. 6.7. Letter of Credit Unit Operating Expenses, Revenues, and Staff

this job than in a functional position. For example, the IBG letter of credit work station had a motivating potential score of 134.9 versus a 47.96 in the IBG treasury preparer position, as measured by a job diagnostic survey devised by the author. Therefore, if the theory base is valid, the desired results of productivity, service quality, and job satisfaction should accrue.

It may be too soon to measure the full impact of this series of changes on customers. But figure 6.7 shows the effect of these changes on operating expenses, revenues, and staff size. In the letter of credit unit, revenues have nearly quadrupled, while expense has remained constant over a five-year period. During this time, staff size has been reduced by 80 percent. Staffing for the entire organization (see fig. 6.8) has been cut by 50 percent during the same period. Most similar institutions have been satisfied to keep the number of employees constant.

The tests have now been completed, and Citibank is proceeding to move forward with the work-stations management concept. It expects that future installations in other areas will also be successful.

THE RESULTS

Three key measures have been examined to determine whether Citibank improved productivity. First, this organization managed to hold expenses of production constant over a seven-year period, at a time when costs were rising at a rate of 15 percent a year. This significant improvement is shown in figure 6.9

Moreover, the work-station format contributed to profits. The savings in operating expenses amounted to a $110 million contribution to profits for 1976, when a 15.2 percent annual increase in cost (the rate of increase ex-

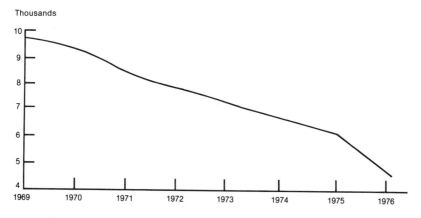

Thousands

Fig. 6.8. Production and Staff Functions — Staffing Level

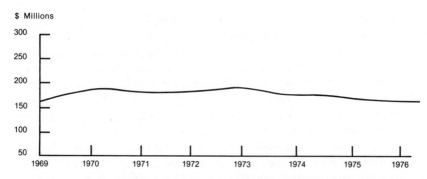

Fig. 6.9. Cost Centers: Production and Staff Functions – Expense

perienced during the 1960s) was projected. If the 1969 cost figures had been allowed to climb at the historical rate of 15.2 percent annually, they would have reached $450 million by 1976. However, since this effort assisted in containing costs at a constant level, it has been estimated that the pretax savings were $220 million and the after-tax savings were $110 million.

These three measures show how changes in organizational and job structure, coupled with improved technology, can result in dramatic improvement. In this instance, the proper combination of organizational and technological changes has yielded these improvements. Improvements of this scale may not be possible in other organizations, but they will never know until they look closely.

The letter of credit unit of the International Banking Group was the starting point. It took one and a half years to move from the manual system to the work-station format. Since that initial effort, the concepts have spread across other operational units. This has required additional time, but the results in other units have been equally dramatic.

Both Matteis and Jaffee emphasize that such radical changes cannot and should not be made quickly. They have learned about the complexities inherent in organizational development issues and refrain from forcing the issue. Even with the total of close to seven years required, Jaffee feels that they may have moved too quickly.

The Work-Effectiveness concept is a tool any organization can use to develop improvements in cost, income, or staff size. It is a tool that is controlled by management rather than by those outside of management. It can be adopted at the top level of an organization or in a lower-level department. That is a decision of management.

The objective of Work Effectiveness is to provide managers with tools *they* can use to improve organizational productivity and effectiveness. At Citibank, managers have used these tools to do exactly that – with results that are self-evident.

7.
The Development of General Motors' Team-Based Plants

Richard L. Cherry*

BACKGROUND AND EARLY HISTORY

Any history of self-managing work groups within General Motors must first acknowledge the supportive context within which these innovations have occurred. The early and continuing quality-of-work-life efforts in GM (discussed by Landen and Carlson in chapter 12 of this book) have provided the framework which sanctioned, encouraged, and nurtured the development of these innovations.

In 1972, three major overlapping events occurred which directly fostered the implementation of semiautonomous work groups in GM by 1975.

Packard Electric-Clinton

In 1972, the Packard Electric Division received approval from the corporation to build a new plant manufacturing wiring harnesses in Clinton, Mississippi, away from its major Warren, Ohio, operations. This location was selected, based on many factors, such as tax abatements, state assistance, and lower energy costs, which would provide the division with a more competitive pricing strategy in an increasingly competitive market. Between 1972 and start-up in 1973, the Clinton plant management developed an approach to people which could be described as "good human relations." A major characteristic of this approach was the increased emphasis on communications, including employee participation in monthly departmental meetings. More attention was given to employee recruitment, selection, and training than in the past, including the first use of assessment centers in

*The author wishes to acknowledge the assistance of Dr. D.L. Landen, director, and Dr. William Duffy, senior consultant, organizational research and development, General Motors Corporation, in the preparation of this chapter.

selecting some hourly (quality inspector) employees. Efforts were made to maintain an open atmosphere in which all employees were on a first-name basis, employee birthdays were recognized, and a climate of mutual trust was developed. The 1977 QWL Executive Conference described the approach as "recognizing employes as contributing adults and allowing them the opportunity to participate as partners in the decision-making process." This was also the first GM plant to implement such symbolic concepts as a common employee entrance, a parking lot without reserved parking for managers, and a single cafeteria shared by all.

The achievements obtained in the Clinton plant through this approach served to reassure other GM managers that increased concern for employee involvement could result in gains for the organization as well. By 1977, it was possible for the then director of personnel for the Mississippi operations to report at the QWL Executive Conference: "The achievements of the past four years at Packard Electric–Clinton, in safety, efficiency, quality and 'presenteeism' confirm that our quality of work life concepts approach is a most effective method of managing a business."

GM Canada–Oshawa

The second major event occurred between 1972 and 1974 when Dick Ault of the corporation's organizational research and development (ORD) department consulted with GM Canada on the design of a new maintenance-free battery plant to be built in Oshawa. A task force was appointed to design this plant using a sociotechnical system (STS) approach. The STS approach to plant planning emphasizes the simultaneous and integrated design of the plant's technology and social system (e.g., organizational structure, reward systems, communication networks) to achieve a carefully thought out set of plant goals. This was the first time STS had been used within the corporation. Employees were to be transferred from an outdated facility to the new battery plant. Unfortunately, strained union–management relations at the time (and premature publicity on the project) resulted in suspicion and apprehension regarding the task force recommendations for new plant design and the ideas suggested for self-managing work teams were rejected. However, three major learnings resulted from this project. First, the positive contributions to be gained by using corporate ORD consultants in designing new work settings was established. Second, STS as a viable and useful tool in the design (if not implementation) of complex new work settings within GM was tested. Finally, as part of the task force's early work, visits by task force members and ORD consultants were made to several companies and plants which had, or were considering, new plant designs incorporating more innovative participative approaches to people. This background information was to prove invaluable in future new plant design efforts.

Delco-Remy Fitzgerald

The third major event occurred with the appointment in 1973 of Edgar E. Ward, Jr., as plant manager of the proposed Delco-Remy battery plant to be built in Fitzgerald, Georgia, with a projected start-up date of March 1975. Ed Ward came to the task with a history of success and accomplishment as a plant manager in other Delco-Remy plants. His father had also worked for General Motors as a plant manager in the same division, and Ed was comfortable with managing a manufacturing operation and working closely with people on a one-to-one basis. He had, in the past, attempted to involve all employees to the extent possible within the context of the traditional management–union environment existing in Delco-Remy's older plants. Ed eagerly anticipated the opportunity to begin a fresh start on a "clean sheet of paper" and agreed at the start to use a consultant to assist him and his staff in the design of the new Fitzgerald facility. Rich Cherry, then with the organizational design department at GM, was chosen for this job.

THE FITZGERALD EXPERIENCE[1]

In September 1974, a live-in, week-long, off-site meeting was held with the consultant and the design or "start-up" group to begin developing their plans for the new plant. On the Sunday night start of this meeting, the then general manager of the division, Ed Czapor, visited with the group and offered his support and encouragement for creative and innovative new ideas around the design and management of this plant. At this first session, the newly appointed members (few of whom had worked together before) got acquainted with each other on a more personal basis and explored their manufacturing experience, their philosophies and beliefs about people and work, and their dreams or ambitions for the new plant. Much of the week was spent using experience-based exercises to explore different points of view about what people (including themselves) wanted from work and their assumptions about the role of management. The exercises dealt with communication skills, decision making, organizational structure, phases of new plant development, and the impact of technology on plant design and employee performance and motivation. Most of the week was devoted to team skills training and, eventually, team development.

About midway through the week, members agreed to operate as a team and developed ground rules for working together (fig. 7.1), which they would review after a three-month "trial." Part of that commitment included a decision to handle any requests from divisional staff which would affect the responsibility areas of three or more team members by meeting as a total team before acting on the request. This decision was to have a major impact on the perception of divisional management that set Fitzgerald apart as "dif-

Delco-Remy
DIVISION OF GENERAL MOTORS CORPORATION

SUBJECT: Team Behavior Commitments   DATE   September 16, 1974

FROM: The Team

TO: The Team

In building an effective management team, one of the most important steps is to determine and exhibit appropriate team behavior. Thus, we the Delco-Fitzgerald team are committed to the following characteristics:

1. We will work for consensus on decisions, objectives, and plans.

2. We will share openly and authentically with others regarding our feelings, opinions, thoughts, and perceptions about problems and conditions.

3. When listening, we will attempt to hear and interpret communications from the sender's point of view.

4. We will trust, support, and have genuine concern for other team members.

5. We will respect and be tolerant of individual differences.

6. We will utilize the resources of other team members.

7. We will encourage comments on our own behavior.

8. We will understand and commit ourselves to team objectives.

9. We will not engage in win/lose activities with other team members.

10. We know that integrity of line authority must be maintained to keep an effective team.

This contract is null and void after November 11, 1974.

Fig. 7.1. Team Ground Rules

ferent . . . if not strange" since consensus seeking did not routinely occur across plant management staffs.

Any clear-cut decision to operate the plant using self-managing work groups was postponed until the team could visit with other organizations, including Packard Electric's Clinton plant. A major obstacle to a ready decision in this area was the impact of the technology to be introduced into the new plant. Delco-Remy would be using manufacturing processes for producing a maintenance-free battery that were basically untried except on a small, pilot-scale basis. One task for the team, then, was to visit with those operations currently developing and testing these processes to see how, or if, self-managing teams could be utilized. The clear intent of the team, however, was to seek ways to implement this concept rather than reasons for its rejection. The possibility of using an STS approach was discussed in depth and the general consensus of the team was that this approach, while potentially valuable, would take more time and effort than they felt was available to get the plant underway. Also, there was general agreement that the plant layout and technology, while untried, were fairly well determined by divisional staffs and that it would be difficult and costly to effect changes at this point.

A major output from this meeting was a preliminary philosophy and goal statement for the new plant (fig. 7.2). This and the other decisions and learnings from the week were shared with the divisional general manager and his staff the following week, including the likely possibility that Fitzgerald would be a plant using self-managing team concepts. While some members

---

The primary goal of Delco-Fitzgerald is to be the best battery plant in the world. This will be achieved through innovative employee relations philosophies and the involvement of the total work force in matters affecting them.

Additional goals as well as philosophies at Delco-Fitzgerald are directed towards satisfying the needs of those affected by our operation:

Our Customers
Our Employees
Delco-Remy Division
The Community
Local, State and Federal Government
Our Stockholders

Through the effective use of human, financial, and material resources available to us we will work towards the following:

- to manufacture a defect free battery in high volume while staying responsive to changing market needs.
- to provide safe, steady, and meaningful employment for our work force.
- to encourage involvement and participation by our employees in an atmosphere of trust, communication and opportunity.
- to be an active citizen of Fitzgerald and the surrounding area, and do our share to promote the growth and prosperity of South Georgia.
- to follow policies that will fully implement Equal Employment Opportunity.
- to contribute to the profitability and return on the investment of Delco-Remy Division, General Motors Corporation and our stockholders.

Through the above we will be able to make greater market penetrations, maintain good employee relations, sustain a high level of product quality, and minimize costs. The net result will create a high quality of work life for the Fitzgerald teams and an efficient and profitable plant for Delco-Remy Division, General Motors.

Fig. 7.2. Delco-Fitzgerald Goals and Philosophies

of the divisional staff were skeptical at this point, in general, there was agreement on the philosophy and goals, and support and encouragement were given for further consideration of the team concept.

Following this sanctioning meeting, many two- and three-day meetings continued with the consultant and the design team with the major objective or target a completed employee handbook before the first hourly wage employee was hired. Of particular interest to this consultant was the low-keyed role played by Dave Jones, the personnel director of the plant. Instead of assuming responsibility for major areas in the handbook, Jones worked primarily as coordinator, ensuring that all members of the design team shared in the decisions as well as in the responsibility for planning and executing subsequent activities that would later be included in the handbook. His behavior was a model of shared responsibility with team members rather than a too-typical protection of "territory and turf." This model was to prove instructive as other team members began to explore how responsibilities might be shared in their own functional areas as well.

Although Fitzgerald did not use an STS analysis, the planning process used in working through major design decisions for this plant is similar in many respects to what is now part of a standard consulting framework for new plant designs of General Motors. Consequently, this design process will be discussed in the context of decisions and activities for this plant.

THE PLANNING/DESIGN PROCESS

Part of the organizational planning process used in working with new plant design groups was adapted and modified from a working paper by Richard E. Walton[2], in which he described the systematic features of organizational innovations. The planning model described in this chapter (fig. 7.3) seeks to achieve an organizational system in which each part is congruent with the rest. Underlying this planning process are three important considerations:

1. There is no one best system of organizational design. What is best for one plant may not be best for another plant.
2. There is an ongoing interaction among the parts of the system. A change in one part of the system can have significant impact on the entire system.
3. Each of the parts must be developed systematically to reinforce consistency of operations and facilitate employee involvement.

Stages of Development

An additional comment concerning this design process is related to the major stages of development in a successfully evolving plant organization. At

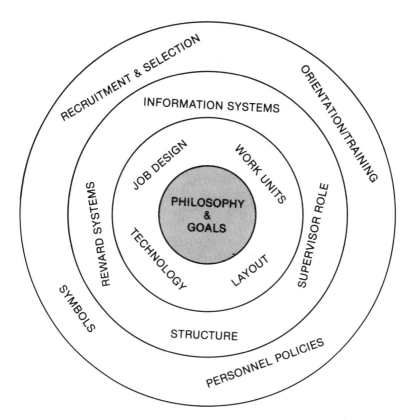

Fig. 7.3. Planning Process for New Plant Concepts

this point at Fitzgerald, the design team was at stage 1, design. The next stage, stage 2, is concerned with the start-up of the operation. After stage 2, the organization moves into a period of time labeled steady state, or stage 3, when such primary indexes as quality, efficiency, employee attendance, and safety are at satisfactory and predictable levels. Steady state is not achieving all the goals and objectives established by the operation in the design state but, rather, obtaining an acceptable level of predictability around these goals. The last major stage, stage 4, is maturity. At maturity, the organization is maintaining, if not exceeding, its goals, and the time is right to consider moving the organization into even more effective patterns of operation through such steps as increased worker participation, increased capability, and/or market penetration.

In the design stage, the focus of design efforts is on steady state rather than start-up. Implementing highly participative work systems during the typical crisis conditions of start-up is inappropriate to both the organization's long-term survival and the readiness level of new employees hired into the organization. In essence, then, the design team at Fitzgerald was designing around concepts, many of which would be implemented, gradually, only as the plant entered into a steady state of operations.

Philosophy and Goals. To achieve an organizational system in which each part is congruent with the rest, careful consideration must be given to basic values, principles, and objectives held by the divisional and local unit management. The development of a philosophy and goals, then, is a necessary first step in the planning process. The philosophy and goals are statements reflecting the local management's beliefs about people and work and the relationship between those beliefs and the plant's objectives. As noted, Fitzgerald management was careful to have its philosophy and goals sanctioned by the division before proceeding further with the design process. In addition, the planning process described tends to be a constraining one, as decisions made early in the first concentric circle restrict or narrow the selection of congruent options within the next outside circle, and so on. Following the development of goals and philosophy, the design process moves outward to the next concentric circle.

Technology and Layout. The first area to be considered (in this circle) deals with the technology employed in the manufacture of the product, i.e., the process used to transform raw materials into finished products. Technology, of course, has a major impact on plant layout, job design, and the structure of work units. In general, the more complex the technology, the fewer options concerning manufacturing flow or layout, the development of "whole" versus "fragmented" jobs, the use of teams versus individual assembly, and the number of job classifications. Both technology and layout in the Fitzgerald case were considered as "givens" even if the technology was a somewhat unknown entity during the planning process. Visits to locations pilot-testing the production process convinced most members of the design team that it would still be possible to develop plant production teams. A major area of concern regarding the plant layout was the lack of planning for meeting rooms. The team decided that two small rooms allocated for traditional supervisory-employee sessions could be used for this purpose. In addition, the plant manager suggested that teams could also use his office for meetings, during which he would tour the plant or use an unoccupied work/desk area.

Job Design and Work Units. Job design (how work is arranged to accomplish the responsibility of the job) and work units (how people and jobs are integrated to achieve operating objectives) were considered together as a single unit by the Fitzgerald management team. These areas deal primarily with how plant operating employees and their responsibilities could be linked in performing plant operations. The planning team, at this point, made its first real commitment to a self-managing work-group concept for plant operating teams. In part, this was accomplished by assigning two responsibility levels. Some responsibilities would rest with the production teams while others would be shared—at least initially—with the management team. The objective was to avoid premature loading of responsibilities onto production teams until they were technically proficient in the production operations and were willing to assume these additional responsibilities. (Figure 7.4 illustrates this approach as used in a later plant design.) At the same time, this provided some members of the design team with a necessary

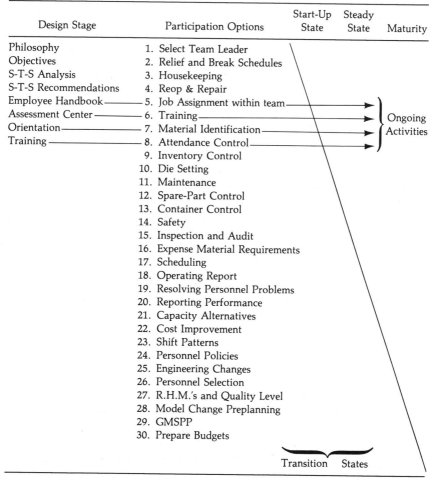

Design Stage	Participation Options	Start-Up State	Steady State	Maturity
Philosophy	1. Select Team Leader			
Objectives	2. Relief and Break Schedules			
S-T-S Analysis	3. Housekeeping			
S-T-S Recommendations	4. Reop & Repair			
Employee Handbook	5. Job Assignment within team			
Assessment Center	6. Training			Ongoing
Orientation	7. Material Identification			Activities
Training	8. Attendance Control			
	9. Inventory Control			
	10. Die Setting			
	11. Maintenance			
	12. Spare-Part Control			
	13. Container Control			
	14. Safety			
	15. Inspection and Audit			
	16. Expense Material Requirements			
	17. Scheduling			
	18. Operating Report			
	19. Resolving Personnel Problems			
	20. Reporting Performance			
	21. Capacity Alternatives			
	22. Cost Improvement			
	23. Shift Patterns			
	24. Personnel Policies			
	25. Engineering Changes			
	26. Personnel Selection			
	27. R.H.M.'s and Quality Level			
	28. Model Change Preplanning			
	29. GMSPP			
	30. Prepare Budgets			

Transition   States

Fig. 7.4. Responsibility Chart

Source: Adapted from the Packard Electric Division, Brookhaven, Design Task Force, 1974.

sense of "control" over plant operations, a sort of "safety valve" just in case their as-yet-untested assumptions were not verified in practice.

Team boundaries were to be established, at first, using "best estimates" of what seemed appropriate until experienced teams could later decide for themselves the best way to establish the teams. Shared responsibilities included hiring of new team members for the operating (shop floor) teams; maintaining EEOC requirements; assessing individual team-member performance; and administering discipline up to, but not including, employee discharge. Operating team responsibilities included meeting established production goals, checking and maintaining quality standards, routine maintenance and minor repairs, training of team members, housekeeping, coordination of effort across teams, job assignment within the team, selection of the team leader, maintenance of safety programs, and keeping track of time for hours worked. Inherent in this list of responsibilities were the following decisions: quality control would be a team responsibility and not the responsibility of the quality control department, although the quality control resource would be available through a member of the management team; a team would be on site, but its role was twofold (nonroutine maintenance and training of operating team members to perform routine maintenance and minor repairs—everyone was a janitor and no one was a janitor); job rotation was possible; each team would have a team leader; and no time clocks would be used in the plant.

Once planning was completed with respect to the technology, work units, job design, and plant layout, the next phase in the planning process was approached. This phase involves determination of the structure of the organization, the role of the supervisor, the pay system, and the plant's information systems.

Structure. In Fitzgerald, the organization structure consisted of four major groupings of teams: support team, area coordinators' team, technical service teams, and plant operating teams (fig. 7.5). In addition, all teams had the following common characteristics:

1. *Collective responsibilities.* Each team would share responsibility for the performance of the total Fitzgerald organization.
2. *Meaningful goals.* Each team member was expected to help meet the goals set for the team and participate in the setting of additional team goals.
3. *Feedback on performance.* Each team member was expected to participate in developing information and data concerning the team's performance.
4. *Team leadership.* All teams would have a leader or representative.
5. *Rewards.* The same rewards would be available for all members within the team.

The Fitzgerald plant organization has the following team structure:

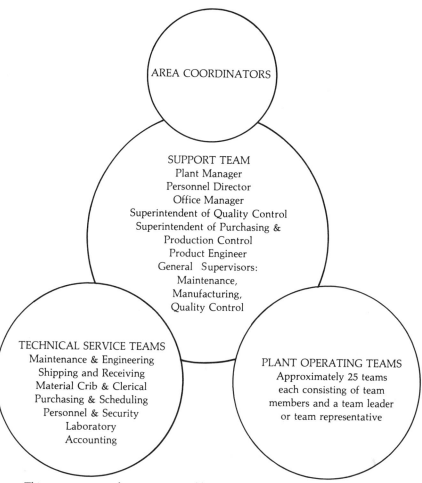

This structure may change as required by our experience in running the business.

Fig. 7.5. How Your Plant is Organized

This structure reflected the intended increased autonomy of the work teams and the supportive interaction of the various segments of the organization. In addition, the structure, if arranged within the context of a traditional hierarchical format, was flatter, with fewer levels between top management and the hourly employees. The area coordinators represented a hybrid of two classification levels found in a typical GM manufacturing plant (first- and second-level supervisors) and, consequently, had available a broader range of salary movement within the coordinator classification.

Supervisor Role. Given the nature of the decisions reached by the Fitzgerald design team up to this point, it became clear that the role of leadership within the operation was to be more supportive and facilitative than in traditional GM plants. Part of this decision was reflected in the nomenclature used to describe the teams themselves, i.e., support and area coordinator teams. The support team's purpose was defined as providing resources for the other teams, developing personnel policies, and coordinating activities in all areas of the plant operations. The major function of an area coordinator was defined as coordinating and facilitating the activities within and across various teams, including the support team. In addition, the changing role of leadership as the plant moved from start-up to steady state was acknowledged. Since their plan was to have the plant operating teams eventually handle many of the traditional duties of the supervisor, it was expected that supervisors would devote more time to training, employee development, communications, and coordination of activities among teams once the basic technical skills were mastered by the operating teams (i.e., a change in emphasis away from technical to human-resource management).

Reward System. Apart from the proposal to design, start up, and manage a complete manufacturing operation using self-managing teams, the proposal to use a pay-for-knowledge scheme for plant operating teams was, perhaps, the most radical departure from traditional operations within General Motors. Historically, the emphasis has been on seniority and, to a lesser extent, on skill levels acquired leading to multiple classification levels. Although this plant would be starting as a nonunion facility, the potential that this pay scheme would establish a precedent for union facilities was a major consideration for corporate and divisional management. (An acceptable compromise was reached which allowed pay-for-knowledge to be used, providing the wage scale or range was within the current GM-UAW contract and that the first two levels following hiring were tied to seniority as well as to task accomplishment.) Under this system, team members increased in wages as they acquired increased job knowledge until they reached level 4, team rate, where they were expected to know all the jobs in their team. After level 4, they were then eligible to move (with an increase in rate) to another team, acquiring new job knowledge until they were at level 6, plant rate, where they were expected to know all the jobs in two different teams. Team leaders under this system were paid an additional increase over their obtained level for the period in which they were selected by their team for this position.

A major concern raised by the design team related to the possible unfairness of assignment to teams having higher or lower technical skill requirements. If a new team member was assigned to a low-technology team, he or she could reach team rate much sooner than team members assigned to high-technology teams. This was resolved with the concept of plant rate since, while it was true that it would take high-technology team members longer to reach team rate in their team, they could "catch up" by moving to a low-technology team when they were going for plant rate. Conversely, initial assignment to a low-technology team could result in faster progression to team rate with slower progress to plant rate.

Information Systems. Two primary vehicles were established to provide effective two-way communication throughout the plant. The first of these, predicated on the underlying philosophy of the plant organization, was "feedback" defined as follows:

> *Feedback* is the best way to develop understanding between all members of the Delco-Fitzgerald team. It is essential to accomplishment, progress, and personal satisfaction. Two important requirements for effective "feedback" are that team members be willing to let the total Delco Team know what is on their minds and that the Delco Team be willing to listen.[3]

The second major vehicle for communications was the Delco–Remy Fitzgerald Handbook, used for purposes of orientation and periodic review, with special attention to philosophy, goals, and team responsibilities.

The final phase in the planning process was to determine approaches to recruitment and selection, orientation and training, the development of plant policies and practices, and the use of symbols.

Recruitment and Selection. Fairly standard recruitment processes were followed in Fitzgerald. Applicants were asked to contact the state employment agency, and preliminary applications were "wide-screened" by the state and then by members of the support team. Innovation occurred in the selection process. All applicants (salary or hourly) were asked to complete an assessment center screening following successful completion of the interviews. With the exception, then, of the original design team members (now the support team), all employees in the plant completed an eight-hour assessment. Salary and production level applications were not separated in the assessment. All applicants were provided with the opportunity to receive feedback on their performance in the assessment center.

Orientation and Training. Unlike other plants in General Motors at that time, Fitzgerald elected to conduct the training program before a formal orientation. Training was considered to be a part of the selection process. This training was designed to cover many of the traditional areas typically considered in a start-up process including a history of GM, Delco–Remy, why the plant was in Fitzgerald, and the major manufacturing processes involved in battery production. In addition, much of the training was devoted to communications, decision making, and group problem solving. The training was conducted by members of the support team, totaled 31 hours, and was generally held from 6:30 to 10:00 p.m. three nights per week. Both in content and length of training, Fitzgerald represented a marked departure from traditional GM new-hire training practices. This format also allowed potential employees to get to know the support team in a facilitating, learning style and had the additional advantage of starting to develop group cohesiveness among training class participants. Roughly one out of ten applicants would be hired at start-up.

The first full day of employment was devoted to orientation. At this point, the handbook was reviewed in depth, emphasizing the philosophy, goals, and objectives of Fitzgerald. Because of the longer preemployment contact these employees had had with support team members, it was possible to more closely relate the training and the behavior of the support team members to the plant philosophy.

Plant Policies and Practices. Most of the major changes which were to take place in this area have been discussed, with the biggest change occurring in the use of pay-for-knowledge. Posted shop rules were replaced by a single motto or plant slogan — "People Helping People" — along with a shared responsibility to review and assess improper conduct by fellow employees. Time cards would be completed by employees replacing time clocks. In addition, the tool room would not be manned by a guard or employee for "security." Instead, employees would sign their names for what they needed and the record would be used to maintain inventory control. Operating team shifts were also to be allowed flexibility in scheduling hours so that the morning shift might come in earlier the day before a holiday to allow the third shift to start their holiday earlier also.

Symbols. While the plant design included two entrance doors in traditional fashion, it was agreed that all employees would use the same common entrance. A single refreshment area in the plant would be used by all employees. The traditional "police" uniforms of the security guards were not to be used. Instead, security decided on blue slacks and blue shirts with an optional tie. Ties for management were also optional. Of more importance, perhaps, was the question of space availability for teams to meet. Since the plant had not been designed for a team concept, it was necessary for teams to use rooms (including the plant manager's office) which were "inside" the traditional "turf" of the clerical and salaried supervisory work force. Other symbols initiated at Clinton, such as open parking, name tags, and the use of first names for everyone, were also adopted.

THE FITZGERALD EXPERIENCE: HIGHLIGHTS AND RESULTS TO DATE

While on an increasingly less frequent basis, consultant contact has been maintained over the past eight years through either ORD or the division consultant. Following are some of the major highlights of this period.

Early Start-Up Issues

Aside from the predictable problems associated with the start-up of any new facility, Fitzgerald had to struggle with the introduction of both a new processing technology and a new concept of management. Both major replacement of equipment and rearranged layouts occurred in working out efficient manufacturing processes. One clear signal that the plant had achieved some measure of a "high commitment" work system was the almost frantic concern on the part of newly formed plant operating teams that they were somehow responsible for the inability to manufacture a stable battery product. This led to two dysfunctional outcomes. First, plant operating teams, at least initially, put pressure on the area coordinators for advice, and the advice received was typically autocratic in direction since the coordinators were experiencing high levels of frustration themselves. Second, as the advice of coordinators failed to result in improvements in productivity, a loss of respect occurred on the part of the operating teams for many of the coordinators, especially those coordinators who were most directive. While early efforts were made to train coordinators to appreciate a more participative style, these efforts were perceived by coordinators to be largely irrelevant and an interference in their work. The loss of respect by the plant operating teams was difficult to change and still exists on the part of some operating team members today—in part, at least, because some coordinators are less capable and participative. In general, however, by 1978, concepts and training relating to participative-management processes were viewed as necessary and highly relevant by area coordinators.

Two interrelated problems frustrated Fitzgerald and the support team for most of the first two years of operation. The first was the relationship between the skilled trades (a technical service team) and the plant operating teams. In a very short time after start-up, it became clear that skilled trades employees felt they could dramatically increase the ability of the plant to manufacture an acceptable battery if only plant operating team employees would leave the machinery alone. This approach was counter to the charter and role of the operating teams, and many conflicts developed between these two groups concerning failures to meet production schedules. It became necessary for the support team to monitor this relationship and balance out these two objectives.

The second problem was safety. As employees were learning routine maintenance and repair of their equipment, along with their jobs, accidents occurred with such frequency that Fitzgerald was at the bottom on safety in 1975 when compared across 128 GM units.

Given the pressures for start-up, safety, quality, and production, the relationship between the division staff and the plant deteriorated. This relationship at the beginning was one of minimal sanction by many staff heads. Fitzgerald was considered by them as a somewhat esoteric "experiment," and efforts by the support team to explain why they were managing as they were sounded defensive when contrasted with current plant performance results. By early 1977, it was necessary to deal with this issue. Divisional staff personnel were interviewed concerning their impressions of the plant, and this information was discussed in an off-site meeting with the support team. Based on these interviews, the support team designed strategies for developing a better relationship between themselves and the division and established objectives to measure these over the next year. (One of the most important of these, incidentally, was to stop "preaching the gospel" of participative management and concentrate, instead, on discussing continuing improvements in bottom-line results.)

Changes in Leadership

Except for the personnel director (who has chosen to stay and work in the plant) and a member who retired, all of the original seven members of the support team have been either promoted or moved to positions of responsibility equal to their responsibilities at Fitzgerald. In August 1979, Ed Ward was replaced as plant manager and moved on to start up another Delco-Remy plant before returning to Anderson as manufacturing manager for all battery plants in the division. Some original members of the area coordinating team have moved into the support team, and some plant operating team members moved into positions as area coordinators. None of these changes has appeared to affect adversely the operating performance of the plant or the underlying philosophy and concepts.

Recent Changes

From the outset, the philosophy and team responsibilities captured in the handbook have been open to modification and revision as the plant gained in experience and new members were added to the work force. Beginning in 1979, operating teams became involved in the preparation of budgets, and that involvement has grown to assume a major responsibility area (fig. 7.6). These teams are now developing their own forecasts on labor efficiency and

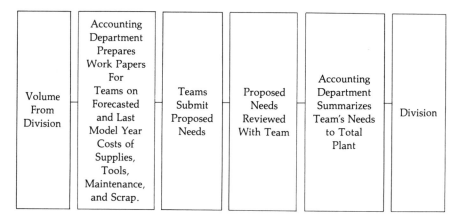

Fig. 7.6. Delco-Remy-Fitzgerald Team Involvement Budget Preparation.

scrap and have been consulted heavily in proposed capacity expansions ranging from layout to equipment requirements. Operating-team members have now assumed the largest share of responsibility for the assessment-center program and operating team safety representatives prepare their own safety procedures, hold safety meetings, and conduct safety talks during weekly team meetings.

Based on the most recent sensing interview (conducted in February 1981), area coordinators report being valued more than in the past, by both the plant operating teams and the support team, and have a clearer understanding of their roles and responsibilities (along with a greater appreciation and interest in gaining additional training in human resource skills).

Attitude of Employees

Since start-up, Fitzgerald management has maintained an active and receptive interest in the quality-of-work-life attitudes of all employees within the plant. These have been assessed through either periodic sensing interviews, as noted above, or attitude surveys. Given the shaky and fragile nature of the start-up, the support team was especially reassured to find that the quality-of-work-life attitudes in an initial attitude survey completed in the first six months of operation were more positive in this location than elsewhere in General Motors. Also, from the first administration of GM's quality-of-work-life survey in 1977, this plant has consistently reported significantly higher overall QWL scores for hourly and salaried employees than have been obtained from either the total GM salaried work force surveyed or a more exclusive sample of salaried work force employees com-

	GM Salaried Norms	New Plant Salaried Norms	Fitzgerald Salaried	Fitzgerald Hourly
Overall QWL	3.40	3.59	4.81	3.68

Fig. 7.7. Quality-of-Work-Life Survey Results, October 1979.

pleting the questionnaire in other (though not all self-managing) new plant locations (fig. 7.7).

This is not to imply that problems have not been revealed through the interviews or surveys but that the approach has been to resolve these problems rather than to ignore them or deny their existence.

Recently, with the severe downturn in demand, this plant faced its first potential layoff in January 1982. Operating teams were asked to meet and decide through consensus, whether employees should be laid off on the basis of traditional seniority practices (for a period up to four weeks), or if an overall reduction in work hours for all employees would be acceptable. All production teams agreed with reduced work hours for all, with 96 percent of the individual employees concurring with this decision.

Other Results

As shown in figures 7.8, 7.9, and 7.10, Fitzgerald's progress in improved quality and scrap (factory-reported defects) has steadily improved over the

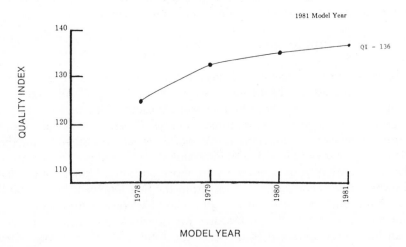

Fig. 7.8. Quality Index — Fitzgerald

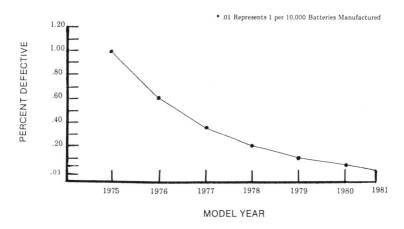

Fig. 7.9. Batteries—Factory Defects, Car Assembly Plant, Allied & Non-allied Returns

past seven years. When compared with the five other Delco–Remy battery plants in the United States producing this product, Fitzgerald has been ranked in the middle for the past two years on overall performance and quality measures, and it has consistently experienced an upward trend in these measures. It is, overall, the third most profitable battery plant in the division (a measure effected by the product models manufactured at Fitzgerald, which are generally not as profitable as those manufactured by the other plants), and their unit cost per battery is the lowest within the division.

In an area where 50 percent turnover per year is standard, Fitzgerald has lost only 11 of 232 employees over the past two and a half years. Absenteeism runs 4 to 5 percent less annually than comparable battery plants, with controllable absenteeism at 2 percent compared to 4 to 5 percent in the other battery plants. Safety is no longer reported on a company-wide basis, but this area has also improved considerably over the first two years of production.

Wilmington	100% member of T135 Club All five model years
Lakewood	100% of T135 Club All three model years
J.C. Penney	Rated Level 4—The highest grade attainable
Atlas	Rated excellent—The highest grade attainable

Fig. 7.10. Quality—Customer Feedback, Model Year 1980.

SEMIAUTONOMOUS WORK GROUP PLANTS IN THE SOUTH: DIFFUSION OR FAILURE?

Background

By 1979, General Motors had started up 16 new component manufacturing plants across the southern half of the United States, which employed between 100 and 550 employees in each location. Admittedly, definitions of "traditional," "participative," or "semiautonomous work groups" as system descriptions of organizations are ambiguous and subjective. A major criteria would have to be that, in "semiautonomous" plants, top local management agrees to operate and "model", on a daily basis, the team concepts in their own behavior with one another.[4] Other factors which would have long-term significance as well include a reward system that is perceived as equitable (in which everyone in a team is eligible to share in those rewards); a philosophy communicated through management behavior which openly acknowledges, plans for, and actively encourages increasing *authority* within work teams as their responsibilities increase; and participation by all employees in selection, assessment of employee performance, work assignments and work schedules, quality, and other areas affecting the quality of their working life.

Given these criteria, of the 16 new plants, 5 fully incorporated or extended the work-group concepts in place in Fitzgerald. Also, based on these criteria, five GM plants (some of which have been "touted" in the past by the media as "team concept" facilities) do not qualify. Such descriptions mislead, since the focus singles out only one aspect of a highly complex organizational system. These five plants might be best described as "mixed" — taking some parts (like the establishment of teams) without incorporating the other major factors.

Of the six remaining plants that could be classified as "traditional" in approach, two major reasons seem to account for their design decisions. In four cases, two plants each were part of a geographical expansion on two original (and "traditional") plant sites which had started production between 1973 and 1975. In one of these three-plant locations, the decision was clearly a reflection of the division's position with regard to innovation in quality-of-work-life efforts. In the second case, having one plant already in a "traditional" mode seemed to lock in the decision to proceed as in the past. In all cases, however, it must be noted that all six plants are noticeably more concerned with the quality of work life of employees than the majority of plants in their back-home, midwest divisional locations.

Union Involvement

The "Procedure for Preferential Consideration for Hiring at Specific Plants" (paragraph 96), established between the UAW and General Motors was announced in September 1978. This agreement supported the movement of union-represented employees from other GM plants to the new southern locations. The impact of this (and subsequent) agreements regarding the movement of represented employees into these locations was, and continues to be, significant.

In three of the six "traditional" plants, employees are now represented by a union. Of the five "mixed" plants, one was successfully organized within 14 months of start of production prior to the paragraph 96 agreement. The remaining four organized very quickly following this agreement.

Five plants had a well-developed team-concept *system*, but three of these had a relatively longer time period in which to implement the concepts. In these three plants organizing attempts have been unsuccessful to date. The remaining two plants were organized, and union and management continue together to implement and expand team concepts. This partnership has increased the receptiveness by both groups to these ideas and concepts as new GM plants have come on stream in the Midwest.

Managers of New Plants Network

As early as 1974, informal meetings were taking place between plant managers of then-existing southern plants to share their experiences and their intentions for QWL efforts within their locations. By 1976, these "managers of new plants" meetings had been formalized. They met every six months, generally on site at a particular host plant location for a two-day meeting. A typical agenda included a tour of the plant and, depending to some extent on the organizational concepts implemented, follow-up meetings with individuals and groups of employees at all levels.

On a few occasions, GM or outside people were invited to participate for part of the meeting. Most often, however, these meetings were deliberately restricted to the plant managers themselves, and one or two ORD consultants. The role of the consultant was two-fold: (1) to facilitate and design the structure of the meeting process, and (2) to establish and maintain a nonevaluative atmosphere in which individual managers could share their problems and accomplishments.

As GM announced more new plant approvals, both domestically throughout the United States and internationally, newly appointed plant managers would be invited into these meetings as well. Here they heard firsthand from their peers what had been tried, what was working, and what was not. These meetings served many purposes. By establishing personal contact, managers felt more comfortable contacting other managers on the telephone about ideas and advice and scheduling plant visits with their design groups to these locations. Also, because of these meetings, they knew more clearly whom to contact about what issues.

In addition, the reassurance, support, and encouragement from other managers who had tried innovations proved to be of tremendous value in encouraging the newly appointed managers to consider adoption and adaptation of these concepts in their own plant locations.

International Diffusion of Concepts

The potential diffusion of semiautonomous work-group concepts in other, non-U.S. locations is still sketchy. In Mexico, one component plant has adopted these approaches, apparently quite successfully, over the past two years. The remaining eight or nine new plants in Mexico are either still in the design phase or have decided to operate in a more traditional fashion.

As GM expanded overseas in the late seventies, semiautonomous-work-team concepts have been implemented in the following countries: France (2); Northern Ireland; and Austria. In addition, these concepts are currently being considered for new plants underway in Spain and Australia.

SUMMARY

The successful institutionalization of work teams in new GM plants has been associated with:

- Designing the plant as a system of interdependent functions tied into and checked out against a clearly articulated and shared quality-of-work-life philosophy.
- Designing the staff and management functions as a support system for shop floor work teams.
- Plant management modeling the behavior and norms supporting the plant operating philosophy.
- A reward system that supports the plant goals and operating guidelines.
- A planned and supportive sanction group in the top management of the division.

Diffusion of work teams to other plants has been associated with:

- The development of a sanction group role for the top management of the division in a successful plant planning process.
- A successful start-up and a consistent performance which meets plant goals; especially if the effectiveness of the work-team system is clearly demonstrated.
- The acceptance of successful team-based plants in the South as models and "mind openers" for plant planning teams in many GM divisions.

Union Involvement in Team-Based Plants

A 1979 agreement between GM and the UAW virtually assures that hourly employees in new automotive plants started by GM will be represented. Accordingly, many new plants now starting up in the North involved the local union in plant planning. In other cases, union representatives were involved through frequent discussions with members of the plant planning team. In some cases, officials of the local union were members of the plant planning team.

The union's role in the operation of team-based plants is being worked out by each plant in its own way. A central issue here is the role of the union committeeman in team operations, particularly in the unusual event that a team member is disciplined.

While the team may counsel a member, the first-level manager, usually called the advisor, is responsible for formal discipline. A team member may use the services of the union committeeman whenever there is a need. In contrast to the committeeman's traditional role, this union official often acts as a facilitator for work-team meetings, problem-solving sessions, and so on, as does the team advisor. The nontraditional committeeman's role has many elements in common with that of the team advisor.

Impact of Work Team Organization on the Supervisor's Role

The most difficult role change in a team-based plant is from traditional production supervisor to an area advisor for a group of shop floor work teams. Advisors are usually chosen through a process of self-selection and careful screening. They are then trained in participative management, group facilitation, and problem-solving skills, often together with the union committeemen. Walton and Schlesinger have provided a good discussion of problems implicit in the advisor's role in the new team-based plants in a recent article.[5]

Advisors are responsible for quality, cost, schedule, and people development goals, as well as boundary management for their groups. Their style should become more participative and less directive as work teams gain skills. The dramatic increase in the scope of the advisor's role and in the skills needed to do it well often lead to feelings of ambiguity and confusion. In this area, as in so many others, top plant management must provide a flexible support system for advisors which is designed to help them grow into their roles as the organization moves from steady state to maturity—a maturity which in a truly effective system is the beginning of a continual evolution.

NOTES

1. As the first and longest running, self-managing work-group plant in General Motors, more attention will be given in this chapter to this pioneering effort than subsequent Southern plants which later embraced these concepts. Also these later plants differ little in the major concepts and practices implemented within the Fitzgerald operation.

2. Richard E. Walton, "Innovative Restructuring of Work," in *The Worker and the Job: Coping with Change*, edited by Jerome M. Rosow (Englewood Cliffs, N.J.: Prentice Hall, 1974).

3. Handbook, Delco-Remy, Fitzgerald, Georgia.

4. While it is certainly possible for a plant to be designed for long-term survival where top local management operates as a team and the plant production employees have more or less traditionally defined jobs and job responsibilities, efforts to promote team concepts on the shop floor when local management operates in a traditional way are highly susceptible to early failure.

5. Richard E. Walton, and Leonard S. Schlesinger, "Do Supervisors Thrive in Participative Work Systems?" *Organizational Dynamics*, Winter 1979, pp. 25–38.

8.
The Limits of Laissez-Faire as a Sociotechnical Change Strategy

Eric Trist and Charles Dwyer

Over a period of 10 years, from the later 1960s to the late 1970s, a number of QWL projects involving the use of semiautonomous work groups were tried out in several locations of a diversified manufacturing concern.* This may be described as a multiplant company of reasonable size, common in most industries at the present time. By the time the recession of the mid-1970s was over, almost all of these projects had faded out. It was widely assumed in the corporation that the recession itself was the main cause of the fade-out; work groups had been dismembered beyond remedy by bumping and layoffs. One or two executives in central personnel were not so sure that the explanation was that simple and asked us to conduct an independent inquiry into what had happened. They felt the findings might help them to determine what policies might best fit the needs of the 1980s.

We were given access to the extensive documentation which existed in the company concerning these projects. We paid field visits to the seven locations involved, where, in addition to work observation, we carried out an interview survey and held group discussions with senior plant management, general foremen, foremen, and workers, on the background of a comprehensive questionnaire. Between 60 and 70 work-group projects had taken place at these locations, some of which were large. Between 600 and 700 workers had participated. As a result of the visits, during which we interviewed 100 employees evenly split between management (including

*In this extensive project, the assistance is acknowledged of Joseph McCann and John Selsky, then Ph.D. students at the Wharton School, and Dr. Bob Drehr, then of Drexel University. The project was carried out under the auspices of the Management and Behavioral Science Center (Wharton School) of which Emeritus Professor Trist is chairman and Professor Dwyer is director. The authors are entirely responsible for the interpretation of the data presented and the views expressed.

149

supervision) and the work force, we compiled analytical reports on each site, which we checked out with those concerned on a subsequent visit. At this time, only two of the projects were still active and, soon afterwards, one of these was terminated. The only remaining active project was different from the rest in that it was a green-field site, a small quasi-independent operation designed from the beginning on sociotechnical principles. The projects which faded out all represented attempts to introduce work groups piecemeal into existing work establishments.

Several levels of skill, including white-collar as well as blue-collar personnel, were involved. In almost all cases, some improvement took place, even if slight. In a number of cases, the degree of improvement was considerable; in a few, substantial. Usually, work-group projects were initiated in their own areas by interested line managers in order to obtain better results in situations which had sometimes become critical. These managers had learned something about the promising results obtained in many industries with forms of job enrichment involving semiautonomous work groups. They wanted to find out if they, too, could secure improvements. They made full use of central personnel as internal consultants. By and large, the efforts they made, though thoroughgoing, were individual efforts. There was not much evidence of active support at the plant-manager level or of active interest on the part of senior management above plant level. Foremen varied in their reactions. Team members were usually positive.

THE LOCATIONS PERSPECTIVE

Isolated Projects

The first semiautonomous work group emerged during 1967 in the development group at Location A. The manager of product engineering gradually gave extended responsibility to a group of nine draftsmen who evolved into full-fledged designers. By and large, the experiment was successful. The groups persisted for four years, until the manager left in 1971.

The development group project was concerned with transforming a group of draftsmen from detailers into designers. The product engineering manager believed that this was necessary to secure economies and increase productivity and, as far as possible, the capacities of the men. More than 90 percent of the assignments came to be handled by the draftsmen, leaving the engineers free to concentrate on large projects and theoretical work. Occasionally, an individual would lack the creativity or was too inflexible to fully make the required change. Individual differences therefore had to be taken into account.

Those participating believed that larger groups would be more difficult to develop in this mode than smaller groups, though not impossible. A change in management style to a more participatory mode was entailed, with the manager no longer acting as a "boss." The project began in the "job-enrichment" tradition, but transcended it in that there was participation, the involvement of the entire group in unit activities, and an explicit change in the nature of the managerial role toward a participatory mode. The change in job content was major, not minor, and involved an altogether higher level of responsibility for group members, continuous learning about larger organizational issues, interpersonal relations, and ways to improve the work group's performance. In one case, it had gone so far that patents were filed for a design developed by the group. The union did not object to these projects, nor was it obstructive. It was viewed as informally cooperative.

The same concept was extended to a wire shop, model shop, and optical shop.

The program cut operating costs drastically and improved morale and productivity. The designers filed only two grievances on matters that were quickly corrected. Yet, the project was allowed to lapse when the initiating manager departed in 1971.

The second project in 1969 also took place in Location A in a unit making a heavier type of equipment. It was initiated by the operations manager. A group of 12 skilled welders and fitters was given responsibility for the planning, scheduling, and control functions necessary for their work. So great was their involvement in the project that they attended a skills-improvement seminar (with their foreman) during a strike which took place soon after the team was formed. The experiment was judged "remarkably successful" by those concerned because it had changed the labor relations climate and saved 50 percent in overhead. Declining business caused the team to be disbanded in 1972. No attempt was made to restart it later.

The success of the welding team stimulated a wider development in 1971 in an area making a complex type of product in Location B. This occurred in a crisis situation in which the department was under threat of closure, and the manager of manufacturing engineering was the initiator. Dramatic reductions were obtained in the time required to build complex products. In one case, while planned time to complete a product was 1,600 hours, it actually had been taking more than 2,000 hours. Completion time was reduced to 1,300. In another, there was a 42 percent productivity gain; in still another, a 30 percent productivity gain was accompanied by a 33.3 percent reduction in quality rejects and a 50 percent reduction in absenteeism.

One project led to another, and a works council was formed in 1973 to cover all 60 employees in the area. Despite these successes, groups were discontinued in 1974 when the initiating manager left. The effort at Location B was a more comprehensive endeavor than those attempted at Location A and is as impressive as anything reported in the literature concerned with a complete but small complex operation. Yet it failed to impinge on plant or higher management.

The pattern revealed by these successful initial developments may be summarized as follows. The nature of the work is complex. The workers are skilled. The union cooperates, or the objections of union officers are ignored by the men involved. The initiator is an interested line manager, below the level of plant manager, who is in difficulties over his bottom line. He involves central personnel in a consultative role. The projects grow in scope but are limited to the area of the initiating manager. Though they persist, with substantial economic success, for three or more years, they fade when he leaves. In organizational pattern and value base, these sporadic efforts were alien to the prevailing managerial culture.

Multiple Projects

The second pattern to appear was that of multiple projects in one plant which develop intensively over a short time period, and then fade. It began at Location A. Seven groups were introduced in processing between January and March 1972 by the manager formerly involved with the welding group. Three more groups were later added in other products.

These projects began to become "experiments" in a more self-conscious sense. Hard data on performance were sought, with before-and-after measures and control groups. There was a concentration on measurement. Central personnel was more prominent, though the initiation of projects by interested managers persisted. The workers tended to be less skilled. Various operations of a more routine kind began to be included.

Location C. This pattern "exploded" at Location C where no fewer than 13 groups were introduced during 1972 and 5 more were introduced in early 1973. While almost all these efforts were modestly successful, they were short-lived.

The write-up concerning work groups at Location A had come to the attention of the personnel manager of Location C in mid-1971. He discussed it with a member of central personnel and the shop operations manager, who had become enthusiastic about the possibilities apparent in work groups and was beginning to implement them in his area. The personnel manager began a program of foreman training. The training consisted of role modeling in group relations skills. The shop operations manager attended the meetings and general foremen seemed supportive and took part as group leaders in some of the off-site training. The plant manager remained neutral with respect to work-group experiments. Many foremen felt that it was the shop operations manager's idea and that it was merely one more management gimmick that would leave the site when the shop operations manager moved on. Numerous "management techniques" had been tried over the years and most had been perceived as "failing" — dying out within a few months.

The foremen who had been through the training were asked to volunteer to try work groups in their areas. Only four or five did so, but their groups were regarded as quite successful. Unable to obtain volunteers for more groups, the shop operations managers selected a number of foremen who were *told* to try the work-group approach.

In due course, the shop operations manager was moved to another location, and the personnel staff turned their interests to other functions. The business climate worsened, causing layoffs and bumping as well as pressures for production and reinforcing supervisors in their desire to revert to older and more comfortable supervisory styles. The groups faded.

Yet, they had been modestly successful during their 18 months of existence. Efficiency measures were available for 11 of the 12 groups started in 1972. For the 11 reporting, results were positive for all except one: 4 represented increases of up to 4.9 percent; 2, up to 9.9 percent; and 4, over 10 percent. The negative result was 7.5 percent. Measurement periods were between 6 and 12 months.

The 1972 program was developed with an enthusiasm which was caught in a report by the personnel manager reflecting the excitement of those leading the endeavor. He and the shop operations manager had started thinking about work groups some three years earlier when they stood looking at the picket line which formed religiously every day in spite of the inclement weather. They had wondered how they might motivate the employees to work that enthusiastically after the strike was over.

It is amazing that something begun so well should have ended so dismally. The interviews are retrospective and took place three years later. Yet vivid feelings were expressed. The negative attitudes make a strong contrast with the positive picture in the personnel manager's earlier report.

There were widely divergent views among management as to what work groups were, their desirability, and under what conditions, if any, they might be reinstituted. The most knowledgeable person still on site was the personnel manager. While he was still enthusiastic about the concept, he did not believe that it could be reintroduced successfully. There was inadequate management support, some of the foremen involved were opposed, and there was fairly widespread employee disillusionment based on experience.

Knowledge about work groups was not widespread among management, but those who were concerned with the experiments expressed a cautious optimism. As one moved to the foreman level, the sense of having had a positive experience decreased and the range of views widened. At one end were views such as "It was a game," "No one took it seriously," and "I already had a work group in operation and calling it a group didn't change anything." At the other end, there was at least one foreman who was enthusiastic, supported the concept strongly in his own area, and believed that it was effective. There was also resentment expressed by some that the work groups were imposed by the shop operations manager and, as such, were resisted or given only reluctant cooperation. One employee's comment reflects this perception — "All of a sudden we were a work group." The concern that imposition did take place was accompanied by a strong belief that the concept could not be successfully forced. There must be both a shared sense of the need for, and the desirability of, work groups along with a shared sense of ownership of them.

"Nobody would define what 'work groups' meant." Several employees expressed the feeling that "it was not clear what was going on." At best, it was seen as an opportunity to "treat people like people, to be honest and open with employees, to facilitate communications, to listen to what employees had to say, to keep them informed, and to develop mutual respect."

By far, the most intense responses came from a group of six women, all of whom had been members of work groups and most of whom were long-term employees. Some indicated quite favorable experiences — "It worked for us" — and regretted the dissolution of the groups. For some, the dissolution was the consequence of their operation's moving overseas. For others, there was the quite clear belief that the groups were allowed to fade out by the inaction of hostile or indifferent foremen or were simply abolished by management when lines were reorganized.

Concerns were also expressed that the groups had a great deal more to do, including paper work and much of the foreman's job, with no increase in pay, and that some members had to "carry" other employees who would not cooperate in group activities. In short, it would take a great deal of effort, over an extended period of time, to convince these employees of the desirability of reinstituting work groups. They said they would require unambiguous evidence that there was serious, significant, and sustained support of the concept throughout the management ranks (particularly at the foreman level), a clearer concept of what a work group was supposed to be and do, and a long-term commitment to maintaining them through difficult times.

The employees compared present conditions with the plant atmosphere five years ago when the first groups were started. They had found the atmosphere then very positive, supportive, and pleasant. They indicated that in the past they looked forward to coming to work, but now they hated to come to the plant each morning. They felt that the engineers were a particular source of difficulty, for example, "They tell you what to do whether it's right or not and you have to do it." "They are never on the line." "They take the credit while we do the work." "They look down on us and make us feel stupid." "Even though they are often wrong, we can't correct them."

Similar points were made about management, for example: "They don't come out into the plant very often." "They have no faith in the workers." "They try to push off everything they can on us." "They don't give us any support, they don't care." "We are dumb people to them." "You can't talk to the managers."

The employees were drawn from the surrounding area, which is a small city/rural environment. They were not hard-line unionists nor a group ideologically in conflict with management. Rather, compared to an earlier period, they saw themselves in a significantly less desirable work environment. Union officials had been briefed regarding the formation of several groups. Among the officials mentioned were the president of the local and the shop committee chairman. No objections appear to have been raised.

A manager who had recently come to the location, and who had had extensive experience with work groups at Location A, began to develop production measurement groups in his area of responsibility. These had many of the characteristics of the work groups. The strategy was to get them more naturally assimilated into the area.

Those interviewed reported attitudes typical of employees whose hopes have been raised, only to be dashed. They showed acute sensitivity to any suspicion of management manipulation, while the management interviewees showed the strength of foreman resentment over coercion.

That there should be those willing to try again is testimony to the durability of the belief that there is something inherently worthwhile in work groups. Restarting in such an environment, however, is clearly more difficult than starting where such past experiences had not taken place.

Location D. The pattern of multiple experiments exploded again in Location D with even greater intensity. Between the spring of 1973 and the fall of 1974, 19 work groups were introduced at Location D. For almost all of them, some degree of success was reported. Yet, as at Location C, they faded.

If their demise was linked to the recession, our interview material suggests that the negative character of the organizational context was also relevant. An organizational climate survey had been carried out to explore attitudes concerning work groups and greater employee participation in decision making. Most of the 21 general foremen and 71 foremen taking part were negative in various degrees. No systematic attempt was made to deal with these attitudes.

The Location D effort was the most deliberately experimental of the programs. Sophisticated attention was given to research design despite rough operational conditions. Measures were numerous and rigorous, putting an extra load on foremen. Control groups did not know they were control groups, even when under the same foreman, which increased the level of internal foreman conflict. There was no lifting of the pressure for production while the groups were finding their way and settling in. In this sense, they were not treated as experiments.

A resident consultant from central personnel was much in evidence. He was there at the request of the plant manager who, like the other managers mentioned, was looking for new ways to improve performance in a situation which was no better than marginal from an economic point of view. He was familiar with what had happened at Locations A and C.

Location D was the first plant at which initial interest at the plant manager level was reported. With his sanction, it was possible to conduct experiments in all areas of the plant. This showed that semiautonomous work groups could make improvements under a wide variety of technical conditions. The plant manager, however, did not continue to give the support he provided at the beginning. He was too preoccupied with the immediate economic problems of the plant. Sustaining the groups once they were established would have taken time he did not have. A lot of additional work was created for foremen through extra record keeping and training. The needs of the groups did not fit in with many traditional operating procedures and measurement practices. New problems of compensation began to emerge. The problem of coping with these wider issues was too great given the immediate operational pressures which worsened as the recession deepened. The projects, therefore, remained too much under the "ownership" of the consultant, despite his assiduous attempts to transfer this ownership to management.

After numerous interviews at all levels (group members, foremen, and others), it became evident that the primary process problems during group operation were found at their "boundary," to some extent with the group's links to upper and to lower levels, but primarily at the interfaces with support groups. Maintenance, personnel, materials suppliers, work planners, "instructors," and timekeepers were all cited at Location D. Because these units did not take part in group goal-setting efforts, were not included in group meetings, and were not evaluated along with the groups, they had little reason to respond in a timely manner to group needs. Group members were allowed to contact these units directly, but several respondents indicated that these support units sometimes continued to deal exclusively with the foreman rather than with group members.

Location D was the first nonunion plant in which work groups were tried. There is, however, little evidence that unions were serious obstacles to the formation of work groups at any of the unionized locations. There was a surprising amount of cooperation by the stewards directly involved, even when there were misgivings or outright objections by other union officers. Improved performance from group methods would help, they hoped, to keep jobs that were threatened.

Management preference on the sites studied was to proceed with a mini-

mum of formality in order to avoid raising difficult issues with the bargaining unit. This was in keeping with the way in which projects arose in the
areas of interested managers rather than through a plant-wide effort which
would bring the union committee as a whole into play. Nevertheless, the
emergence of a works council at Location B represented a move in the direction of more formal labor-management cooperation in the areas of quality
of working life and productivity.

Location E. This location was a twin plant site where eight work groups
were rather rapidly introduced during 1974 in the packaging areas. Each
foreman had between 50 and 80 people under his control, and the areas
were considered "problematic." The packing-area jobs were all entry-level
positions, the work force was young, and the employees had short service.
There was a constant flow of workers, high turnover, and constant bumping. The work load was dictated by the production rate of the rest of the
line, with the packing area at the end. The workers were expected to pack
whatever was produced.

Entry areas of this kind, where the work is entirely unskilled and where
exposure to disruption of all kinds is greatest, are not auspicious sites for
work groups, especially in an inaugural phase. Management apparently had
little idea of what it was getting into and had no strategy for assessing conditions needed for success. There was some training of foremen in terms of
role modeling and team building, but this was done in parallel with the setting up of the work groups rather than as a preparation for them. Group
members were not offered training.

Groups were introduced on three shifts in the packing area in one plant
and on two shifts of a similar area in the other. In one plant the majority of
the first shift favored the group approach, but the union steward encouraged resistance. This was due to an antagonistic relationship he had with
the shift foreman. In June, a new foreman was assigned to the packing area
and, at the initiative of the employees, a group approach was reintroduced.
Following a series of meetings, several work changes were initiated and a
trip was made to the other plant which had what was considered a more
organized packing area. Following a shutdown, there was a 50 percent turnover. This, together with a series of drug problems, brought the group-
approach activities on this shift to a halt. Acceptance of the group approach
was better on the second shift and enthusiastic on the third. Meetings were
held throughout the spring. However, the activities of these two groups also
stopped after a shutdown and the high turnover (70 percent on the second
shift) that followed.

In the other plant, work groups were introduced in January 1974 in the
packing area on both shifts. During the initial period of two to three
months, one team worked well. Better cooperation between incentive and
day-work employees was noted. There was greater autonomy, and partici-

pation and cooperation were in evidence in a rearrangement of the packing area. According to our interviews, these gains were short lived. After start-up, the groups experienced a number of "personality clashes" as older and younger workers were brought together under the bidding system. Group activity faded under strict work-rule adherence when bumping brought an infusion of higher-seniority workers into established groups. Nor was the piece-rate system conducive to the more cooperative group model.

There was little reference to any training. The comments were that whatever was done was not very successful. The members themselves were seen as generally cooperative, especially in the beginning and on two of the shifts. One shift was considered very problematic — it was a young, antagonistic work force, with poor work habits and a lot of absenteeism, and it was "very much into drugs." This latter group did begin to develop as a more disciplined, cohesive team after a foreman change. This was a promising result, considering the poor quality of the group. However, by then, layoffs, plant shutdown, and turnover had decimated the original group.

Location E represents the most extreme case of the introduction of work groups in a negative organizational context, at an inauspicious moment. Management appears to have regarded them simply as tools to be slotted in where convenient — in case they might help out with one or two immediate headaches. The work groups at this location were begun when the phase of multiple experiments had already passed its peak in the other locations and the disruptive effects of the recession were already in evidence. Groups started under these circumstances at an inexperienced site had little chance of surviving.

Yet the groups themselves were promising, despite personality conflicts in two teams and poor timing for introduction in another. The disrupting forces were largely external. Realization of this seemed to be the basis of the not altogether unhopeful attitudes of the respondents concerning restarting teams under more settled conditions.

This pattern of multiple projects, intensively developed at one site only to fade after some 18 months (even though moderately successful) suggested to us that the laissez-faire approach adopted contained a strategic error. There was no systematic organizational support, no preparedness for system-wide implications, no working through to an overall concept to which plant management as a whole could become committed. The failure to persist of these economically successful, intensive, multiple experiments represented to us the limits of laissez-faire as a change strategy.

A Training Framework

Location F. By and large, the projects, so far described were initiated under conditions of strain as regards maintaining production at an economic level.

In some cases, the economic situation was one of crisis. (This was apart from the recession, which came later.) It constituted a main reason for the initiating managers to try something new and for the workers to cooperate to preserve their jobs. But Location F was expanding in 1972 when work groups were started. The need was to take full advantage of a positive business opportunity. This also provided a situation which could encourage innovation.

What was done differently at Location F compared with other sites was to embark on an unusually thorough management training and development program before work groups were introduced. This went considerably beyond the "role training" offered to foremen at Location A and elsewhere. Not only foremen and general foremen but management personnel above this level were included. No fewer than 150 members of staff went through a 13-week program (three hours a week) in three years, designed by an external consulting firm. The introduction of work groups was not delayed until all 150 had completed the program, which was continued after their inauguration.

The aim was to change managerial style toward a more open and participatory mode. Such a change is consonant with the philosophy of work groups. The scope of the training program indicated a not inconsiderable management interest for moving in this value direction. It provided a wider support base than existed on other sites, even if this was not so throughout the entire plant.

Another difference was that Location F did not follow the pattern of rapidly introduced multiple experiments. Only two groups were formally instituted. A third had spun off naturally and was not known as a work group. Account must be taken also of the fact that the training program led quite a number of foremen informally to allow their teams considerable freedom of a work group type.

No attempt was made to secure elaborate measures, which were a strain to collect; to insist on control groups, often difficult to identify; or otherwise to create a climate of self-conscious experimentation, though the dearth of data now became too great. The process was one of slower and more natural assimilation.

The problem was to discover why the rate of diffusion was not faster under conditions which suggest this may have been possible, considering the scope of the training effort. It was postulated that the pace of the training effort was too slow. Three years is a long time. At one point the union was the obstacle. This inclined management to keep the work-group idea implicit and rely on the training of the foremen to work things out informally.

Yet for one group, output was up 31 percent and rejects down 37 percent in the first year. This has been maintained with several innovations. In the other group doing sophisticated work with nonexempt personnel, overtime was reduced from three-to-six hours a week to six hours for the whole of the first four and a half months of operation in the new mode, with two members off sick. In spite of this, the groups were allowed to die.

Something more is needed than either the pattern of multiple experiments or the training framework provided. In the first instance, intensive development of multiple experiments failed to arrest fade-out. In the second, extensive preparation through a well-designed training program failed to occasion widespread diffusion.

A Green-Field Site

Location G. This location represented a development of a different kind from any so far attempted. It was a new plant (1973) designed from the beginning on work-group principles with an organizational structure and management philosophy consistent with them. Though a very small operation (less than 100 personnel in all), it was an entity in itself. This is a very different situation from being a component in a larger established operation. That it should have been brought into existence at all suggested that, for the first time, someone in the line above plant level had some interest in testing (in the comparative safety of so small an operation) the validity of moving toward the full organizational alternative now available to the conventional manufacturing setup. Yet some anxiety was voiced concerning future support from management above plant level.

Suffice it to note that all personnel were salaried, that the management structure was "flat," that specialist staffing was minimal, and that far-reaching responsibility had been delegated to the groups. Like a number of other new plants set up along innovative lines in the United States, it was nonunion. There are, nevertheless, an increasing number of cases in which unions have participated in the design of such plants.

Location G weathered its own start-up and survived the recession. It outperformed a sister plant which is older and more conventional. People said they liked working there, but they were, of course, the kind of people who like to work in this way, as were the managers who had chosen to develop the plant along these lines.

A relatively large and heterogeneous manufacturing corporation cannot depend too heavily on the odd new plant it sets up from time to time in order to discover its preferred organizational path into the future. It seemed significant, therefore, that small steps were being taken spontaneously to restart work groups — at Location C, for example, where a good deal of participation had continued informally. Moreover, one or two managers formerly associated with work groups appeared to be intent on introducing them in other locations where they were now working. Interest in setting up such groups had been expressed by three small plants "when the time was ripe." The supply of initiating managers had far from dried up. Such managers were beginning to create a network of increasingly experienced individuals who, though dispersed, remained in informal contact.

Despite severe setbacks and the phenomenon of project fade-out, the work-group concept had survived the recession in this corporation as in most others which have seriously explored its application and development.

INTERVIEW SURVEY PERSPECTIVE

This perspective treats the findings of the interview survey as a whole across all sites (except one which was not available for interview).

It was important to interview management members as well as work-group members — not only the foremen directly involved but also general foremen and plant and personnel managers. Roughly equal numbers of the work force and management were interviewed in a sample of 100. Some nongroup members were included, as their perspective also was relevant. Though Location D was overrepresented, it is doubtful if this is unduly distortive.

The 80 questionnaire items are grouped (not always in consecutive order) under headings which describe six broad areas: program design, implementation, internal processes, support, evaluation, and termination.

Managers were interviewed individually, while members of the work force were sometimes interviewed in groups. In such a case, a member of the research team first took the group through the questionnaire, then discussed matters arising with them. With managers, this type of discussion took place during the administration of the questionnaire.

The level of cooperation was high, but the experiences of work groups were "cold"; the groups had ceased functioning two to three years previously. Not unnaturally, since the experiences were being recalled from so far in the past, some respondents could not answer a number of the questions. Also, there were those who did not feel able to express an opinion on some of the broader issues. This was particularly true of work-force members. Therefore, varying numbers gave answers, though most respondents answered most questions.

For the present analysis, the four points of the scale have been collapsed to two — those agreeing and those disagreeing. Each of the six sections is introduced by an overview statement. The questions pertinent to the section are then given, along with the number of respondents agreeing or disagreeing. A short commentary is added which makes use of the qualitative material.

A correlational analysis was carried out, but due to the small numbers and the dubiousness of assuming normal distributions, the results are inconclusive. Therefore, it has been omitted from the present discussion.

Despite the limitations of the data, the interview survey discloses a number of important findings and a great deal of suggestive material. It gives a picture of how work groups were experienced by those who took part in them or were closely associated with them in a managerial capacity. Under the circumstances, the extent of the recall is remarkable, as well as the strength of the views and feelings expressed, leaving no doubt as to the impact of work groups on those who had experienced them or the importance they attached to the concept. This picture complements that obtained from site visits, which is described in the first half of this chapter. Many of the views commonly put forward in the literature were voiced by this group of operating people who between them seemed to have learned the alpha and omega of work-group functioning. Too little of this knowledge and wisdom was used by those responsible for initiating and running the programs. The corporation did not know of the wealth of experience that had been built up. The process of organizational learning had scarcely begun.

Program Design

Strong views were expressed concerning the principles on which work groups should be designed (see table 8.1):

Voluntarism. Involvement in work groups should be voluntary. Nothing good would come out of attempts to force people to participate.

Selectivity. The best strategy is to select suitable areas rather than to proceed plant-wide from the beginning.

Diffusion to the Whole Plant. On the other hand, there was concern about experimental groups becoming privileged, especially in the work force, where any form of divisiveness is feared. The prospect of diffusion to the plant as a whole should be kept under consideration from the beginning. Ultimately, having part of a plant on work groups and part not is likely to produce difficulties regarding equity.

Inclusion of Management in Evaluation. Plant management and general foremen as well as foremen and group members should be considered as part of a total effort. Therefore, the performance evaluation of these higher ranks should include a judgment on how well work groups within the scope of their responsibility are doing.

Payment. Additional pay for group members as compared with non-group members was not recommended. Special pay would give rise to envy and jealousy and be disruptive. However, pay schedules should be sensitive to employees acquiring new skills and adjusted accordingly.

Sharing in Savings. When productivity increases or cost savings are obtained, the benefits should be shared between the "company" and all employees concerned — both workers and management — and on a plant-wide basis.

Recognition of Individual Performance. Though work groups focus on group efforts, the individual needs to be recognized too. Contributions to a group are often differential.

Allowance for Group Differences. The differences in performance among work groups tend to be considerable. This must be accepted. It means that no program can remain uniform.

Implementation

Implementation is concerned with how well the program design is placed in operation within the actual workplace (see table 8.2). Some principles stated were:

Training. The amount and adequacy of training given key participants (unit workers, foremen, general foremen, and others) on group concepts and processes were viewed as critical.

Feedback. Provision has to be made for adequate feedback to group members and management (i.e., methods for providing information about group performance). Effectiveness has to be periodically checked and reported to group members if motivation is to be maintained and corrective actions taken.

Site Selection. The selection of "appropriate" work units and plant sites is a key factor in long-term success.

Goal Clarity. Clarity of both management's and the group's expectations (goals) regarding the use of work groups is essential for success, as is their congruence and compatibility.

Start-ups were felt to have been rather ineffective. While there was agreement that group-member selection and site selection was good, greater attention to these factors would be needed for future efforts.

The training needs of foremen and group members were also significant concerns. While perceived as adequate, the training of foremen was, upon closer inspection, uneven and too short, according to the interviews. Group members' training was seldom provided, although it is crucial if truly effective groups are to develop.

Table 8.1. Program Design

		Response	
Question	Agree	Disagree	Commentary
35. Participation in work groups should be voluntary.	59	18	There is substantial agreement that participation should be voluntary rather than required. Greater cooperation and motivation are secured through a voluntary program.
37. For work groups to be effective, the whole plant should use work groups.	30	41	The balance of opinion was against going plant-wide immediately. The minority who favored a plant-wide strategy were group members and some foremen concerned with equal benefits and advantages.
47. Even though they are not a part of the work group, general foremen should be evaluated in part by how well their work groups do.	64	11	Respondents overwhelmingly agreed that general foremen hold some measure of responsibility for the performance of their work groups.
48. Even though they are not a part of the work group, senior plant managers should be evaluated in part by how well their work groups do.	63	7	Respondents overwhelmingly agreed that senior plant managers' performance evaluation should be kept at an individual level, distinct from group evaluations.
49. Individual members' performance should be evaluated as well as work-group performance.	58	17	Most group members and management personnel agreed that some performance evaluation should be kept at an individual level, distinct from group evaluations.
52. There was a lot of difference between the work groups.	41	11	By almost 4 to 1, respondents agreed that the differences between work groups were substantial. Work-group members perceived differences the least, probably because they had less exposure to other groups. Differences in type of work as well as in people were mentioned.

54.	As a group member, I had a lot of freedom to do the work the way I wanted to.	34	21	Most respondents felt they had freedom in job design with work groups, though a good many felt they didn't. Work-group members at Location G perceived freedom to a much greater extent than any other group.
72.	Work group members should not be paid more than non-work-group members.	51	16	Respondents generally agreed that group members should be paid the same as non-group members. But note the different attitude to question 73.
73.	Work groups should share in the savings they generate for the company.	40	21	By a 2-to-1 margin, respondents felt that groups should share in savings they produce. However, there is a real split between supervisory/management levels, who disagree, and group members, who agree with the statement.
77.	*How important is it to know how well other work groups are performing at this plant?	54	26	Knowledge of other groups' performance is important. Respondents at Location D felt especially strongly about this.
78.	*How important is it to know how well work groups are performing at other plants?	42	28	The patterns of response were similar to question 77. General foremen and management were more apt to feel it was important to know about work teams in other plants.
80.	*How important is it for other workers to know how well the work groups are performing?	51	15	Respondents attached importance to this, too, though to a lesser degree than for question 78.
81.	*How important is it for work group members to know how well non-work-group members are performing?	35	25	Across all sites and all levels except one, respondents attached importance to this, too, though the degree was less than for question 80.

*Note: Responses measure whether it is very important or *not* very important.

165

Interviews indicated great interest in ways to improve group meetings; the inclusion of support groups in these meetings is one way of improving them and the development of group skills another.

Additionally, while management felt that they had adequate information on group performance, work-group members believed that they themselves did not have adequate information on results. In terms of group goals, there was much greater agreement that goals were clear. Work-group performance was perceived to be good by twice as many respondents as those who felt performance was not good.

Internal Processes

This area is concerned with internal group activities and attitudes toward these activities (see table 8.3). The adequacy of group meetings, the attendance of key "others" (general foremen, management, support units, and so on), and their roles in these meetings were key elements. The importance given to goal setting, the level of conflict internally and interunit, and the level of interest in groups once they had been operating for a while were also stressed.

One of the most important findings of the entire study was that it is essential for both short-term and long-term group effectiveness that support units, such as maintenance, be included in group meetings. Also, management's role in regulating and smoothing relationships between units needs to be more explicit. Management should also be willing to alter plant rules and policies that inhibit the functioning of work groups. This was rarely done.

Many people lost interest in maintaining their work groups once they had operated for a while. This was said to be caused by unresolved problems such as:

- Constraining rules and regulations
- "Support units," such as maintenance and engineering, that did not support the groups
- Feelings that the commitment and support of management were diminishing
- Poor communication horizontally (within a level) and vertically

These were all external constraints. Work groups did not often break down for internal reasons. It was said that there was little intermember conflict and excellent group spirit, and that group meetings were open and on the whole constructive.

Some operating principles suggested were:

Line Management Involvement. Successful work groups cannot, it was said, be solely promoted by the personnel department. Line management

Table 8.2. Implementation

	Question	Response Agree	Disagree	Commentary
1.	The start-up of the work group was effective.	31	46	Start-ups were generally perceived as rather ineffective.
2.	An effective choice was made in selecting foremen for work groups.	44	13	General consensus was that foremen selection was effective.
3.	Effective choices were made in selecting the work-group members.	43	22	On balance, work-group members were thought to be well selected. Individual experiences were highly varied, however.
4.	Effective choices were made in selecting the plant sites (i.e., their own site) for work groups.	50	12	Most respondents were pleased that their site was selected for a work-group experiment, though there was some evidence of dubiousness in retrospect in the managerial ranks.
5.	The work group's foreman was well trained for his position.	46	21	On the whole, the training of foremen was perceived as adequate. Most respondents, however, held no standards of comparison. Verbal comments expressed considerable dissatisfaction with foreman training.
6.	Training should have been available to workers who were part of work groups.	65	22	Opinion was strong that group members should receive special training, especially among group members themselves. They did not receive adequate training for truly effective group functioning.
7.	More work groups should have been added in the plants as the first teams gained experience.	54	14	The balance of opinion favors rapid addition of new groups. This opinion was very strong among group members and rather strong among foremen, with general foremen and management opinion more reserved.
8.	Work-group meetings were effective.	59	22	Group meetings were believed to be generally effective. Interviews, however, suggested that they could have been more operationally effective, but in themselves they were satisfying to many.

Table 8.2. (Cont'd)

	Question	Response		Commentary
		Agree	Disagree	
9.	Management had adequate information on work-group results.	42	23	General perceptions were that management had adequate information on the performance of work groups. Lower levels, however, thought that management's information was not as adequate as management perceived it to be.
10.	Work-group members had adequate information about work-group results.	43	36	There was less agreement that group members had adequate information, with most group members themselves believing that they did not. Foremen and general foremen tended to believe that groups did.
39.	The goals of the work group(s) were clear to me.	62	29	Twice as many respondents agreed that work-group goals were clear. They reported a wide variety of goals, both economic (productivity, cost reduction) and behavioral (morale, absenteeism) in nature, with no consensus as to which were most salient.
56.	Generally, the work groups performed well.	55	26	The majority opinion is that work groups performed well.
59.	Our work group never really got going well at all.	26	39*	On the whole, perceptions were that groups did go well. This corresponds with responses to question 51. Nevertheless, a sizeable minority did not.

*Note: Statement is negatively stated and responses under "disagree" represent the positive response.

has to be directly involved in monitoring, evaluating, and helping solve problems.

Group Meetings. Provision of a place and sufficient time to hold meetings were regarded as essential. A minimum level of group skills for members is "a must."

Group Decision Making. Decisions directly affecting a group should be placed before it to get advice and, when possible, a solution. When this is not possible, the reasons why a decision affecting the group was made should be provided.

Goal Setting. Development of a process for setting clear goals is essential. This process could be determined with input from others. Goals, such as productivity, could be framed in both short-term and long-term ways. Long-term goals would include those extra things the group would like to accomplish given sufficient time.

Role Clarity. A clear understanding of each member's role, the foreman's role relative to the group, and the place "others" (management, support units) have in supporting the group were regarded as essential.

Inclusion of Others in Meetings. Responses to questions 74a to 74d indicated the need to include foremen, general foremen, management, and non-group members (e.g., support units) in group meetings with varying degrees of frequency to share information and solve problems at an intergroup level.

Lateral Communications. Communications among groups, group/non-work-group units, and foremen allow information and new idea sharing. Ways to encourage these types of communication need to be created.

Support

This area is concerned with how much underlying support there was for the work group idea (see table 8.4). The majority of respondents believed, despite all the obstacles, that work groups were feasible in their locations and that with some effort they could be maintained. This latter belief was one of the most emphatic opinions given in this inquiry. It implied that the basis of underlying support did indeed exist, while the termination of most of the groups indicated that the support was not effectively mobilized. Some of the key constraints have already been listed; they were in the organizational context rather than in the groups themselves.

Table 8.3. Internal Processes

Question	Response Agree	Response Disagree	Commentary
20. Anything could be brought up at work-group meetings.	72	15	Meetings were perceived to be open by nearly all respondents.
21. Goal setting was an important part of work-group meetings.	56	20	Responses indicated that goal setting was an important group function.
22. The work groups developed a "group spirit."	63	21	Most groups did develop group cohesion and identity.
29. The compatibility of group-member personalities influenced team performance.	69	11	There was general agreement on the importance of member compatibility in how well the group performed.
33a. *How often did disagreements with other work-group members hinder performance?	21	51	Conflict was infrequent between group members.
33b. *How often did disagreements with foremen hinder group performance?	7	54	Perceptions were that conflict was infrequent between foremen and work groups.
33c. *How often did disagreements with general foremen hinder performance?	7	33	Perceptions were that conflict was infrequent between general foremen and work groups.
33d. *How often did disagreements with management hinder performance?	5	26	Perceptions were that conflict was infrequent between management and work groups.
33e. *How often did disagreements with "others" hinder performance?	12	29	Perceptions were that conflict was infrequent between work groups and "others."

No.	Statement			Comment
57.	Once the work groups were running for a while, everyone started losing interest.	37	31	Respondents were split over whether apathy developed in the work-group programs. Management levels perceived apathy more than worker levels did.
65.	There were many things outside the work group's control that affected group performance.	52	11	There was much agreement across levels that external factors did affect work-group performance negatively. Factors cited were numerous, including maintenance, supplies, production pressure, bumping, lack of support from management, and poor interface control.
74a.	Work group meetings should be open to foremen.	50	2	Respondents felt overwhelmingly that meetings of work groups should be open to foremen. The foreman level itself felt strongly about this.
74b.	Work group meetings should be open to general foremen.	52	10	Again, there was high agreement that group meetings should be open to general foremen. Interestingly, general foremen themselves did not feel strongly about this.
74c.	Work group meetings should be open to senior plant management.	46	17	Group members felt that meetings should be open to senior plant management, but the majority was somewhat smaller.
74d.	Work group meetings should be open to non-group members.	54	26	Whereas a majority of respondents felt that non-group members should be permitted to attend work-group meetings, there was a sizeable minority who felt they should not. Management personnel tended to agree that meetings should be open to non-group members.
75a.	*How frequently should foremen be at group meetings?	58	6	Respondents agreed by a wide margin that foremen should attend team meetings very frequently.

Table 8.3. (Cont'd)

Question	Response Agree	Response Disagree	Commentary
75b. *How frequently should general foremen be at group meetings?	35	26	Respondents felt that general foremen should attend meetings less frequently than foremen. Group members, however, felt general foremen should attend "frequently," while supervisory levels felt they should attend from "infrequently" to "almost never."
75c. *How frequently should senior plant management be at group meetings?	25	35	Of the three levels of management, respondents felt that senior plant management should attend group meetings least frequently. Group members welcomed management more than supervisory levels did.
75d. *How frequently should non-group members be at group meetings?	29	31	Respondents were split evenly on this issue. Those desiring participation by non-group members wanted them there primarily to improve relations with support and maintenance groups.

*Note: Responses are for frequent (agree) versus infrequent (disagree) attendance at meetings.

Respondents felt that as one went up the management ladder the clearness with which support was offered diminished. This confirmed the answers to corresponding questions in other sections.

An emphatic opinion was that management's attitude to work groups should be thoroughly assessed before any program was embarked upon. If management acceptance and commitment were not obtained, the work-group concept had little chance of success.

People thought of support in two ways: (1) as commitment to work groups because of their inherent benefits and the chance they offered workers for a more active involvement in the organization; and (2) as interest in them solely because of their positive effects on productivity. Work-group members and foremen tended to interpret support in the first sense; general foremen and management tended to interpret it in the second sense. A basic misunderstanding about the goals and purposes of the programs usually existed between higher and lower levels. These attitudes were not irreconcilable. In the long run, a successful program depended on their reconciliation.

Three important principles surfaced regarding support:

Creating Support for Work Groups. Acquainting work units, foremen, and management with the benefits of using work groups should be undertaken through training programs, discussion with others with group experience, films, and so on.

Commitment to the Work-Group Idea. Assessment of tangible, long-term support must be made before implementation. Voluntary adoption of the group mode by a work unit is one sign of support. The commitment of resources (time, money) is another.

Maintaining Support. More than just commitment is needed to keep groups viable. Ongoing training; timely, adequate feedback on performance; clear goals; and role clarity for those involved are also needed. Rewards for goal accomplishment and incentives for participation need to be present and explicit.

Evaluation

Evaluation addresses the types, source, frequency, and effectiveness of the measures of performance used by work groups. In addition, this dimension includes a set of questions about changes in work behavior and attitudes associated with the work-group program (see table 8.5).

The perceptions of the respondents with respect to work-group performance measures revealed a great deal. For instance, a majority of respon-

Table 8.4. Support

	Question	Response Agree	Response Disagree	Commentary
31.	*The way things are set up around here makes the work-group idea impossible.	25	45	In the majority opinion, the difficulties encountered were not so great as to make groups impossible. Difficulties mentioned included worker movement, the type of unit task, the measurement system utilized, and low support.
61.	Plant management's attitude toward work groups should be assessed before work groups are formed.	62	5	Respondents overwhelmingly agreed that management's attitudes should be assessed before implementation of a work-group program. This had not been done systematically.
62.	The foreman's role in helping work-group activities was clear.	50	29	While respondents as a whole agreed that the foreman's role was clear, perceptions of foreman role clarity declined at the group-member level.
63.	The general foreman's role in helping work-group activities was clear.	32	26	Respondents felt there was less clarity about the general foreman's role.
64.	The senior plant management's role in helping the work group was clear.	32	25	Senior plant management's role was perceived as the least clear of the three supervisory levels.
69.	With some effort, work groups could be maintained in this plant.	58	10	Respondents agreed by six to one that groups could be maintained with effort. This is consistent with question 31.

*Note: Statement is negatively stated and responses under "disagree" represent the positive response.

dents felt that performance criteria were clear (question 41), although 39 percent felt they were not clear. There was a decline in these feelings about measurement clarity from the management level to the work-group level, which indicated a problem in maintaining communications down the line. This was also borne out in question 46, where management and supervisory levels felt that group members knew how well they were doing better than the members did. In other words, supervisory levels felt they were communicating feedback to a greater extent than members were receiving it. There was, as a result, little association between how clear respondents perceived the performance measures to be and how well they perceived themselves to be functioning.

Respondents perceived the same types of performance measures as those being used. Emphasis was placed on the standard economic measures, such as productivity and efficiency, scrap, absenteeism rates, and quality control. What may be an indication of a participative attitude was the fact that two or more levels appeared to have determined these measures (question 44). The respondents disagreed on how often these measures should be taken. Performance was apparently assessed with varying frequency and emphasis. Of the 67 respondents who answered question 44, 42 agreed that the actual measures were good.

With respect to changes in attitude toward work (questions 51a to 51d), some change was perceived among work-group members and foremen; little change was perceived among general foremen and non-work-group members. Those who perceived the most attitude change were also those who felt most strongly that the performance measures were good.

Three important points to consider regarding evaluation are:

Criteria Development. Group members, foremen, and others (e.g., management) should develop performance criteria collectively; ownership of the measures and results would thereby be shared.

Feedback. An important part of evaluation was providing results to the groups. Feedback must be timely and constructive. Thought should be given beforehand, preferably when criteria are developed, as to how this information is to be provided.

Inclusion of Others in Evaluations. Survey results indicated that other individuals and groups (foremen, general foremen, management, support units) should be included in work-group evaluations. How this might be done could be negotiated with these individuals and groups. As noted elsewhere, evaluation of individual performance in terms of contribution to the group effort is also needed.

Table 8.5. Evaluation

Question	Response Agree	Disagree	Commentary
41. The ways of judging work–group performance were clear to me.	38	25	On balance, respondents as a whole said that the measurements taken were clear to them. They were, however, less clear to group members than to management. Interview material disclosed a great variety in measures recalled: productivity, scrap, absenteeism, suggestions submitted, etc.
44. These were good measures.	42	25	There was, on the whole, agreement that the performance measures used were good ones. It was stated that usually two or more levels took part in devising these measures.
46. Work-group members pretty much knew how well they were doing.	60	16	There was strong agreement that groups knew how they were doing. Responses indicated that supervisory levels felt they were giving more performance feedback to work-group members than the members felt they were receiving. The time span between measurement-taking ranged from once a week to once a month.
51. During the period in which the work groups existed, I noticed definite changes in how members thought about their own work:			A large number of respondents noted changes which they experienced as beneficial in member behavior. Foremen perceived changes in groups more than members themselves did. Changes in foreman behavior were also noted by the majority of respondents, less so among general foremen. For non-work-group members, perceptions were evenly divided. This showed that some change was noticeable in support groups. The amount of perceived change fell off as distance from the groups increased.
a. group members	50	13	
b. foremen	38	10	
c. general foremen	23	13	
d. other non-work-group members	17	15	

Termination

This area is concerned with the perceptions of respondents in regard to the reasons why the groups stopped functioning, how they felt about termination, and what they felt would be necessary for them to be started up again (see table 8.6).

Several important observations from the data can be made. First, three out of four respondents who answered question 25, especially at lower levels, did not want work groups stopped. Secondly, interview material showed that layoffs and personnel changes were not the only reasons why groups terminated. In many instances, the teams simply "fell apart" after a while. They did not receive the ongoing, committed interest and effort that they required if they were to be assimilated into the fabric of the workplace. This effort and interest diminished after a period of initial enthusiasm. Thirdly, most respondents stated that they would like to have the teams started up again. Given what we believe to be moderate levels of success overall, this response illustrates the viability of the work-group concept and its ability to gain and maintain broad-based support. It confirms the answer to question 69 in the previous section as well as question 25.

Several foremen felt caught in a bind. Two sets of objectives that could not be satisfied simultaneously were being communicated to them from their superiors: (1) get the work groups functioning; (2) maintain performance levels. This placed a considerable burden on them since an additional set of responsibilities (establish the groups) was placed on them in addition to their regular duties (performance maintenance). Several foremen felt that they were receiving neither the moral nor the resource support to address effectively this new set of demands. Moral support — interest and involvement in the functioning of the groups — did not come from their superiors; and resource support did not come from equipment, maintenance, personnel, suppliers of materials to the groups, or plant planners.

Many respondents felt that, initially, there was much enthusiasm for the program among group members but that their interest declined as the program continued. Other experiments with work groups have shown that, over time, they increase employees' autonomy, participation, and interest on the job. The combination of the two factors noted (lack of moral support and lack of resource support) was a major reason for the attenuation of interest in sustaining the groups and brought about their dissolution. The difficulty in establishing a new work structure without the support that was seen to be required made people give up and programs fold.

Finally, what would it take to start the groups again? Respondents seemed confused on this point, but clearly there was a need for commitment from management as well as from workers themselves. The interview survey suggested the following requirements:

- A clear and coherent program design
- Thorough preparation of management and training of foremen and group members
- A selective implementation effort
- Continued, concerted management support
- The plant-wide diffusion of new concepts and ways of operating
- Some special assistance from inside or outside the plant at the group and foreman levels during implementation and periodically thereafter to develop skills

FURTHER DEVELOPMENTS

A Corporate Review

During the fall of 1978, a review of the material summarized in this chapter was held at corporate headquarters. Four functional vice-presidents were present as well as a number of other staff people. No line managers were present, however. A full half day was set aside to consider whether a new beginning should be made with work-group projects with explicit corporate support, or whether it would be best to remain inactive or even to discourage fresh attempts.

The findings occasioned considerable interest as few of those present had been aware of the extent of the group activities that had been taking place or of the positive results obtained, more often than not, in spite of the tendency of the projects to fade out. The location perspective suggested that, if work groups were to be started again in the laissez-faire manner that had characterized them in the last ten years, they would in all likelihood fade out again. The perspective of the interview survey suggested that, if they were restarted in a more strategic manner, with corporate support, the wealth of experience about the do's and don'ts that had been accumulated by the managers and workers immediately concerned would provide a solid foundation on which to build the type of future effort that could become self-sustaining. A persistent belief in the potential benefits of work groups both for job satisfaction and productivity lingered in a number of participants (especially the workers) despite the vicissitudes and disappointments encountered.

We suggested that the work group by itself was too small a unit to bring about lasting organizational and performance improvement. The data made it plain that all the systems of an operating plant, or similar self-standing workplace, were involved in one way or another in work groups. The organizational context had to change at the same time if the enduring results for job satisfaction and productivity possible through semiautonomous

groups were to be realized. This implied the working out of a new philosophy of management based on participative principles in which each level
within a plant would have to redefine its role to some extent as regards the
others. A number of operational practices, control systems, measurement
procedures, and reward systems would also require modification. A new
type of cooperative relationship with the union would have to be evolved in
areas not previously thought to belong to labor relations. Work improvement through QWL had to be envisaged as a long-term effort. For plants to
be secure in venturing along this road, they would have to know that there
was stable commitment to it in the corporation above plant level.

Most of those present were inclined to accept these views at least to
some degree. Work improvement through QWL was indeed a long-range
strategic undertaking requiring a large investment of management time and
energy and a large investment in the training and development of the work
force as well as of those in the supervisory and plant-management ranks.
This was a daunting prospect. The company, some of those present pointed
out, had other formidable priorities in the technological field regarding new
products and new manufacturing processes. The changes entailed would
strain the capacities of operational managers for the foreseeable future.
These managers could not be asked to undertake a major parallel task,
especially as their views on QWL were contradictory. Our systems of
management practice, they said, had stood the test of time and in labor relations, at least, both sides knew where they stood.

Several leading corporations had been evolving large-scale programs in
QWL in the last few years. Let them do the pioneer work, was a view advanced by some strong voices. We would hang well back in the pack watching what they were doing and learning from it. Then, if and when the time
was ripe for us, we would mobilize the very considerable internal and external resources we could command and move forward quickly on a wide
front.

Though this was not a decision-taking meeting, and there was a wide
range of opinion, it was apparent that no one was about to make any policy
proposals to get QWL supported at the corporate level. No formal encouragement of QWL projects was to be expected for the present from those in
high-level staff positions, whatever their personal views. Any prospect of
corporate sanction seemed a long way off.

An Innovative Affiliate

Nevertheless, this meeting did not signal the end of work-innovation projects, even in the shorter run. A supporter appeared in a high-level line
manager. The chief executive officer (CEO) of an important affiliate, which
had considerable autonomy, took up the challenge. He had been convinced

Table 8.6. Termination

		Response	
	Question	Agree	Disagree	Commentary
24.	It is clear why the work groups stopped operating.	31	24	Somewhat more respondents said they were clear why work groups stopped than weren't, but almost half did not answer the question. Additional interview material disclosed considerable confusion and ignorance.
25.	Work groups should not have stopped operating.	45	16	When the question of group continuance was negatively stated, almost three times as many believed that groups should not have been stopped. This opinion was very strong among group members and foremen, with reservations among general foremen and management.
26a.	*How do you think group members felt about ending the work groups?	23	32	Members, on balance, wanted work groups to continue. Many felt frustrated and disappointed that they ended, and a number became pessimistic that conditions favorable to a restart could be obtained.
26b.	*How do you think foremen felt about ending the work groups?	22	27	Foremen, on balance, also wanted work groups to continue. Several foremen said that they felt "trapped" between groups and management.

Table 8.6. (Cont'd)

Question	Response Agree	Response Disagree	Commentary
26c. *How do you think general foremen felt about ending the work groups?	21	14	General foremen tended to be perceived as more adverse than not to the continuation of groups.
26d. *How do you think senior plant management felt about ending the work groups?	20	11	Management was also perceived to be rather adverse to the continuation. of groups.
26e. *How do you think non-group workers felt about ending the work groups?	22	7	Non-group workers were even more adverse. (For this question and the others in this set, the wish to continue falls off as distance from the groups increases. Some respondents felt that experimental results did not justify continuing the groups. Most, however, felt that it was apathy that prevented a restart. Restarting would require interest, support, and commitment that did not currently exist.)
30. I would like to see the work groups started up again.	53	12	When the question of continuation was positively stated, four times as many respondents wanted work groups to start up again as those who did not. This opinion was uniform across levels and sites.

*Note: Responses are for ending (agree) versus continuing (disagree) the work groups.

for some time of the importance of the value changes taking place in the wider society, especially in the attitudes of the younger generations entering the work force. He was preoccupied with the need to press forward with organizational as well as technological change if the involvement and commitment of employees at all levels were to be obtained. This commitment and involvement he regarded as essential to assure the levels of innovation and productivity he deemed necessary for the survival of the business in a world of increasing competition, complexity, and uncertainty.

He had appointed one of his senior vice-presidents to make a survey and critical assessment of innovative projects across the whole field of human resources in North America, Europe, and Japan. The first author of this chapter met this vice-president at an intensive QWL workshop and was invited to work out with him a strategy for assessing the willingness and preparedness of managers in the affiliate to undertake projects in work innovation. The vice-president felt it was essential to start with the senior executives, functional as well as operational, around the CEO, but he did not think it would be appropriate to begin with a meeting of these key individuals as a group. They were not ready for it. Accordingly, the first author held long, unstructured interviews of two to three hours with each of the 12 most senior executives.

These interviews disclosed a widespread awareness of the situation described by the CEO, a willingness to move in a direction which would integrate the human and technical needs of the enterprise, but very great differences in their beliefs regarding whether it was appropriate for them to do so in the immediate future of their own businesses. Some had all-absorbing priorities in products or markets; others had a union which was implacably adversarial and had just elected a new leadership of the same kind; others had too many managers of the old school to want to proceed very far until more of the younger generation were in positions of greater responsibility. These views echoed some of the opinions expressed in the corporate review. Yet the conviction was general that QWL was the right direction in which to move in the longer term.

In a report to the CEO, the first author suggested a strategy of selective development in contrast to laissez-faire. Laissez-faire had failed in the corporate parent, and the findings were discussed in the report which the CEO circulated to his senior managers. To assess the acceptability of the new strategy and to begin to define its operational meaning, the CEO asked each of his two group vice-presidents to hold meetings in retreat with his senior managers. Each of these meetings was scheduled for a day and a half. He himself would attend as required, as would the first author.

These meetings confirmed the need to proceed with work innovation, whether called QWL, some other name, or no name. Each senior manager would be responsible for developments in his own area. The method was adopted of listing the constraints and opportunities in each section of the

business. Through this, an attempt was begun to identify specific criteria for
site selection. When a site seemed appropriate to senior management, the
question of its desirability and feasibility would be taken up with local
management. Nothing would be forced. Only if there was a genuine wish to
proceed on the part of local management would action steps be taken. Then
the question of involving the union would arise in those plants that were
unionized.

It was recognized that more internal resources would have to be developed. One of the ablest of the younger plant managers and one of the ablest
of the younger personnel managers, both of whom had begun to accumulate experience in this field, were appointed to nourish developments
in work innovation throughout the affiliate and to assist selected sites.

As regards external resources, one independent center and one university
center have been involved, together with a consulting firm with special experience in the problem-solving methods which have been developed in
Japan.

During 1979, two projects were launched, one of which has survived
severe market vicissitudes. Both have now become substantial, and a third
project has been started.

These and other projects in this affiliate and emerging endeavors in other
divisions of the corporation are picking up the efforts of an earlier network
of activist managers. How they fare will constitute the story of the eighties
as distinct from the story of the seventies with which this chapter has been
concerned. It will reflect the growing strength of the QWL enterprise
worldwide as evidenced by the international conference on "QWL in the
'80s" held in Toronto at the end of August 1981. It will also reflect the growing stringency of the current recession and the longer-range slowing down
of economic growth. In relation to these, the experiences of QWL projects
in the recession of the mid-1970s, such as those reported in this chapter, are
worth attention.

The economic climate has indeed changed. Improvements in productivity
have become imperative, but we now know that employee involvement and
commitment, desirable for their own sake, are essential to achieve them. At
the first annual conference of the Philadelphia Area Labor–Management
Committee, held in November 1981, Rex Reed, the vice-president for labor
relations and corporate personnel of Michigan Bell, put it this way in his
keynote address: "The time has come to change the managerial culture of
America" to one of participation, i.e., power-sharing.

The case reported in this chapter shows some of the complexities of trying
to take the first steps toward this basic cultural change in an endeavor in
which every corporation must find its own path. A great deal has been
learned, even if there is still more to learn. Meanwhile, the more experiences
of what has so far taken place that are publicly shared, the more rapidly will
organizational learning accumulate in industry as a whole.

9.
The Bolivar Quality of Work Life Program: Success or Failure?*

Barry A. Macy

The Bolivar project is a collaborative effort of Harman International Industries (HII) (formerly the Jervis Corporation and now part of Beatrice Foods) and the United Automobile Workers of America (UAW) to jointly determine organizational change and improve certain social-human principles. Its goals were many, but one stands far above all others. This goal was "to create an example applicable to many American companies, one which could be adopted as a model by unions."[1] Michael Maccoby, director of the Harvard Project on Technology, Work and Character, and head of the external resource group at Bolivar, categorized the goal of the Bolivar project in the following manner:

To create an American model of industrial democracy: a model that is acceptable to unions and that might stimulate future union–management efforts. The project is based on the view that a national movement to improve the quality of work is unlikely to succeed without union–management support and that

*This chapter is based on reports from people at the site combined with independent observations and data from the University of Michigan, Institute for Social Research (ISR), Quality of Work Program. It represents a summary assessment at Bolivar. The ISR assessment of the Bolivar experiment by Macy, Ledford, and Lawler is scheduled to be published by Wiley–Interscience in 1982. Support for this chapter was provided by the Ford Foundation and the Economic Development Administration, U.S. Department of Commerce.

Portions of this chapter stem from a paper presented by the author at the Thirty-Eighth Annual Meeting of the Academy of Management, August, 1978, in San Francisco, California, and from an article in the *Proceedings of the Thirty-Second Annual Meeting, Industrial Relations Research Association,* 1979, pp. 83–93.

The author acknowledges the assistance of Belinda Petty, research associate, Texas Center for Productivity and Quality of Work Life, Texas Tech University, in preparing this chapter.

union–management leaders are practical people who can't be expected to struggle for abstract concepts like 'humanized work' or self-management without something concrete to point to. If the project is successful, the workers and management . . . will develop programs that not only change the character of their work but that also can be adopted by unions as goals for collective bargaining.[2]

The Work Improvement Program (WIP) at Bolivar, one of a series of cooperative union–management quality-of-work-life (QWL) projects,[3] was intended to provide a model for improving factory life and optimizing employee development. The WIP involved a total existing factory (in contrast to a newly built factory) located in Bolivar, Tennessee, a small rural town southeast of Memphis, with no special selection of workers. A central element of the program was that the top and local management and the top and local union, together with the third-party social scientists,[4] jointly try to improve the quality of working life according to the principles of security, equity, individualization, and democracy.[5]

QWL BACKGROUND[6]

The Bolivar QWL project discussed in this chapter is a collaborative union–management organizational redesign project (see fig. 9.1). Such projects usually have a common structure, but each project's goals and processes are unique. Most projects have an advisory committee composed of union leaders, top management and other representatives. The advisory committee develops a letter of agreement between the company and union, which specifies the relationship between the QWL project and their collective bargaining contract. This agreement, called a "shelter agreement," also provides an escape clause to let either party out of the project and a guarantee that no employee will lose his or her job or suffer reduction in pay because of the project. In addition, this agreement provides for joint ownership of the QWL project by union and management.

The advisory committee also locates a site for the project and helps set up a joint labor–management committee, called a quality-of-work-life committee at that site. The local committee, working with the advisory committee, employs a third-party social scientist as a consultant to act as a resource person(s) for the QWL committee and the project. In order to implement the project in a particular organization, most QWL committees set up either representative or participatory subgroups. For example, at another QWL site, these were autonomous work groups (participatory); at Bolivar, core groups of foremen, job stewards, and other employees from the work area were formed; at TVA, the site QWL committee appointed 13 union–man-

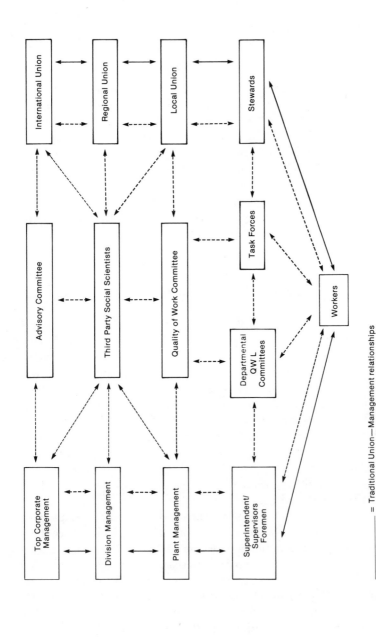

Fig. 9.1. Joint Labor-Management Quality-of-Work-Life Influence Process: New Structures, Processes and Relationships

_____ = Traditional Union—Management relationships

·········· = Cooperative relationships

agement task forces, with over 100 people directly participating in the change program.[7]

Cooperative redesign projects require a new problem-solving structure between union and management that must coexist with the traditional bargaining structure. Schlesinger and Walton suggest that union-management parties are a network of "stakeholders" to QWL projects.[8] Consequently, each party has a set of unique risks and coping strategies associated with its participation. The central panel of this "ladder" (see fig. 9.1) indicates the additional structures and processes characteristic of a cooperative QWL project. This new structure stimulates new relationships and processes between the parties throughout the system. Therefore, two separate interventions, a QWL committee structure and process in addition to the social science consultant's change activities are instituted at each of the quality-of-work-life sites.[9]

THE BOLIVAR COLLABORATIVE CHANGE PROGRAM: SEVEN DIFFERENT PHASES

The change program at Bolivar had seven different phases.[10] Phase 1 (January 1972 to March 1973, 15 months) involved preproject discussions and negotiations with Sidney Harman, then president of Harman International Industries, later under secretary of the United States Department of Commerce, and now president of Harman International again; E.T. Michael, former regional director, Division 8, UAW; Irving Bluestone, then vice-president, General Motors Department, UAW, and now University Professor of Labor Studies at Wayne State University; and Michael Maccoby, director of the Harvard Project on Technology, Work and Character.

Phase 2 (April 1973 to February 1974, 11 months) was the beginning of the actual on-site change program at the Bolivar plant with the introduction of an on-site participant–observer in the plant. The major activity, besides having the participant–observer work as a full-time hourly employee in the inspection department, was one of collecting and interpreting data on plant conditions by means of a two-hour structured interview. The results of this survey phase were published in a *Final Technical Report* dated February 15, 1974, written by the original project staff (Maccoby, Sheppard, Herrick, and others).

Phase 3 (March 1974 to January 1975, 11 months) consisted of the establishment of experimental groups by the on-site staff to try new approaches to restructuring work and seek ways to expand the WIP.

Phase 4 (February 1975 to December 1975, 11 months) saw the Earne
Idle Time (EIT)[11] experiment go plant-wide following an official ratifica
vote by the UAW local union. During this period, 33 core group

composed of a foreman, job steward, and other employees, were created. In addition, during this phase, the WIP added an in-plant school (e.g., classes in blueprint reading, welding, Bible studies, black studies) to complement the EIT program.

Phase 5 (January 1976 to December 1976, 12 months) introduced joint determination of some plant efficiency rates by the UAW and HII, sharing of limited product and profitability information, and an effort to formulate plans for a joint Cost-Saving-Sharing Program (i.e., modified version of a type of Scanlon Plan). During this phase, the need for continued third-party involvement (i.e., the outside third-party social scientists, called the project staff) and the permanency of the joint labor–management QWL committee (at Bolivar, called the Working Committee) were discussed and debated at length.

During phase 6 (January 1977 to February 1978, 14 months), the Bolivar project was undergoing a "self-renewal" searching process of how the plant should institutionalize and internally diffuse ongoing organizational change in order to be self-regenerating and maintain a self-functioning joint labor–management process. It was at this time that Sidney Harman, a powerful force behind the project at Bolivar, had relinquished the presidency of Harman International Industries and had become under secretary of commerce for the United States. Therefore, a powerful leadership force at the top of Harman International was withdrawn from the Bolivar experiment. The effect of this upon the site and its collaborative labor–management programs and processes for organizational change was dramatic, especially in regard to the local plant site and the international union.

Phase 7 (March 1978 to present) required several major transitions by the Bolivar project. The departure of the third-party consultants, specifically Maccoby and Ramsey, began during this phase. This departure brought with it a dramatic change in the structure of the project, namely, an effort to function without outside assistance. Subsequently, due to the influence of the general plant manager and vice-president, Arthur McCarver, the EIT program became group-based and secondary to other programs, such as the education and employee orientation programs. Even as these changes occurred, the true essence of the initial Bolivar project continued in the assembly-line department under the direction of Paul Reeves, superintendent of the assembly line. Through his training, the assembly group was, in

itself. This phase was also substantially affected by an
causing one-third to one-half of the work force to be
term effect of each of these recent changes remains to be
project's life seems to have run its course.
hend the Bolivar quality-of-work-life program, it is im-
familiar with the plant setting and project history of the
rt as well as the relationships and philosophies of the key
lved in the project.

Setting

When the Bolivar QWL program began, the physical conditions of the plant were poor. In the early 1960s the original owner, the Jervis Corporation, had moved the auto-mirror factory from Michigan to Bolivar, Tennessee, a small rural town located approximately 60 miles east of Memphis. The factory consisted of three abandoned World War II Quonset huts, which were modified into a single plant. The facility was poorly ventilated, disorderly, and noisy. A shortage of storage space and the pace of production had resulted in parts and materials being pushed into every available corner. Many of the machines were in poor repair due to lack of replacement parts. Machines were kept in running order via ad hoc repairs utilizing wire and roughly cut pieces of metal. Fumes from die cast, plating and paint, and towmotors permeated the plant, even though efforts had been made to blow away the most noxious ones. Pools of water dotted the floor. In the winter, there was inadequate heating; in the summer, there was no air conditioning, with temperatures sometimes reaching 120°F inside the factory. Apparently comfort, and sometimes safety, had been ignored in order to maximize production and profits.

Conditions were poor from a human standpoint as well. The relationship between the company and the union, as well as the one between management and hourly workers was one of little trust or cooperation. A typical example of this lack of cooperation occurred on an assembly line where three women assembled the knob-and-cable mechanism which allows a driver to adjust the side mirror without rolling down the car window. One day an industrial engineer brought each woman a tray of grease. Each was instructed to dip the knob into the grease before installing it in the usual fashion. The women protested, contending their gloves would get too greasy to exert the necessary downward pull on the cables to fasten the knobs securely. Also, the women would not be able to avoid smearing grease on the outside of the mirror shells, nor would they be able to wipe the grease off due to the fast pace of the line. At the time, the engineer ignored their comments. However, weeks later, the grease trays were removed because of the problems the women had predicted. Numerous examples could be cited about the lack of cooperation and trust between workers and management as well as between the company and union members.

After attempts to avoid unionization in the early 1960s, the Bolivar plant was unionized by the United Automobile Workers of America (UAW) in the late 1960s. The traditional relationship between labor and management was adversarial, but Sidney Harman, the chief executive and principal owner of Harman International (of which the Bolivar plant was one component), espoused quite a different philosophy of management. From 1963 to 1971 Harman pursued interests congruent with his philosophy. He taught history and aesthetics to deprived black high school students, became president of Friends World College (an experimental, loosely structured Quaker institution on Long Island), and earned a Ph.D. in organizational psychology from the Union College Graduate School. However, during this period Harman exerted only a minimal influence over the company.

After Harman International posted consecutive losses in 1970–1971, Harman resigned the presidency of Friends World College to turn his full attention to the company. Harman became deeply interested during his graduate work in the philosophical and psychological foundations of work. He became convinced of the necessity for "work humanization" or improving the quality of working life for employees. He also believed that Harman International was a prime setting for experimentation in this area. He began his efforts to improve the quality of working life for employees at the JBL Division of Harman International in Los Angeles. Through several weekend "Open Houses," employees and their families became familiar with the plant, the products produced, and the employee's role in making the products. The major result of these experimental weekends was a significant enhancement of employee self-esteem. Subsequently, Harman found a strong correlation between the level of employee self-esteem and the quality of work the employee produced. The JBL Division expanded experimentation by giving small groups of workers the responsibility for their own decisions on quality control. Harman was pleased with the progress of the experiments at JBL.

HISTORY OF THE BOLIVAR PROJECT

The seven historical phases of the Bolivar project are described here, followed by an assessment and discussions of the results.

Phase 1—Negotiations and the Decision to Participate

In April 1972, the Department of Labor sponsored a conference on the humanization of work, which allowed people from business, labor, government, and the academic world to meet and exchange ideas. Harman represented the business world. On the union side were three key officials of the UAW: Irving Bluestone, Douglas Fraser, and Donald Ephlin. Neal Herrick represented the Department of Labor. The academic members included Michael Maccoby, a psychologist and student of Erich Fromm who headed the Harvard Project on Technology, Work, and Character; and Harold Sheppard, a researcher at the W.E. Upjohn Institute for Employment Research. The mix was an effective one. Maccoby, Sheppard, and Herrick had all investigated worker alienation and were interested in applying their ideas and skills to a real situation involving humanization of the workplace.

The union members voiced a willingness to participate in such a project if the union had a role of equal importance to that of management. At the conference, Herrick circulated a proposal calling for joint action-research programs involving unions and organizations. Harman was receptive to the idea due to his early successes at JBL.

After this first meeting of the key principals in the Bolivar experiment, Harman and Bluestone testified before the Kennedy hearings on worker alienation. Bluestone was impressed with the fact that both he and Harman had called for the *same* action steps involving companies and unions—namely trying new ways of achieving industrial democracy on the factory floor. Following the hearings, Bluestone pulled Harman aside to discuss their almost identical philosophies. They agreed that the purpose of collaborative union-management quality of work life projects was not to increase productivity, but to enhance employee self-esteem and job satisfaction. Harman and Bluestone agreed, in principle, to combine their similar philosophies about work into an action-research project at the automobile mirror plant in Bolivar, Tennessee, where the UAW represented the work force.

An incident in September 1972 in the Bolivar plant's polish and buff department acted as the catalyst that quickly brought the project conceptualized by Harman and Bluestone into being. Second-shift polish and buff workers at the Bolivar plant had for years taken a coffee break at 10:30 P.M. One night a buzzer, which signaled break time, malfunctioned by going off at 10:00 P.M. Management sent word to the 40 workers that their new break time was now 10:00 P.M. At first, the workers complied. Several days later, the UAW shop steward led 16 men in ignoring the buzzer and taking their break at the usual time, 10:30 P.M. For the next several evenings, John Lyle, then the plant general manager, and other managers met individually with each of the 16 workers to determine the reasons for their insubordination. The managers had to decide whether to regard the incident as trivial or to treat it seriously. The reputation of the workers in polish and buff was that of a maverick group who produced only 60 to 70 percent of their quota much of the time. Finally, Lyle consulted a labor attorney. The attorney recommended that the 16 men be suspended for a day without pay, and that the shop steward be fired. Lyle followed the recommendations.

Sidney Harman became aware of this buzzer incident shortly after it occurred. Though he had never before intervened in the internal affairs of the Bolivar plant, he felt the time had come to act. He sent his executive vice-president, Sanford Berlin, to consult with UAW officials in Detroit. Shortly thereafter, due to the influence of Berlin, Lyle reinstated the shop steward and made up the lost pay to the other workers involved in the incident.

Harman also contacted Irving Bluestone. He expressed his desire to begin a kind of program, originally called a job-satisfaction program, that they had already discussed. Bluestone had already contacted E.T. Michael, the UAW director for the Bolivar region. Within the next two weeks, Bluestone arranged a meeting of Harman, Michael, and Ray Casteel, the UAW regional representative to the local Bolivar union. Separate meetings were also conducted with plant management and supervisors. Harman and Michael agreed to jointly sponsor a program cooperatively run by the company and the UAW. Harman, with Bluestone's approval, solicited Michael Maccoby, director for the Harvard Project on Technology, Work and Character, as one of the project directors to help ensure impartiality. The stage was set to introduce the program to the workers.

Harman, Bluestone, Michael, and Maccoby agreed that voluntary acceptance of a work improvement program was vital. In order for acceptance to occur, the workers and the UAW local union leadership had to be apprised of the nature of such a program. Similarly, the management at Bolivar had to be convinced that such a program would be a worthwhile endeavor. On October 5, 1972, Harman and Michael addressed a meeting of all employees at the plant. In broad terms, they explained the concept of allowing workers to participate in the decision-making process. A hand vote was taken. About 50 percent of the employees voted in favor of participating in the program. No one raised a hand in opposition. Employees were informed that the program would be introduced only after careful and cautious preparation by both parties.

Before the process for the project could be developed, the purposes and goals of the project had to be identified and agreed upon by Harman, Maccoby, and Michael. These preproject discussions and negotiations marked the initial phase of the collaborative change program. The initial purpose of the program was to seek new approaches and, where indicated, new work redesign so all people in the company would experience increased satisfaction and increased self-realization. Somewhat later, a second purpose was developed: to create a model of industrial democracy acceptable to unions. If the project was successful, the workers and management could develop programs that not only changed the character of their work, but also could be adopted by unions as goals for collective bargaining. It was agreed upon, from the beginning, that the program would not bring in specialists to redesign the workplace. Instead, the Bolivar workers and management would decide together upon the necessary changes to fulfill the primary goal of the program.

During this initial phase, a shelter agreement was drawn up and later signed by the company and the union. It stated that the primary goal of the project was increased job satisfaction. In the agreement, the structures and duties of an advisory committee as well as a working committee were outlined. It also stated that participation in the program was voluntary, and that no worker could lose job, pay, or seniority as a result of the program, whether he or she participated or not. In addition, the agreement indicated that the purpose of the WIP was *not* to increase productivity. This agreement read in part:

> The purpose of the joint labor-management Work Improvement Program is to make work better and more satisfying for all employees, salaried and hourly, while maintaining the necessary productivity for job security. The purpose is *not* to increase productivity. If increased productivity is a by-product of the program, ways of rewarding the employees for increased productivity will become legitimate matters for inclusion in the program.[12]

The Bolivar shelter agreement did not take the place of the collective bargaining agreement and it did not allow for the contract to be undermined or broken. Irving Bluestone and other UAW leaders made sure of this.

During this initial phase, Harman, Bluestone, and Maccoby established four principles to guide the restructuring of the workplace.[13]

1. *Increased Security.* The first area of security involves health and safety, which we intend to improve by creating the best possible environment, with a minimum of hazards. Security against loss of job is more difficult to achieve, as the Harman Automotive Division is part of a market which is subject to fluctuations that are beyond our control. No one can promise that workers will never be laid off. In the *overall* sense, security from loss of job depends on effectively operating the plant to assure recovering the major portion of the available business, so the plant continues in business and continues employing workers.
2. *Increased Equity.* By making the distribution of work, the organization of work, the rewards of work, and the rules under which we work as fair and as reasonable as they can be.
3. *Increased Individualization.* By recognizing that all people are not the same, but have different interests and needs, and by increasing the opportunities for people to develop in their own ways.
4. *Increased Democracy.* By giving each worker more opportunities to have a say in the decisions that affect his life, including his work life.

From the start of the program, a secondary goal was to reorganize the way the Bolivar plant traditionally operated. It was recognized that, if managers remained locked into a hierarchical bureaucratic system, there was no way to improve the quality of work life for hourly workers. The union and management agreed that the principles outlined above should govern the work life of hourly employees and managers alike. Agreement on the purposes, goals, and principles governing the Bolivar WIP program brought to a close the initial phase of the project.

Phase 2 — The Study Period

The second phase of the Bolivar WIP program (April 1973 to February 1974) concentrated on the process of the change effort and saw the beginning of the on-site change activities. This phase mainly entailed gathering attitudinal and observation data through structured interviews at the Bolivar plant. Maccoby assembled a staff of social scientists and interviewers.[14] In May 1973, the staff interviewed a sample of 60 Bolivar workers for approximately four hours each, in an effort to understand different attitudes and perceptions among the work force. The data gathered were analyzed, and Maccoby formed six major Bolivar character types. This analysis led to the design of a two-hour structured interview. During July and August of 1973, the two-hour interviews were given to 300 workers and seventy salaried personnel. The final outcome of the interviews was documented in February 1974 in the form of a *Final Technical Report*, known as the "telephone book" consisting of 429 pages. The report was made available to workers, though few read it. A statement from the report typifies some of the early issues of the WIP at Bolivar:

> Foremen and supervisors have small offices at various places in the middle of the factory. Around the periphery of the production area, there are storerooms, storage areas, loading docks, and the cafeteria. The offices of the managers, engineers, and clerical workers are in the front of the building, sealed off from the production area. They are cleaner, quieter, and air-conditioned.
>
> All of this is inside on one floor under one roof encompassed by three quonset huts which were left over from World War II. The production floor is dirty and disorderly, compared to many large factories belonging to richer companies. Like most engaged in this kind of work, it is noisy. A shortage of storage space and the pace of production which overworks the luggers and towmotor operators results in parts and materials being pushed into every available corner and sometimes strewing out into the aisles. No time is allowed for anyone to keep his work area clean and orderly. . . . There are holes in the roof, and pools of water on the floor. In winter, there is inadequate heating; in the summer, no air conditioning. Comfort and sometimes safety have been ignored in the all-out effort to maximize production and profits. Only recently has management started to improve the physical conditions of the plant.
>
> The drive to cut costs and to stay within narrow profit margins had also meant a lack of formal training programs for workers and supervisors. Training, if any, takes place on the job.[15]

This is only an example of the frankness and comprehensiveness of the *Final Technical Report*. It includes other areas such as the initial survey results describing attitudes and perceptions about equity, work, democracy, supervision, working conditions, counterproductive behaviors, the union, health and safety, and many others.

During the fall of 1973, an ad hoc committee (the Working Committee was initially suggested by Neil Herrick), composed of five management employees selected by management and four union representatives selected by the local union president, as well as the local union president himself, was formed to consider solving plant problems jointly. In addition, the Advisory Committee became a permanent structure during this period.[16]

The first meeting of the Working Committee included discussions concerning temperatures in the plant, air pollution, ventilation, safety and health, parking problems, congestion at the time clocks, institution of a credit union, and other issues. Maccoby characterized this ad hoc committee as the "beginnings of communication and cooperation between management and union leaders who before met only as adversaries, bargaining about wages or arguing about grievances."[17] In November 1973, this ad hoc committee became known as the Working Committee (WC) and started to meet, with the assistance of the WIP project staff, to consider joint organizational changes at Bolivar.

The development of these new structures (such as the Working Committee), new relationships, and new problem-solving processes played a critical role in the development of the Bolivar Work Improvement Program. In fact, they were the critical aspects responsible for the initial survival of, as well as the continuation of, the WIP at Bolivar, enabling it to continue on through 1980. Maccoby characterizes these new structures, processes, and relationships as starting at the top of the company and the union, and requiring a new style of leadership in both. Specifically, he states:

> The [Bolivar] project required a new style of leadership both in management and the union. Managers needed examples of how to analyze problems cooperatively (in such a way that both sides gain) without weakening their position in adversary collective bargaining.[18]

It is worth noting that the WIP program probably could not have survived without the Working Committee, the three-member top-level Advisory Committee, and the initial core groups (described later). For example, during the life of the Bolivar program, many crises occurred, mistakes were made, personality conflicts were obvious, and individual feelings were sometimes ruffled. However, with the full support and involvement of the top leadership from the company and the union along with the local Working Committee, these incidents were resolved without threatening the goals and pre-1981 survival of the project.

In addition to the Working Committee's efforts and the initial collection of the survey data, Robert Duckles, a member of the WIP project staff, spent three months as a full-time employee of Harman International, working as an inspector in the inspection department. (He was assisted by his wife, Margaret Duckles, during this period.) This firsthand experience on the factory floor as an on-site participant–observer proved to be an invaluable aid during subsequent phases of the Bolivar project.

The pace of the project slowed after the planned departure from the plant of Robert and Margaret Duckles, partly because of contract negotiations during the winter of 1973–1974. After completion of contract negotiations, the WIP proceeded into an experimental phase.

Phase 3 – The Experimental Period

The experimental phase, the third phase of the Bolivar project, began in March 1974, with the return of the Duckleses[19] to the Bolivar plant as full-time on-site project staff members. Their initial task was to feed back the survey data gathered from the interviews and reported in the "telephone book," as well as to educate workers, management, and the union about different methods and approaches available for improving the quality of working life. The Bolivar work force did not show much interest in the results of the survey phase: only a handful of the workers ever saw or wanted to see the results included in the *Final Technical Report*.

During the same month, a seminar was held at the Bolivar plant to initiate experiments within various departments. The three-day seminar was led by Einar Thorsrud, director of the Norwegian Industrial Democracy Project in Oslo, Norway. Also contributing were Berth Jonsson, director of corporate planning at A.B. Volvo, and other WIP project staff members. In April 1974, experiments were instituted by the Working Committee and the project staff, with 42 volunteers from the polish and buff, assembly, and preassembly departments, to try out new approaches to job redesign. The Duckleses, along with John Lyle, later to become chief plant engineer, acted as resource people for the three experimental groups. This was the beginning of the Earned Idle Time (EIT) experiment. In essence, EIT was a method, devised by the workers,[20] whereby the work force (individuals or groups) could go home or (initially only) produce extra production. For example, if a worker had reached production, he or she could go home with eight hours' pay after only five hours' work.

By June 1974, when the original Advisory Board of the project met at the plant to review the experimental phase, it became clear that the experiments were a success from the workers' standpoint. However, the experimental groups had raised new problems of what to do about productivity gains that created inequities among union members, job security issues, and how to relate these new changes to the collective bargaining structure. For example, the three experimental groups made some changes in work methods and procedures, and they also introduced a new reward system (i.e., going home early). Initially, the groups were allowed to choose one of the following three rewards if they reached their production standard on any particular day:

1. Go home early with pay for a full day's work (Earned Idle Time).
2. Earn extra pay for extra work based upon group performances (a bonus).
3. Earn bonus hours for whatever a group wanted to do in the plant (e.g., attend education classes, go to the cafeteria to socialize, or other activities).

The result of these worker reward options, or "having a say in the decision-making process," was that the experimental groups increased their productivity and, in some cases, decided to go home early. The majority of other hourly workers at Bolivar became upset because of what they regarded as an "inequity" and voiced demands that everyone in the plant be included in the experiment. Because of these inequities, Irving Bluestone came to Bolivar in June 1974 for a special union meeting to discuss the Work Improvement Program and the experimental groups with the local leadership and membership. He encouraged the local union to cooperate and "try" the experiment since the program was truly "an experimental project." After considerable debate, the union agreed to cooperate during the experimental phase. Had it not been for Bluestone's encouragement and strong support, it is the author's judgment that the program could have failed at that time. Subsequently, with the urging of both Bluestone and Sidney Harman, the Working Committee decided it would not expand the experimental programs to the entire plant because of a number of problems (e.g., inequity, scheduling, lack of standards on some jobs, and so on).

During this phase, some important shifts occurred among managers at the plant. Sidney Harman was displeased by the "traditional way" in which the plant's affairs had been handled and decided to reorganize. General Manager John Lyle, who was contemplating resignation,[21] was persuaded to accept the position as chief engineer of the company's automotive division. He was an engineer by profession and was attracted to the challenge of this new job. He actively participated in the Work Improvement Program, including classes he later taught to employees in engineering, time-study methods, and music as part of the new experimental program.

Initially, Harman chose an outsider to replace Lyle, but he did not perform successfully in the position; after approximately three months, Harman selected Arthur McCarver, a Bolivar native. McCarver, a Bolivar management employee, came to the plant in 1965, when it was owned by Jervis, and started in a low-level job. Over the next several years, he worked in many departments. Subsequently, McCarver was promoted to be assistant general manager. However, he had no training in finance or administration. To overcome this handicap, Sidney Harman promoted William Dawson, controller of the plant, to general manager with the understanding that he would train McCarver. McCarver became general manager in 1975, with Dawson assuming the position of vice-president of the automotive division, which included responsibilities for some of Harman's foreign operations, as well. Seemingly, the potential problem of having three general managers, past or present, working together never materialized; rather, each man contributed his own special skills to help the plant, and the Work Improvement Program continued to flow as smoothly as possible.

In early September 1974, a group of Bolivar workers and managers, UAW officials, project staff members, and various others visited factories in Sweden and Norway as a means of gaining ideas concerning job redesign and industrial democracy for the project. It is interesting to note that workers and managers from the Bolivar plant considered the major benefit of the trip to be the opportunity to observe problems that could, and should, be avoided. However, the Bolivar work force thought the European approach to work and their methods of work design would not work in the United States, particularly not at Bolivar. As a result of the Scandinavian trip, the Bolivar management requested that the project be continued until all departments were part of the Work Improvement program. Also, to counter the EIT program, the UAW suggested that initial investigations begin into setting up an educational program at Bolivar.

During subsequent months, the demand for experimental group expansion in terms of Earned Idle Time seemed to reach an intolerably high level; however, the 1974–1975 recession hit the plant, and the situation was dramatically changed. The plant shut down for a short period of time and the experimental groups were decimated because of large plant layoffs during the downturn in the automobile market. It should be noted how hard hit the company was by the economic downturn in the auto industry during this phase. A third of the work force was laid off during December 1974, and January 1975. Yet, the Work Improvement Program was not abandoned by either the company or the union. In fact, it was expanded and further developed. Maccoby calls this "spirit" and "structure."[22] This might better be called increased levels of communication, trust, and faith at the top corporate level, the UAW International level, and at the Working Committee level. Top corporate and local plant management kept the work force informed about the situation created by the economic downturn through the Working Committee, and the workers accepted these facts as economic necessity. During this period of economic adversity, the company and the union jointly sent a letter to laid-off workers inviting their participation in a future in-plant school. Therefore, increased levels of communication, trust, and faith were demonstrated. Once again, these new structures, processes, and relationships were critical to the Work Improvement Program.

Phase 4 — Plant-Wide Change

Even with the massive layoffs which resulted from the recession in the fall of 1974 and early 1975, the growing pressures from the workers (i.e., those who were left at the plant) outside the three experimental groups increased. In February, 1975, it was decided to expand the Work Improvement Program gradually to include the entire factory. This decision signaled the beginning of phase 4, which lasted until January 1976. This diffusion was accomplished by means of the creation of a "core group" in each department to analyze work and develop ideas for work improvement. The goals of the 33 core groups throughout the plant were:

1. Expand the WIP to include all production (direct labor) departments along the general guidelines of the three original experimental groups.
2. Begin meetings and experiments in the indirect labor and management departments.
3. Start a broad educational program for everyone who was interested.

This core group involvement in the change process was undertaken with layoffs exceeding 300 (approximately 33 percent of the hourly work force). The on-site participant–observers were engaged in holding meetings with the 33 core groups, each composed of specific people from product work-flow areas or interdependent departments in the plant, to inform all of the people in the group about the WIP, and to see if they wanted to participate. These core groups were composed of an immediate supervisor or foreman, a shift steward, and people appointed or elected by the department from which the core group originated. These core groups were informed about the WIP by the project staff through weekly meetings which covered how, when, and where the WIP originated, the progress of the program, and where it was headed. The Bolivar plant devoted over 1,100 paid hours throughout the eight to ten weeks of this core group orientation. The core groups were to carry this same message to members of their departments.

During this same period of core group start-up and orientation, the Working Committee, top company management, and UAW officials discussed the ever troublesome issue of what to do with EIT.[23] This problem was finally resolved by a procedure which allowed workers and foremen in each department to propose an EIT plan for how such earned time would be gathered and used. The guidelines for departments suggested that EIT might be used to leave the plant early, to discuss work-related matters, or to attend education programs.

According to WC policy, any Earned Idle Time plan had to be approved by the committee. This procedure was approved through the collective bargaining process, thus reaffirming the union's role in determining rewards. In April 1975, the union conducted an official ratification vote to decide the "fate" of the WIP. Following a plant-wide union membership vote held in the plant cafeteria, the WIP and the EIT experiments went plant-wide. The vote was 80 percent for and 20 percent against the WIP (i.e., 325 union members voted "yes" and 79 members voted "no"). This positive vote for the WIP (specifically for the EIT plan) did not have the full support of some members on the Working Committee, top company leaders, and union officials. However, because the local membership wanted it, these powerful forces decided not to block it, based upon some of the program's principles (e.g., individualization and democracy).

To counterbalance the Earned Idle Time program, a free in-plant education program, or school, began during this phase. The school at the Bolivar factory stemmed from three forces: (1) the experimental groups, (2) the "charge" given to the core groups, and (3) a "felt need" by some members of the Working Committee, the project staff, and the Advisory Committee to make the WIP something in addition to "going home early." The school had courses ranging from industrial engineering to first-aid to typing to music. These courses were held during time gained by workers when they reached production standard and were held before or after the beginning of each shift.[24]

The courses at the Harman school were those requested by the workers. In some cases, workers, managers, foremen, and outside third parties were the teachers. The school had the cooperation of the Hardeman County vocational education program, which paid for teachers of approved courses. Loren Farmer was hired by the Working Committee to serve as a member of the project staff in coordinating the various educational programs at the plant. During the in-plant school start-up, the WIP seemed to slow down again; consequently, a search for alternatives began to take shape.

Phase 5 — Plant-Wide Change Continues

Phase 5 (January 1976 to December 1976)[25] brought a new dimension to the WIP. In search of other work innovations (e.g., alternatives to EIT) and to meet current economic situations (i.e., losing a potential sales contract to a nonunionized company), Harman International and the UAW jointly determined some plant efficiency rates and shared limited profitability information for an "A Body" type mirror.[26] The company and the International
/ measured various efficiency rates at Bolivar. The objective
r the original company bid (by lowering the various component
omprise the product costs, such as scrap, downtime, mainte-

nance and repair, and manufacturing supplies and ensuring that efficiency rates were neither loose nor tight). If this joint union and management effort was successful, a possible savings of 70 jobs to the union and a return of the "A Body" business to Bolivar was feasible.

The International UAW and the Bolivar plant controller met to discuss various methods to decrease the HII "A Body" bid. During their discussions and subsequent meetings, the company shared profitability information with the UAW.[27] In addition, the plant management, in conjunction with top corporate officials and the UAW, raised the standard rates on some jobs. Consequently, the "A Body" contract was awarded to the plant. It is very doubtful that the company could have reduced its original bid on the "A Body" mirror and received the contract without the direct intervention by the union and the WIP.

This collaborative "A Body" bid effort brought the company and the union into hard discussions for a potential joint Cost-Saving-Sharing Plan (CSSP). The CSSP, a type of Scanlon Plan, was to include aspects of quality, downtime, maintenance and repair, and supplies; unfortunately, the company and the union were unable to agree on the component elements and the formula base for the CSSP. Initially, the company wanted the bulk of the savings, if any. The union would not agree to this proposal. Also, top corporate and local management could not decide on which component elements should be in the Cost-Saving-Sharing Plan. Another major issue, besides the lack of agreement on an equitable split of the savings, was that local management opposed Sidney Harman's CSSP concept. Local Bolivar management did not want another incentive plan in the plant. The combination of these factors spelled doom for the Cost-Saving-Sharing Plan from the outset.

Phase 6 — Searching for Self-Renewal

During this phase (January 1977 to February 1978), the continued need for the outside third party's (i.e., the WIP project staff) involvement, the institutionalization or permanency of the WIP and the Working Committee, and the need for core groups were debated at considerable length. This was not the first time during the previous five years of existence of the Bolivar project that permanency and the continued involvement of the third party had been discussed. In fact, the on-site project staff had intended to leave at least two additional times prior to this phase. Each time, however, the Working Committee and the Advisory Committee requested them to continue their work at Bolivar. The continuation of the third-party team at Bolivar significantly led to the site's continued dependence on the change team, greatly diminishing the potential for institutionalization at Bolivar.

During May 1977, the project staff raised some possible future alternatives regarding the permanency and self-renewal of the WIP. In discussion with the Working Committee, the following four alternatives were suggested by the project staff:

> *Alternative 1.* Let the Work Improvement Program come to an end in December of 1978 or before. This does not have to mean an end to what we started; earned time could continue and the education program could continue. The *structure* that continues would be only to maintain what has already been started, just as the credit union has a structure to keep it going.

> *Alternative 2.* Everything that's been accomplished continues. The *structure* of the Work Improvement Program—the core groups, the Working Committee, and the Advisory Committee—continues to function, including for the purpose of offering opportunities for ideas that come up to be expressed and discussed. The purpose of the structure is to respond to such ideas but *not* to initiate them.

> *Alternative 3.* The structure of the program—core groups, Working Committee, and the Advisory Committee—takes the initiative to develop new programs which are presented to employees for their reaction, discussion, and refinement. Where there's clear interest, the programs are put into effect. The Cost-Savings-Sharing Plan, the development of profit centers in the plant, and [the former controller's] proposal at the last Working Committee meeting for offering a variety of service resources are all programs of this type.

> *Alternative 4.* The structure of the Work Improvement Program, particularly the Working Committee, encourages the means and the process by which people can analyze their work process and situations, and develop alternative ways of doing them. This alternative does not get in the way of doing any of the others. It is the alternative that is the most difficult and requires the most work and requires the most initiative on the part of the Working Committee.[28]

The project staff seemed to feel that alternative 4 was more precisely in line with the original four principles and ideals or values of the Work Improvement Program. They seemed to be suggesting that these alternatives for self-renewal should be studied and investigated by the Working Committee in order to pave the way for institutionalization of the WIP at Bolivar. However, local plant management thought alternative 1 was the correct action.

Of course, one of the crucial aspects of that renewal effort would be trying to answer the following questions: (1) Are the members of the Working Committee the only people interested in, and committed to, seeing the WIP continue? (2) Does the Working Committee initiate change or wait for the Bolivar work force to initiate change? (3) Where should the WIP leadership emanate from (i.e., top corporate and top union leadership, the project staff, or within the Bolivar plant)? At that time, there were strong indications that the Bolivar work force was only interested in the Earned Idle Time plan. If that was the case, did people on the floor really want the WIP to continue? And if so, in what form and how?

In an attempt to elaborate on alternative 4 above, the on-site project staff stated:

> For this alternative, participants must be sought out. We cannot just wait for people to come forward. Time has to be set aside for people to work on this alternative. Time and place for the discussions to take place has to be *structured* and it will *not* happen spontaneously. This alternative involves listening to people, listening beyond just having an open ear. It involves asking questions and stimulating people to think about their work so that everyone works together. The process involves people meeting on a regular basis to do the following: (1) describe what they do at work; (2) understand the reasons for their jobs and the way their work is done, to get information about what they do not know or understand; (3) to learn the process of running a business; the reasons for particular methods, standards, supplies, equipment, etc.; (4) to examine all of this critically; (5) to weigh and think about the alternatives to the present situation; (6) to try out new ways of doing things if any that seem better come out of this discussion; (7) to evaluate all the effects of the alternatives that are tried.[29]

As the Bolivar WIP began its sixth year, the above questions were some of the critical issues constantly nagging the WIP and presenting significant negative forces to institutionalization or self-renewal of the project.

Several other critical events occurred during phase 6 of the WIP program. In January of 1977, Sidney Harman was selected as under secretary of commerce in the Carter Administration. Because of the divestiture guidelines for presidential appointees established during this time, Harman had to either dispose of his shares of stock in Harman International or place them in trust. Shortly after Harman's appointment, Beatrice Foods Company acquired Harman International Industries, Inc.

In February of 1978, the end of phase 6, another important event occurred: The Duckleses officially left the Bolivar WIP. They were replaced by Richard Ramsey as the on-site third party. With the change in personnel came a change in WIP project-staff philosophy. Ramsey sought to encourage the project to establish local leadership as well as new formal structures, procedures, and processes. However, he met with strong resistance from Maccoby and the local management.

During this time, some members of the Working Committee and union officials recognized that a paradox in democracy existed in the WIP. Early in the project, the employees had voted for plant-wide institutionalization of EIT. To be able to leave work early was a highly valued commodity. However, not all employees were eligible for the same amount of EIT. New pressures came within the EIT system as well. The pressure to work faster to complete the job led to resentment of the system. Moreover, negative consequences of EIT included more psychosomatic and other types of illnesses (see results section later in chapter). Many employees disliked the EIT system, yet the majority had decided to accept EIT as a means of increasing their quality of work life. It became apparent that democracy in some cases only guarantees that desired goals are acted on, not that desirable goals are obtained.

Phase 7—Major Transition Period

Phase 7 of the Bolivar WIP (March 1978 to present) included several critical transitions in the Bolivar WIP. Third-party withdrawal had been a topic of discussion throughout the project. During the first part of 1979, specific steps were initiated to begin the withdrawal of the Harvard project staff and to formulate self-renewal plans and designs for the WIP. The structure of the project staff also changed to fulfill its new role.[30] The role of the project staff was changed to that of administrator/organizer of the ongoing experiment. The project staff, which was now directly responsible to the Working Committee, received a budget for the first time during this phase, and the management of the WIP rested solely in the hands of the Working Committee. Previously, it seemed that the project staff rather than the Working Committee managed the project. Another key event was the change in the EIT program from an individually earned reward to a group reward system and the increased importance placed by senior management on such projects as the enlargement of the education program and the institution of alcohol abuse and employee orientation programs as compared to EIT. Generally, the UAW favored or went along with many of these employee-assistance programs.

Even as these plant-wide changes occurred, some of the essence of the quality-of-work-life project at Bolivar continued in the assembly area. Paul Reeves, superintendent of the department, one of the three original experimental groups, had initiated an intervention on the assembly line. In an attempt to bring about more employee participation in decision making and increased employee responsibility, he had allowed line workers to observe and then function as group supervisor under his supervision. As the workers became more familiar with the functions of a supervisor, they were given the responsibility for controlling their own work actions. The group was, in effect, self-managing.[31]

This phase was also plagued by another recession, causing one-third to one-half of the work force to be laid off. This significant event, as well as the others described in this phase, had critical and even death-dealing effects on the WIP project. Post-1981 results remain to be seen. Clearly, the WIP of the early and middle 1970s is not present at Bolivar today. The early structures, processes, and relationships were not permanent. The key actors (Harman and Bluestone) played a major role throughout the program until they departed. Local management and union leaders never took key leadership roles and rarely reinforced or supported the WIP's structures, processes and relationships. These unfavorable forces were vital factors severely limiting the WIP's institutionalization and diffusion at Bolivar.

The preceding discussion emphasizes the various historical phases of the Bolivar project. Each of these favorable or unfavorable critical events in the Bolivar quality-of-work-life project had a direct impact upon the various successes and failures of the Bolivar experiment in trying to create a model acceptable to American unions and their managements. In part, each event was a favorable or opposing force for change at Bolivar.

SUMMARY ASSESSMENT OF RESULTS

Independent ISR assessment of the Bolivar QWL Program has been operational at Bolivar since the summer of 1974; complete interpretations and findings concerning the happenings at Bolivar can be found in Macy, Ledford, and Lawler.[32] However, various behavioral and performance data and certain attitudes and perceptions during past phases have been assessed.

Some of the outcomes of the Bolivar QWL experiment are presented in the following sections.

Behavioral and Performance Outcomes

Using the criteria developed by Macy and Mirvis,[33] ten "hard" employee behaviors and performance variables were distinguished and grouped into two broad categories: (1) participation–membership — absences, leaves, turnover, and internal employment stability; and (2) performance on the job — productivity, product quality, grievances, accidents and illnesses, unscheduled machine downtime and repair, and material and supply overuse. An eleventh measure — employees sent home from the workplace due to lack of work — was used as an indication of managerial effectiveness.

Using these measures across the first five intervention phases of the Bolivar experiment (55 months), the following changes were measured: job security, healthy working conditions, financial security, job security founded on organizational performance and, finally, cost-benefit assessment. Each group of changes will be discussed briefly.

Job Security. The Bolivar change program has resulted in positive changes in the area of job security. More jobs were created, as the employment level rose 55 percent. Once the change program was underway, the cooperative union-management climate stimulated an effort to develop a joint bid on a particular product, and the company and the UAW established joint efficiency rates with the goals of both increasing employees' QWL and improving job security. Ultimately, this cooperative venture saved 70 jobs. Voluntary turnover rates declined by 72 percent while involuntary turnover (e.g., discharges, retirements) rates decreased by 95 percent.

Healthy Working Conditions. In terms of healthy working conditions, the results of the Bolivar project have been mixed. Occupational Safety and Health Administration (OSHA) accident rates declined 60 percent, while minor accidents declined 20 percent even with the presence of many new and inexperienced employees. Rates of short-term absences due to sickness declined 16 percent. However, not all changes were favorable, as the rate of minor illnesses rose 41 percent and the rate of medical leaves increased 19 percent. The negative results, such as the increase in minor illnesses, might have been caused by the substantial increase in hourly factory employment during the project. The new workers, as a group, were relatively young in age and new to factory life. In addition, the paid-personal-time program required the work force to attain standard production before going home or attending educational classes. This pressure to increase production could have increased the probability and actual occurrence of minor illnesses.

Financial Security. Indicators of financial security showed little change throughout the Bolivar experiment. The average hourly wage rate remained constant over the five phases analyzed, and the wage rates relative to area standards did not change. Of course, during this time, the wage rates for the whole country did not increase relative to real wages. The fringe benefit package increased a small amount. Proposals for the introduction of a gain-sharing compensation plan (a negotiable issue) were discussed for about three years, but none was adopted.

Job Security Founded on Organizational Performance. Job security based on plant performance increased significantly under the Bolivar QWL program. Output per hourly employee per day, adjusted for inflation, rose 23 percent. Two other measures of productivity — efficiency and standard performance — verify this positive change in plant performance. On the product quality side of the financial ledger, net product reject cost rates declined 39 percent, while the rate of customer returns decreased by 47 percent. Net plant product scrap decreased by 16 percent. Once again, not all results were positive, as the rate of manufacturing supplies rose 22 percent and the rate of machine downtime increased slightly. A major factor contributing to these costly increases was the paid-personal-time program. Employees now
y minute of machine downtime. This increased communication
y employees is due to the fact that machine downtime is sub-
n the standard production rates to obtain the production quota.
yees must meet the standard before earning paid personal time,

they are motivated to report every minute of downtime. What is so striking about productivity and quality at Bolivar is that both of these performance measures increased during the same period. Moreover, these performance measures have held these positive and significant trends for approximately three years. While some of these gains are attributable to technological and capital inputs, many of them can be attributed to the cooperative labor–management change programs.

Cost-Benefit Assessment. The cost-benefit calculations for the Bolivar project reflect the program costs and program benefits per hourly employee per phase, summed over the 55 months. They show a net discounted benefit per hourly employee to the Bolivar plant of over $3,000. The cost-benefit calculations show the net benefit of the WIP to be $111,077. When expressed as a benefit/cost return, the estimate is $1.24 return for each dollar spent. The calculations also reflect the input of changes in the size of the work force over the 55 months of behavioral and performance assessment. The net benefit per hourly employee is estimated to be $3,157 and the benefit/cost ratio to be $6.32 return for each dollar spent per employee. Of course, there are multiple reasons for this positive net savings. Nevertheless, the Bolivar plant improved its effectiveness through a combination of positive forces, including the cooperative QWL program.[34] More will be said about the different forces affecting this improved effectiveness at Bolivar in the next section of this chapter.

Employees' Quality of Work Life and Environmental Indicators

Other outcomes from the cooperative union–management program at Bolivar have also been assessed. From systematic surveys, 13 indicators of the employees' experienced quality of work life and 24 measures of job and work environment (organizational) characteristics known to be associated with higher quality of work life were assessed.[35] Table 9.1 provides a summary of some of the attitudinal changes that were found at Bolivar. Although these data refer only to UAW members, they are fairly representative indicators of the different types of Bolivar employees surveyed.

The attitudinal findings in table 9.1 show that the gains have been more than offset by losses or no change. It must be remembered, however, that over the extended period studied, some unmeasured changes occurred in Bolivar employees' levels of aspiration and expectation. These changes were enhanced by the change program, and later conditions were probably judged more critically than the earlier ones. When asked a series of questions pertaining to the goals and outcomes of the program, Bolivar employee responses were generally positive about the beneficial impact of the QWL program, its desirability, the effectiveness of the union–management rela-

Table 9.1. Assessment of Bolivar Quality-of-Work-Life Indicators and Work Environment Characteristics

Gains	No Change	Losses
	QUALITY OF WORK LIFE	
Less alienation	Job satisfaction	More reports of physical stress symptoms
Treated in a more personal way	Job offers opportunity for personal growth	More reports of psychological stress symptoms
Job involved more use of, or higher level, skills	Working conditions	Less satisfaction with pay level
	Work equity	
Job is more secure	Fringe benefits	Less satisfaction with pay equity
	WORK ENVIRONMENT	
Supervisors more participative	Role conflict	Supervisors are less work-facilitating, supportive, and respectful
	Job variety	
More work-group participation	Supervisory closeness, favoritism, and feedback	
More employee influence over task-related decisions	Work-group feedback	Less satisfaction with work group
More adequate work resources	Employee influence over work-schedule decisions	Less association between work performance and reward received (3 indicators)
More work-improvement ideas provided by employees	Association between job security and intrinsic motivation with work performance	Less job feedback
	General organizational climate	
	Work-improvement suggestions	

NOTE: Assessment based on 85 matched UAW members; for gains and losses significance level defined as p ≤ .05.

tionships, and the ability of the UAW to represent membership concerns. For example, 60 percent found the QWL program to be desirable; a majority found the QWLC (i.e., the on-site union–management committee responsible for designing and implementing change) to be effective without domination by either party; and 67 percent found that the change program strengthened the local union. In addition, 90 percent of the union membership was satisfied (33 percent very satisfied, 57 percent somewhat satisfied) with the local union in 1976 compared to 78 percent (35 percent very satisfied, 43 percent somewhat) in 1973 — figures substantially higher than the satisfaction level of a national sample of blue-collar union members with their union during this period.[36] Moreover, union membership at Bolivar has increased from 65 percent to above 90 percent, and 100 percent of the union members responded affirmatively when asked: "If there was an election today on whether or not the union should be kept at HII, how would you vote?"

The above Bolivar results and other outcomes not reported here seemed to indicate strongly that the Bolivar work force preferred to use joint union–management programs to deal with quality of work life and other important domains of their life at work.[37] Recently, many other case studies have indicated the same trends and seemingly similar results with other unions and companies.[38]

Assessment Summary

In summary, the Bolivar attitudinal results are mixed. There were gains, losses, and no changes in employees' quality of work life and environmental characteristics. However, as contrasted to the survey findings, the behavioral and performance findings showed, in most cases, dramatic improvement. The evidence is that (1) jobs objectively became more secure, (2) productivity and product quality rose, (3) OSHA accidents decreased at a faster rate than the industry average, (4) minor accidents declined, (6) manufacturing supplies and machine downtime increased, and (7) employee earnings held steady. Two other rates — grievances and absences due to lack of work — decreased 51 and 94 percent, respectively.

The Work Improvement Program and the positive behavioral and organizational performance gains seem to have had some practical implications for both the company and the union in their contractual process. The company's 1976 contract with the UAW was signed earlier than ever before and benefited both the company and the union membership by reducing the need for higher product inventories while maintaining the same employment level. These bargaining sessions, as contrasted to previous ones, were accomplished in an atmosphere of mutual cordiality, creativity, and trust. Absent was the win–lose philosophy and counterthreats of gamesmanship that often accompany labor–management bargaining. This is not to indicate that the adversary relationship between the UAW and HII has vanished. It has not! The union still grieves contract issues; however, the spirit (i.e., capacity for local problem solving in which grievances are handled) has improved.

Generally, the behavioral data (absenteeism, turnover) and performance (productivity, product quality) findings are positive, while a comparison of attitudes during 1973 and 1976 indicates mixed results at best. This surprising finding, as opposed to the generally positive behavioral and financial indicators, brings important methodological questions to mind. For example, had only the standard method of survey methodology been utilized at Bolivar as contrasted to multiple methods (i.e., hard company-record data, on-site structured and unstructured interviews, naturalistic observations, and surveys), the independent assessment would not have provided an accurate picture of the various changes.[39]

DISCUSSION

The past four years have been difficult transitional ones at the Bolivar plant. The key participants have withdrawn and, in August 1979, the Bolivar management, with the consent of the Working Committee and the UAW, decided to discontinue the provision of the on-site third-party consulting/resource team. Thus, after almost six full years of constant on-site professional staff support to assist with the design and implementation of the change program, the company and the union tried to be independent of professional assistance. At the current time only the group EIT program, some education classes, and Reeves' experiment with self-management remain at Bolivar. In essence, the viability and permanency of the change effort are highly questionable, if not nonexistent. For example, one of the plant's managers recently told the author that if a stranger were to visit the Bolivar plant today, he or she might never know that the plant ever had a quality-of-work-life program.

As for performance results, it seems clear that productivity and product quality increased significantly for the aggregated Bolivar performance indicators. Generally, the paid-personal-time program made it necessary to reach standard in most departments, whereas this rarely occurred before; therefore, efficiency and output per hourly employee per day, adjusted for inflation, increased throughout the plant. In addition, ISR on-site observations indicated that some departments or work groups do function with less regimentation. The foremen police less, leaving it up to the employees in the group to decide when to stop or start something. Before the program started, the workers were closely supervised, whereas some work groups now operate with three basic norms: (1) the workers should be left alone and not bothered; (2) the workers should produce to standard; and (3) the workers should produce quality parts. The process and procedure to meet these norms were left up to the workers. There was a feeling on the part of the Bolivar management that the majority of the employees felt more involved in their jobs and were more interested in their work. They also seemed more interested in housekeeping and, because of their pride of ownership, more intent on producing a quality product.

It was also interesting to note that many groups spent their earned time discussing their work and possible ways to improve it. Within a group, there was a strong sense of teamwork, possibly giving the job more meaning. One member of a group said that this was the reason he no longer came to the plant feeling that "I can't face it." One line of the original assembly experiment recorded all of their delays, together with the reasons for each delay. This kind of report (never done before) was extremely useful in correcting the delay problems in the assembly department. But again, the EIT caused many problems (see table 9.1, especially physical and psychological stress symptoms).

Overall, the Bolivar project produced a number of important results. Perhaps the most impressive thing about the project was that an initial climate of experimentation, trust, and faith was produced in the organization. This statement is made from the numerous on-site observations, rather than from the attitudinal data previously discussed. One of the great unknowns in organizational change research is how this climate is brought about. The major unknown at Bolivar was and continues to be whether or not self-renewal and permanency of the cooperative change effort lie in the future. At the present time, institutionalization of the change effort and internal (as opposed to external) diffusion of the program at Bolivar look dim.

Perhaps the biggest change at Bolivar, besides some of the behavioral and financial results, was the initial support of the project by local management and local union representatives and the general commitment by top corporate and top union officials. At the start, the Bolivar project had strong corporate support but lacked strong commitment and support from the local management. Over the course of the project, there was a marked increase in cooperation and support at the plant level, and the resulting union–management ownership of the program was beginning to show many benefits. However, local management never wanted the same goals as did the corporate office. In fact, the corporate office, in what turned out to be a vital mistake, forced many decisions upon local Bolivar management. On the other hand, it was clear that the UAW felt a high level of ownership of the project and clearly felt responsible for what happened as a result. This orientation of joint problem solving produced a relationship between top union and management which was usually characterized by the question "How can we get things accomplished?"

The heavy UAW involvement at Bolivar made it a particularly important experiment. It was both a complicating and reinforcing factor — reinforcing in the sense that this organized union pressure for planned organizational change meant the Bolivar program probably proceeded faster than it would have in a nonunion situation. The union commitment almost guaranteed that something would happen. The union — hopefully — will continue to encourage Bolivar's management to keep some semblance of the WIP. However, with Bluestone's retirement from the UAW, there seems to be no strong force at the regional or international level to make change happen at Bolivar.

As far as system-wide change is concerned, the major question becomes one of cause and effect: Did the quality-of-work-life experiment cause the Bolivar system to change? The answer is a definite yes. However, how much change was related to each of the independent variables is very difficult to measure. Nevertheless, the author firmly believes the Bolivar system was changed through a combination of positive factors, including the quality-of-work-life project.

As with any organizational change effort, there were some nonexperimental effects that also influenced the behavioral and performance results. At Bolivar, five nonexperimental variables were identified:

1. Increased managerial effectiveness and the collection of a group of engineering/designer oriented innovators working with the line management.
2. A more favorable product/sales mix (i.e., more production quantities of particular product lines coupled with working near maximum plant capacity).[40]
3. Technological improvements/advancements and capital investment (i.e., die cast automatic extractors and other minor jigs and fixtures, some stimulated by the program).
4. Marketplace/customer demands and the automotive division's sales and engineering staff's expertise and willingness to take risks in order to obtain more business.
5. The 1974–1975 automobile and auto supplier industry business recession tended to bring the company, the union, and the employees closer together rather than dividing them; thus, the recession enhanced the cooperative problem solving and further developed a strong sense of group cohesiveness that was initially created by the quality-of-work-life experiment.

These five nonexperimental factors coupled with the cooperative change effort were the six major factors that influenced the Bolivar system to change. However, the above five factors were all related (directly or indirectly) to the intervention. For example, the experiment definitely affected the increased managerial effectiveness of the management. This was evident to the assessors many times throughout the six years of the experiment. Privately, many managers would indicate to us: "Look at everyone who's watching us — the corporate and division offices, the union, the employees, ISR, and so on. We had better get our act together." In addition, the national, state, and local press; radio; and television coverage of the experiment, together with the many outside visitors (sometimes from foreign countries and their parliaments), influenced the local management to further improve working conditions and ensured that the system was operating effectively. Moreover, absences (i.e., due to lack of work) which are a measure of managerial effectiveness, decreased 94 percent during phases 1 through 5. This total system pressure at Bolivar for better working conditions, a good quality product at low cost, and increased quantity of production at higher efficiency rates was enormous during this period.

Generally, there were long-term positive participation benefits from situations very similar to what Kahn labels as the positive effects of a "Hawthorne" situation.[41] Also, the experiment influenced managerial effectiveness by means of joint union–management meetings to solve production, machinery, and quality problems. Moreover, as a consequence of the Earned Idle Time intervention and an accompanying rule that a poor quality product would be reworked and added to a subsequent day's production quota, some employees acted as inspectors to ensure good quality parts. This combined production and inspection task ensured that the earned-time participants would always be able to acquire personal time.

Joint employee–management meetings also occasionally generated worthwhile suggestions and innovations from the work force. In order to implement many of these suggestions, the company had to spend only minimal amounts of capital. This joint problem-solving climate positively helped the adoption of machinery improvements.

The technological improvements at the site most likely had a direct effect on product quality. In addition, the increased sales/production requirements at the plant resulted in increased company resources to better enable the system to produce a quality product at a low price. These increased resources (e.g., minor capital expenditures for the most part during phases 1 through 4) acted as an "enabling function," which in turn influenced productivity and product quality. Because the plant was primarily a labor-intensive facility, the addition of fixed capital had only a small effect upon the performance changes.

In the final analysis, most of the major capital investment and subsequent improvements did not commence until the end of the last analysis period — phase 5. Their effect on system performance did not begin right away because of the lead–lag purchase/installation/efficient operation cycle.

Therefore, their effects upon Bolivar system performance are judged to be minor — contributory, but of minor significance.

Another factor which was interrelated with the site performance changes during this period was the 1974–1975 recession. The effect of this recession on the management and employees at the site was (surprisingly) somewhat beneficial rather than totally harmful to the joint cooperative change effort. It eventually brought about joint rate setting, joint product bidding, a saving of approximately 70 jobs at the plant, and many other consequences. The change effort initiated at the plant in 1973–74, followed by the economic recession of 1974–75, brought the management, the union and the employees closer together. Their economic and job security were dependent upon the outcome of this cooperative venture.

In essence, the cooperative change effort indirectly influenced three of the five nonexperimental factors — increased managerial effectiveness, technological advancements and improvements, and the increased union–management cohesiveness. In turn, these variables directly influenced the improvements in the Bolivar system.

These five nonexperimental forces and the change effort's effect on the system are shown in figure 9.2. This figure indicates that the quality-of-work-life intervention had both a direct (solid line) and an indirect (dotted line) influence on changes in the system during 1972–76. During 1977–79 (data not mentioned), it continued to have these same positive effects. The experimental cooperative QWL effort indirectly influenced the direct positive effects that managerial effectiveness, technological advancements, capital improvements, and the 1974–75 recession had on improved system performance. The two other nonexperimental variables that directly influ-

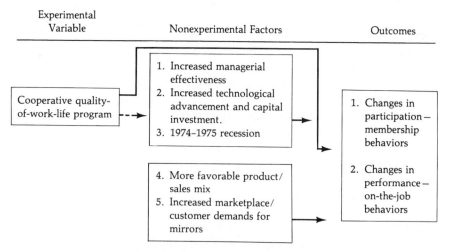

Fig. 9.2. Major Forces Influencing the Bolivar System to Change: 1972–1979

enced system performance changes were the more favorable product/sales mix and increased marketplace/customer demands for the plant's products.

CONCLUSION

After assessing the pluses and minuses of the nine-year change experiment at Bolivar, the author tends to believe that there has been a net gain in the work system and concrete opportunities for employee growth. There is little question as to the positive and beneficial behavioral and financial outcomes for the company. In almost every instance, the behavioral and financial indicators have maintained their phase 4 or phase 5 levels or have improved during subsequent phases.[42] However, the total financial benefits to the employees have yet to materialize. In addition, physical and psychological stress symptoms increased due to the Earned Idle Time program.

Nevertheless, it is this assessor's independent estimate and judgment that from 50 to 75 percent of the performance improvements at the site were caused by the direct effect of the intervention, coupled with the intervention's indirect influence on the three indicated nonexperimental variables. Therefore, the majority of the improvements in the Bolivar system performance were caused by the intervention. The lack of an experimental research design and a validated production function to trace the impact of programmatic and nonprogrammatic variables makes this an "educated" judgment at best. Of course, had it not been for the more than two-fold increase in sales, increased Bolivar resources, and the changes resulting from the quality-of-work-life program, these gains brought about through the "enabling" function would have been very doubtful. In some respects, had these not been in place during the experiment, the likelihood of significant performance gains would have been very small.

Nevertheless, there are sufficient data to encourage caution about the institutionalization and diffusion of the Bolivar change effort and the ability of the internal system to generate the capacity for self-renewal, if not plain survival mechanisms.

When looking at diffusion or the spread of work innovations such as the Bolivar project, the following assumption is critical: if innovation is successful or effective, it will be adopted and used by others inside and outside the organizational entity from which it originated.[43] In terms of diffusion to others outside the HII system, the Bolivar change effort has been a tremendous success. The UAW relied on the Bolivar site to provide learnings (both successes and failures) for future change attempts with other companies such as General Motors and Ford. Many other companies, other international unions, and others from all walks of life visited Bolivar from 1975 to 1980. Countless other unionized workplaces have adopted similiar collaborative union–management models to improve the quality of work life for employees. Regarding external diffusion, Bolivar was an unqualified success.

However, in terms of institutionalization inside the Bolivar organization, the results have been the opposite of those expected. Most union leaders and managers would expect that a changed organizational system, such as Bolivar, which is working better than the one it replaced would be recommended by supervisors and workers. Experience at Bolivar, however, shows that this is not generally the case. Workers like the paid-personal-time program (over 75 percent of the hourly work force in phase 5 and over 90 percent in the following years can earn paid personal time); foremen and supervisors, who do not receive any personal time, see the program as the cause of such problems as cheating on production figures, increased scrap (causing the supervisor to become a checker of quantity and quality). It is possible that the paid-personal-time program benefits derived by the hourly workers are nullified and offset by competing and conflicting management and productivity demands. This issue is demonstrated by the comments of a high-ranking Bolivar manager and an assembler in the assembly department. The manager observed: "Getting out of the plant is the overriding factor in the program for the people. It has been in their minds ever since the project started."

A woman in the assembly department indicated that "she liked to go home early but ever since the paid-personal-time program started, she and her co-workers felt nervous, unfriendly and fidgety toward one another."

In conjunction with these critical questions, six factors seemingly had a depressing effect on the Bolivar system in the period between 1975 and 1980. First, there was the Working Committee's dependence upon the outside third-party project staff to convene most Working Committee and core group meetings, to act as secretary for the Working Committee agendas, and to generally probe into the Bolivar system for possible future work innovations. The local plant management felt that it was too busy with other management problems (e.g., making production, reducing scrap, and so on) to carry on the required everyday change activities associated with the project. Second, the Working Committee seemingly wanted the Bolivar work force to initiate work innovations and bring these ideas to them. This might have been possible if the core groups had been working and effective bodies or mechanisms for organizational renewal; unfortunately, they have not been meeting regularly for over four years. Third, the company and the UAW could not agree upon the components, formula base, or split of possible savings for the Cost-Saving-Sharing Plan. After over three years of formulating plans and figures, the question of how to combine the contractual collective bargaining process with the benefits of the quality of work life project died on the vine. Fourth, Sidney Harman, a strong company force behind the program from the beginning, and Irving Bluestone, an equally strong UAW force, have relinquished their respective positions. Thus, their strong support, commitment, and active involvement are absent from the advisory committee, top corporate management, and the international union. Fifth, a second recession occurred in 1980–1981 requiring layoffs of one-third to one-half of the Bolivar work force. And, finally, senior management exhibited little interest in developing a fully operational cooperative union–management program which might lead to innovative work redesign and reward systems.

One can easily ascertain that not all the Bolivar results have been positive; however, it is the author's opinion that the Bolivar plant and its union will never return to their original, preexperimental condition, but have instead incorporated in their normal functioning the values and some of the methods of joint union–management problem solving that have been learned.

Irving Bluestone, former vice-president, UAW, General Motors Department, indicated in an interview:

> I think when evaluating this cooperative union–management program at Bolivar, you have to think within the perspective of the total program. This program has had problems attendant to it all throughout. We expected that there would be. You're really revolutionizing a system of work process to which people on both sides are unaccustomed. As you know, to bring about change is extremely difficult. There are always those who resist it. Overall, we expected some unhappiness, by reason of the program. You've got to look at this unhappiness in the total perspective — considering the total employment and the general reaction to the quality-of-work-life program.
>
> My feeling is that — on the whole — the general reaction has been constructive. The workers do appreciate more today than they did before their own input into what goes on in the plant.
>
> I would think that under the present circumstances of a new firm (Beatrice Foods) taking over, and if they said, "As of Monday, this program is going to be stopped and we're going back to the Frederick Taylor type of work procedures," that we'd have one hell of a time at that plant.
>
> I think by and large there has been a ready acceptance of what this Program has meant in establishing a new kind of work life at the plant — that's what's important.

From the company's standpoint, some of these same benefits have developed since the QWL program began. Responding to the question, "Have labor–management relationships improved at the plant?" the HII plant personnel director said:

> Yes, very definitely. We're able to communicate and work out our problems. We have grievances, but in less numbers. We still recognize problems and we

work out these problems by effective communication and trust. We've not had anything go to arbitration in about four years. The fact of learning how to communicate has been one of the greatest benefits of the program. In a labor-management relationship, both parties effectively communicate through establishing trust.

It has caused a lot of us to work harder because you have to keep up with more things (i.e., has the worker obtained his or her quality and production?).

We've worked hard at communicating with each other and working together on an effective safety program. We're getting more involvement — we're getting people being honest and sincere.

In addition, I think working with people more . . . being more sensitive has changed people's perspectives. Instead of the old hard line relationship of the boss saying: "I'm the boss — you're the employee — you'll do it as I say," now a lot of that has been diminished. Foremen are asking their employees what their feelings are: "What do you think about this and that? What ideas do you have to improve work?"

It seems clear that, in terms of improving the labor–management relationships at Bolivar, the project was a "win–win" success story.

As in most organizational change efforts, there have been both positive and negative consequences that can be attributed to the Bolivar Quality of Work Life Experiment.[44] In some instances these consequences were directly linked to the cooperative change effort; in others, the linkage was indirect.

Is this kind of cooperation a wave of the future? Some believe so — others do not. One trend seems very clear. The time is ripe for the U.S. industrial relations system to seriously consider cooperative union–management programs, like the one at Bolivar, along with their traditional contractual and collective bargaining processes. At any rate, the many and varied changes that have come about at the Bolivar plant surely present an interesting and meaningful outcome for a project whose initial goal was to improve employees' quality of work life.

NOTES

1. Michael Maccoby, Harold Sheppard, Neil Q. Herrick, and others. "Final Technical Report: The Bolivar Project," submitted to the National Commission on Productivity, February 1974, p. 1.

2. Michael Maccoby, "Changing Work," *Working Papers*, March/April 1975, p. 44.

3. During the 1970s, many of the cooperative union–management projects in the United States were started as part of the Quality of Work Program of the Institute for Social Research (ISR) at the University of Michigan and the American Center for Quality of Work Life (ACQWL) of Washington, D.C. The role of ACQWL was to initiate broad-ranging joint quality-of-working-life projects by soliciting the support and interest of individual managements and unions. In most projects, ACQWL established the structure of a joint labor-man-

agement committee at participating sites and served as third party during the project start-up and initial planning stages; an independent consultant and/or third-party social science consultant team was usually chosen by the union or unions and management as the intervention team once the change project began. At the Bolivar project, however, ACQWL did not perform this function. The primary role of ISR, although not in all projects, was to independently document individual projects and to evaluate and assess their impact on organizational effectiveness; individual worker outcomes, such as satisfaction and safety; and the union as an organization. Funding for the overall effort was provided through grants from the Ford Foundation and the Economic Development Administration, U.S. Department of Commerce.

4. In the later stages of the Bolivar project, the WIP staff consisted of Michael Maccoby, director of the Harvard Project on Technology, Work and Character and director of the Bolivar project; Robert Duckles and Margaret M. Duckles, who were on-site participant–observers, or educator–researchers; and Richard Ramsey, the last on-site change agent. In the early stages of the Bolivar project, Maccoby served as codirector of the project along with Harold Sheppard, formerly with the W.E. Upjohn Foundation and now with the National Council on the Aging, and Neil Q. Herrick, formerly with the U.S. Department of Labor, the Ohio Quality of Work Center, and the National Center for Productivity and Quality of Working Life and presently at the University of Arizona.

Besides these key external resources, others on Maccoby's external Bolivar staff were Dennis M. Greene, Katherine A. Terzi, Cynthia E. Margolies, Rolando Weisman, Sue Thrasher, Leah Wise, Barry A. Macy, Gerald Ledford, and Loren Farmer.

5. N.Q. Herrick and M. Maccoby, "Humanizing Work: A Priority Goal for the 1970s" in *The Quality of Working Life*, vol. 1, edited by L.E. Davis and A.B. Cherns (New York: The Free Press, 1975).

6. Material on QWL cooperative efforts, structures, processes, and outcomes are from J. Herman and B. Macy, "Labor–Management Relationships in Collaborative Quality of Working Life Projects," a paper presented at the Quality of Work Life Assessment Conference, University of Michigan Institute for Social Research, Ann Arbor, Michigan, July 14–15, 1977; and B.A. Macy, "Labor–Management Relationships and Measures in Cooperative Quality of Work Life Projects," paper prepared for the Quality of Work Program, Institute for Social Research, University of Michigan, November 1979.

7. Barry A. Macy and A.J. Nurick, *The TVA Quality of Work Experiment* (New York: Wiley-Interscience, forthcoming).

8. L. Schlesinger and R.E. Walton, "Work Restructuring in Unionized Organizations: Risks, Opportunities, and Impact on Collective Bargaining," in the *Proceedings of the 29th Annual Winter Meeting of the Industrial Relations Research Association*, Atlantic City, September 16–18, 1976, pp. 345–51.

9. For further details, see Michael Maccoby, "The Quality of Working Life: Lessons from Bolivar," unpublished paper, Institute for Policy Studies, Washington, D.C., 1976; and Margaret Duckles, Robert Duckles, and Michael Maccoby, "The Process of Change at Bolivar," *Journal of Applied Behavioral Science*, March 1977, pp. 387–99.

10. These phases are the conceptual change stages of the Bolivar experiment; however, they are not exactly the same phases used for the assessment of behavioral and performance outcomes. See assessment section later on in this chapter.

11. The EIT was a program set up in the plant by the Working Committee whereby hourly employees can leave their job and go home or attend education classes when they reach standard production. It was diffused from the three experimental groups in phase 3 involving 42 hourly employees, to a plant-wide experiment in phase 4.

12. Robert Duckles, "Humanizing Work: The Bolivar Project," *Survey of Business*, University of Tennessee, May/June 1977.

13. Herrick and Maccoby, "Humanizing Work: A Priority Goal for the 1970s."

14. The author was one of the 1973 interviewers during this work on the behavioral and per-

formance assessment methodology mentioned in the results section of this chapter. In June 1974, Macy began his work on the independent assessment team at the University of Michigan, Institute for Social Research.

15. Maccoby, et al., "Final Technical Report," 1974, pp. 11–12. By the end of Phase 4 of the Bolivar WIP, the environmental conditions cited in the above report were improved.

16. At this time, an advisory board provided advice and made policy recommendations to the Working Committee. Initially, the Advisory Board's membership was Irving Bluestone, vice-president, General Motors Department, UAW; Harvey Brooks, dean, Harvard School of Engineering and Applied Physics; Sidney Harman, president, Harman International Industries; Berth Jonsson, Volvo Goteborg; John Lyle, chief engineer, Harman International Industries, Bolivar; Michael Maccoby, director, Harvard Project; E.T. Michael, regional director, UAW: Lubie Overton, president, Local 1303, UAW; David Riesman, Harvard University; Ben Stephansky, director, W.E. Upjohn Institute for Employment Research; and Einar Thorsrud, Work Research Institute, Oslo, Norway. During phase 4, the advisory board became the Bolivar Advisory Committee, composed of three members: Irving Bluestone, Sidney Harman, and Michael Maccoby. Starting with phase 5, this advisory committee was composed of Irving Bluestone, UAW; Herbert Paige, Harman International; and Michael Maccoby, WIP project staff.

17. Maccoby, *The Quality of Working Life*, 1976.

18. Ibid., p. 6.

19. Margaret Duckles was officially approved as a full-time project staff member by the Working Committee shortly after this time. Prior to this time, she had assisted her husband with WIP activities.

20. EIT was not new to the Bolivar plant. Early in the 1970s, the Bolivar workers had attempted such an experiment, but local management did not agree with the work force and subsequently returned to a standard eight-hour day.

21. John Lyle actually resigned for a few days during this time until Sidney Harman and others persuaded him to return in an engineering capacity.

22. Maccoby, *The Quality of Working Life*.

23. It must be remembered that neither the UAW International nor Bolivar top local management wanted an EIT program. It was designed and supported by the hourly work force. Bluestone thought that it was a form of a speed-up or just working harder instead of smarter. For example, Bluestone did not know the EIT was in force at Bolivar until he heard about it on the European trip. Local plant management had already tried EIT in the early 1970s and did not like it. However, Sidney Harman and the WIP project staff indicated that if the workers wanted it, they wanted it too.

24. It was decided by the Working Committee, with strong advice from the three-member Advisory Committee, not to allow workers to gain a financial bonus by increasing output above the standard because this would lead to loss of job security for individual workers. As of 1978, over 70 percent of the direct and indirect labor force at Bolivar were receiving EIT and going home early. There still is no financial incentive option in the WIP. According to a Bolivar Education Committee report, approximately 20 percent of the work force have attended educational classes.

25. The Bolivar WIP, as of August 1977, continued to search for new directions and self-renewal. The seven distinctive phases are conceptualized according to change activities for analysis and report writing purposes.

26. A particular type of Bolivar mirror worth approximately $5 million in sales.

27. It is interesting to note that local plant management was dead set against this idea; however, they were overruled by Sidney Harman.

28. Bolivar Working Committee transcript, May 17, 1977.

29. Ibid.

30. Ramsey did not agree with Maccoby or the Duckleses about the role of the project staff. He thought the third-party staff should provide for independence rather than dependence.

Consequently, he tried to force the Working Committee to perform many of the duties that the Duckleses had previously performed.

31. Michael Maccoby, *The Leader: A New Face for American Management* (New York: Simon & Schuster, 1981), ch. 4.

32. Barry A. Macy, Gerald E. Ledford, and Edward E. Lawler, III, *An Assessment of the Bolivar Quality of Work Life Experiment: 1972–1980* (New York: Wiley-Interscience, forthcoming).

33. B.A. Macy and P.H. Mirvis, "A Methodology for Assessment of Quality of Work Life and Organizational Effectiveness in Behavioral-Economic Terms." *Administrative Science Quarterly*, June 1976, pp. 212–226, and Macy and Mirvis, "Organizational Change Efforts: Methodologies for Assessing Organizational Effectiveness and Program Cost Versus Benefits." *Evaluation Review*, June 1982.

34. Macy, Ledford, and Lawler, *An Assessment of the Bolivar Quality of Work Life Experiment*.

35. Part of the assessment of the Bolivar change program consisted of two surveys—one from June to July 1973, before the introduction of the change program, and the second in November 1976, after its introduction.

36. R.P. Quinn and G.L. Staines, *The 1977 Quality of Employment Survey* (Ann Arbor; Survey Research Center, University of Michigan, 1978). A general discussion of the entire survey results can be found in an article by Staines and Quinn, "American Workers Evaluate the Quality of Their Jobs," *Monthly Labor Review*, January 1979, pp. 3–12. For a more in-depth discussion of union attitudes, see T. Kochan, "How American Workers View Labor Unions," *Monthly Labor Review*, April 1978, pp. 23–31.

37. Macy, Ledford, and Lawler, *An Assessment of the Bolivar Quality of Work Life Experiment*.

38. Citations of these numerous studies are available from the author on request.

39. A review of this type of assessment strategy, design, and methods employed at Bolivar and other sites is found in Stanley Seashore, Edward E. Lawler, III, et al., *Observing and Measuring Organizational Change: A Guide to Field Practice* (New York: Wiley-Interscience, forthcoming).

40. The ISR assessment team collected and analyzed sales data and other variables, but the company considered these data confidential and therefore they are not reported.

41. R.L. Kahn, "*In Search of the Hawthorne Effect*," in *Man and Work in Society*, edited by E.L. Cass and F.G. Zimmer (New York: Van Nostrand Reinhold, 1975).

42. The 1980–1981 recession has seriously influenced the behavioral and performance indicators since 1980.

43. Paul S. Goodman, *Assessing Organizational Change: The Rushton Quality of Work Life Experiment* (New York: Wiley-Interscience, 1979).

44. Macy, Ledford, and Lawler, *An Assessment of the Bolivar Quality of Work Life Experiment*.

10.
The Rushton Quality of Work Life Experiment: Lessons to be Learned*

Paul S. Goodman

INTRODUCTION

Employees' Views — 1974

Well you're your own boss . . . you go to your own section . . . run things your own way . . . talk things out when you have to . . . seems jobs now are divided more equitably . . . everything is kept up better. . . . Before when a timber [safety timber] was down, you'd say the hell with it. Now you do something . . . it's your section.

Union 1974

It's [the program] trying to get everyone to do the next man's job [job switching] . . . doing a real good job. . . . The place is kept better . . . men seem to care. . . . If something's wrong we fix it . . . everyone's part of it. . . just jump'n to do it.

Union 1974

We are more or less without a boss. . . . We try to cut down on accidents, increase productivity . . . it benefits everyone.

Union 1974

Had its good points but never reached its potential. . . . Guys in sections just sit around . . . no desire to do anything.

Union 1976

Well, it worked . . . it worked in 2 South, not in the other sections. . . . If

*This chapter was supported in part from earlier grants from the Ford Foundation to the Institute for Social Research, University of Michigan; and Office of Naval Research, Contract N0014-79-0167.

anything, the program is going backwards. Only real improvement was in safety and that did come from the program.

Management 1976

Don't mean much now . . . program is back to where it was [in the beginning]. All the joint committee meetings are a lot of talk . . . don't get nothing solved. . . . Program good if it were run as it was intended to.

Union 1976

The above statements were drawn from interviews collected in 1974 and 1976 by the evaluation team at the Rushton Mining Company. They present a representative picture of the feelings and beliefs of employees about the experimental program at Rushton. The purpose of this report is to tell the Rushton story — what changes were introduced, what were the results, and what lessons can be learned from this "quality-of-work-life" (QWL) experiment.[1]

Before beginning, it is useful to know the context in which the Rushton project developed. Experiments in new forms of work organization have proliferated in the United States since 1970. These have taken many different forms, and their impact on work, the work environment, worker attitudes, organizational effectiveness, and labor-management relations is potentially very significant. Rushton is one of these experiments.

In 1972, a series of labor-management demonstration projects were initiated by the National Quality of Work Life Center. The purpose of these experimental projects (which Rushton and the United Mine Workers of America participated in) was to find new ways to organize work and work organizations in order to increase the productivity of the organization and the quality of working life of its members. The focus of the projects was at the national level. It was expected that the demonstration projects would have a broad influence on how work would eventually be organized in this country.

These projects are distinguished from other attempts to improve the utilization of human resources within the firm in the following ways: (1) there is a dual focus on improving productivity and also the quality of working life in such areas, for example, as safety, opportunities to develop new skills and greater job satisfaction; (2) there is an attempt to restructure several aspects of the organization simultaneously rather than just one aspect such as a job or a pay system. A QWL experiment restructures authority, decision making, rewards, communication systems, and other aspects of organizational life rather than any one dimension. The focus of this multidimensional change is generally to provide more democracy in the workplace and greater control for the worker over his or her environment; (3) there are joint labor-management problem-solving groups created to diagnose organizational problems, introduce changes, monitor the changes, and make adjustments. These groups are the mechanism for change. The joint ownership of the project and involvement by labor and management are key factors in every project. The above three characteristics distinguish current QWL experiments from other forms of organizational change such as job enrichment, supervisor training programs, pay incentive systems, and so on. The QWL projects are major experimental efforts to find new ways to organize work. Rushton was one of the first QWL experiments.

My Point of View

In 1974 I signed a contract with the Institute for Social Research at the University of Michigan to independently evaluate the Rushton project. The design of the first QWL experiments required an independent evaluation team. This was separate from the research team, which served as the external consultants to management and the union. Funding for the evaluation team and research team came from separate sources.

The major activities for the evaluation team were to design, collect, analyze, and write up the results of the experimental intervention at Rushton. We had complete access to all company data. We attended and made transcripts of all major meetings, with the exception of a few consultations between research team and management and, of course, union meetings. Access was available at all times for interviews with labor and management. At the end of three years, vast amounts of information on job attitudes, productivity, costs, absenteeism, safety, strikes, and so on, were accumulated from five attitude surveys, four years of daily economic data, extensive on-site observations, and interviews. While our work was intensive, we did not contribute directly to the decisions relevant to the experimental program at Rushton. Our role was to observe and record but not to intervene.

Despite our independent measurement of this project, it could be that our values affected the outcome of our evaluation. That is, if we ideologically supported a particular form of change, we might be more likely to present data supportive of that type of change. Therefore, my own values relevant to this and similar projects need to be stated. They are the following: I think management and labor should experiment with new forms of work organization. We need to think of new ways to structure work in order to improve both the economic well-being of the firm and the psychological well-being of the workers. There is clearly no one solution. We need a period of experimentation in order to identify approaches which will work in specific situations. Eventually, the projects will have to meet the test of economic viability, or organization "owners" will have to change organizational goals explicitly to permit trading off social or psychological benefits for economic benefits. I am not a proponent of the theoretical framework (sociotechnical approach) or the major substantive change (autonomous work groups) that characterized the Rushton project. Therefore, while I support the general principles of finding new forms of work organization, I am not an advocate of any of the substantive changes introduced at Rushton. Basically, I do not see that my value position or that of others on the evaluation team led to biasing the results.

Was Rushton a Success?

While the question "Was Rushton a success?" is interesting, I think it is really the *wrong* question to ask. The Rushton project was an experiment in uncharted areas. It was a new experience for the consultants, the company, and the union. There was to be no simple success or failure judgment; rather, the task was to determine what conditions lead to success, what problems are likely to occur, and how to deal with those problems.

RUSHTON MINING COMPANY

General Background

Rushton Mining Company, located in Osceola Mills, Pennsylvania, is a medium-sized coal mine producing steam coal for a major power utility. Prospecting for the mine began in late 1962, with actual operations commencing in 1965. The mine is part of a mining corporation owned by the utility company which provided the initial backing for the mine. While the mine is part of a larger corporate body, from its beginning it was run as a fairly autonomous unit. Even after the utility company took over formal ownership in 1974, the Rushton mine was run as an independent unit, with Warren Hinks, the founder and president, serving as the principal decision maker.

At the time of the QWL experiment, there were approximately 180 employees. Of these, some 30 were classified as managerial; the remainder were production workers and members of the United Mine Workers of America (UMW). By the end of 1976, there were approximately 200 employees of which 35 were managerial. The average age of the work force was approximately 35, and the average educational level was tenth grade.

Organization. The president is the final authority and operationally makes most of the critical decisions. A plant superintendent and a general foreman supervise the daily underground operations. Underground operations are divided into sections where mining occurs. A section is divided into three crews, each of which includes a foreman, six production workers, and a maintenance man. Mining at Rushton operates on a 24-hour basis.

The other major operations of the mine include a cleaning plant, which prepares the coal (e.g., separates rock, washes, and dries) for shipment to the utility company, and maintenance. Supervisors from both these areas report to the mine superintendent as do other staff positions, such as the safety director, training director, and purchasing agent.

Technology. Mining has been often described as a transportation system. That is, the technology of the mine is organized to transport coal from the face to the consumer. The work flow starts with the activity of removing coal at the face and transporting it to a conveyor belt, which carries coal from inside the section to outside the mine. There it is transferred to the cleaning plant for processing and then transported (by conveyors) to a finished coal pile. Subsequently, it is loaded on coal cars for transportation to the power company. This technology is critical to understanding the experiment at Rushton and will be further delineated when we discuss the focal unit for the experiment — the mining section — of which there are four at Rushton.

Social Context. Rushton is located in a small rural community (population approximately 1,670) in the north central part of Pennsylvania. The work force is fairly well distributed over the adjacent towns in this rural area. Driving to the mine from Pittsburgh, one passes through towns such as Ramey, Frugality, Coalport, and Tippletown. Although there are not a large number of mines near Rushton, most of the men (70 percent) have come from mining backgrounds. Rushton is in a relatively isolated cultural area, where most of the miners were born and raised.

Union Relations. The mine was started as a nonunion mine. In 1967, there was a major strike over unionization which concluded with the establishment of a local of the United Mine Workers of America. During this early period, labor–management relationships were bitter and punctuated by many strikes. In the early 1970s, there was a moderation of strike activity and more cooperation in labor–management relationships.

The local union carries out the daily implementation of the collective bargaining agreement through its officers (e.g., president, vice–president, etc.) and committee structures (e.g., safety committee). District officials monitor the local union activities in an assigned geographical area and report to international headquarters. Collective bargaining and general union policymaking occur at the international level. Rushton is not a member of the employers association which negotiates the national contract, but adopts the contract as its own.

Focus of the Experiment

The experiment at Rushton was first introduced into one mining section. A section is the major mining unit; it operates on a 24-hour basis and contains three crews which rotate shifts weekly. Each crew has a continuous miner operator and a helper. The continuous miner is a large (approximately 25 feet long) and expensive piece of machinery which scrapes the coal from the seam. Two car operators then transport the coal to a feeder. Meanwhile, two bolter operators place bolts in the roof to hold the strata together to prevent a roof fall. When special work is required (e.g., moving belts), general laborers are assigned to the regular crew. The foreman and a maintenance man who reports to the maintenance supervisor bring the total to eight men in each crew in each shift.

The physical conditions in the section are generally unfavorable. There is complete darkness. The ceiling height is around five and one-half feet, wet areas are common, and dust levels are noticeable.

From the physical conditions and technology, the following observations can be made: (1) the physical working conditions are hostile; (2) there is a high degree of uncertainty (e.g., chances of roof falls, changes in the coal seam) surrounding the mining operations; (3) the physical conditions and darkness restrict the supervisor's ability to direct the work force; (4) there is a high degree of interdependence within a crew (i.e., if the continuous miner stops, production stops); (5) there is a high degree of interdependence between crews in the same section (i.e., failure to coordinate increases the problems of production downtime and lower production); and (6) there is a high degree of interdependence between the mining crew and outside operations (i.e., failure to coordinate supply needs leads to long delays as supplies are sent into the sections).

In the fall of 1975, the focus of the experiment changed. It was extended throughout the mine to include the cleaning plant, inside general labor groups, and the outside general labor groups, which are technologically quite different from the mining sections. Since these work groups were not the prime focus of the experiment, their technological features will not be described here.

Decision to Participate

The initial stimulus for Rushton's participation in a QWL experiment came from a training program conducted at Pennsylvania State University by Grant Brown in early 1973. The president of Rushton was attracted by some of the novel ideas presented in the session. At the same time, Davitt McAteer from the United Mine Workers of America had learned about Eric Trist's work in the British coal mines and had contacted Trist. McAteer was examining new approaches to improve safety in the mines. Subsequently, Brown, Gerald Susman (a former student of Trist and now at Penn State), and Trist met in New York in March 1973 and agreed to form a research team to pursue an action research project in the coal industry. Then the research team met with Ted Mills, a member of the National Commission on Productivity and Quality of Working Life (later director of the National Quality of Work Life Center) to discuss whether the commission would be the neutral sponsor of the project. Meetings with the president of Rushton; his co-owner, Mike Cimba; the research team; and Ted Mills explored the feasibility of conducting a quality-of-work-life experiment at Rushton. Finally, with Ted Mills serving as the catalyst, the presidents of Rushton and the United Mine Workers were brought together. In April, 1973, they signed a letter approving the goals of a quality-of-work-life experiment and agreeing that each of the parties could withdraw as he saw fit. Funding for the project came from the National Commission on Productivity and Quality of Working Life and later from the National Quality of Work Life Center, affiliated with the Institute for Social Research, University of Michigan.[2]

Why did the company enter this agreement? The Rushton president's values weighed heavily on his decision to participate. Autonomy, responsibility, and freedom of choice were essential dimensions in the Rushton quality-of-work-life experiment. These are values that were frequently articulated by Warren Hinks. At a more practical level, Hinks was concerned with attracting young miners to Rushton in the future. The problem is that younger, better educated miners bring higher expectations to the job, yet the current state of work in mining is not congruent with these expectations. Hinks saw the experimental project as a way of attracting the younger workers.

From the international union's point of view, the experiment at Rushton was attractive since it attempted to improve safety conditions and practices. It was the union's initial interest in finding new ways to improve safety that opened the door for joint labor–management collaboration. Also, the experiment reflected some of the values of the current union leadership; the union has been undergoing a process of democratization which parallels the attempt at Rushton to democratize decision making at the workplace.

THE QUALITY-OF-WORK-LIFE EXPERIMENT

General Framework

There are two general frameworks that guided the quality-of-work-life experiment at Rushton. First, there is a theoretical framework which draws heavily on sociotechnical analysis. Basically, this orientation views an organization in terms of two systems — technical and social. The basic thesis is that an organization is more effective when there is an optimal fit between these systems. Proponents of this position have argued that managers and consultants traditionally have focused on only one of the dimensions (i.e., the technical). To incorporate the sociotechnical analysis in a mine, one would have to look for a joint fit between the two systems. The technology of mining is characterized by high degrees of uncertainty, high interdependence, and little opportunity to directly supervise or control the work force. Given this technology, the research team for Rushton (Trist, Susman, and Brown) needed to design a social system which would facilitate coordination and flexibility of the work force to meet uncertainty and to provide control at the appropriate levels of decision making. Autonomous work groups were selected as the prime design strategy. This strategy, in part, delegates greater levels of authority, responsibility, decision making, and information to the work group so that the members can be more responsive to changes in the environment.

A second general framework — the action framework — was created to implement the theoretical design; it was built around a labor–management committee. This committee was composed of the major union officers and different levels of management at the mine. The character of the membership was jointly agreed upon by union and management. At a meeting of this group, one would find on average some 20 to 22 participants, including members of the research team. This labor–management committee served as the executive mechanism of the experiment. That is, this group would diagnose existing conditions, develop a change plan, institute the plan, evaluate its outcomes, and modify it. The research team's role was to help establish and provide guidance for the project through the labor–management committee. The committee began its activities in August 1973. A proposed plan for the experiment at Rushton was voted on and approved by the local union in the fall of 1973; the final revised plan was introduced in December 1973.

Nature of the Change

The following are the major characteristics of the experimental program developed by the research team and the labor–management committee:

1. *Goals.* There were five major goals: increased safety, increased productivity, higher earnings, greater job skills, and job satisfaction.
2. *Focal unit.* The major unit of analysis was the section. By focusing on the section instead of the crew (e.g., in terms of performance evaluation), less between-crew competition and more cooperation was expected.
3. *Autonomous work groups.* The responsibility for daily production and directing the work force was delegated to the crew.
4. *Foreman's job.* With responsibility delegated to the men in the crew, the foreman was no longer responsible for production. The foreman's prime responsibility was safety. This change was introduced

because the research team felt there was a basic contradiction between safety and production objectives. In addition, he was to become more involved in planning activities and integrating the section with the rest of the mine.

5. *Job switching.* All men were expected to exchange and learn other jobs within their crews so that the crew would be multiskilled. That is, the crew would develop the flexibility to be able to staff any job. Movement between jobs did not require bidding as would be the case under the regular contract.

6. *Pay.* All members of the experimental section received the same rate and it was the top rate for the crew. The rationale for the high rate was that the men had increased responsibility for production and maintenance of equipment. Also, they agreed to learn to perform multiple skills.

7. *Additional crew members.* The traditional crew consisted of six production men. In the experimental section, two support men (to lay track, transport supplies, etc.) were added to the crew. These two support men were traditionally drawn from the general labor force and were assigned to a section only when support work was needed.

8. *Joint committee.* A smaller labor–management committee (five members from each side) was instituted 75 days after the experiment began to supervise the daily operation of the program. The larger labor–management committee remained intact; its responsibilities were to deal with broader policy issues.

9. *Grievances.* Grievances were not initially processed through the traditional machinery. The expectation was that grievances would be resolved within the experimental section. If they were not, they were to be brought to the joint committee. Failure to resolve the grievance at this point would lead to the use of the traditional grievance machinery.

10. *Training.* A major part of the change effort was to move the men toward being professional miners. A training program on safety practices, ventilation, roof control, and other potential problems was to be a major part of the change effort.

11. *Allocations of financial gains.* No gain-sharing plan was worked out in the initial agreement. Rather, some general principles were established. If no gains resulted, the company would assume all the costs from the experiment. If gains did occur, the company would be reimbursed, and the remaining gains would be allocated between labor and management.

These characteristics made the initial plan for change a significant document for several reasons: first, it represents a contract between labor and management outside the existing union–management contract; second, both union and management gave up rights they had previously enjoyed (for example, certain rights over job bidding procedures, rights to direct the work force); and third, the changes discussed above represent a major alteration in how work was conducted at Rushton.

In July 1975, a new document was drawn up to extend the principles of autonomous working to the whole mine. This document and the original one were the same in terms of philosophy, goals, and procedures; but some changes were required because the original sheltered experiment was over and the new plan was mine-wide. There was stricter adherence to building the 1975 document in line with the existing labor contract, particularly in handling grievances. The top pay rate received by the experimental section was changed so that the men would initially receive the top rate in their work area but after 90 days would have to "qualify" (i.e., demonstrate specific job skills) to receive this rate. The 1975 proposal also reflected some of the experiences from the first experimental group. For example, procedures to call labor-management meetings were spelled out in greater detail.

The principle of voluntary autonomy was a new concept in the second document. It established that work areas could voluntarily determine the degree to which they would adopt autonomous practices.

Critical Historical Events

In the fall of 1973, labor and management drew up a document (discussed pp. 229 to 230) which charted the course of the initial experiment. This was a very dramatic and significant event in that both parties for the first time were able to work through a complicated proposal in a problem-solving rather than an adversarial atmosphere.

The experimental program was launched in December 1973. One section (2 South) was selected as the experimental group and the miners were given the option to volunteer into that section (37 volunteered). The reasons for volunteering were many:

I was in water [in another section] and I wanted to get out [to the experimental section].

You'd get $5 more a day.

I didn't want to leave this section [already in experimental section] and the program intrigued me. I had 60 days to change my mind.

I'd like to be a professional miner.

Some reasons for not volunteering included:

> I had no desire to work without a boss . . . I like having a boss.

> I didn't know much about it . . . things done automatically . . . right?

> I don't want no part of it. . . . A guy should have a boss. . . . don't give him complete freedom. . . . I like things the way they are.

Reasons for volunteering primarily focused on getting more money, staying in 2 South, or getting into the experimental section because of its better physical conditions. None of the volunteers really understood or embraced the concept of autonomy. Those not volunteering preferred to stay with their own crew, or had a surface job and did not want to work inside, or did not like the idea of not having a "regular boss."

Once the experimental section was staffed, the research team conducted a series of six day-long training sessions in December and January. These sessions focused on the technical aspects of mining (e.g., laws relevant to roof control, ventilation) and the basic concepts of the autonomous work groups.

Following the training sessions, conferences were scheduled every four to six weeks. The conference, a critical part of the Rushton experiment, was an all-day meeting of all members of the experimental section plus members of management, union officials, and the research team. The conference had four functions: to review past performance, to provide communication opportunities across crews, to solve problems, and to plan. Some of the issues discussed in these meetings included coordinating supply needs, determining the proper role for the foreman, and dealing with overtime problems. Shortly after the section conferences started, a mini-labor–management committee was initiated. This committee — composed of five members (three from the experimental section) of labor and five of management — had the responsibility of resolving day-to-day problems that arose within the experimental section. Some of the problems were of a technical nature — how to prevent flat tires — while others concerned coordination problems among the three crews in the section. Besides being a smaller group, the mini-labor–management committee differed from the section conference in that its job was to deal immediately with day-to-day problems.

A series of Friday foremen's meetings were also instituted at this time. The foreman's role was affected most immediately by the experiment, and the meetings were instituted to help the foremen adapt to their new roles. Participants in this group included the three foremen of the experimental section, members from management, and the research team. Meeting activities focused on clarifying the new roles and facilitating communication among the foremen and between the foremen and management.

Along with these three new problem-solving groups, which were important parts of the change effort, the original labor–management steering committee which drew up the document for change remained intact to deal with general policy issues. In the third quarter of 1974, Rushton's president decided to introduce a fourth operating section into the mine. The parent company needed more coal and, compared to other mines owned by the corporation, Rushton was operating at a lower cost per ton. Therefore, Rushton was asked to open another section (5 Butt).

There was no consultation with the research team about this decision, and indeed there was no plan to make 5 Butt an experimental section. When the research team learned about the new section they proposed that it be an autonomous section. One major rationale for their proposal was that they did not think the program could survive if all the other sections were not autonomous. They felt that hostility toward 2 South (the experimental section) from certain levels of management and the other mining sections was growing, and that there were doubts within the experimental section whether the project would survive. The introduction of a new autonomous section would serve to counterbalance these forces. Basing his decision on the above argument from the research team, the president agreed to make 5 Butt an experimental section. The decision was then brought before the labor–management steering committee on September 9, 1974, since this group was designed to deal with policy issues. Discussion in the meeting focused on whether the new section should be autonomous, the bidding procedure for the new section, problems with inexperienced miners in the new section, and other issues. At the conclusion of the meeting, there was at least implicit consensus that 5 Butt would be the second experimental section and that this matter should be brought to the local union hall for a vote. A special meeting was called, and the local voted 26 to 5 to support 5 Butt as an autonomous section. Of those attending this meeting, 17 were from 2 South (the original autonomous section). Since participation in union meetings is generally low — around 20 percent — the bloc voting of the South section obviously had a strong bearing on the outcome. The plan was to open the new autonomous section in October. The document for the first experimental section was to be the guiding document for developing 5 Butt into an autonomous group. Bids were put up for the new section. Since not enough men bid into the section, some relatively inexperienced miners — "yellow hats" (men with less than a year's experience) — were placed in the new section. This staffing problem was not anticipated, and it was to cause subsequent problems within 5 Butt and within the mine.

The training program for the new section followed the same procedure as the first autonomous section's training. The teachers included members of the research team, management, and outsiders; the miners met as a section. The only major difference was in the timing of the training sessions. For the first experimental group, the six training sessions were concentrated in a two-month period, with most held within the first four weeks. The new section's sessions began in October 1974 and continued into February 1975. This spread in training was partly caused by the national strike, which precluded training in November, but it also reflected the design of the research team.

During this time the research team set up special meetings for members of top management at the mine. The rationale for this new effort was that the quality-of-work-life experiment could not be successful unless it was actively supported by management. Up to this period, top management had participated in the many different meetings and conferences which were a part of the Rushton project, but it was still not committed to the program.

Another interesting event at this time was a call by members of a crew in 2 South for the removal of their boss and a member of the crew. The crew members felt the foreman was being too directive and not following the autonomous work group guidelines of giving the men the right to direct the work force. The crew member was cited for unwillingness to switch jobs with other members of his crew. This event was important because it was the first time the experimental group felt powerful enough to assert its authority on disciplinary matters, which traditionally were initiated by "the boss." The preliminary resolution of this issue was that the foreman and crew member would behave in accordance with autonomous work group principles.

Perhaps the most dramatic event during the period was a challenge from the union that either the whole mine participate in the experiment or none of the mine participate. This challenge was raised by the union president during the South section conference in March. He said that the union (in their last meeting) had passed a resolution demanding that the whole mine participate in the program or that no one participate. The basic issue was the inequity in wages among the sections. Members in the 2 South and 5 Butt sections were getting higher rates than other men in the mine doing the same jobs. In particular, the 5 Butt section had been staffed with a number of "yellow hats" and, since these men were getting top wages, the feelings of inequity were exacerbated. Members in the experimental sections reacted differently to the union resolution. Some said that management should just pay the men in the other sections more. Other members of the 2 South section pointed out that pay was not the issue — the concept of working in an autonomous work group was more complex and demanded more work and responsibilities, thereby justifying the higher pay. The company president's reaction was the following:

> I do not think there should be an ultimatum. I realize there are jealousies. We're in an experiment. We shouldn't be stampeded. If the whole mine had to go autonomous I would say no. I couldn't pay the high rate. It will take time. One

section at a time. Our goal is to make the coal miner a professional. I don't want to be stampeded.

The union president's response was "If these men [union members] want something, that's what they are going to get. The men in the South section are not running this mine." The discussion during that meeting continued without any resolution of the major issue. The men did decide to bring the problem up at the next union meeting.

The next major event was the union meeting on the first Sunday in April. The union membership determined that a new document specifying the mine-wide operation of the experiment should be drawn up by the steering committee and voted upon by the union members after the miner holiday which occurs in July. The ultimatum by the union was softened since slightly more than four months were now available to introduce the program.

The task of developing a document that would fit the whole mine was begun by the steering committee in April. Meeting biweekly, they began to draw up an acceptable program. Many issues, such as how to deal with grievances, pay rates, job movement within areas of the mine, and job bidding, occupied members of this committee. Parallel to the steering-committee meetings, a set of communications meetings were instituted in which the president of Rushton was actively involved. Their purpose was to explain the nature of the program and the document, and to obtain ideas from the men that could be introduced into the document. The meetings held during this period represented approximately 480 worker hours.

On August 20, 1975, with all the miners voting, a mine-wide quality-of-work-life program was defeated in a close vote (79–75). This vote signaled the decline of the QWL program. (An analysis of the reasons for this vote will be presented in a later section of this report.)

The reaction to the "no" vote was obviously one of disappointment for members of 2 South, 5 Butt, some union officials, the research team, and the company president. The company president said:

> I had a slight pang of disappointment but . . . I have been preparing in my mind for either eventuality. . . . It shows a lack of understanding—what is good for the working man. I don't see the vote shutting off the experiment. I don't see why management can't come up with new policies but keeping within the contract and still forwarding the autonomous idea.

This position did, indeed, become the description of what was to happen. The experiment was not over; management took over the program and implemented it throughout the mine. In the week after the vote, the superintendent convened a meeting of the steering committee members. The president made clear his intention of continuing the program within the context of the labor–management contract. At the end of the meeting, a common position of the members was reflected in the following announcement issued by the union.

Due to the recent vote, the autonomous joint steering committee has been abolished; but under Article 16, Sec. g, p. 67 of the contract a new committee has been formed called the MTDC (Mine Training and Development Committee) which is strictly a management committee but may have union representation.

The management now retains the right to direct the work force. All wages will be paid according to the contract rates and Article 19, Sec, E. j; two extra support people will be assigned to each crew under the direction of the foreman to provide the same opportunity as 5 Butt and 2 South.

Classes on mine law, mine safety, and section performance will continue under the direction of the company.

All foremen and general men will remain the same until a training program is arranged.

This announcement was significant because it signaled a new direction in the experiment. The official labor–management program was canceled, but management elected to continue the program for the whole mine. It had this right under the contract. Essentially, the same program implemented in the first two sections was to be extended to other work areas in the mine. In the announcement, the right to direct the work force was retained again by management and the miners' pay went back to union contract rates. The program now was *management-initiated*. The union officers, however, did agree to cooperate.

On September 8, a meeting of the new training and development committee was held. The goal was to draw up a revised document which would provide the guidelines for extending the "program" to the whole mine. The focal issue in this meeting was to determine the appropriate pay rate for different job skills — the same issues that had plagued steering-committee meetings before the vote. The position of the union was that people had voted against the program because the routes to the top rates and the qualification to obtain these rates were inequitable. They argued that the first two experimental sections had been given top rate immediately, with no conditions for qualifications. This same procedure should be extended to the two other mining sections and the other work areas. Management's position was that people should be paid for services rendered. The original decision on pay was made in the context of an experiment; now that the experiment was over, management felt new approaches for payment should be considered.

The final resolution was to pay the men the top rate for their work area. Some redefinitions of work area (e.g., outside and cleaning plant) were drawn up to provide the men more opportunities for job switching and for higher rates. The qualifying period was changed to 60 days and, if any of the men decided not to participate in the program after that period, they would revert to their contract pay rate. Concerning his decision to pay the top rate, the president said:

> I firmly believed we should pay for services rendered. The thing that bothered me was to pay people not deserving. . . . If they didn't cut it I wanted the right to cut them out. . . . I also felt we wouldn't make progress [with the men] if we didn't pay the top rate.

It is interesting to note, and this point will be discussed later in more detail, that there was no procedure established for determining in 60 days if the men wanted to continue to participate in the new training program.

Another major decision of the training and development committee meeting was to begin a training program for all the workers who had not been in the first two experimental sections. Training was to represent one of the major activities of the extended program for the next six months. Training began in late September 1975 and continued through to April 1976. The substantive part of the training was much the same as in the training programs for the first two autonomous work groups.

A new phase of training for managers suggested by the research team and the company president began in January 1976. One of the issues discussed after the vote was the need to improve supervisory skills.

In their December union meeting, the local agreed (no formal vote) that their officers could continue working in the training and development committee to shape a new agreement. This provided some legitimation for the labor–management activities to continue.

During the period following the "no" vote, the research team remained active in the project, attending the major meetings and playing a major role in design and implementation of the training programs.

From September 1975 through April 1976, there was a marked change in labor–management relations. Six walkouts occurred during this period compared with none in 1974 or in 1975 up to September. The most critical confrontation occurred in April 1976, when a walkout occurred which challenged the existence of the experimental program at Rushton. The issue concerned the assignment of a person to a job that was up to bid. A union officer said: "The job should have been given to the senior man. . . . The men got mad and walked out. At the special meeting they voted to stay out. They figured arbitration just takes too long." Some of the union men set up pickets at other mines owned by the Rushton president. Management reacted by suspending the picketers and removing some of them from the union mine committee (i.e., the grievance committee which is part of the contract) and from the Rushton labor–management committees. As one manager put it, "We feel some of the union guys say one thing to us when we are in the quality-of-work labor and management committees but say another when they get back to the men. . . . We've really had it."

The district and international unions became involved and a representative from the international threatened to withdraw support from the existing program. Eventually, the dispute was resolved; the suspensions were withdrawn; and the man assigned by management to the job retained that job, while other job opportunities were given to the senior individual who did not get the job. It is fair to say that the walkout, though resolved, created a good deal of ambiguity about the future viability of a quality-of-work-life program at Rushton.

After the strike, there were no other major crises for the rest of 1976. Most of the activities during this period were to introduce new procedures to ensure the viability of the program. The research team spent much time trying to work up a gain-sharing formula. An attempt was made to institute a goal-setting program for foremen (e.g., monthly production goals) and to initiate more planning activities by the foremen. A full-time union person was designated by the labor–management committee to work on safety and other related mine problems and then report back to the committee on his activities. Examples of other activities were: regularizing the meeting time for the mini-labor–management committee; setting up a new leadership training program for the first-line supervisors, and (for the research team) conducting interviews with high absenteeism individuals.

Despite these activities, interest in the QWL program continued to decline in 1976 in both the original experimental sections and other parts of the mine. In 1979, we returned to the mine to interview the workers for another purpose. There was no evidence that any of the institutions (e.g., labor–management committees) or roles (e.g., new foreman's role) remained. The quality-of-work-life experiment was no longer functioning.

RESULTS[3]

It is important for the reader to understand the context of the results to be presented. Rushton is one of the most comprehensively evaluated organizational experiments. We have had complete access to all the relevant data systems. For each major area (e.g., safety) we have developed several different types of measures and collected data for these measures over the course of the experiment. In some areas, such as economic analysis, we had to develop sophisticated economic information systems. Thousands of worker hours have been invested in the development and analysis of the economic and attitudinal data, using new models and analysis procedures to get at whether the experiment had an effect. Assessing organizational change is a complex task. In the past, we think other researchers of organizational change have been somewhat cavalier in determining effects of organizational interventions. The reliance on case studies, for example, really does not get at the question of whether an experiment has an independent impact on organizational effectiveness. Our strategy has been to bring the best scientific tools to the examination of effects of the Rushton experiment. The investment in time and resources has been substantial. The message to the reader, then, is that, while the results here are in summary form, they are based on sophisticated, quantitative, and qualitative analyses of large amounts of data over a three-to-four-year time period. The performance of the experimental section(s) is always contrasted against baseline periods. Similarly, control groups (other mining sections) are used to tease out the effects of the intervention. The results are arranged along the following dimensions:

1. *Constituencies.* There are three major groups in the project — the company, the union, and the miners. Since the benefits and costs of the program to the company are different from those to the union, it is necessary to consider the results for each group. In this analysis, the union and miners are treated as one group.
2. *Goals.* On what dimensions should we evaluate the Rushton project? We have decided to evaluate the project according to the five goals stated by the participants as the reasons for initiating the Rushton project. These are increased safety, greater productivity, greater earnings, increased job skills, and more positive attitudes toward work.
3. *Time.* The experiment is divided into four time periods. The baseline period runs from January 1973 to December 3, 1973. The first experimental period begins on December 3, 1973 and continues until the national coal strike (November 1, 1974). The third period begins December 1974 and continues until the vote on August 20, 1975. The last period runs from the end of the vote to January 1977. This period includes the expansion of the quality-of-work-life program to the entire mine.

Results for the Company

The following results are presented for the major goals of the company.

Job Attitudes. The intervention was designed to increase favorable attitudes toward work. Analysis of the data from the baseline period to the vote indicates significant changes in attitudes from members in the first experimental section (South) which can be directly attributed to the QWL experiment. The miners felt they had greater opportunity to make decisions on their own and that their jobs offered more variety. They viewed their crews as more productive, cohesive, and innovative (using the other sections as controls). Supervisors were perceived to have become less directive and coworkers more likely to provide recognition. The second experimental section, which really started after the national coal strike, exhibited some of the attitude changes found in the first experimental section. The miners in this section felt their crews were more productive, innovative, and had more say about how the work was to be done. The overall changes, however, were not as strong as in the first experimental section. All during this period (baseline to the vote), there was little if any significant change in the other mining sections or in the other work areas in the mine.

After the vote, the plan was to extend QWL concepts to the whole mine and a training program followed. The "new" autonomous mining sections showed significant increases in the perceived autonomy of their jobs and viewed their work groups as more cohesive or generating more ideas. These changes (after the vote versus before the vote) indicate the program had some effect on attitudes. However, the changes were not as pronounced as they were when the first experimental section was launched.

During this same period, there were some opposite changes in attitudes in the first two experimental sections. In the South section, the miners felt they had lost control over deciding how the work was to be divided up and how the work was to be done. A similar but less pronounced downward shift occurred in the second experimental section. (The reasons for this decline will be analyzed in the next section.)

Safety. A major goal of labor and management was to increase the level of safety. Many indicators, such as accident rate, lost-time accident rate, costs of accidents, frequency of violations, and on-site observations, were used to assess changes in safety behavior over the course of the experiment.

The general conclusion is: In terms of number of accidents, the first experimental section performed better than the other mining sections up to the national coal strike. During the second experimental period, the sections were about the same. Accidents increased from the vote to the end of 1976 but the rate and absolute number were smaller in the first experimental section. Violations are another indicator of safety. During the first experimental period, from December 3, 1973 to the national coal strike, the violation record in the South section was substantially better than in the other two mining sections. From December 1975 on, there were no significant differences in violations across the sections. We also had mining experts rate section safety violations on a scale from 0 to 100. The first experimental section always received the top safety rating. At the end of the experimental period, December 1976, the South section rated 90 to 95, the next section (East) was 88, and the other two sections (one of which was the second experimental section) received a relatively low rating of 70 to 80. We asked all employees in the mine, union, and management their opinions about whether the QWL project had an effect on safety. Both union and management perceived the program as improving the level of safety.

Job Skills. The program was designed to make the men professional miners. This meant that each miner would be familiar with mining and safety practices, know the law, and be able to perform multiple jobs. Training, section conferences, and job switching were the major vehicles to reach the objective.

It is clear from objective measures, such as the number of classroom hours, questionnaire responses from management and union officials, or ratings from outside experts, that the level of job skills increased at Rushton. The change is particularly apparent in the South section. As the experiment progressed, members of the South section were temporarily assigned to other sections when they were short of key personnel. Since the South section had members capable of performing multiple tasks, it was possible to lend skilled miners to other sections and still be able to mine in their own section.

The degree of change in job skills in areas other than South was less because training was more spread out and fewer section conferences were held (a forum for training). Also, the miners' attitudes toward the program were less positive in other sections and this probably detracted from learning.

Productivity. We have carefully examined whether the experimental intervention increased productivity (i.e., tons of raw coal) at Rushton. The most appropriate econometric techniques have been brought to bear on this question. In the analysis, we have focused on the first experimental section (since it had the highest priority of being successful), comparing it against the baseline and other possible control groups.

The general results do not indicate a major increase or decrease in productivity. The fact that productivity did not decrease is significant because there were increases in safety behaviors which often lead to productivity declines. Our best estimate is that there was a slightly positive effect on productivity on the order of 3 to 4 percent. These positive differences are not statistically significant and thus we must be cautious about this estimate.

Extensive cost-benefit analyses have been conducted. The production benefits were weighted against the investment costs of introducing the experiment (e.g., lost time for section conferences) and costs of operating the experiment (e.g., the cost of increased crew size). The results of this analysis indicate that benefits slightly exceeded costs.

The failure to significantly increase productivity is not surprising given the nature of mining and the intervention. First, the mining environment is hostile, and the workers have little control over the physical environment. The effect of noncontrollable variables (i.e., physical conditions) and the related high degree of uncertainty makes it difficult to increase productivity substantially. Second, our on-site observations indicate that the experiment did increase the level of energy the miners put into their work. However, most of that extra effort was devoted to safety rather than productivity goals. Third, the intervention at Rushton did not put a high priority on increasing productivity through joint problem-solving efforts. That is, if we review all the labor-management meetings, there was no major effort to find new ways to increase productivity through changes in the mining process or procedures, or through modifying equipment. Alternative organizational strategies which focused on productivity problem solving might have increased productivity.

Indirect Effects. The experiment had several indirect effects on the internal functioning at Rushton that were not included as major goals in the original QWL document. There was much more communication both horizontally and vertically. Previously, communication was primarily from top to bottom. Because of the experiment, there was a more pronounced follow-up of ideas from bottom to top and also laterally. Coordination between the experimental crews was substantially improved by formalizing intercrew communication while crews were switching. This was a new behavior brought about by the experimental intervention. The experiment also served to identify possible managerial talent; several miners in the experiment moved into managerial positions. Also, it served to provide special training to managers who were not the initial focus of the intervention. The program's orientation of learning and experimenting encouraged other organizational changes (e.g., a new preventive maintenance program) which were not related to the intervention.

On the negative side, the program did increase levels of stress for the first-line supervisors and other members of the mine management. (This issue is discussed in detail in the last section of this chapter.)

Results for the Union and Miners

The following results are presented for the major goals of the union.

Earnings. Since the program paid top wage rate, some members in the experiment received wages over and above the regular contract wage.

Safety. As previously discussed, safety improved (see preceding discussion).

Job Skills. Miners in the experiment increased their job skills (see preceding discussion).

Job Attitudes. There was a significant increase in positive attitudes in the first experimental section and then a slight decline after the vote; some positive changes occurred in the other sections (see above discussion).

Indirect Effects. The experimental intervention did not affect the organizational structure of the local union or the rate of participation in union affairs. It did, however, increase the level of conflict within the union because of the pay differentials in the experimental sections.

There were no changes in traditional indicators of labor–management relations at Rushton such as number or content of grievances. Walkouts, a common problem at most mines, are another indicator of labor–management relations. During the first experimental period (December 1973 to December 1974), there were no internally initiated walkouts. An impending long national coal strike later in 1974 probably reduced to some extent workers' propensities to walk out and lose wages during 1974. However, the program did create a new understanding between labor and management which also contributed to the absence of walkouts. This came about as labor and management were able to meet together frequently in a new social arena that was not characterized by the traditional adversary relationship. In late 1975 and 1976, the rate of walkouts increased to the baseline level. None of the incidents initiating the walkouts were related to quality-of-work-life program issues. However, the labor–management mechanisms of the program were not able to contain the walkouts.

REASONS FOR CHANGE

Clearly, there were changes at Rushton — particularly in job attitudes, job skills, and safety. These changes occurred in the first experimental section during the experimental period from December 3, 1973, to August 1975. Why did these changes occur? What factors contributed to these changes? Are there any principles that could be generalized to other settings?

The following two factors could have made a difference but probably are not major reasons for the change:

1. Members of the first section volunteered to participate, and this might have led to a selection bias. We were aware of this problem and questioned these people about their decision. Most of the men volunteered to get more money or to leave sections with poorer physical conditions. Their motivation to participate in the experiment was not based on their interest in the ideological aspects (e.g., greater autonomy) of the experiment. Indeed, most knew little about the new program. Since practical matters (e.g., more money) rather than ideological considerations affected their decision to par-

ticipate, the volunteer selection bias really does not explain why behavior changed in the first experimental section.

2. Sometimes subjects in an experiment react because they are in an experiment rather than because of any features of the experiment (this is known as the Hawthorne effect). However, the experiment at Rushton covered a 20-month period. It is unlikely that the reactive features of an experiment would persist long enough to explain the results we have reported.

The following four factors are probably better explanations of the changes that took place in the first experimental section.

1. The knowledge of the workers about mining and safety practices was substantially increased through formal training, section conferences, and foremen's meetings. The important point is not that lots of training was offered but that it was absorbed by the men. This newly acquired knowledge was an important condition for the changes that occurred. Knowledge about safety laws is a precondition for improving safety behavior.

2. The experiment removed many of the negative incentives attached to work behavior. A major problem in mining is close supervision and constant pressure for production from the foremen. The work of a miner is relatively autonomous, even without an experimental program, and these supervisory practices increased tension at work. By changing the foreman's role to concentrate on safety, and buffering the foreman from production pressures from his boss, the source of tension between supervisor and worker was removed. As one miner said: "There's no one breathing down your back any more — you make your own decisions."

3. Opportunities for feedback were increased. New social arrangements in the form of section conferences and mini-labor–management meetings provided frequent feedback to the workers about their performance (e.g., accidents, violations, production costs). Now the miners knew how they were doing. Previous to the change, this type of information was only infrequently given to foremen. Without feedback, it is difficult to change one's behavior.

4. The QWL program brought about a new set of rewards for workers commensurate with the greater levels of responsibility they had assumed. If we look at the interview protocols, there is a shift from talking about "the" crew or section to talking about "our" crew and section. Greater pay was tied into taking this greater responsibility. The section conferences and other meetings provided a direct opportunity for management, union officers, and the research team to recognize and reinforce changes in the workers' behavior in respect to items such as safety or intercrew coordination. Through job switching, workers had the opportunity to develop new skills. As one miner said: "I don't have to just run the car all the time . . . yesterday I did brattices (ventilation work). . . . I've learned how to lay track." Through the committee membership, some of the workers

were able to test out their leadership skills. Two committee members from the experimental section eventually became foremen. The point is that the structure of the program created a new set of rewards — some related to membership in the experimental group, others to the worker's performance — which reinforced change.

These were changes that affected individual miners. However, changes were going on simultaneously to make the section in which the individual miner worked more cohesive. The more cohesive the group, the more, in turn, it could affect the workers' behavior. The changes in crew and section described below had a marked effect on individual performance in the first experimental period in the South section:

1. The program tried to reduce conflict among the crews by providing greater opportunity to communicate (and thus coordinate) as shifts were changing. Section conferences and mini-labor–management committee meetings were used to resolve problems between crews (e.g., who should do clean-up). Also, there was an attempt to change the basis of performance evaluation from the crew to the section. The rationale was that section-wide evaluation should minimize within-crew competition. All these program changes created an opportunity for cohesiveness to develop.

2. The autonomous-work-group concept led to greater interaction among the men, greater opportunities to make joint decisions, and greater control over their environment. This, in turn, led to more positive feelings about work and stronger identification with the experimental program. Again, this is another necessary condition for the development of a cohesive group.

3. The first experimental section was launched with an intensive set of meetings. This helped create a strong section identity, which also increased the feelings of cohesiveness.

The stronger feelings of group cohesiveness developed because of changes in the experiment which, in turn, placed new forces on the workers (1) to adhere to the concepts of the program (one crew asked that its boss be removed because he was being too authoritarian), and (2) to work toward the program objectives (e.g., safety).

We can summarize our explanation of why the experimental program caused changes in the work behavior at Rushton by looking at safety. There is no question that the program led to a substantial improvement in safety behavior. The workers invested a great deal of energy in bringing it to the experimental section and keeping in compliance with the law.

What caused this change in behavior? The training program provided knowledge about safety practices, but this is common to all other safety programs. What distinguished the Rushton program was that the motivational state of the workers also was changed. Making the foreman's role safety- rather than production-oriented minimized the negative reinforcement workers usually received from their bosses when they wanted to do safety versus production work. The meetings provided formal feedback on how safety behavior matched safety goals. The meetings also provided a problem-solving arena where new safety practices were developed and provided a direct opportunity to positively reinforce good safety behavior. This is absent in most traditional safety programs. Lastly, the autonomous work group concept increased feelings of worker responsibility for achieving high safety levels.

WHY DID THE PROGRAM LOSE ITS EFFECTIVENESS?

Although the QWL project at Rushton was initially successful, it was not sustained over time. Program changes and policies can be expected to evolve over time, but the argument here is that Rushton's program changes and policies have not remained viable institutions.

To analyze why this came about, we will separate it into two parts: First, why was the change that had successful consequences in the first experimental section not sustained over time; and, second, why was the project not successfully extended to the rest of the mine? For both questions, the major reasons will be summarized in order to keep this chapter a reasonable length.

Why Was the Change in the First Experimental Section Not Sustained?

Before we look at some of the reasons, it is useful to provide some evidence that QWL effects in the first experimental section declined. In August 1976, when we conducted our last attitude survey, questions were asked about whether a QWL program was still in operation and what the concepts of the program meant to the participants. The majority of respondents in the first experimental section reported a decline in the QWL effort. Most discussed the program in the past rather than the present tense. During this three-year period on-site observations of the sections have been conducted. The last on-site report indicated a decline in interest in the QWL experiment. Also, as part of the evaluation effort, we have developed transcripts of all the major meetings. If we compare the beginning meetings to the 1976 meetings, there was a substantial change in the interest in the program. Many other sources of evidence confirm the decline.[4]

The following points attempt to explain why the decline occurred:

1. The meetings, particularly the section conferences, were curtailed in 1975 and even more so in 1976. These meetings were a very important part of the program. They were a major source of feedback, an arena for problem solving, a means to ensure intercrew cooperation, and a mechanism for providing direct reinforcement and recognition. Moreover, the development of a section identification was built on experiences in these meetings. By curtailing the meetings, an important source of motivation was withdrawn from the South section. One reason the meetings were curtailed was because new events were capturing the time of the research team. The unexpected opening of 5 Butt as an experimental section in 1974 represented a major time commitment. Planning for a mine-wide program (April to September 1975) represented the second major commitment. Extending the project mine-wide required another major commitment. Given a limited set of resources, the research team could not deal with both the new demands and the South section. Another reason for the curtailment of the South meetings was that management was resistant to any additional meetings because of the proliferation of meetings that did occur and that affected production in 1975. What is not clear is why there was no concerted effort to provide attention and reinforcement to the South section, especially after the vote. For example, there could have been short meetings led by at least one member of the research team in the section on a crew-by-crew basis. This would have provided the necessary contact without substantially affecting production. We feel this reduction in the number of South section meetings substantially changed the motivators available to workers in that section and subsequently their behavior. Other mechanisms to sustain the South section were available within the constraints provided by management.

2. The vote rejecting a mine-wide autonomous work-group program clearly reduced the viability of the program in the South section. From its inception in December 1973, the South section had been the object of criticism from the other miners who claimed that pay rates and other privileges enjoyed by the experimental section were inequitable. Initially, this hostile environment probably contributed to the solidarity of the South section. However, the vote was a statement by the union membership to stop the program. While the management attempted to extend the program to other areas of the mine, there was a good deal of ambiguity for members in the South section as to whether they were an autonomous group or not. This ambiguity contributed to the decline in the experiment's effects. What is interesting is that there was no concerted effort after the vote to save the South section.

3. While there was a surprising amount of stability (i.e., low turnover) in the first experimental section, there were changes in personnel. Two of the

foremen left for other jobs at the mine. (They were replaced through promotion by men in the experimental section.) Other workers also moved to more responsible jobs (e.g., belt examiner). These job movements and the subsequent replacements were natural occurrences. The problem was that the replacements did not have the same training experiences as the original experimental members and that there was no special training for the replacements. The consequence was that the new workers tended to dilute further the original impact of the QWL program.

4. An analysis of the section conferences held in 1975 and 1976 for the South experimental section indicates that many of the miners perceived these meetings as ineffectual. The basic complaint was that a lot of talking occurred in the meetings but that few decisions were actually implemented. This reaction by the workers could simply be a symptom of their growing discontent with the program. On the other hand, one of the basic themes of the meetings over the last three years was the problem of following through on decisions made in the meetings. There had never been a good feedback mechanism to report on whether actions taken in the meetings were actually instituted in the mine. Thus, there was no formal basis for corrective action.

5. The South section did not operate in a vacuum. It was influenced by the activities of the other sections. If the plan to extend the QWL program mine-wide had been successful, many of the work practices and values developed during the initial experimental period might have been maintained.

6. The original Rushton agreement called for a gain-sharing program. Discussions for developing such a program began in 1974. By the end of 1974 no program had been approved. It is clear from our interviews and discussions with the workers that the failure to produce a gain-sharing program contributed to negative attitudes toward the entire QWL program.

Why Was the Experiment Not Successfully Extended to the Entire Mine?

By the first quarter of 1976, the quality-of-work-life program at Rushton had been extended mine-wide. As we have noted in the results section, the new intervention initially had some effect on attitudes and behavior, but the effect was not as pronounced as it had been in the first experimental section. At the end of 1976, however, the data from our periodic interviews, on-site observations, and the labor–management committee meetings indicate the program was not a viable set of institutions. If the president of Rushton withdrew from active involvement, the program would not continue. Program institutions, such as the labor–management committees, did not have a life of their own that would enable them to continue as integral parts of Rushton's operations without their initiator and chief supporter (i.e., the president). There was no person at the mine, equally respected by management and labor, who could administer the program after the external research team left. Most important, our interviews with management and union leaders as well as workers in the first experimental sections indicated that they did not see a "program" going on at Rushton at the end of 1976.

The following factors attempt to account for the fact that the program was not extended successfully to the whole mine:

1. The "no" vote on August 1975 against a plant-wide QWL program was a clear statement against extending the autonomous-work-group concept. The 79 to 75 vote was not close in the following sense: All the members of the first experimental section, most of those in the second section, and some of the other members associated with the labor–management committee probably accounted for most of the "yes" votes. Those rejecting the program, then, represented almost all of those voting who were not directly involved. That is, the majority of those not in the program and to whom the program was to be extended voted against it. Why did the vote come out the way it did? Again there are many complicated reasons, but the following are probably the most critical:

- There were no opinion leaders to support the extension of the program. With the exception of the president, many members of management were indifferent or opposed to it. The bosses in the nonautonomous sections (as of September 1975) were also indifferent or opposed. Within the union leadership, support for the program was mixed. It is fair to say that there was no one from management or from the union who served as a leader or advocate for the program.
- Some members of the work force, because of prior labor–management conflicts, expressed low levels of trust toward management. Rushton is a relatively young mine (1965) and its current organization was preceded by a bitter conflict. Feelings from that earlier conflict still persisted and affected the acceptance of QWL ideas.
- The original quality-of-work-life document and program (December 1973) created inequities within the mine. Members of the first two experimental sections were getting paid higher wages for the same work. The negative feelings this generated led to general resistance to the proposed mine-wide program.
- The document drawn up for the mine-wide program contained provisions different from the earlier document, and these generated conflict for those miners not yet in the program. One of the new provisions required that a miner meet certain qualifications before receiving the higher rate of pay. Despite the fact that almost all the miners met the qualification requirements, the "qualification test" was perceived as unfair by the miners since it was not required of the first experimental section.
- The process of explaining the new program was ineffective. The com-

municators in the first series of "communication" meetings were perceived as the "professors from Penn State." They were not well known by the members of the nonautonomous sections, and it is fair to say that they were not seen as highly credible communicators. The second series of meetings was conducted by union officers only. However, none of them could substantially influence union opinion; in addition, in the meeting we observed, the union leaders did not make strong personal commitments toward the program. The nature of the communication itself detracted from the program. First, the program document was complex; few miners read it. Second, most of the communications were one-sided — that is, they emphasized the benefits to the workers. This one-sided communication generated feelings of skepticism. Third, there were too many people in the early meetings to permit effective communication. Another difficulty was in the model of persuasion which depended on communicating some very abstract and complex ideas and concepts. There were few opportunities for members in the nonautonomous sections to gain some concrete understanding of the program. There was an exchange of foremen (into the autonomous sections) but this occurred late in the diffusion process and only a few participated.

2. Management's decision to initiate a mine-wide QWL program in August 1975, despite the vote, probably reduced the effectiveness of extending the program. A basic theme from the beginning of the experiment was joint decision making and ownership of the project. Management's unilateral decision to continue the program after the vote alienated some members of the nonautonomous section despite the fact that the union officers were willing to cooperate with management. The degree of alienation is difficult to assess since it was not possible to reinterview the miners after the vote and since the company's offer of top wages plus two extra support people per crew probably minimized any immediate negative reactions. From the data we were able to gather later, those who were opposed to the program held their views more strongly after management's unilateral action.

3. The inducements for the workers to participate in the program were less than when the experiment began in 1973. Because of a change in the national coal contract in 1974, more members of a crew received the top rate, so fewer crew members benefited from the top-rate provision in the mine-wide program. Also, the expansion of the program on a mine-wide basis required hiring additional miners, most of whom were relatively inexperienced. These miners, often referred to as "yellow hats," filled the extra support positions in the (formerly) nonautonomous sections. Their lack of experience complicated the process of setting up the new program. In the original experimental section, the additional support people were experienced miners.

4. The demands of a mine-wide introduction in five different work areas minimized the effectiveness of setting up the program. The training meetings were spread out over long periods of time, and each received only a portion of the research team's time. In the first experimental introduction, there was an intensive series of training sessions and section conferences. This helped develop an identification with the program and the section and, thus, a commitment to the concepts of the program. We feel that the strategy of simultaneously introducing the program rather than working intensively with one section at a time seriously detracted from effective installation of a QWL program at Rushton.

5. A mine-wide program requires the cooperation of all levels of management. A basic theme throughout the interviews collected in the last quarter of 1975 and throughout 1976 was that certain members of the mine management who were critical of the installation of the program were uncooperative. Although these individuals did not support the program from the beginning, the effect of their lack of support was not critical until the program was extended to the entire mine.

6. Again, the lack of development of a gain-sharing program contributed to negative attitudes toward the QWL program.

CONCLUSION: CRITICAL ISSUES IN DESIGNING AND IMPLEMENTING QWL EXPERIMENTS

In conclusion, I will highlight a set of critical issues that bear on the successful design and implementation of a QWL experiment. These observations are drawn from the Rushton project and from other experience.[5]

Statement of Explicit Goals

If labor and management intend to join together in a quality-of-work-life experiment, it is necessary for them to state an explicit set of goals or objectives that will guide both the design and evaluation of the project. This is also a way to "reality test" the intentions of the participants.

The Acceptance of Common vs. Complementary Goals

Common goals are those that are equally accepted by labor and management. Safety is an example of a common goal at Rushton. Complementary goals are trade-off goals, for example, productivity and wages. In this case, each goal represents the interest of one party, and by achieving one goal the other can be satisfied. Common goals are more congruent with joint problem-solving behavior — a necessary ingredient in all QWL experiments —

than complementary goals. Determining the appropriate trade-off between productivity and wages will more likely evoke adversary behaviors which are incongruent in QWL projects. Therefore, QWL projects built solely on complementary goals will probably be less successful than those that include common goals as well.

The Specificity of QWL Program Characteristics

Most change programs have some new organizational form and procedures associated with them. We are interested in how formal these arrangements are. For example, are meetings scheduled in advance? Are procedures written down? In general, we have found that programs with more formal mechanisms and procedures attain higher levels of institutionalization.

Sociotechnical Orientation

Most QWL experiments are directed toward increasing productivity and the quality of working life by restructuring the social and technical systems of an organization. One concern we have is that many of the consultants to QWL projects are primarily trained in changing the social system rather than the technology. Even at Rushton, where a mining engineer was part of the research team, there were no major interventions in the technical system by the research team or by the experimental groups. There were attempts, however, to improve the communication systems within the mine and to improve planning. Both of these activities should bear on the effectiveness of the technical system. We are arguing, however, that there was little emphasis on technical problem solving by labor and management to increase productivity. There was little planned experimentation going on in the section to improve the technical system. We feel that more balance between technical and social innovations is necessary if a project is to achieve its dual goals of increased productivity and improved quality of working life.

Design of Labor-Management Committees

Labor-management committees are an integral part of any QWL project. They are responsible for the overall design, implementation, and monitoring of a program. However, little attention has been paid to the design of these committees. What is an optimal size? What should the membership be and how should it change over time?

At Rushton, the membership on the major labor-management committee was fairly stable. Except for natural job movement and changes in union offices (via an election), the membership remained much the same throughout the experiment. Also, the union officers on the committee worked on outside (e.g., maintenance) rather than inside mining jobs. This situation probably limited the diffusion of the project. Since members of the nonautonomous sections did not play a role in the design and monitoring of the first experiment, it is not surprising that there was a good deal of misunderstanding about the experimental concepts at the time of the vote.

Another issue concerned the place of union-management problems (e.g., grievances) versus quality-of-work-life problems in labor-management committee discussions. After the "no" vote at Rushton, discussions about grievances took a more dominant position in the discussions of the major labor–management committee. These discussions had a more adversarial orientation, and they precluded work on QWL problems.

The above issues have been raised to demonstrate the importance of the design of labor–management committees. Unfortunately, the design and functioning of such committees have received little attention. Obviously, there are no easy prescriptions for the form these committees should take. What we think is necessary is an explicit consideration of alternative designs of labor-management committees. Some of the topics that should be analyzed include: (1) the goals of the committee (problem solving, policymaking, coordination); (2) the size of the group (which should be related to the goals); (3) the place of traditional union–management topics (i.e., grievances) in a QWL labor-management group and mechanisms to control discussions of grievances versus quality-of-work-life matters; and (4) the kind of training that is necessary to make QWL groups effective.

System-Wide Change versus Pilot Projects

The strategy in some QWL projects is to introduce pilot projects in one work area, shelter the intervention, operate it until initial success is demonstrated, and then diffuse the QWL activities throughout the organization. This strategy is typically used when resources (e.g., the consultants' time) are limited or when the consultants want to learn about the intervention in one area before extending it to other areas. At Rushton, there was a major focus on the first experimental section. A logical consequence was that the research team became less in touch with the rest of the mine, and the rest of the mine became more alienated toward the experimental section because of its perceived advantages (e.g., more pay).

Another strategy would have been to introduce change across the whole mine from the outset. This would have minimized the alienation and counterimplementation strategies that appeared in the Rushton experience. The problem with this strategy, however, is that it requires more resources.

While there is no easy solution to this issue, the following course of action is desirable: Whenever possible, introduce change system-wide. Pilot or experimental projects are easy targets for counterimplementation strategies. If intervention must be at a subunit level because of limited resources or organizational size, a diffusion strategy should be incorporated into the initial change effort and should be initiated early in the change effort.

Consultant's Role

Many QWL efforts will require initially the services of consultants external to the focal organization. The key issue is whether the organization becomes dependent on the consultants which was in some sense true at Rushton. If the organization develops its own capability to initiate and create change, the QWL activities will be powerful and viable.

Congruence Between Organizational Change and Organizational Values

Implicit or explicit in most QWL programs is a set of values such as autonomy, personal control, responsibility, democracy, and participation. Sometimes, these values are incongruent with the traditional values of the organization. The greater the incongruency between the new QWL values and the existing organizational values, the more likely the change will be rejected and the less likely it will remain viable over time.

Problem Areas in Implementing Change

Introducing a quality-of-work-life experiment in an organization is a complex task. There are bound to be many unanticipated consequences. In this section, we will identify some of those problem areas. These are derived from the Rushton experience but have appeared in other QWL experiments.[6]

First-line Supervision. A basic theme in most QWL projects is giving workers more control over their environment — usually in the form of more responsibility. It has been argued that changes in control do not really redistribute responsibilities from one segment of the organization to another; rather, the total influence structure is expanded. However, many jobs are changed and stress on the job is increased for certain positions. The first-line supervisor is initially affected the most. At Rushton, the foreman's traditional activities of supervising production were withdrawn and responsibility for new and unfamiliar activities (e.g., planning) was introduced. As a consequence, levels of job stress increased.

Meetings were introduced at Rushton to help the foremen make the transition to their new roles. These meetings served to alleviate stress and clarify the new job. However, to introduce changes in the foreman's role, direct on-the-job training is necessary. The foreman, in conjunction with a trainer, needs to practice and receive feedback on these new behaviors. This was never fully accomplished at Rushton.

Middle Management. Changes at the section and first-line supervisor level at Rushton reverberated throughout the organization. Middle and upper management roles also had to change. Often, as was the case in Rushton, these positions are not integrated early enough into the change program. Nevertheless, people in these positions experience greater ambiguity and stress, similar to that identified for first-line supervisors. This can affect performance and the acceptance of the experiment. The critical issue seems to be that, when introducing a total system change, interventions must occur simultaneously at different organizational levels.

Individual Differences. A problem at Rushton and in all QWL projects is how to introduce organizational change and, at the same time, be responsive to individual differences. The change program at Rushton called for greater levels of responsibility and autonomy, and this did affect worker behavior. These changes, however, were not welcomed by all workers. Some preferred a highly structured work environment; others did not want to switch to jobs that they did not feel competent to perform. The challenge to QWL experiments is to introduce a general program that is tailored to individual differences. The Rushton mine-wide document acknowledged the workers' right to not participate in an autonomous work-group framework. However, a specific mechanism to permit this choice to be made was never implemented at Rushton or other sites. No one mechanism would be suitable for all sites; but, nevertheless, an explicit mechanism tailored to each experiment needs to be developed.

Union Leader–Member Relationships. The labor-management committee is the principal mechanism for integrating union and management efforts in most QWL projects. Through frequent meetings, participants have reported developing a better understanding of each other — a consequence which should facilitate traditional labor–management negotiations. On the other hand, the frequent association between management and union officers outside the traditional collective bargaining arrangements did raise feelings of distrust in the union membership toward their leaders at Rushton. This, in turn, encouraged the leaders to behave in any way that was dysfunctional to the program but which enhanced their position with their men.

Member Relations. At Rushton, the change was introduced in a particular section. This strategy had two implications for the internal functioning of the local union. First, the experimental section was different from the other sections in terms of pay for the same work and other resources. These differences generated feelings of inequity which led to conflict among the union members.

A second unanticipated consequence was that the experiment created a new potential power structure within the local union. In the Rushton project, some of the experimental groups voted en masse at union meetings; in the past, most of these men had not attended meetings. The point is not that this emerging power structure was good or bad but that it represented a possible challenge to the existing power structure and, thus, a potential source of conflict, insecurity, and resistance.

Local-International Relations. Most activity in quality-of-work-life experiments such as Rushton occurs at the local level, while the final legitimation comes from the international level. This poses an interesting dilemma. On one hand, at the local level, union and management have a mandate to innovate. On the other hand, and especially if the new labor–management arrangements are considered far beyond the boundaries which could be incorporated in a future collective bargaining agreement, the international may view the local QWL project as only experimental and temporary — quite independently of the success of that project. Without long-run legitimation, the local project is unlikely to survive. This can result in conflict between the local and international if the local wants the project to continue.

Another unanticipated consequence is that political activities within the international can affect the viability of the local project — again, quite independently of the success of that project. The political battles in the UMWA headquarters affected the degree of support the international provided to the Rushton project. In turn, this probably affected the successful expansion of the program. When the international staff contributed to the Rushton project (e.g., in drawing up the mine-wide document), the contributions were viewed as positive by all parties. However, the total amount of support was quite low.

It should be noted that relations between corporate headquarters and local plants can parallel international–local union relations. This was not true at Rushton where, although the mine is part of a larger corporation, most of the decisions were made by the mine president. In other organizational arrangements with more centralized decision making, conflict between the local plant quality-of-work-life activities and corporate policy may occur.

Making the Change Last

One of the most critical issues in all QWL experiments is whether the new forms of organization will persist over time. Once the research team leaves the organization or the novelty of the project subsides, there is a tendency for behavior in the organization to revert back to a state of equilibrium that existed prior to the experiment. This problem of maintaining change has been a major theme in our discussion of the Rushton experiment.

What conditions facilitate the persistence of a change program over time? While there is no simple answer to this question, the following factors are probably important.

Training. QWL programs will last if training is initiated *over time* rather than just in the early phase of the effort. Training needs to be directed at new organizational entrants as well as existing organizational members. At Rushton, the decline of the section conferences paralleled the decline of the program.

Commitment. QWL programs will last if there is total system commitment. At Rushton, there was commitment at the top and at the employee level, but not at the level of middle management. Also, opportunities for recommitment should be provided during the life of the project.[7] At Rushton, the vote against the program was clearly a sign of lack of commitment from the work force.

Reward System. For QWL programs to last, there needs to be some balance between monetary and other rewards (e.g., autonomy). Also, problems of inequity need to be minimized.

Diffusion. For a QWL program to last, it needs to be quickly diffused in the relevant organizational unit. At Rushton, there was delay in diffusion and the process was not successfully implemented.

Feedback and Change. For change to be successfully maintained, there must be some feedback mechanism to report on whether the new forms of work behavior are being performed, and some corrective mechanism to recalibrate the changed behaviors. At Rushton, these feedback and recalibration mechanisms were not in place.

CONCLUSION

The goal of this chapter has been to provide an objective account of the Rushton quality-of-work-life experiment. A description of Rushton was presented to provide a context for the experiment. Then the features of the experimental intervention were delineated. Some of the critical decisions were enumerated to indicate that an organizational experiment is really a dynamic series of interventions rather than a single change. Decisions about starting up a new experimental section, and developing a mine-wide program were some of the major decisions that shaped the Rushton experiment, but these were not planned when the experiment was launched.

The results of the experiment point to both benefits and costs for the company and union. The better safety record, positive job attitudes, and higher level of job skills benefit the company. For these benefits there were costs in setting up and running the program.[8] The union also realized benefits in terms of better safety, increased earnings, and more training for its members. The "costs" to the union related more to increased tension within the union than to financial costs.

It is really up to the reader to make the final judgment about whether the cost-benefit ratio justifies participation in QWL experiments. My position is that it is too early to use a hard cost-benefit calculation to determine the feasibility of QWL experiments. Rushton was a new venture. It was a high-risk project that tried to substantially reorganize how work was done. There were few, if any, precedents to guide the Rushton project. It was truly an experiment.

What we should learn from the Rushton experiment is not *what* worked but *why* it worked — not *what* did not change (e.g., productivity) but *why* it did not change. We now know some of the major problems in conducting QWL experiments and possible approaches to resolve these problems. The last part of this report has dealt with these matters. The point is, if people can learn and build from the Rushton experiment to a new level of organizational experimentation, then the project and this report will have been of value.

NOTES

1. This is a condensed version, which highlights only the major events. See Paul S. Goodman, *Assessing Organizational Change: The Rushton Quality of Work Life Experiment* (New York: Wiley-Interscience, 1979), for a more detailed account.

2. While an agreement was being developed between Rushton Mining Company and the United Mine Workers of America (UMWA), a parallel agreement was being developed between the UMWA and a second coal mine. The latter mine differed from Rushton in that it was larger and publicly owned. This two-mine strategy represented an explicit attempt by the research team to focus on the industry rather than on a single company. This report will examine only the Rushton experience. The local union at the second mine eventually decided not to participate (see E. Trist, G. Susman, and G. Brown, "An Experiment in Autonomous Working in an American Underground Coal Mine," *Human Relations*, 1977, pp. 201–36.

3. The section on "Results" is a nontechnical review of the results from the Rushton experiment. Detailed models, analyses, and tables on which this review is based are available for the interested reader in Goodman, *Assessing Organizational Change*.

4. Ibid.

5. Paul S. Goodman and Edward E. Lawler, III, "New Forms of Work Organisation in the

United States," in *New Forms of Work Organisation*, Vol. 1 (Geneva: International Labour Office, 1979); Goodman, *Assessing Organizational Change*; Paul S. Goodman and J.W. Dean, Jr., "The Process of Institutionalization," in *Change in Organizations*, edited by Paul S. Goodman (San Francisco: Jossey-Bass, 1982); and Paul S. Goodman, and J.W. Dean, Jr., "Why Productivity Efforts Fail," paper presented at the American Psychological Association Convention, Los Angeles, 1981.

    6. Goodman and Lawler, "New Forms of Work Organisation in the United States."

    7. Paul S. Goodman and J.W. Dean, Jr. "Why Productivity Efforts Fail."

    8. Paul S. Goodman, *Assessing Organizational Change*.

11.
The Topeka Work System: Optimistic Visions, Pessimistic Hypotheses, and Reality

Richard E. Walton

INTRODUCTION

Seven members from General Foods' pet food plant in Topeka, Kansas, appeared as a panel before the International Conference on the Quality of Work Life in Toronto, Canada, on August 31, 1981, and discussed the history of their work organization. During this presentation and in my subsequent interviews, these individuals confirmed that the innovative work system installed in 1970 was continuing to function along the highly participative lines established then. They also described recent renewal activities, which had reversed the decline in member commitment that I had observed in 1976 and reported in print.[1]

Many conference participants were surprised to learn that the work system was still operating, in general, according to its founding principles, because they had heard that Topeka had "gone traditional." This perplexed the Topeka delegates, most of whom had been in the plant throughout the last decade. The system had indeed encountered many problems, including friction with corporate headquarters, loss of its founding managers, and rivalry between the original plant and a second plant built on the Topeka site. But these difficulties, and the moderate decline in commitment which accompanied them, *never* altered two basic "bottom-line" realities for stakeholders in the Topeka work system: first, the plant continued to be unusually productive and profitable due to its work organization; and second, it remained a superior workplace because of its self-management, pay-for-knowledge, and egalitarian provisions.

Early accounts of Topeka have been authored by Lyman Ketchum.[2] My own detailed description of the Topeka design and a systematic analysis of the chronological history of the first six years also exists in published form, and I will not repeat that material here.[3] Rather, I will seek to put the Topeka story into perspective and in the process, bring its history up to date. My primary focus is on the work system of the original plant on the Topeka site, the dry dog food plant.

At the time it was launched, the Topeka work system was seen as a radical departure from customary practice, an innovation invested with the hopes and dreams of those who planned it. In the first part of the chapter, subsequent reality will be compared with elements of the planners' optimistic visions. The Topeka system was widely publicized in print and frequently used for illustrative purposes in educational seminars, especially in the early 1970s. While the system inspired many observers, it drew the fire of others, who directed a broad array of criticisms at its approach. In the second part of the chapter, the pessimistic hypotheses of the early critics of Topeka will be examined in light of the history of that plant and of other similar systems.

THE OPTIMISTIC VISIONS OF THE PLANNERS

The Topeka system was first conceived in 1968, just about the time the media began to identify growing worker malaise in the United States and Europe—the "blue-collar blues." Rates of absenteeism were up sharply, and incidents of sabotage were on the rise. Several managers from the General Foods (GF) plant in Kankakee, Illinois, had been asked to plan a new pet food plant to be located in Topeka, Kansas. I joined that planning group, which included Lyman Ketchum, who had responsibility for both the Kankakee and Topeka plants; Edward Dulworth, the person named to manage the new Topeka plant; and a few others who would play key roles in the new plant. Both Ketchum and Dulworth later left GF and currently serve as experts on work restructuring—but that is getting ahead of the story.

We were resolved to create a very different type of workplace—one that would be extraordinarily effective in business terms and that would, to an exceptional degree, meet the evolving needs and expectations of the new work force. Our plant design was regarded as radical and counterintuitive at the time because we acted contrary to the received logic, initiated with the Industrial Revolution, by which productivity increases were sought through a progressive fragmentation of tasks, deskilling of jobs, separation of planning and implementation, control of the individual worker, reliance on external and formal controls, and pay pegged to the specific job. We proposed a work system in which normally separate jobs were combined to create whole tasks, skill requirements were deliberately increased, teams were made collectively accountable for a segment of the work flow, pride and peer pressure were substituted in part for external and formal controls, and pay was geared to what a worker knew and could do. Supervisors were to facilitate and lead, not direct and control. We tried to minimize status differences, rather than following the customary practice of using them to reinforce hierarchy. The plant organization was not to be a "pure" democracy, but it was to be highly participative, providing workers with a voice regarding a very broad range of matters that affected them.

Today these design concepts are not radical — in fact, they have become the conventional wisdom of the growing numbers of managers and (some) union officials who have subsequently designed new plant organization with both productivity and quality of work life in mind. But the fact that it was a radical departure in 1970 has helped shape the history of Topeka.

Back to the vision itself.

1. We believed that if the projected work design were accompanied by a clearly articulated philosophy which emphasized human development as well as business performance and if the plant were led by managers with the requisite attitudes and skills, the result would be a work system characterized by high human commitment.

2. We envisioned that workers would value the variety in work, the freedom from close supervision, the membership in work teams, the opportunity to learn more jobs, the managerial perspective which they would acquire, the openness to speak their minds, and the opportunity to exercise influence. We believed that, as a result, absenteeism and turnover would be relatively low, human skills and abilities would be better utilized, and economic performance would be superior to other General Foods plants and to the performance expected by upper management when they approved the capital expenditure for the new plant.

3. We, the planners, also expected that, while high enthusiasm would be easier to generate initially than to maintain, it would be possible to institutionalize and perpetuate the unique patterns of behavior that were generated. We assumed that the organization would have a high capability for self-diagnosis and for making midcourse corrections.

4. We assumed that the roles we had designed for first-line supervisors, called "team leaders," would be challenging and satisfying.

5. We envisioned that the managers in the plant would find the task of establishing and managing this pioneering work system personally satisfying and professionally rewarding; and that, if the system proved to be an effective one, managers in the plant would be given choice promotional opportunities elsewhere within the corporation. This vision was linked to another one — diffusion.

6. We envisioned the Topeka system as a pilot organization which, if successful, would be endorsed by upper management and extended to

other plants and facilities. This diffusion would be a confirmation of the practices of the Topeka organization. We did not give much thought to the potential influence of the plant beyond the General Foods organization.

The first four visions were generally fulfilled or overfulfilled, and the hopes of the second two were disappointed. We will explore how and why.

The Vision of High Commitment

Before we explore how effectively the Topeka organization generated and maintained commitment, let us consider why commitment is crucially important in this type of organization.

The distinguishing feature of the Topeka work system is that a high commitment by workers is the basic presumption of the design. I have elsewhere used the label "high-commitment work system" to describe a system designed to generate high commitment, to utilize fully high commitment for gains (human and business), and to depend upon high commitment for its effectiveness.[4] In contrast, a conventional plant that provides close supervision, simplified tasks, narrow job descriptions, detailed procedures, and formal controls is designed to function adequately even when member commitment is moderate to low. It provides relatively few ways for the organization to benefit from high commitment, and it has relatively low power to elicit such commitment.

As part of a research project completed a few years ago, I attempted to reconstruct the historical trend lines of commitment in four innovative work systems, including Topeka.[5] My judgments were based on clinical observations, gathered during periodic visits to each plant, including Topeka. I interviewed, as well as worked with, fairly representative samples of each plant's population and observed a variety of ongoing activities that characterized the plant's day-to-day working patterns. My assessment of the Topeka plant's trend line for worker commitment through 1976, when I last visited the site, is represented by the solid line in figure 11.1. The dotted line indicates my estimate of the trend between 1976 and 1981, as reported by the seven Topeka individuals interviewed in September 1981 and confirmed by other observers knowledgeable about the plant. During the first year and a half, commitment rose to an extraordinary level, and it continued at a relatively high level over the next ten years. However, a significant decline and recovery took place around the system's third anniversary, and then the system suffered a gradual decline until about 1978 when an upward trend set in. How do we explain these ups and downs?

Why did extraordinarily high commitment develop in the first few years? This set a very high index of commitment, a fact which must be borne in

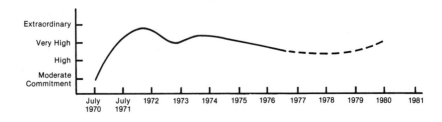

———————— Based on periodic visits to plant.
– – – – – – – Based on interview of seven members of Topeka organization in 1981.

Note: "Moderate commitment" is intended to describe the kind of commitment found in a conventional plant that is generally well managed and is progressive in its personnel problems and practices. A "moderate" level of commitment is below what I judge to be adequate to sustain over the long term the type of work structure employed by the Topeka plant. "Extraordinary commitment" represents the uppermost standard in my observation of innovative plants during the 1970s. "Very high" and "high" are convenient labels for intermediate points on the scale.

Fig. 11.1. Pattern of Development of Member Commitment in Topeka Plant Organization.

Source: This diagram and the other two diagrams in this chapter are based in part on material in Richard E. Walton, "Establishing and Maintaining High Commitment Work Systems," in *The Organizational Life Cycle: Issues in the Creation, Transformation, and Decline of Organizations*, edited by John R. Kimberly, Robert H. Miles, and others (San Francisco: Jossey-Bass, 1980).

mind when we refer to declines and recoveries in subsequent periods. First, the designers of the work structure fortunately had made correct assumptions about what workers would value. The work teams did become a potent force, enabling workers to achieve a high degree of freedom from supervisory control and providing them with the means for self-regulation. The participative features were successful in generating identification with the enterprise. The acquisition of new job skills was experienced as personal growth. The pay increases, which were linked to mastery, did produce a sense of equity, and other design features contributed as expected.

Second, plant management did an exceptionally skillful job of implementing the design. As I have learned from studying the start-up of other innovative plants, implementation errors are more often the source of problems than are design errors. The Topeka managers possessed skills and attitudes highly consistent with the design, and they carefully and forcefully articulated the philosophy of the work system. Thus, workers were confronted with a compelling, even inspiring, conception of how work was to be organized and managed. When events or circumstances were perceived by members as a test of some particular premise of the system (delegation, trust, equity, responsiveness) management made choices that confirmed the validity of the premise in question. The importance of this aspect of implementation cannot be overstated. Managers previously trained to manage in a conventional control-oriented manner often will inadvertently take individual actions that tend to contradict the philosophy underlying a high-commitment work system. In Topeka's very important formative period, managers rarely took such contradictory actions.

Third, the emerging evidence that the plant would excel in business results reinforced both the effort and the operating mode of the work force.

Fourth, national publicity acted to strengthen member commitment to the "Topeka concept." The plant had become the most publicized American example of a solution to the blue-collar blues. A journalist's account of his visit to the plant was featured on the front page of the *New York Times* on February 3, 1973. Along with work innovations at Volvo, in Sweden, it was the subject of NBC's "First Tuesday" program—sixty minutes of prime television time. My article analyzing this "prototype" plant and its initial successes reached over 100,000 subscribers of the *Harvard Business Review*.[6] The plant work force had generated an image which they wanted to maintain. They had become associated with concepts of work and workers which they wanted to prove correct.

These four factors—design, implementation, business results, and public image—continued into the future generally to support member commitment. But there were omissions in design and implementation as we shall see.

Contributing to the temporary decline in 1973 were (1) neglect of the need to orient new members of the organization; (2) delay in interteam movement and, hence, pay advancements; (3) diversion of management attention to the start-up of a second plant on the site; and (4) the fact that the sponsoring manager to whom the plant reported sought and received staff assignment, resulting in local concerns about the future of the Topeka system. Management reversed the drop in commitment by corrective attention to the first three factors.

To understand the moderate, long-term decline that set in thereafter, we need to examine how Topeka managed some dynamics that I have found to be inherent in the maturation of plants, especially those with high-commitment work systems. These dynamics arise because the developmental tendencies affecting the plant's task technology are opposite to the developmental trends of the plant's human resources.[7] From initial start-up to normal operation, a plant's task technology evolves from uncertainty to relative certainty, from a greater to a lesser need for problem-solving capability. During start-up, pieces of equipment have to be adjusted and debugged. As the equipment becomes progressively more reliable, there are fewer operating variables, and adjustments occur within a narrower range. Eventually, decision rules evolve to handle the more common variations.

In contrast, the new plant's work force develops from a lesser to a greater possession of technical skills and knowledge, and from lesser to greater group problem-solving capacities. The group must acquire the relevant technical skills, and knowledge about the product and the manufacturing system. Moreover, the group's affinity — trust, respect, and the ability to communicate efficiently — takes time to develop. These two opposing trend lines as I observed them in Topeka are shown in figure 11.2.

During start-up conditions, the technical skills and problem-solving capabilities possessed by the work force fall short of those required to operate the technology at high efficiency. I call this deficiency the "potential skill gap." It is a "potential" gap rather than an actual deficiency, because certain organizational measures can minimize the extent to which the actual tasks are or are not beyond the skill levels of operators. For example, this actual gap can be minimized by temporarily assigning experienced engineering and

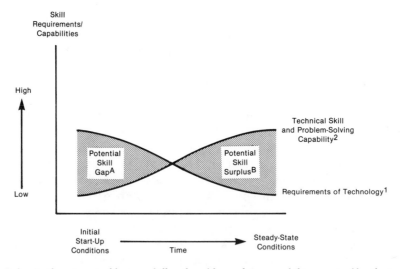

1. Refers to the amount of human skill and problem-solving capability *required* by the task technology. It is shown to have declined after technology is debugged and stabilized.
2. Refers to the amount of human skill and problem-solving capability *possessed* by the work force operating the technology. They are shown to rise as a result of learning.
A. Reflects the extent to which the work force capabilities fall short of the technical skill and problem-solving requirements of one task technology.
B. Reflects an excess of work force capabilities over the inherent requirements of the technology.

Fig. 11.2. Developmental Pattern of Technology Requirements and Human Capabilities at Topeka.

manufacturing talent to the new organization during start-up and by providing more detailed assistance and direction to the work force.

This potential skill gap narrows as the technology becomes routinized and therefore less demanding, and as the work force's capabilities increase. At some point, their accumulated capabilities will equal and then exceed the requirements of task technology. A "potential skill surplus" then grows and stabilizes when the work force's learning curve flattens and the technology cannot be further routinized. Again, I call this skill surplus "potential" because the organizational design could utilize work force knowledge and skill to a greater or lesser degree. For example, participative problem-solving processes are a way to tap a greater fraction of the accumulated human capabilities in the system.

Let us briefly sketch how Topeka's organizational design evolved and affected the skill gap and skill surplus. In the beginning, given a new work force, management provided a relatively high degree of technical and organizational direction, gradually decreasing this direction as the work force acquired technical and problem-solving skills. In effect, the start-up organization evolved from greater specification of structure ("mechanistic") to a more flexible, open structure ("organic"). However, this trend was reversed when the plant emerged from its start-up mode and management introduced more mechanistic features in response to the imperative of volume operation.

By mapping these structural trends onto the patterns of technology requirements and human resource capability already diagrammed, we can now visualize how the organizational structure served partially but not completely to close the skill gap and skill surplus (see fig. 11.3).

The "net skill gap" refers to the extent to which the current work structure is consistent with greater skills, attitudes, and group problem-solving capacities than those that actually exist. In effect, work organization is less structured and specified than existing skills warrant. One effect of this gap is to induce development through trial-and-error learning. And some risks associated with the gap are that effectiveness will suffer, frustration will mount, and the credibility of the structure will decline.

The "net skill surplus" refers to the extent to which greater skills and problem-solving capacities have been developed during start-up than are required, given the technology and design of roles and decision-making processes. One adverse consequence of this underutilization during normal operation is that loss of challenge will detract from the attractiveness of the work system and, hence, from workers' commitment to it.

The Topeka case well illustrates these dilemmas and their consequences. In the dry dog food plant, management permitted a net skill gap initially in order to start relations in a participative mode and emphasize learning rather than immediate performance. After the human resources became

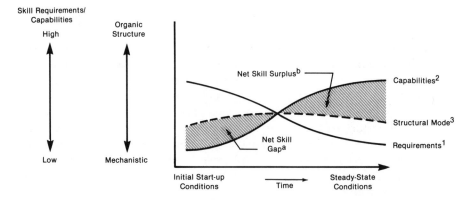

1. Refers to the amount of human capability *required* by the task technology.
2. Refers to the capability *possessed* by the work force.
3. Identifies the degree to which the structure includes organic versus mechanistic elements. It is shown to have become increasingly organic (as skills developed) during start-up period and then to have reversed its trend, as more mechanistic elements were introduced under normal operating conditions.
a. Reflects the extent to which the current structure "assumes" greater skills and problem-solving capability than curently exist. This concept focuses on the "net" skill gap which exists after taking into account the structural solution, rather than the "potential" discrepancy between the skill requirements of the technology and the skill bank currently possessed by the work force. The same distinction applies to our conception of the skill surplus.
b. Reflects the extent to which greater human capabilities exist than are "assumed" by the current structure.

Fig. 11.3. Developmental Patterns of Technology, Human Resources and Structural Form at Topeka.

well developed, workers' skills actually exceeded the amount required to function in the more certain environment, even taking into account the participative philosophy. The effect of this later net skill surplus was that members' sense of challenge and achievement suffered, and some letdown occurred, along with a moderate erosion of interest.

These dilemmas cannot be completely avoided. Compared with other systems I have observed, I believe that the pattern of work-structure development at Topeka dealt reasonably well with the opposing developmental trends of task technology and human resources. The human resources gap in the first year was considerable but not excessive. Moreover, this gap was planned, and management resisted the market demand for the product to allow for learning to take place. Later, when the work was under control and when a surplus developed, the plant resisted any mechanistic and bureaucratic development for which there was not a strong rationale. The net result was some underutilization of resources and a certain amount of individual disappointment, but neither was so serious as to cancel the work force's earlier assessment of the work system.

This analysis helps explain why there was a "peak experience" early in 1972 (see fig. 11.1). This was the period in which work-force capabilities just matched the requirements of task technology, and the structure perfectly accommodated both. The workers enjoyed feelings of challenge and mastery. They had now harnessed the equipment, and it still engaged all of their faculties to do so. The technical self-doubt and frustration which accompanied the skill gap was behind them, but the declining challenge of increasingly routinized task procedure was still ahead of them. The development of the skill surplus was delayed somewhat as the new can plant drew people with high skill out of the dry plant work force.

This analysis also helps explain the decline beginning in 1974. Strong forces act to decrease one's intrinsic interest in the work as an organization matures unless there are natural occurrences or planned changes which create new requirements to tap one's accumulated knowledge and problem-solving capabilities and further develop them. In Topeka's case, there was a long period after the dry plant reached an operational steady–state in 1974 when the absence of a number of externally stimulated changes — no new products, no expansion, no new-process technology — helped perpetuate a skill surplus and promote a sense of stagnation. There also was an absence of planned initiatives to address these conditions.

The upswing in commitment that began in 1978 reflects both the fact that some new demands on the dry plant had been made (new products and expansion) and that organizational renewal activities were initiated. The pattern of initiatives instituted to make the work system evolve will be addressed in the section below dealing with institutionalization and change.

The Vision of Economic and Human Benefits

Here I will elaborate on our vision of the positive "bottom-line" results in terms of both business economics and work-force satisfaction.

Herman Simon, the Topeka site manager since 1976, and Randy Castelluzzo, personnel manager at Topeka for a period in 1980–81, report as follows:

The work system has, in economic terms, been "unequivocally successful":
- Productivity has improved each year except one. GF now uses a rather sophisticated formula for measuring productivity that takes into account every manufacturing cost element, and Topeka has demonstrated consistent year-to-year improvement by this measurement.
- Overhead costs for the size of the organization and volume are relatively low, because of the small number of supervisors and support departments.

- Product quality has always had one of the best ratings in the corporation. The organization has been responsive to change, met all business commitments, responded to periods of high-volume demand and demonstrated understanding, patience and cooperation during periods of curtailment.[8]

These claims have been confirmed by corporate accountants asked to give top management an objective reading of the economic achievements of the Topeka work system. Based on their data, I estimated the annual incremental benefits due to employee motivation and participatory problem solving during the early 1970s to be $1 million — a significant premium considering the size of the plant population (about 100 employees) and the size of the capital investment.

Most indices of worker benefits are similarly positive, albeit less quantifiable. The work force has benefited from pay rates that are higher than those General Foods would have paid in a conventionally organized plant, and that are comparable to the best employment alternatives in the local community. Similarly, employment security has been enhanced because of the business effectiveness of the first Topeka plant and because of the company's policy commitment to exhaust all alternatives before resorting to a layoff. Positive human conditions were found by Robert Schrank of the Ford Foundation. In 1973, he found high levels of worker participation in decisions, freedom to communicate, expressions of warmth among the workers, commitment to the job, and individual self-esteem.[9] Another study of Topeka in 1974 confirmed these findings of positive attitudes. According to Edward Lawler, of the Institute for Social Research, the "data show high levels of satisfaction and involvement in all parts of the organization. In fact they show the highest levels we have found in any organization we have sampled. I specifically compared it with other small organizations and still found it superior."[10]

According to my own observations, these positive aspects were declining in 1976. After a visit in the fall of 1976, I reported:

By general agreement it was still a very productive plant and a superior place to work, but the "quality of work life" had slipped. And while the majority still supported — by their own behavior — the unique strengths of the "Topeka work system," an increasing minority did not. Slippage occurred across a broad front of attributes: openness and candor; helping among team members; identification with plant management; confidence in General Foods; perceived upward influence; effective leadership within teams; and cooperation between shifts. In addition, there continued to be serious doubt about the ability of teams to make objective judgments about members' qualifications for pay increases.[11]

These positive human conditions were unfavorable only relative to earlier highs, not relative to jobs elsewhere. Reportedly, these positive features have strengthened again in the past several years.

In totaling the benefits and costs for members of Topeka-type work systems, one ought to assess the effects that extend beyond the workplace. In an unpublished study of another similarly designed work system, a researcher found that the problem-solving skills and self-confidence gained at work were then tried out in the family setting. Their new work roles raised the consciousness of women employees in working-class families, many of whom undertook to change their decision-making roles at home from passivity to activity and their marriage-role relationship from subordinacy to equality. Many male workers in this plant practiced their new listening skills at home, with implications for the quality of family relationships. On the negative side, workers tended to take their work problems home with them and to experience stress related to task difficulty. In effect, they experienced many of the psychological gains and costs associated with professional and managerial work. Anecdotal evidence suggests that these conclusions apply to Topeka as well.

The Vision of Institutionalization and Change

The planners assumed that the organization would have the dual capacity for continuity and change. The Topeka system was rapidly and successfully institutionalized. Within 18 to 24 months, behavior patterns were firmly established, many participative principles had been deeply internalized, and the basic elements of the designs were accepted and defended by a large majority of members.

If the system's institutionalization was impressive, its capacity for self-directed change was disappointing. The quick recovery from the drop in the third year did display a capacity for self-diagnosis and corrective action – a capacity that was no longer evident during the subsequent decline between 1974 and 1978. The reason for the decline relates importantly to the mounting skill surplus (with implications of boredom) referred to earlier, and the lack of natural challenges – to the dry plant work force – such as new products or expansion. But why were there no major efforts to confront this decline?

Three factors explain this low capacity for midcourse corrections. First, the founding managers had left, and their replacements were cautious about tampering with a system that was performing very well. This is a leadership omission. Second, and more important, there were no regular plant-wide forums in which basic design questions could be raised. The planners had provided for extensive participation at the team level, relative to day-to-day functioning, but had not proposed institutional mechanisms for periodic reassessments of the total system. One might label this an omission in the structural design. Third, and the most fundamental reason, the planners and founding managers had not effectively implanted the idea that the work system would need to evolve continually. Such evolution could be derived only from experience, and ideally there would have existed a widely shared responsibility for promoting this evolution.

By 1981, however, there was an indication of an increased capacity for renewal and evolution. During 1978–1981, there had been many dialogues about design questions, and members showed a growing interest in their "roots," which caused many of them to review the rationale of the planners of the Topeka design. Members also exhibited a growing interest in the experience and analysis of other innovative work systems. Ad hoc committees were created to deal with design and philosophy issues, and members participated in outside educational programs.

Supervisory Roles

The planners envisaged a supervisory role that could be satisfying and rewarding. In the early- and mid-1970s, I found that supervisors often were the target of criticism from some team members because they provided too much guidance, and from others because they provided too little. Team leaders felt isolated because, as a group, they had not developed a pattern of mutual support. They did not attempt to influence higher plant managers. They were expected to develop the self-management capabilities of their teams, but they were not given assurances that other career opportunities existed. They engaged in task forces and developed broader knowledge and skill, which further sharpened their concern about the absence of other career opportunities.

In 1979, the Topeka staff concluded that, while the flat structure was cost effective, it did not by itself provide adequate opportunities for professional development or for career advancement for team leaders. They planned a team leader development program, with team leaders themselves taking the lead. The program included "familiarization assignments" of six to twelve weeks in other functional areas and "job rotation assignments" of 18 to 24 months. As of June 1981, three team leaders had participated in familiarization assignments, and two had rotated to other positions. Management expected this developmental program to result in some permanent assignments to higher level positions. In the meantime, Topeka management sought, this time successfully, a higher salary-grade position (above the Senior Team Leader position), which could be earned by team leaders who developed broader, plant-management capabilities.

Ed Dulworth recalls that, as early as 1972, steps were taken to provide team leaders with growth experiences — experiences which "led to significant progress elsewhere in GF and outside GF." He reported: "All of the past team leaders I've talked to through the years rate it as the best experience they ever had and excellent career development." On balance, I am persuaded that the early vision regarding the team leader position was realized.

Vision of Confirmation and Advancement for Topeka Managers

Was the experience rewarding for Topeka managers above the level of Senior Team Leader? It was, I gather, personally satisfying and professionally developmental, but the expected advancement opportunities in GF were not forthcoming. Why not?

Friction developed between Topeka management and corporate executives. Many ingredients in the situation contributed to the friction. Topeka's success, for one, was threatening to other managers whose leadership style was built on opposite principles. Moreover, the plant management's demands for autonomy in certain areas and its requests for exception from other corporate procedures was resented by such staff groups as personnel, accounting, engineering, and quality control. And many corporate executives simply did not understand the Topeka system.

For their part, the Topeka managers did not develop an effective strategy for educating and winning the support of higher management and staff groups. The Topeka managers simply reacted spontaneously in expressing their exasperation with these corporate groups. With the benefit of hindsight and on the basis of my experience with other pioneering plants in which external relations were handled very differently, I conclude that we who planned the system as well as the Topeka managers were partly to blame for not devising ways to avoid this friction — which eventually polarized the plant and the corporation.

The effect of this friction was to sour the career opportunities within General Foods for most of the original Topeka managers. By 1976, all but one had left the company. I believe that they generally prospered in their new assignments, but clearly their GF careers suffered from their association with this pioneering and locally successful work system.

Vision of Diffusion of the Approach

We assumed that if the work innovations were successful in Topeka, they would be endorsed by upper management and emulated by other GF plants. But the case is not that simple, as my subsequent research has documented.[12] Many dynamics may act to frustrate the intracompany diffusion of work innovations.

My judgment is that the amount of work restructuring in General Foods has been neither greater nor lesser than the amount one might have expected if the Topeka project had never occurred. A number of other work-innovative initiatives arose in GF during the 1970s, but probably no more than have occurred on the average in other comparably progressive, large American corporations. Top management has expressed support, but the evidence of support is again no more than the average. While some plant managers were positively encouraged by what they knew about Topeka, others were effectively innoculated against the spread of this type of innovation to their facilities. But "Stonewalling Plant Democracy," the title of a *Business Week* article on General Foods' managerial response to Topeka's success *in* Topeka, was an exaggeration, and misleading.[13] (The content of the body of that article was reasonably accurate.) In fact, some GF officials were actively supporting the spread of such innovations. One of the reasons why the Topeka approach did not spread throughout GF was because some company executives labeled the Topeka system a "problem" for the corporation, despite its apparent economic and human successes. Equally important, there were no natural champions for the underlying philosophy among top corporate officers, as there were, for example in Cummins Engine Corporation and General Motors during the early 1970s — two companies with good diffusion records.

Yet, as weak as Topeka was as a stimulus to further innovation within General Foods, the plant became a compelling example for many management teams from other corporations who visited Topeka and whose own plant innovations were inspired by what they observed.

THE PESSIMISTIC HYPOTHESES OF CRITICS

In trying to make sense out of this pioneering work organization, we will find it as instructive to compare Topeka's actual history to the early projections of the skeptics as to the optimistic visions of its planners.

Questions, doubts, and fears were expressed early in the 1970s in reaction to a description of the Topeka system. The "challenges" to the Topeka concept fall into three clusters: (1) the first cluster questioned the general applicability of Topeka principles; (2) the second questioned the ability of this type of high-commitment work system to survive; (3) the third projected new problems created by such systems if they were effective. In responding to these challenges, where Topeka itself doesn't provide evidence bearing on a critic's hypothesis, I will draw on the experience of high-commitment work systems in other United States companies.

Topeka Is a Special Case — the Approach Is Not Generalizable

When we planned the ambitiously participative work system at Topeka, we appreciated that many conditions were especially favorable to the experiment. The question was, were they necessary conditions? I thought not, but it was inevitable and appropriate that others would question the general applicability of the Topeka approach. I recall at least seven pessimistic hypotheses.

The Size Hypothesis. "Topeka employed only one hundred. It can work in a small plant, but not in plants of several thousand." We have observed, however, that the same principles *have* worked in plants of several thousand—for example, in Procter & Gamble's paper division and General Motors' assembly division. Largeness may be a liability but not a decisive one.

The Task-Technology Hypothesis. "Topeka employs continuous process technology which defines easily enriched jobs. The Topeka approach works if mental as well as physical skill requirements are inherent in the task, but it would not work with highly routine assembly line tasks." Yes, the task technology does limit the options which one can consider for organizing and managing work—it affects the relevance of work teams, it limits the range of discretion that can be delegated, and it determines the amount of economic benefit that will accrue from a more positive work culture. Thus, the Topeka work design, taken as a literal model, is not applicable across the board. However, the underlying principles of whole tasks, self-management, egalitarianism, facilitative leadership, and so on, have been found to apply to a very broad range of tasks. Moreover, although the Topeka design is not an all-purpose one, it is striking how often similarly inspired work systems in diverse contexts have incorporated two of its central design elements, namely, work teams as the basic organizational building block and pay increases for acquired knowledge.

The Location Hypothesis. Initially, skeptics asserted that there was something uniquely favorable about the work ethic in the rural Midwest. But, in fact, similar designs have produced similar reactions by workers in New England, the Deep South, California, Mexico, Scotland, India, and in both rural and urban environments. Work-force values, expectations, and skills vary, and these must be taken into account, but early interpretations of the Topeka proposals exaggerated the effects of these locational differences.

The Favorable Labor Market Hypothesis. "Topeka managers could review ten applicants for every person hired. The Topeka system depends upon selecting the relatively small fraction of the labor pool who happen to have the particular skills, attitudes, and intrinsic motivation that fit the system." In fact, similar designs have worked in new plant start-ups with less favorable labor markets. More convincingly, successful new projects started up in facilities adjacent to conventionally managed plants often have been manned by employees who transferred from the traditional plants. Individual differences, like locational differences, must be considered, but they are less constraining than the planners, myself included, believed earlier.

The Nonunion Hypothesis. "The Topeka approach is only possible in a nonunion environment." One argument was that unions would oppose job-content changes that blurred traditional job jurisdictions, and work processes that blurred traditional worker–manager distinctions. Although unions have been suspicious of such work designs, with increasing frequency unions are dropping their automatic opposition to them. Today, work reforms jointly sponsored by union and management are as ambitious and becoming as successful in restructuring the workplace as those initiated in nonunion environments.

The New Plant Hypothesis. "Only in a new plant start-up is the Topeka approach feasible." Indeed, in existing plants, it is not appropriate to try to revamp *all* elements of the work design, which could consciously be redesigned for a new plant. General Motors' Tarrytown plant is an example of successful change to a participative approach in a large, unionized, established plant. Tarrytown confirms that similar philosophies can be applied in established as well as new plants, but it also confirms that the work design and implementation tactics will vary widely and that the time required to establish the new work culture is very different in an established versus a new setting.

Unique Leadership Hypothesis. "The managers involved in Topeka had uniquely supportive human values and leadership skills." Critics argued that without comparable leadership, in other situations, the Topeka design would fail. I agree, in part. I have painfully observed how poor leadership *during the formative stages* of the work system can completely undermine the otherwise positive effects of the work design. (Later it is less important, as I will argue below.) In any event, experience has contradicted the assumption that the type of leadership available to the Topeka plant is a special case. The necessary values and skills were much more widely available in management, union, and worker ranks than was assumed at that time. And, they are even more available today.

Topeka-Type Systems Won't Survive

Another set of hypotheses held that, even if Topeka was not a special case, such systems either contain the seeds of their own destruction or are otherwise vulnerable to a variety of changing circumstances. Although never a committed pessimist on this matter, I have shared many of the concerns reflected in these hypotheses. In a report produced in 1974, initially entitled "Half-Life and After-Life of Work Innovations," I analyzed why about 10 of 12 previously publicized work-innovation projects started in the 1960s had been discontinued or had withered after a successful start.[14] The poor survival rate of these early innovations was certainly discouraging. While some critics concluded from this early experience that "they can't survive," others assumed the problems were correctable — if planners understood them, they could avoid or minimize these threats. What perspective do we now have on these pessimistic hypotheses?

The Hawthorne Effect. One view of the Topeka system was that its positive effects were due entirely to its novelty and to the special attention given workers, called the Hawthorne effect after some early experiments in which this dynamic was demonstrated. The hypothesis was that, when the novelty wore off and the work force no longer received special attention from management and the media, workers would reflect no greater commitment than existed in other General Foods plants.

The Hawthorne effect indeed helped launch the system, but the system survived long after the Hawthorne phenomenon was plausible. This same statement applies to dozens of other similarly inspired systems with which I am familiar, many now more than five years old.

Burnout. The burnout hypothesis is that high-commitment work systems are so stimulating and demanding for both managers and workers that, after a few years, fatigue becomes a factor, leading to forms of self-protective withdrawal. Too much withdrawal of energy by too many members would be fatal to a high-commitment work system.

I have found evidence of burnout in innovative plants, due to the special demands associated with high-commitment work systems. For example, the Jamestown plant of Cummins Engine has produced a video tape to present to prospective employees, the theme of which is that they should know in advance that working at the plant involves stress. Members experience stress because of the higher responsibility they assume, the great demands for communication and involvement placed on them, the exchange of criticism, and the ambiguity inherent in participation.[15] On the video tape, Cummins workers describe the nature of this stress and its significance to them. At this same plant, managers acknowledge that after several years it becomes more difficult to generate the emotional energy required to tackle difficult problems in the highly participative mode which they practice.

At Cummins, and in other plants where I have observed burnout, managers can cope with burnout by moving on to other positions, by rotating lead assignments in the participative process, and by allowing individuals to decrease their own involvement for periods of time without feeling guilty. Of course, as we better understand the causes and consequences of stress related to high-commitment work systems, we should try to find optimum levels of demand and stimulation that take into account the burnout phenomenon.

At Topeka, some managerial burnouts were avoided by the departure of the founding managers after a few years, but I believe both supervisors and team members did experience some significant instances of burnout. The burnout phenomenon is real, it needs to be monitored, but it is manageable.

Iron Law of Bureaucracy. This hypothesis is that Topeka-type systems inevitably gravitate toward the conventional patterns they seek to replace: Rules and structures will develop to solve certain problems and then take on a life of their own. Individuals and groups will instinctively define and attempt to protect some turf — whether it be differentiated roles or special privileges. The initially egalitarian society will become stratified to accord status to those who have accepted more responsibility.

I believe that the hypothesized *tendency* is real but that the hypothesized *outcome* is not inevitable. If one wants to minimize bureaucratization, one must work at it. A number of developments at Topeka could be cited in support of this general hypothesis. In accordance with design principles of "whole tasks" and "delegations," the planners omitted from the original design many traditional specialist roles — in quality assurance, maintenance, stores, accounting, purchasing, and personnel. The functions those specialists normally performed were integrated into the line organization and largely delegated to work teams. After ten years, some specialization *within teams* (among team members) occurred in all of these areas. This specialization was in response to both the task requirements for greater mastery in these areas and team members' desire for additional levels of advancement and compensation. One could argue that this movement toward specialization constituted backing off from the original commitment to "whole tasks" and "generalists," and was, thus, a form of bureaucratization. But it was not so perceived by members of the Topeka organization.

Other proposed changes toward specialization, however, were interpreted by many members as "going traditional." One change affected the screening and hiring of new employees:

The original design involved all the team members in the hiring process as much as possible. Applications were accepted on the site and were kept on file for one year. When a team had an opening, the team members would go through the applications and pull those that they wished to interview. Once the individual was scheduled for an interview, any team member, and many times all the team members, along with the team leader, would interview the candidate. They would then get together and decide which candidates to make an offer [to]. This process, of course, would stop the pacemaker of any corporate attorney in terms of risk under Equal Employment Opportunity legislation.

In 1977, the hiring procedure was reviewed and modified. All applications are now submitted to the State Job Service Office and they maintain applicant flow records for us. Each team has selected a hiring committee which includes one team leader, four team members, and a representative from Personnel. All the members are required to attend an in-house training session on EEO legislation and interviewing skills. Our procedure now is to contact the Job Service Center and request applications which indicate that the individual has the required skills (electrical, mechanical, industrial experience, etc.). These are sent to Personnel where they are screened initially. Those applicants having the required skills, indicated on a hiring request form, are then reviewed with the committee to determine who will be asked in for an interview. Each committee member interviews the candidates and then meets, as a committee, to make the decision on a job offer.[16]

Thus, some functions formerly handled almost entirely by the work team are now performed by the State Job Service and the plant's personnel department. The hiring criteria are more prescribed and the work team has less latitude. One can view the amount of bureaucratization involved here as "backing away from the concept," as did many Topeka team members, at least initially. Or one can examine it closely and regard it as a modest and appropriate increase in specialization and structure. I view the *substance* of the change in the latter way. In this case, the real bureaucratic error was in the hierarchical process by which the change was made. Simon and Castelluzzo explained:

This particular change was not handled as well as it might have been. The managers knew the (hiring) change was necessary, but did not communicate the reasons to the team leaders and the team members. There was no involvement of team members in the development of the procedure so it was not totally understood and certainly not accepted as theirs. The teams viewed the changes of procedure as an issue in which they had no control. This is one change that we would bring about differently if we had the luxury of going back in time.

I believe that this change has been effective in helping us, as an organization, review our direction and identify areas that we need to work on. We have broadened training programs and intend to make them an institutionalized part of the "Topeka" system.[17]

This example helps illustrate the type of slippage in participation and in commitment which occurred from 1974 to 1979 (see fig. 11.1), and shows the beginning of a management resolve to reverse the trend.

Another change, which involved purchasing, can be viewed within the framework of bureaucratization. It illustrates another common set of pressures for an elaboration of rules, required procedures, formal control, and greater specialization.

Corporate auditors made a number of recommendations for the Topeka organization, the biggest of which dealt with purchasing procedures. We did not have a purchasing agent where the purchasing duties could be centralized. In fact, any employee could determine the need for an item, identify and contact the vendor, make the purchase, and receive the item as long as the value was less than a set amount. The auditors pointed out that they found nothing questionable taking place from an ethical or legal standpoint but were quick to show where the risks were. They also mentioned that the purchasing process did not allow us to take advantage of savings by consolidating purchases and billings, using national contracts, and bidding among local vendors. They also added that we were (often) not in compliance with established corporate procedures. The auditors recommended the establishment of a purchasing agent to accomplish their recommendations. This was bolstered by a separate recommendation from Corporate Purchasing to add a purchasing function.[18]

The plant management consulted with team leaders and team members who had the most responsibility for purchasing. These individuals concluded that the concerns and the objectives of the auditors' recommendations were legitimate, but strongly disagreed with the creation of a purchasing agent position. Instead, an on-site purchasing committee was proposed, comprised of those most involved in purchasing, to (1) review national account opportunities and bidding processes; (2) establish and enforce procedures to ensure that the best-value vendor would be chosen; and (3) establish more effective controls. Then, according to Simon and Castelluzzo:

> The difficult part of the task began and that is the effort necessary to convince the corporate management that this alternative would be effective in meeting their needs and still be consistent with the operation of the Topeka organization. The plant manager and controller were successful in gaining our own division management's support to try the local recommendation. We are now living up to our commitment. We have identified considerable savings since instituting the program and have done so without eliminating the input of those affected. Moreover, these changes did improve the control over our purchasing and clearly defined the approval responsibility within the site.[19]

Yet another change (already discussed) created an additional level between the senior team leader and the area manager. It was not a new level in the authority chain, but it was nevertheless a new status level and, hence, contributed to greater stratification.

How should we interpret the above changes? In my view, these limited changes toward specialization and stratification are appropriate responses to identified human and business needs. They do not constitute an unhealthy retreat from founding concepts. Moreover, these changes have been closely scrutinized by members of the Topeka organization, especially at the team-member level, in order to ensure that they did not constitute an unwitting bureaucratization of the system. For me, Topeka's ten-year experience is consistent with the hypothesized tendency, but it also demonstrates the ability of an organization with a widely shared consciousness about the issue of bureaucratization to manage that tendency in the interest of achieving optimum levels of specialization, formalization, and stratification.

"Fragile — Handle with Care." This hypothesis is based on an assumption that several specific forms of external support are necessary for the continuation of a Topeka-type system and that a unique set of internal circumstances must be kept in perfect balance. The opposite hypothesis is that such systems, once established, are very "robust" and difficult to destroy.

Many comments commonly made about high-commitment work systems reinforce the "fragile" hypothesis. I, with others, have emphasized the need for top management's philosophical support, for leadership with values and skills highly consistent with the work system, for as much employment security as possible, for internal consistency among design elements, and for heavy investment in training. Earlier, I assumed — and many others still hold this view — that these conditions were essential not only for the establishment of a Topeka-type system but also for *sustaining* it over time. Now, I emphasize their great importance only for *establishing* the work system.

On the basis of my analysis of Topeka's history and that of other established high-commitment work systems, I am impressed with the robustness of these work systems. If work-force expectations — for participation, influence, dignity, and status — are raised and made legitimate by philosophical statements, then made manifest in certain operational forms (participative procedures and job designs, for example), and then reinforced by practice for a period of time, the result will be a broad and powerful constituency for perpetuating the work system. Topeka continued to function despite mixed philosophical signals from higher management, despite the fact that replacement managers were not in the same mold as first-generation managers, and despite some economic adversity. While there were no significant external threats, there certainly was very little "tender love and care" given to the system from 1973 to the late 1970s.

The history of other high-commitment work systems provides me with even more persuasive evidence favoring the robustness hypothesis — they persist in the face of a total absence of external support, poor leadership, inconsistencies among design elements, layoffs, and long periods of delay in necessary training. A collective ideal, once embedded, is a powerful force — one that enables people to discount discordant signals for a significant period of time, but not, of course, forever.

Diffuse or Die. This hypothesis is that, if the approach does not spread into the larger company and/or industry system, the original organizational unit will become isolated, will be able neither to place its own personnel elsewhere nor to attract new personnel, and will not develop political allies for dealing with staff groups. Isolated, it will stagnate. Stagnated, it eventually will die.

Basically, I subscribe to the hypothesis; but, fortunately, Topeka's experience does not give us a clear test of it. As we noted earlier, there was not rapid diffusion, but there was some. The Topeka plant was isolated, but not completely — it exchanged notes with other plants where work innovations were undertaken. Members of the Topeka organization derived support and confirmation from external companies. Most of Topeka's founding managers were not promoted within the company, but Topeka did get able replacement managers. The second site manager came to Topeka with the clear mandate to build better relationships between the plant and corporation, which he did. Today, the plant is less isolated.

What Will This Lead To?

A third set of hypotheses referred to problems posed by the success of Topeka-type systems.

Ever-Rising Expectations. This hypothesis was that delegation of some functions would lead to an expectation that still other functions would be delegated, that voice in some matters would lead to the expectation of voice in other issues. Although the type of delegation and the amount of voice contemplated in the Topeka design might be appropriate, future worker expectations would include delegation and voice that clearly would not take place. In other words, where does this sort of thing stop?

One of the reasons this fear has not, in my experience, been well founded is that interest in delegated duties and influence is not like a concern for money, of which we would always prefer more. Shared criteria can be applied to determine the *optimum* level of delegation — for example, decisions should be made at the lowest level which is in possession of the relevant information and expertise. Similarly, individuals do not always prefer more influence, if it is clear that with greater influence goes greater responsibility. This principle is soon learned in most high-commitment work systems.

A particular concern voiced by some critics was that shop-floor influences will lead to worker interest in boardroom influence. One could argue the opposite — that the *absence* of shop-floor influence is more likely to lead to demands for worker representation on boards. But it is too early to test this particular hypothesis in the United States.

If the initial delegation and provisions for voice sharpen workers' awareness of these issues and lead to further questions about the appropriate amount of delegation and voice, I regard that as an asset and not a liability. I make an assumption not held by critics — that one can typically resolve such questions by consensus, by reference to both business and human criteria.

If I'm So Smart, Why Ain't I Rich? This hypothesis predicts that as workers are expected to invest more of themselves in their work, they, in turn, will expect increased compensation. The fear was that this expectation for more money often could not be met — either because no real business gains would materialize or because company or union policies would prevent appropriate adjustments in compensation.

The hypothesis, as stated above, is only partly supported by my experience. First, Topeka and other high-commitment work systems with which I am familiar have produced real economic benefits for the company. Second, workers understand that equity can be achieved with several different currencies — ranging from additional job security at a more competitive plant to gain sharing. Third, if there are broader policy constraints, workers can understand and may accept them.

Clearly, I subscribe to a more general version of the hypothesis, one that centers on the idea of equity. In the Topeka system, individual investment in learning and a willingness to work flexibly were compensated by the provision of incremental pay for incremental skills. In addition, the overall superior performance of the plant was indicated by the favorable relationship of the plant pay scales to pay scales in the community at large. A gainsharing scheme would have achieved even greater equity, in the minds of both Topeka managers and workers, and in my mind, as well. But the fact that, after ten years, one still has not been installed has not brought the system down.

Unions Will Become Obsolete. Many managers cited the prospect of unions becoming obsolete as an advantage, of course. But some union officials and academics feared that the spread of work reforms illustrated by Topeka would create an open field for management manipulation of workers.

The 1970s provide mixed evidence on this question. The Topeka plant, of course, has not been unionized. To my knowledge, the work force has never evidenced any interest in a union. Comparable experience in other new plants has led managers in some companies to view these systems as a way of avoiding unions — maybe eventually getting rid of the unions they have. On the other side of the issue, there is an increasing amount of joint union–management activity supporting Topeka-type work systems, especially in the auto industry, but also in rubber, steel, and telecommunications. Thus, there is a trend toward an effective integration of the essential ingredients of collective bargaining and of high-commitment work systems.

These work systems are, therefore, involved in two opposite trends: one integrating them into collective bargaining relationships and the other positioning them in opposition to collective bargaining. I believe both trends will continue. Which will be stronger? The more that work innovations supported by both union and management are successful and visible, the less likely that American managers who now deal with unions will resort to a strategy of eliminating or preventing unions, and the better the prospects that a healthy, free trade-union movement will persist. I personally would not argue that every work force in every facility should be unionized, so long as adequate provisions exist for employee voice and due process, and so long as employees can exercise an informed choice about unionization. Because I value pluralism in the workplace, as in the larger society, I would deplore the loss of an effective trade union movement.

Loss of Management Prerogatives. Some managers were alarmed when they first learned of the "radical" Topeka work system. They regarded the blurring of traditional worker and management roles as yielding on "prerogatives," with negative implications for management status, legitimacy, and effectiveness.

I do believe that one effect of the Topeka-type system is, indeed, to undermine the concept of "management prerogatives," as traditionally formulated. These systems are causing a revision in assumptions about what actions management may take unilaterally and what actions should be open to influence by other stakeholders. However, I believe the changes in decision-making processes, if well conceived and implemented, have positive rather than negative implications for management status, legitimacy, and organizational effectiveness. This certainly is true in the Topeka case — after more than a decade.

CONCLUDING COMMENTS

Why do the pessimistic hypotheses reviewed here seem less persuasive today? By 1981, contrary evidence has accumulated, and there is a recognition that the general Topeka-type approach has wide applicability, and that such work systems have continued over many years. In addition, the hypotheses are actually becoming less supportable as the societal context becomes more favorable to the new approach. In the early 1970s, the approach was considered radical and deviant; therefore, it actually needed more favorable conditions for continuation. Today, the approach is becoming normative and is less in need of special support.

Perspectives of Key Actors

I invited comments on a draft of this manuscript from a number of the individuals who played key roles either in the founding of the Topeka plant system or in its later development, or both. Some of their comments relating to dates and other facts have been reflected in the final draft of this chapter. Other perspectives of these key actors are presented here.

Herman Simon, Donald Lafond, John Shimp, and Randy Castelluzzo. Herman Simon has had overall responsibility for the Topeka site since 1976. John Shimp currently has responsibility for production planning, traffic, and quality assurance. He came to Topeka in the mid-1970s. Don Lafond is manager of the can plant. He was a member of the management team that designed and started up the dry plant. Randy Castelluzzo was personnel manager at Topeka from 1979 to 1981.

Their comments emphasized the importance of the "skill gap" and "skill surplus" concepts in understanding Topeka's history. I will paraphrase.

> The applications of these concepts to the dry plant are accurate. The skill surplus was a real issue and we didn't give enough thought to it. The dry plant personnel did grow above and beyond the work required to operate the plant and so they became disenchanted.
>
> In the can plant, we took steps to minimize the potential skill gap — steps which we did not need to take in the dry plant. We beefed up the engineering and manufacturing talent, we drew skilled operators from the dry plant, and we also provided more detailed assistance and direction. Why? Because in this second plant, the meat ingredients and the canning technology presented us with more technical difficulties. These difficulties and market uncertainty also delayed the development of the "skill surplus."

A comment by Don Lafond gave his personal perspective:

> The can plant, not the focus of Walton's account, is an interesting story in itself. While the can plant was started in a more traditional mode, in my opinion, members of the can plant today have as much, if not more, understanding of, and commitment to, the Topeka concepts; they are more willing to give interpersonal feedback, and to try to evolve the system. Today, there is some reseeding of can plant members back into the dry plant.
>
> As the single managerial linkage with the founding of the Topeka system, I've played a particular role in attempting to keep our organization true to the original ideas. It's taken energy and I've sometimes felt lonely.

Edward Dulworth. Ed Dulworth was the first manager of the Topeka site and currently is vice-president for manufacturing of Topps Chewing Gum, Inc. In addition to confirming that the above treatment was a balanced one, in his view, Ed reflected as follows:

> Looking back, as I often do, the Topeka experience was a fantastic learning and feeling experience — and I'd take the trip again! We did many things — good and bad — but it was always alive and active — hardly ever dull. The most important

thing to me is that we did create something that has survived well because it's attractive to its members. I take great satisfaction knowing that and knowing its contribution to the larger industrial society.

I've spent a good deal of my last five years working toward the same goals at Topps with some success. I play the politics better today and understand the process more. I should, given the scars!

Lyman Ketchum. Lyman is the person most responsible for the fact that the Topeka innovation ever occurred. After helping found the Topeka system and supporting it for several years, he left General Foods to become an independent consultant on work systems design. After reading the manuscript, he offered a number of comments, a few of which provide slightly different interpretations of Topeka's history.

I don't agree with the single-trend line of commitment proposed here. There were so many currents there, it was a complex wave system. Maybe you never can capture the full complexity of commitment and its many causes. Also, there is some additional complexity to the history of skill gaps and surpluses. For example, in the can plant, there were four, not one, start-ups. When the skill surplus developed in the management ranks, we moved one of our key managers, Bob Meck, out of the line and into consulting with others in the community and with other GF plants. That is just one way we coped with skill surplus.

The report treated the plant's publicity as strengthening a public image which the work force sought to uphold, but the publicity also had its negative effects because when a few operators appeared on TV, some others became envious.

I believe we started the dry plant far more participatively and closer to the eventual organic design than Walton's account suggests.

I am troubled about burnout as a concept that applies to innovative work. In traditional plants, stress is related to boredom and conflict, and its manifests itself in drugs, alcohol, and all the rest. Sure, there is stress in innovative plants, but is it damaging? I want to see more evidence.

All in all, I would not trade the experience for anything else. Some of the waves Topeka created are still breaking on shores I've never heard of. And I continue to learn from those at Topeka how much it has added to their lives. This is enormously satisfying.

NOTES

1. Richard E. Walton, "The Topeka Story," *The Wharton Magazine*, Spring 1978, pp. 38–48.

2. Lyman Ketchum, "A Case Study of Diffusion," in *The Quality of Working Life, Volume Two: Cases and Commentary*, edited by Louis E. Davis, Albert B. Cherns, and Associates, pp. 138–163 (New York: The Free Press, 1975); and Proceedings of the 1976 Professional Development Conference, American Society of Safety Engineers, Atlanta, June 14–16, 1976.

3. Walton, "The Topeka Story"; "Establishing and Maintaining High Commitment Work Systems," in *The Organizational Life Cycle: Issues in the Creation, Transformation, and Decline of Organizations* by John R. Kimberly, Robert H. Miles, and Associates (San Francisco: Jossey-Bass, 1980), pp. 208–90.

4. Ibid.

5. Ibid.

6. Richard E. Walton, "How to Counter Alienation in the Plant," *Harvard Business Review*, November–December 1972.

7. Walton, "Establishing and Maintaining High Commitment Work Systems."

8. Herman R. Simon and R.F. Castelluzzo, "General Foods, Topeka: Ten Years Old," a presentation to the International Conference on the Quality of Working Life, Toronto, Canada, August 31, 1981.

9. Robert Schrank, "On Ending Worker Alienation: The Gaines Pet Food Plant," in *Humanizing the Workplace*, edited by Roy Fairfield (New York: Prometheus Books, 1974), pp. 119–40.

10. Edward E. Lawler, G.D. Jenkins, Jr., and G.E. Herline, "Initial Data Feedback to General Foods, Topeka Pet Foods Plants: Selected Survey Items," unpublished paper (Ann Arbor, Mich.: Institute for Social Research, University of Michigan, 1974).

11. Richard E. Walton, "The Topeka Story," p. 45.

12. Richard E. Walton, "The Diffusion of New Work Structures: Explaining Why Success Didn't Take," *Organizational Dynamics*, Winter 1975, pp. 3–22.

13. "Stonewalling Plant Democracy," *Business Week*, March 28, 1978, pp. 78–82.

14. Richard E. Walton, "Innovative Restructuring of Work," in *The Worker and the Job: Coping with Change*, edited by Jerome M. Rosow (Englewood Cliffs, N.J.: Prentice Hall, 1974).

15. Interestingly, this stress can be thought of as produced by "overstimulation," whereas the stress in conventional plants is produced by the opposite condition of tedium and boredom, that is, "understimulation."

16. Simon and Castelluzzo, "General Foods, Topeka: Ten Years Old," p. 11.

17. Ibid., p. 12.

18. Ibid., p. 13.

19. Ibid.

III:
Corporate Strategy

12.
Strategies for Diffusing, Evolving, and Institutionalizing Quality of Work Life at General Motors

D.L. Landen and Howard C. Carlson

INTRODUCTION

Like taxes and death, change is inevitable. But change differs from those other two inevitabilities. We may not be able to do much about taxes, and ultimately we can't do anything about death. But we can do a great deal about change. We can understand its dynamics. We can utilize its energizing force. We can guide its direction. We can either impede or accelerate its speed. One of the functions of this chapter is to view change as a positive force and to see how change can be helpful in creating better institutions of work.

Another function of this chapter is to examine the issue of diffusion. More precisely, some strategies by which workplace innovations can be spread or transferred successfully from one organizational entity to another will be discussed.

A third function of this chapter is to discuss various means by which change/improvement efforts can be transformed from the status of "an experiment" to an established, accepted way of operating an enterprise.

Some Principles

As noted, the focus of this chapter is on change, its diffusion, evolution, and institutionalization. While these will be discussed separately, it first needs to be established that these are not independent events or activities. All of these variables are interdependent. It is neither feasible nor practical to think of diffusion, evolution, or institutionalization independent of change. They cannot occur without a capacity on the part of individuals and organizations to alter values, norms and behaviors; i.e., to change, consistent with what is required in order to make limited workplace innovations more broadly and fundamentally a basis for enterprise operations and performance. By the same token, diffusion cannot occur without the evolution of broad institutional acceptance and support for initial innovations. The more extensive this support, the greater is the likelihood that diffusion will occur.

By the simple extension of the above reasoning it can be asserted that organizations cannot institutionalize that which does not exist. Therefore, when we speak of making acceptable that which has been atypical, we are implying that the novel has now become the norm. One way of thinking about the subjects discussed in this chapter is to view them as elements in a larger, organizational learning system which triggers a process of making acceptable the unacceptable, standardizing the temporary, and normalizing the novel.

Definition of Terms: Diffusion, Evolution, and Institutionalization

Other writers have either offered definitions of these terms[1] or have discussed organizational conditions that contribute to their success or failure.[2] For purposes of this chapter, we will use these terms in the following manner:

Diffusion is more than merely the spreading of innovations from one work unit to another. It is also something that goes beyond the successful outcome of an alternative work system. Diffusion implies that there is a compelling force within the larger organization to see the principles and rewards enjoyed and practiced by a significantly larger proportion, if not all, of the workplace. In this concept of diffusion, a judgment is made by those observing but not involved in the limited work innovation project that they too would like to be provided the same opportunities to shape the nature of their work activities. Moreover, viewing diffusion from this perspective implies that change/improvements seek their own level of acceptance and penetration. If an innovative process is appropriately handled, its impact should be apparent and its purposes and "mechanics" should be broadly understood, accepted, and appreciated.

While this concept of diffusion is much broader than that typically advanced by change theorists, it is still best applied in accounting for the spread and adoption of innovations from one specific work unit to another, e.g., from one department to another within the same plant, or from one plant to another within a larger organization.

We will use the term *evolution* in attempting to account for higher-order, global processes of diffusion (e.g., in speaking of progressive states of development for General Motors as a whole).

In a similar fashion, *institutionalization* implies not only the acceptance of an organization's principles and goals but a strong commitment to the organization and all that it represents. It should carry the connotation that the people in the organization not only adhere to the organization's values and goals, but that they enthusiastically embrace and foster them. That means a level of harmony has been achieved between what the organization stands for and what the people believe in and want to be identified with.

In a more operational way, Goodman and Dean have defined institutionalization as made up of three elements, "performance of the change program behaviors, persistence of these behaviors, and the incorporation of these behaviors in the daily functioning of the organization."[3] Goodman and Dean also stress that institutionalization exists in degrees rather than as an absolute. They have identified five factors that contribute to the degree of institutionalization: (1) knowledge of the behaviors; (2) performance of the behaviors as reflected in their frequency and extensiveness; (3) preferences for the behaviors; (4) normative consensus, or the awareness that others are performing the behaviors or feel they should be performing the behaviors; (5) values, or a general agreement that people ought to perform these behaviors. In summary, Goodman and Dean state, "A program is institutionalized to the extent that it has progressed from the levels of knowledge and performance to preferences, norms and values."[4]

Before turning to a closer look at what is involved in diffusing, evolving, and institutionalizing change, it will be helpful to ground the reader in the experience of General Motors.

Planned Organizational Change in General Motors: Some Historical Background

Most people in GM would mark the fall of 1968 as the beginning of organizational development in General Motors. It was in November of that year that Ed Cole, then the president of GM, held a meeting with Rensis Likert (director, Institute for Social Research [ISR]), Lou Seaton (vice-president, personnel staff), and D.L. Landen (director, organizational research and development). The purpose of this meeting was to explore the idea for a joint organizational development project involving ISR and General Motors.

It was agreed at that meeting that a proposal would be jointly developed and, if mutually agreed upon, also jointly implemented and administered. After a year of planning, staffing, and preparation, an extensive OD effort was undertaken involving four GM locations and over 20,000 employees. There were four primary reasons for carrying out this project:

1. For some years, GM had been conducting plant-level studies that

clearly showed significant correlations between various measures of organizational performance (i.e., absenteeism, grievances, discipline, efficiency, and quality).

2. Other studies not only confirmed these correlations but demonstrated that supervisory leadership style was also correlated with these performance outcomes.

3. Following a tour of 120 GM plant locations, the president, Ed Cole, was struck by the fact that two organizations in the same community — building similar products, with common technologies, structures, union agreements, and corporate policy — could range so widely in their performance.

4. All participants shared a strong desire to demystify the field of management and to demonstrate more objectively what distinguished effective from ineffective managers, and successful from unsuccessful organizations.[5]

During the course of this joint project, which was "terminated" in 1973, regular meetings were held with all project personnel, the involved operating managers, and various corporate executives including the president. The purpose of these meetings was to keep all parties up to date on what was occurring and, most importantly, to assure their support and their advocacy of OD concepts and strategies. Consistent with this philosophy, upon completion of the project, a presentation was made to GM's board of directors.

It should also be stressed that "all of the GM eggs were not in one basket." Running parallel with the GM-ISR project were a number of other projects. A study of the content of the production supervisor's job was being carried out at the Saginaw Steering Gear Division. The Oldsmobile Division in Lansing, Michigan, was involved in a varied but interrelated array of projects — an absenteeism action research program, a productivity/quality improvement process, an analysis of the impact of "desirable/undesirable" jobs on employee behavior, and a longitudinal study of the organizational variables that shape the attitudes and subsequent behavior of car assemblers. In addition, an extensive job-satisfaction study was being carried on in GM by the organizational research and development department to assess the findings reported by the U.S. Department of Labor in its 1970 "Tri-Annual Study of Working Conditions in America."

In 1971, another important event occurred. The personnel staff was divided into two separate staffs — industrial relations and personnel administration and development (PAD). Dr. Stephen Fuller, long-time professor of management at the Harvard Business School and a regular consultant to General Motors, was brought in as vice-president of the PAD staff.

One of the purposes of this restructuring was to place importance on developmental activities equal to that which had been historically accorded labor relations. This move, among other things, communicated a shift of priority and emphasis to the operating managers of the corporation. It represented the first major step toward diffusing and institutionalizing what had been learned from the GM–ISR project.

In 1972, at the request of Irving Bluestone, director of the GM Department and vice-president of the International UAW, a review of the GM-ISR project was held with Bluestone and his staff. While this was primarily an informational meeting, it served to emphasize in Bluestone's mind that the UAW should be directly involved in the activities being carried out unilaterally by GM under the banner of organizational development.

In the 1973 national contract negotiations, this goal of Bluestone's became a reality. The union submitted a quality of work life demand that led to the creation of the GM-UAW National Quality of Work Life Committee. The goals and structure of the committee were set forth briefly in a letter of understanding that appears in the appendix of the National GM-UAW Contract. In essence, the letter states that the role of the National QWL Committee will be:

> designed to improve the quality of work life, thereby advantaging the worker by making work a more satisfying experience, advantaging the Corporation by leading to a reduction in employe absenteeism and turnover, and advantaging the consumer through improvement in the quality of the products manufactured.

While the membership of the committee has changed over the years, its primary goals are as they were first set forth in 1973. This is an important consideration when one speaks of institutionalization. The principles and goals on which QWL was founded in GM persist today. They are generally accepted by local managers and union people alike. It is apparent to anyone who wants to ponder the evolution of QWL in GM that certain principles and goals transcend events and personalities and have a virtually immutable quality. This continuity of purpose, however, should not be construed to mean that many things have not changed or that the principles and goals of the National QWL Committee would not be altered if circumstances dictated some modification. The more critical point is that, as one seeks "to spread the word" in large and complex organizations, the chances for success are far greater if the "rules of the game" have some level of permanence to them.

In 1971, Dick Terrell, then executive of the Car and Truck, Body and Assembly Group, convened a meeting of the top executives of those divisions to (1) discuss some of the human problems being experienced in the corporation; (2) review the status of the GM-ISR project; and (3) initiate a process of experimentation/innovation in organizational development designed to be responsive to the human/employee issues which gave rise to the meeting. This meeting spawned a series of such meetings now referred to as the National QWL Executive Conferences. The early purpose of these meetings was to impress upon GM managers that the quality of employee relationships was vital to the success of the business. The initial meetings were held in different locations, such as Atlanta, Montreal, and Boston. By holding the meetings near locations where some significant learning was in process, an opportunity was provided to visit pilot projects or to visit with academics who were themselves involved in various workplace projects.

Today's conferences are more elaborate and the presentations far more sophisticated. In the first meeting, one executive spoke of a motivational program that involved giving away turkeys at Thanksgiving. At the second meeting, one executive spoke with pride about the policy of providing pall-bearers at funerals. Despite the naiveté of some of these early presentations and the apparent "window dressing" that some locations attempted to pass off as being innovative and substantive, other divisions were engaged in some significant efforts at organizational change. Soon it became apparent to everyone attending these regular conferences that the emphasis and the issue were not going to go away. More importantly, those divisions taking the whole process seriously were beginning to achieve some significant improvements. The "window dressing" then began to give way to real progress among all divisions.

This point needs emphasizing. One of the critical variables in institutionalizing and diffusing workplace innovations, particularly among operating managers, is for them to know that such innovations will not impair their performance and may very well be the means by which higher levels of performance can be achieved with far fewer employee-relations problems. This conclusion implies two things. First, an educational process is important as a means of challenging traditional mind-sets and pointing managers toward other goals and the resources for achieving them. But since these are very practical and pragmatic people, a second need is to assure that there will be some payoff in terms that they understand and that are important to their concept of what makes for an effective business organization.

Critical to this ongoing educational process were two union-management QWL seminars held in 1975 and 1978. Both of these seminars were sponsored by the GM-UAW National QWL Committee. Each involved from twelve to twenty executives from each organization. Their major function was to provide a forum where QWL issues, objectives, and strategies could be discussed. Presentations were made at both seminars by locations that had some unique process underway. For example, as a part of the 1975 seminar, Irv Bluestone spoke about Harman Industries' Bolivar project. Three spokesmen from General Motors Assembly Division (GMAD)-Baltimore (local union president; chairman, local shop committee; and the plant's personnel director) spoke of an off-site seminar they had participated in, using the resources of the U.S. Department of Labor. By the 1978 seminar, some things of sufficient substance were going on in two locations — Buick Motor Division and GMAD-Tarrytown — to warrant their participation as panels at that year's joint seminar. Aside from their presentations, all participants were involved in experience-based learning exercises similar to those of the 1975 seminar. Both of those seminars were instrumental in encouraging or fostering some learning exchanges. Buick Motor Division and UAW Local 599 launched their joint process as a direct result of the general manager's participation in the 1975 seminar.

The mere fact that the National QWL Committee was sponsoring such seminars and that executives from both the UAW and GM were participating telegraphed to local union and management people that it was legitimate for them to undertake similar joint learning experiences. Today, such "off-site" seminars are commonplace in GM and the UAW. The fact is, locations that have not held or participated in at least one such meeting are the exception today rather than the rule.

In 1972, a meeting was held with the top managers of the Packard Electric Division at its headquarters in Warren, Ohio. The purpose of this meeting was to discuss some possible innovative features for a new wiring harness plant to be constructed by the division in Clinton, Mississippi. This meeting led to the introduction of some modest, but novel for GM, management/organizational practices. For example, all potential new employees went through a one-week vocational/technical training program to learn how to assemble wiring harnesses. This training was done on the individual's own time as a prior condition of employment. Following this training, every applicant went through a four-hour assessment process. The assessment center was designed to identify individual leadership, communication, interpersonal, and problem-solving skills. Once having been hired, every employee then participated in a comprehensive orientation program on the operation, measurement, structure, roles, and performance of a business organization. This strong emphasis on communication, interpersonal relationships, and individual development became a foundation on which the organization was built and on which it operates.

While Packard Electric's Clinton plant represented only minor innovations in workplace concepts and design, it nonetheless did establish a precedent for innovations in new plant designs. This precedent then became the basis for the design of other new plants in Monroe, Louisiana (April 1975); Fitzgerald, Georgia (March 1975); and Brookhaven, Mississippi (January 1977) — this one another Packard Electric plant. In all of these instances, as well as in other new plants — Delco–Moraine, Fredericksburg, Virginia (1978); Delco-Remy, Albany, Georgia (1978); Delco-Remy, Laurel, Mississippi (1976); Delco-Remy, Meridian, Mississippi (1975); Delco-Remy, Muncie, Indiana (1977); GMAD, Oklahoma City, Oklahoma (1977); GMAD, Shreveport, Louisiana (1977); Guide, Monroe, Louisiana (1974); and Hydra-matic, Three Rivers, Michigan (1977) — a common organizational planning process was used. (See chapter 7, fig. 7.3, for a diagram of this planning process). In this series of plants, the Delco-Remy Battery Plant in Fitzgerald, Georgia, represented a major breakthrough in organizational design. This plant is structured around self-managing, autonomous operating teams. The operating teams are supported by technical and administrative teams. The operating teams select their own leaders and, as a group, are responsible for their own budgets, scheduling, maintenance, production, quality, EEO objectives, discipline, and other administrative responsibilities. No differentiating symbols, such as time clocks, privileged parking, or private dining facilities, exist within the plant. Hourly employees are compensated on a pay-for-knowledge/skill basis. The more jobs one learns, the more money one makes. The reward system is appropriately tied to the principle of individual development. The responsibility for determining job proficiency resides with the team members. (See chapter 7 for a more detailed description of the Fitzgerald plant.)

The most critical principle regarding the Fitzgerald plant and other plants is that all of the elements in the organization fit together. The objective is to create a well-integrated system wherein all of the energy and resources are directed toward business and human goals and objectives. It is essential in these and other organizational forms that the culture and structure of the organization are inexorably bound to the philosophy and goals of the organization. To violate this relationship is to damage the integrity of the system and thereby impair its operating effectiveness and the quality of work life.

Since the advent of Packard Electric's Clinton, Mississippi, plant, 80 other plants have been designed and built by General Motors throughout its worldwide operations. In all of these instances, no two plants are structured or operated in precisely the same way. Each plant structure is shaped not only by its own philosophy and goals but by its peculiar products and manufacturing technology. One of the significant values of this development is that these plants and the process by which they come into being have provided General Motors with an array of "laboratories" or "test beds." It is possible to assess objectively both the idiosyncratic and common elements in each plant system as a basis for generating organizational principles which can be applied to the design of other new plants and, more importantly, to the redesign of existing and highly traditional organizations.

As an example of how this learning has been diffused, Packard Electric's Brookhaven, Mississippi, plant as an organization has more in common with the Delco-Remy Fitzgerald plant than it does with its sister plant in Clinton, Mississippi. Beyond this level of diffusion and institutionalization, Packard Electric sought to use what it learned in both Clinton and Brookhaven as a basis for redesigning its traditional plants in Warren, Ohio. As an expansion of this concept, in cooperation with the IUE local union in Warren, a Jobs Committee was created (1978) as a means of jointly designing other new plants in the Warren area, using the process and principles developed and tested at Clinton, Brookhaven, and the several other GM institutions.

This rather general description of GM's experiences serves as a frame of reference for further discussion of the essential nature and conceptual elements of diffusion within a broader process of organizational learning.

Understanding Diffusion

A conceptual framework is required to clear away some of the fuzziness and vagaries of the term "organizational learning." Figure 12.1 presents a perspective or model of organizational learning that is intended to separate out the following:

- *Inputs to Learning (Sensemaking).* How decision makers or members of the dominant coalition in an organization make sense out of their environment (both internal and external) and plan adjustments vis-à-vis that environment in triggering a change and diffusion process.
- *Processes of Learning (Diffusion).* How such inputs to learning create change and desired outcomes and the needed spread of those outcomes to other parts of the organization.
- *Outcomes of Learning (Evolution).* How resulting changes in organization structure, culture, and members begin to extend and affect the larger system of which the organization is a part.

The first, or sensemaking, stage of this model is a modified and expanded version of some key ideas presented elsewhere by Duncan and Dutton.[6] The model holds that there are a series of six major episodes or events, labeled as "sensemaking" when taken together, which will launch a change and diffusion process. Assuming that a dominant coalition employs some sort of monitoring or scanning mechanisms (e.g., control systems or measurements against standards of desirability) what has been called a *triggering episode* may occur at any time. This term is simply meant to describe a significant "something (anything)" that happens in the environment. *Activation* is the way that episode is observed and interpreted to fuel or energize the entire sensemaking sequence. For example, the episode may be detected as a performance discrepancy, a developmental need, or some potential disruption

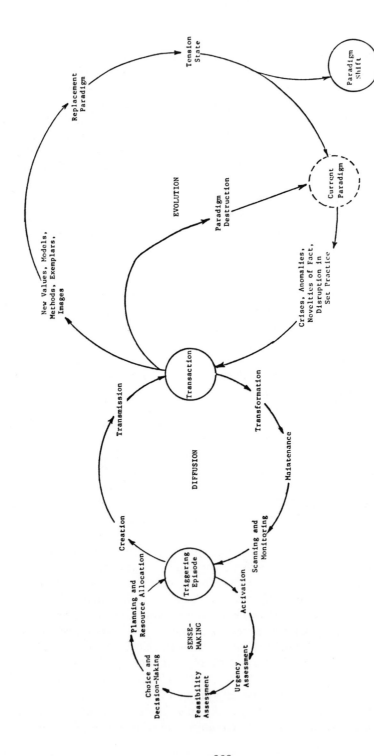

Fig. 12.1. A Model of Organizational Learning

in already established and patterned ways of behaving as an organization or as individuals or groups within the organization. *Urgency assessments* focus on whether decision makers decide to devote further attention to what they have detected. *Feasibility assessments* speak to whether or not these decision makers perceive enough predictability and control to make any change in the organization's response to its environment. Upon completion of such assessments, members of the dominant coalition can then move on to exercise their *choice and decision-making* role in setting the direction, target, and broad QWL strategy for dealing with their environment. *Planning and resource allocation* are obviously needed next steps. Given these inputs, their first-order outcome is simply another *triggering episode* or event that has been planned to launch the intended process of diffusion.

The diffusion process is shown in figure 12.1 as the second stage of the organizational learning model proposed here. This second stage comprises a series of different QWL efforts, each with a basic role or function to perform as events by which the process of organizational learning (i.e., diffusion) produces outcomes. As shown in the model, *creation* is any effort aimed at the search for, experimentation with, and development of new approaches to improving organizational performance and the quality of work life among members of the organization. Following creation, *transmission* is any QWL effort required to disseminate information about the innovation to other parts of the organization (e.g., to other departments within a plant). *Transactions* can then begin to take place, where interactions are initiated between the innovation source group and a potential application or user group or between management and employees, management and union, dominant coalitions in two or more departments or areas of the plant, the innovative plant with another plant organization, etc. Often such transactions are facilitated, mediated, or "brokered" in some way by a QWL/OD consultant. The result is potentially the energy behind a *transformation* of organization structures, technologies, or members by means of adopting, modifying, and implementing specific QWL activities which (at least in part) originated elsewhere. What has been transformed must then be stabilized and reinforced through *maintenance* QWL efforts. Supportive reward systems and information systems are two of the best examples of such maintenance activities. The transformation itself, along with indicators of its continued effectiveness and viability in dealing with the environment, is then tracked over time with a variety of *scanning and monitoring* mechanisms. Such mechanisms will then inevitably point the way to new *triggering episodes*.

In addition to performing the different functions shown in the model, the same QWL efforts can produce diffusion and then potentially focus on the larger organization (e.g., General Motors) of which the diffusion unit (e.g., a plant within GM) is a part. They might also focus on external organizations and on the larger social system. Where these higher-order or more global systems are brought into the picture, more pervasive and complex diffusion processes are required and the term *evolution* is used to denote these processes. The *evolution* stage, as shown in figure 12.1, might well have been focused on gradual, continuous, incremental change in the larger system. However, since a detailed model of the evolution of organizations is presented in the next section of this chapter, figure 12.1 presents the *evolution* stage as more of a quantum, discontinuous shift in the prevailing organizational paradigm of the larger system.

All organizations and social systems have a structure and a culture that tend to prescribe how events are to be viewed and responded to. The dominant paradigm may be operationalized as current and acceptable norms, models, exemplars, methods, or approaches in the organization. Organizations tend to use these current paradigms for viewing and interpreting social reality, both internally and externally. They have problem-solving components which trigger "knee-jerk" reactions alerting the organization's members to events which constitute problems and provide a framework to identify possible solutions.

Our model holds that *transactions* between growing numbers of diffusion units and their larger system begin to sprinkle and then shower the larger system with *new values, models, methods, exemplars, and images* of a "better way." Taken together, these new concepts form a potential *replacement paradigm* (with its own advocates and stakeholders) in some dissonant, tension state with respect to the *current paradigm*. As the current organizational paradigm repeatedly meets *crises, anomalies, novelties of fact, and disruption in current practice*, its restraining power can be expected to diminish and the balance of tension to slip more and more to the advantage of the replacement paradigm. What is often likely to block any such gradual movement to change paradigms, however, is the absence of effective communication between the advocates of these different points of view. But the learning process has the potential to be self-correcting. As opposing paradigm advocates engage in structured transactions, the evolving practicalities of the *replacement paradigm* will become more apparent, more pervasive, and more valued. Hence, when *paradigm destruction* occurs (as it will inevitably, given the increasingly turbulent environment in our society) the newly emergent paradigm will appear to shift rapidly in replacing the current one. This *paradigm shift*, then, completes the model of the anatomy of organizational learning and brings us to the question of how to institutionalize any such change.

However, some important reality factors and caveats should be noted. While the explication of organizational learning processes just provided is the ideal, the reader must be conscious of a whole range of other possibilities. When organizational learning processes do not operate as described here, various effects can be hypothesized as realistic alternatives:

1. *System Drag* — where an inertial component of the diffusion process operates to slow down or halt the pace at which this process can proceed. As just noted, the typical lack of communication between advocates of current and new paradigms will cause system drag.
2. *System Drift* — where the directional or goal-oriented component of the diffusion process is deficient and thus may allow movement or the spread of effect into unwanted or unplanned target areas. For example, the lack of commonly defined change goals or targets might be one factor causing some drift in the joint QWL efforts of union and management people.
3. *System Blockage* — where any one element of the model is arrested or blocked from releasing any energy to precipitate the next element in this process. It appears to be typical of many innovative processes in GM, for example, that after a certain time particular implementation sites reach their limit. The burden of trailblazing is then taken up by other sites where favorable conditions emerge in the broader GM system.
4. On the other hand, when organizational learning processes do approximate the flow and pattern modeled here, it might be suggested that here is a case of *system drive*, i.e., an instance where the trend of change is directional, well focused over the long pull, and reasonably consistent and adaptive under the press of variable circumstances and events.

THE EVOLUTION OF ORGANIZATIONS

Classical organizational theory treats institutions as static entities. It is presupposed under the classical paradigm that the hierarchical organization with its several echelons, line and staff demarcations, concepts of unity of command, span of control, and managerial prerogatives will best assure both the productivity and continuity of the enterprise. Under conditions of stability and predictability, such structures do perform quite well.

As the environment in which organizations exist becomes more turbulent, the institutions, if they are to prosper and survive, must be able to adjust to changing environmental demands and forces. Both Bennis[7] and Toffler[8] have predicted that other organizational forms (i.e., temporary systems and adhocracies) are essential to the vitality of contemporary and future American institutions.

Drucker agrees with equal conviction that the "age of discontinuity" and a shift to a service society impose new demands on organizations. These demands emanate from external forces and from the fact that knowledge and not products is becoming the critical resource that must be effectively organized. Accordingly, Drucker speaks of "knowledge-based or decision-based" institutions.[9] His views parallel those of Bennis and Toffler in that he, too, calls upon managers to create new organizational forms that will provide for and stimulate the integration of knowledge. If decision making is the engine that drives organizations toward their goals and objectives, then it is vital that knowledge normally diffused throughout classically structured organizations be creatively brought to bear upon and within the decision-making process. New structural forms must be instituted to assure that this is accomplished.

A small group of top-level managers may be in the position to formulate broad and long-range company policy, but they are neither responsible nor qualified, by virtue of the kinds of knowledge and expertise they possess, to deal with day-to-day operating issues. These responsibilities must be decentralized, if they are now highly centralized, to the lowest reasonable level feasible. Such decentralization presupposes that the required structures exist to facilitate the shift of responsibilities and *all* related administrative responsibilities and authority, and that people have the competency with which to deal effectively with the newly emerging administrative roles. And, critically, beyond this change in administrative roles, people must have the authority to take appropriate actions consistent with their responsibilities and accountability.

The above description should suggest to the reader that individuals need to be provided with the developmental opportunities that will enable them to perform differently and more effectively. But this developmental process cannot be limited to the individual. Developmental processes must also be applied to the organization. Like individuals, organizations possess developmental patterns. They also are endowed with a potential for growth and development. But such maturational patterns do not simply occur. They must be planned, implemented, and wisely guided. Figure 12.2 is a model of a developmental/learning curve designed to display the sequential steps through which organizations evolve.

The "building blocks" are the base on which all organizations are constructed. Organizations generally begin at this stage of development, and many organizations never evolve beyond this level. Those who manage organizations at this stage of development view the relationship of the "individual to the job" as being the most critical source of improvement. Therefore, it is not surprising that traditionalists commit considerable resources to job training in the belief that both the individual and the organization will be the beneficiaries of the training investment. This may or may not be so. If the focus of education and training is on new organizational concepts, principles, and behaviors, the probability of their being executed is proportional to the amount of investment that is made in altering the nature and culture of the organization so that the "individual/organization" interface is systematically enhanced. Since all organizations are sociotechnical systems,

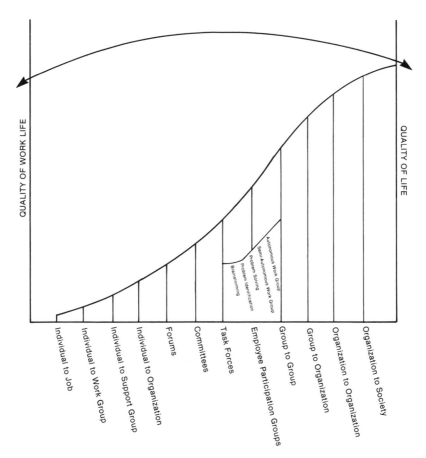

Fig. 12.2. QWL: An Evolutionary, Holistic Process

the system must be the focus of improvement. We should not expect significant changes or improvements in organizational outcomes as a direct product of individual training. The training strategy does not possess sufficient
power to provide for system-wide transformation. Training is logically a
part of a larger change/improvement strategy. But most training is neither
concerned nor designed as a broad organizational development process.
That is one reason why most organizations never evolve beyond this basic
stage of development. The strategies generally employed in conventional
organizations lack the breadth, scope, and power to become "bridging"
rather than "building" blocks.

As figure 12.2 suggests, the process of organizational transformation is
evolutionary. One stage or phase of development is built on a preceding
stage or stages. It should also be recognized that the soundness of the organizational "building blocks" is essential to providing the basis on which suc-

cessful "bridging" or transforming mechanisms can be constructed. And, most importantly, these "building block" stages must not be weakened as a result of introducing transforming mechanisms. They are basic to the building of and further development of the organization. Ideally, the transforming or bridging mechanisms should be designed so that they strengthen rather than diminish the basic foundation of the organization.

Transforming organizations should be viewed as an incremental process. While there may be a strong tendency on the part of many people in an organization to want to make the "quantum leap" from more elementary to more sophisticated organizational structures, most organizations would be wise to proceed in an evolutionary fashion. This approach will help to avoid trying to move at a rate too rapid for both participants and the organization. Since new organizational structures require new knowledge, skills, and behaviors, a graduated process will enable people to acquire these needed qualities to enable them to perform competently.

As can be noted from this figure, as one moves to the right on the developmental curve, power or authority is being more widely diffused throughout the organization. For example, a *forum* provides for a wider distribution of information about the organization, its operations, and the relationship of individuals to the organization. The process is commonly referred to as information sharing. When a committee is established, the communication process is modified from a one-way to a two-way transmittal of information. Rather than simply being better informed by means of a forum, individual members of a committee are asked to contribute their views, opinions, and ideas; and, as participants, they are afforded at least a beginning role in the decision-making process of the organization. Committees can either be temporary or permanent. Permanent committees tend to have more power than do temporary ones, merely because some organizational sanctions exist that permit the members to meet occasionally and presumably take some kind of action, generally outside the boundaries of their regular jobs. A task force represents a stronger organizational commitment. Membership on a task force presupposes that all members will have access to all information required to understand the task and generate intelligent approaches to dealing with the task. But beyond this, an implicit, if not explicit, understanding is that the recommendations generated will be acted upon affirmatively. And if not acted upon, a reasonable explanation must be provided as to why certain proposals cannot be implemented.

A quality circle may be viewed as a permanent task force or a standing committee. A major distinction is that a quality circle is not only intended to be permanent but its members are *empowered* to meet regularly; receive problem-solving training; have access to information, data, and people; and either recommend actions to be taken or implement their own decisions. Therefore, a quality circle represents a significant shift in organizational decision making. Moreover, it is an ongoing and self-adjusting, decision-making system that is freer than task forces or committees from the influence of external whims or capricious contracts.

As quality circles develop greater maturity, the circle members can gradually take on many traditionally supervisory responsibilities such as scheduling work, job assignments, job training, layout arrangements, and requisition of tools and materials. As this participative process evolves, the role of the supervisor will of necessity change. In order to encourage or facilitate this downward shift of responsibilities, new supervisory roles must be encouraged and supported. It is likely the supervisor may become a resource to the newly emerging, semiautonomous quality circles. At this stage of its development, a quality circle should more logically be labeled an employee participation group (EPG), a term commonly used in General Motors.

As the figure shows, an EPG can, over time, become totally independent of the supervisor, since the group will develop its own leadership. It is at this point that a major organizational restructuring can occur. The supervisory role can be moved out of the vertical structure into a collateral organization such as a business team. Thus, one level of supervision is reduced, shifting supervisory work downward and providing for a new support system made up of experienced supervisors who now take on new responsibilities such as planning, plant-wide problem solving, interfunctional coordination, and, generally, "trouble shooting." Through the process of attrition, the number of people in the collateral organization can be reduced and a small nucleus of highly competent generalists can be developed.

The organization at this stage has reached a high level of sophistication and the overall structure has been transformed from a quite traditional one to one beginning to approximate a high-level sociotechnical system. But the process need not end there. The system must be free to evolve to a point where the coordination of group-to-group, group-to-organization, and organization-to-organization relationships is widely spread throughout the organization. Under this type of an arrangement, the responsibility for making the organization perform effectively is a shared responsibility. Every individual under this paradigm is responsible for performing certain tasks, helping to make the group perform effectively, handling intergroup relationships, and having a role in helping the organization achieve its fullest potential.

As in all other stages, the unit of development (in this case, the total organization) can only grow in direct proportion to the development of the larger system of which it is a part. Public relationships and social responsibilities are roles that everyone can help perform and in which everyone has a vested interest. Contrary to historical tradition, people do not live compartmentalized lives. We do not check our value systems at the plant gate or office door. People come to the workplace as total human beings, and the quality of their lives and the quality of their working lives are so intertwined that they defy separation. This model is an effort to help bring that fact into greater clarity.

One last important point needs to be made with respect to figure 12.2. Much of the foregoing is based upon the principle of infinite power. The term "power" is herein defined as the ability to influence individuals and events toward the accomplishment of agreed-upon goals and objectives. As more people gain greater power, the net effect is to increase the power of the organization—to perform, to grow, and to sustain its continuity.

STRATEGIES AND MECHANISMS FOR INSTITUTIONALIZATION: GM'S EXPERIENCE

Turning from the conceptual to the concrete, let us identify the major strategies and mechanisms used in General Motors to initiate, diffuse, evolve, and institutionalize change over the past 14 years. That such strategies and mechanisms have been reasonably successful might be inferred from Burke's observation that GM presents the only example among bureaucratic organizations in his experience of a long-term, sustained change process.[10] The remainder of this chapter is devoted to a thoroughgoing explanation of how this success has been achieved, along with many of the mistakes which give rise to new learning about the problem of sustaining change.

In a brief summary, institutionalizing work innovation requires a number of organizational preconditions:

- A system-wide change/improvement strategy.
- An early-on decision to institutionalize change.
- An organizational culture that encourages and supports innovation.
- A variety of mechanisms that provide an interchange of experiences and learning from one site to another.
- A conscious strategy for shifting and/or decentralizing responsibility, authority, decision making, and accountability from function to function and level to level.
- A flexible reward system that recognizes the changing roles of people in the organization and assures equity of responsibility, performance, and contribution.

A System-Wide Change/Improvement Strategy

While most workplace innovations begin on a limited basis, the likelihood of their being sustained is reduced sharply if the pilot effort does not become more widely diffused to other workplaces within the same system. In the case of General Motors, the initial effort at organizational development was a joint project with the Institute for Social Research at the University of Michigan and involved over 20,000 employees in four different plants. By most standards, this would not be classed as a "pilot project." However, in the case of GM, it was judged as precisely that. The initial change strategy employed a survey feedback model. Over 5,000 salaried employees were involved in the first survey process.

Aside from the data-based developmental process that was launched in each plant location, a number of other innovations were instituted. Some locations focused heavily on team building; others initiated major job redesign projects, particularly around the role of production supervisors; others committed considerable resources to the training of supervisors and hourly employees. The most striking of those early innovations was the business-team concept introduced in the cushion room of the GMAD Lakewood, Georgia, assembly plant.

Despite the variety of innovations spawned over the four years of the project, very few of these innovations were diffused to other locations and very few even became institutionalized in the locations where they originated. One of the primary reasons for this lack of success was that there was no well-designed plan for spreading the process to other GM locations. Consequently, while many top managers were aware of the project, they had only cursory interest in, and no direct involvement with, it. Hence, they held no ownership of the change effort. The only GM group maintaining a strong commitment to the concept was that of the organizational development professionals. At that time, unfortunately, this group had limited access to GM's top operating executives and no clear strategy for gaining their support.

However, in 1971 a meeting was convened of the top operating managers of nine of GM's major divisions to review the status of the project and to discuss a range of organizational issues. At the end of this meeting, the top executive of the group expressed his dismay with the intractability of the personnel and labor problems under review. He also challenged all of those present to return to their divisions and begin some pioneering efforts at involving people in helping to solve some of their operating and human problems. He also appointed a committee to organize a second meeting in about six months, the primary purpose of which would be to provide an opportunity for every division to report on the work innovations introduced over the preceding six months. This process continues today in General Motors. These meetings are now referred to as Annual Executive Quality of Work Life Conferences. They generally involve 250–300 of the top operating executives of the corporation, both domestic and overseas.

Each conference has a theme. The 25 to 50 presentations are all structured to explicate and exemplify the theme as it is operationalized in their respective units. Over the past few years, presentations have ranged from detailed explanations of how joint union–management efforts are improving work attendance to using QWL principles as a basis for developing market and business strategies.

In 1981, GM's International QWL Conference was followed by seven one-day regional meetings. These meetings were organized and administered by local committees and involved presentations by local panels, many of which had union and management panelists. Through this strategy, over 1,600 managers and 265 union leaders were, for the first time, a part of a joint educational experience.

These conferences, along with the routine administration of the QWL survey, regular QWL update reports to executive committees and to the Joint GM-UAW National QWL Committee, annual presentations to the public policy committee of the GM Board of Directors, and a number of other supporting mechanisms described briefly in a later section of this chapter, are the major elements in an overall corporate strategy to make QWL principles the foundation on which General Motors operates its business.

An Early-On Decision to Institutionalize Change

From the outset, one of the most fundamental strategies in GM's approach has been the conscious decision to build OD/QWL principles into the very fabric and operating agenda of the organization. The QWL conferences just described, for example, have been an integral part of GM's calendar since 1971. They have been held even in years of economic restraint when meetings of whatever variety were curtailed to reduce costs.

Another good illustration is the early decision to rely on the selection and training of internal people (usually highly credible, middle management people) as OD/QWL specialists or consultants within their plant, division, and staff organizations. While most other companies have apparently relied on external consultants, it was believed in GM that a kind of dependence can thus be created which would in some ways run counter to the growth needs of the organization.

Finally, another example is what might really be *the* QWL operating norm in General Motors: responsibility for QWL must reside in the line organization (among managers and all other members) and not among QWL consultants or the particular staff (e.g., personnel) in which they are housed organizationally. The widest possible accountability, ownership, and skill development have thus been emphasized instead of limiting such attributes to the internal "experts."

An Organizational Culture That Encourages and Supports Innovation

The early strategy to have every division report at each conference on its new organizational developmental efforts was designed to accomplish four objectives:

1. To diffuse learning from unit to unit
2. To encourage innovation and risk taking
3. To impress upon managers the importance of developing new ways to meet business and human needs
4. To make apparent to all in attendance those locations that were engaged in substantive innovations and those that were "playing games and were attempting to delude rather than inform"

To begin with, about all that became institutionalized was the holding of regular meetings. Some divisions took the challenge and opportunity quite seriously. Their early efforts, while limited in scope, began to show some encouraging effects. For example, one division was able to reduce its absenteeism in a pilot area primarily by means of involving hourly workers in trying to solve the problem. The "startling" insight that evolved was that absenteeism dropped to zero among the people involved in the project *before any solutions were implemented*. It became apparent to practically everyone that the process (in this case, involving hourly workers in a task force on absenteeism) was the solution.

The division in question reported on this project at the 1972 conference. Subsequently, highlights of the project were presented to all top managers within the same division. In neither case did the elements of the project spread to other locations, either within the corporation or even within the same division. In the former case, it was hypothesized that the NIH ("not invented here") factor explained that lack of diffusion. In the latter case, it was learned later (much to the chagrin of many people) that the reason managers at the same location did not duplicate the project was that they were heading up work units used as a basis for comparing changes in the "experimental plant." These managers felt that they had been made to look bad because their innovative efforts, which were focused on issues other than absenteeism, were cast in a negative light. One of the things learned from this experience was, given the existing culture of that division, all projects must be seen as a joint effort on behalf of the entire organization. If comparisons are to be made, either compare before-and-after conditions within the same unit, or use another division or the corporation as a frame of reference.

Over the past decade the support for workplace innovations has grown sharply. Today, the climate for innovations is very apparent. The locations that receive the greatest publicity and, generally, the greatest acceptance are those regarded as learning models at the cutting edge of the quality-of-work-life process. The only exception to this are those locations which receive a great deal of unwarranted publicity when the substance of what they are doing is rather shallow and short-lived.

The current culture in GM places importance on innovations that, over the long pull, will likely improve the organization's competitiveness (in the broadest sense of this term) and also significantly alter the roles of people in relationship to the overall balance of organizational responsibility and decision making. The significant efforts are those that involve a major restructuring of the organization and the process by which it accomplishes its objectives.

Interchange of Experiences and Learning from One Site to Another

Innovations in the workplace, organizational design and redesign, or, more broadly, a vital and comprehensive QWL process imposes upon people throughout any system new roles, new behaviors, new skills, and new value choices. The often-heard cliche that QWL is "just good common sense" or that QWL is nothing other than living by the Golden Rule is far from the truth. While common sense and the Golden Rule may be elements in an effective QWL process, they are not what QWL (or any other label one chooses to use when speaking about workplace design) is all about in principle or in practice.

In order for people to be able to participate intelligently and effectively in any workplace innovation and to support and nurture a process of improvement, they must have some understanding of the values, principles, concepts, strategies, and sustaining forces involved in the process. If they lack this knowledge, they will by nature continue to operate or behave based upon their existing body of knowledge.

There appear to be two schools of thought as to how best to educate or reeducate people about the concepts and techniques of organizational change.

One point of view is to create learning systems such as workshops, conferences, and seminars so people can come together and "sit at the feet of a guru" and engage in a dialectical interchange. This is a quite acceptable educational equation. However, it is predicated on the traditional pedagogical model which asserts that the acquisition of knowledge leads to changes in values and behavior. An alternative approach to this "cognitive" format is to see learning as an "experiential" process. The rationale is that more cognitive learning will occur if certain emotions are experienced before any attempt is made to articulate or to understand the concepts underlying the experience. This approach to learning also has both value and validity.

Like most things in life, there is no simple dichotomy between these two learning models. Both points of view have value when effectively applied. What organizations must do is create a variety of learning opportunities. Some things are learned best by going from theory to practice. Other principles are best learned when they are based on practical experience. Learning systems should be available that not only presume to go from theory to practice or practice to theory, but see theory and practice as having a composite rather than a linear relationship. One of the best ways to forge this composite is to design a learning process around the real work and operating issues of the organization rather than around "games" (experiential learning) or concepts (cognitive learning).

Today in General Motors, there are a variety of learning forums – conferences, seminars, workshops, projects, printed materials, and video tapes. All of these are valuable and important. In addition, there are a number of networks of people who are widely located throughout the corporation and meet together on some regularly scheduled basis.

One such example is the "OD/QWL Heads" network. These are the divisional people who have overall resource responsibility for QWL activities within their divisions and staffs. This group meets quarterly. Each meeting is hosted by a particular division and is generally held at an operating unit of the host location. One reason is that, in addition to the formal agenda covering the two or three days of the meeting, network members have a chance to sit in on QWL activities underway at the location where the meeting is held. Also, local operating people have an opportunity to participate in the "OD/QWL Heads" meeting to learn about projects and progress at other GM locations.

Another network in GM is made up of the managers of plants where nontraditional work systems are operational. Meetings of this group are generally held on a quarterly basis. Their primary aim is to provide a forum where unique organizational concepts can be discussed, exchanged, and built upon. These meetings, like the ones held by the "OD/QWL Heads," are hosted at a particular plant location where it is possible for those line managers to see firsthand what is going on in the host organization and to exchange ideas with the people in the plant.

Another network in the process of being established will be made up of facilitators of employe participation groups (more broadly known as QC or quality circles). This network will be launched at a facilitators conference to be scheduled in the near future. This network, like the others just described, is prompted by a desire on the part of divisional people to have a forum where they can learn from one another and gain encouragement and reinforcement for their initiatives. In some cases, this translates into a support system for needed risk taking.

One final comment on the role of learning systems. Their form and content need to be relevant to the people who are involved. As one means of assuring such relevance, the learning system should be theirs to shape, to control, and to nurture. But, in the final analysis, the best learning comes from doing. The stimulation to test out new ideas can begin through the kind of learning systems described briefly above. However, people must have the opportunity and the encouragement to design and test new systems and the knowledge that, in so doing, they are performing a unique service for the enterprise and for its people.

A Conscious Strategy for Decentralization

The only effective way to think about institutionalization is to view it in the context of restructuring essential organizational variables. If the behavior or roles of people in a work setting are to undergo significant and sustainable change, all critical work activities must be subject to redefinition and modification. QWL must be seen as a process that serves to get decisions made where the issues and problems are, and by the people who have the information, knowledge, and skill.

These points of view are based on the proposition that, in most traditionally structured organizations, too many decisions are made too far from the source and by individuals or groups with limited and, quite frequently, inappropriate data. This form of decision making is too time consuming and generally leads to less than adequate decisions and, therefore, to less than maximal performance.

It is generally assumed that the traditional system of decision making must operate because people further down the organizational ladder cannot be trusted to make sound decisions. The bulk of the evidence today refutes this position. Today's workers are fully capable of making sound decisions about their own work and workplace if they have the necessary information, skill, and opportunity.

As shown in figure 12.3, to achieve this objective of full decentralization requires comprehensive strategies that, over time, will evolve the organization and its structural elements from one "level of authority" to another, more relevant "level of authority." It is apparent from this figure that at least four discernible change strategies exist within General Motors. An eclectic, multivector approach to organizational restructuring may appear to be at variance with an ultimate goal of institutionalization of work innovations. In actuality, the contrary is the case. The aim is not to institutionalize the process but the product of the process. In all instances, the product of the four strategies is the same — "down shifting" responsibility and its associated administrative roles.

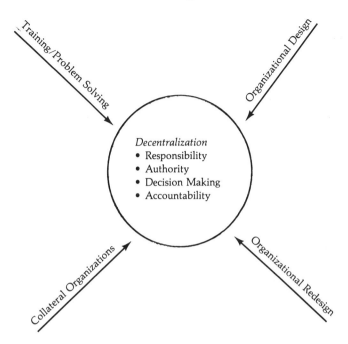

Fig. 12.3. A Four-Vector Strategy

While it may appear from the figure that the ultimate aim is not achieved until the process has been completed, that is certainly not intended. It should be emphasized that the process used to bring about change/improvement must be idiosyncratic to the organization, its stakeholders, its state of development, and its unique philosophy, goals, products, technology, etc. If all of that is true, then it can be reasserted here that *the process is the solution.* The decentralization that appears in the center of the figure occurs incrementally as the process evolves and matures. It is the organic nature of the process that stimulates the "spin-off" of the "decentralized roles." It is also the organic, dynamic, and never-ending qualities of any successful change/improvement process which create the conditions for diffusion and institutionalization.

Using the label "The Four-Vector Strategy" may be quite misleading. It may suggest to some readers that this was a preconceived, corporate developmental strategy. Such was not nor is it now the case. The major function of the figure is to show roughly what has been occurring in General Motors. These approaches were neither preordained nor planned. They just happened. And that fact is important. A great deal can be offered in the way of counsel and advice as to how a change/improvement process might evolve. But in the final analysis, despite all the direction and guidance that can be provided on the process by all participants, the process must have sufficient flexibility and alteration to "just let it happen." The idea is to trust the process. Some clarification and examples of figure 12.3 will perhaps help to make this idea more concrete.

The Training/Problem-Solving Vector. The GMAD Tarrytown plant went through the general pattern of development found in most GM locations: phase I — improving union–management relationships; phase II — providing for increased employee involvement.

Phase I, in the case of Tarrytown, involved joint meetings and, more importantly, joint planning and implementation of a fairly major rearrangement of some assembly operations. This process led to significantly better relationships between labor and management, and the activities in which they were jointly engaged became a vehicle for involving large numbers of workers throughout the operations that were being rearranged (see chapter 5 by Robert Guest for the details).

Phase II, increased employee involvement, was diffused by means of a pilot project in an operation not involved in the earlier stage of the process. Because of the success of both the pilot project and the rearrangement operation as well as the plant-wide visibility given to both, the next logical step was to implement a plan that would involve every employee in the plant. This was accomplished through a three-day training program conducted jointly by 25 two-person teams, each with a union and management trainer, over a period of 18 months.

The challenge conveyed to all 3,800 employees during the training was to utilize newly acquired knowledge of the organization and its operations combined with their problem-identification and problem-solving skills to tackle day-to-day operating problems when and where they occurred.

Fisher Body–Fleetwood in Detroit is following a strategy quite similar to that of Tarrytown. In contrast to Tarrytown, Fleetwood management has invested substantial resources in the education of all managers and supervisors. The initial judgment in this example was that, before any effective efforts could be committed to improving relationships between the management and the union leadership, it was critical to upgrade managerial and supervisory knowledge and skills.

Upon completion of these educational activities, every hourly employee is asked to participate in a two-day team development seminar conducted jointly by salaried and hourly trainers. Following this training, any hourly employee who wishes to become a member of a permanent problem-solving group is provided additional training in problem-solving and decision-making techniques.

The important lesson to be learned from the Tarrytown and Fleetwood examples is that Fleetwood represented a "second generation" model of the Tarrytown process. In the case of Fleetwood, it was recognized early on that, in order for the QWL process to be vital and effective, there had to be some structural mechanisms to assure the continuing involvement of large numbers of employees and the desired shift in problem-solving responsibilities.

Collateral Organizations. As a concept, a collateral organization has unlimited application. While the end product of all change/improvement strategies is to get decisions made at appropriate levels by appropriate people, creating collateral organizations is a very powerful way of restructuring existing hierarchical organizations.

The underlying rationale for any collateral system is that such a system must contain the elements and the qualities of the future state toward which the existing organization should be evolving. A collateral organization is an organizational entity that exists initially parallel with a current structure but differs in terms of purpose, philosophy, culture, norms, roles, and structure. The process of organizational transformation from existing to future-state organizations is to have people spend a portion of their working time in the collateral organization. This arrangement should encourage the simultaneous development of processes — the resocialization and skill development of individuals as they are exposed to a new work culture, and the reculturalization of the traditional organization, as individuals with their newly acquired behaviors and skills begin to apply these characteristics within or to the old organization.

An example of this concept in General Motors is the Parallel Business Planning Organization of the Central Foundry Division. This collateral structure was created to provide a continuing means of maintaining desired focus and priority on long-term business goals. The parallel organization provides a day-to-day means for managers in different locations who represent differing functions at different organizational levels to meet to discuss, resolve, and recommend strategic approaches to future business needs. The parallel organization provides not only the unique integration of managers across traditional organizational boundaries, but also the kind of culture in which the open, free-wheeling interchange of ideas, not typical of the line or tactical organization, is acceptable.

As the parallel organization has matured, it has served to modify the behavior of managers and the culture of the tactical organization. Moreover, since managers are spending roughly 20 percent of their time in the strategic organization, that naturally leaves a vacuum of unmet responsibilities in the tactical organization. These responsibilities, either through delegation or usurpation, provide the foundation for redesigning the jobs of subordinates, thereby elevating their organizational roles.

As a diffusion/institutionalization strategy, collateral organizations have broad application and powerful potential to redesign traditional organizations. It should be a conscious strategy of every organization to capitalize on every opportunity to use temporary organizational systems — councils, committees, task forces — as mechanisms for exposing employees to the norms, behaviors, and skills that will be required in future-state organizations. Such a plan will serve to accelerate the rate at which the current organization is helped to change. The behavior newly acquired in the collateral organization will become the force for evolving the current organization from one state of development to its next most logical state.

Organizational Design. Chapter 7 by Richard Cherry contains a detailed explanation of the concepts and techniques of sociotechnical systems analysis and the organizational design process utilized in GM.[11] The major parts that need to be emphasized here are that (1) this planning process may yield quite different organizational forms; (2) the ultimate objective of decentralized administration is the accomplishment of an early planning objective and operating reality; and (3) the decentralized administrative function assures that the organization performs as it is intended to perform.

The goal of creating new forms of workplace structures and operations had its origin in GM in the planning for the Packard Electric Clinton plant in 1971–72. At that time, a comprehensive plan for designing an organizational system had not as yet been developed in GM. What did exist, however, was a high-level commitment to create an organization more consistent with the perceived needs of contemporary and future organizations.

The Clinton plant was really not that unique. A great deal of emphasis was placed on communication; interpersonal relationships; and selection, orientation, and training. But its primary contribution was not the form, relationships, nor processes of the operation. It was the general awareness and willingness by key division and corporate managers to design and operate alternative organizational forms.

Over the past decade, 80 new operations have come on stream in GM throughout its worldwide operations. Some of these have been quite large systems such as the GM Assembly Division plant in Oklahoma City which, at maximum production, employs over 6,000 employees. Others have been quite small by GM standards, about 250 employees.

As stated earlier, this thread of new plant innovations has provided GM with 80 "laboratories." Some plants have touched the advanced edge of self-managing, autonomous workplaces. Other operations are only marginally distinguishable in form and style from their home plants. This phenomenon alone not only provides for interesting and informative cross-plant comparisons, but also is highly reflective of the basic philosophy on which the QWL process is predicated and by which it operates in GM.

It is the position of the corporation that each operating unit must be free to create its own organizational forms. The people who create these organizations are the people who must administer them. Therefore, it is vital that the operating people not only be free but also be encouraged and supported in creating the kind of organization that is consistent with their philosophy and goals, with the products and technology that will prevail in the organization, and, finally, with their own sense of what is appropriate and their own vision of the future. Such latitude of choice may not always produce the most interesting or exciting organizational forms. It may not even represent a very sound strategy for diffusion. But it does increase the probability that what is created will become institutionalized. Moreover, it precludes the possibility of putting all of one's "work-innovation eggs" in one organizational form, which may only have transient mobility and vitality.

Organizational Redesign. At the system-wide or macro level, everything that has thus far been said in this section could be construed to be an organizational redesign process. Certainly, General Motors is a quite different organization in 1981 than it was in 1971. At various times, top-level corporate executives have encouraged divisional operating personnel to apply the same ingenuity, creativity, and risk taking to organizational design that is applied to product design — and for precisely the same reasons. The business environment, like the market, is subject to all kinds of complex and unpredictable forces. Therefore, designing new organizations and redesigning existing ones require sound, far-sighted management.

Rather than pursue a discussion of the changing nature of GM, two examples of organizational redesign at GM will be cited. The two organizations, to be discussed briefly, were selected from several locations that are equally fascinating and unique. Two of the reasons for selecting these locations are (1) both are moving toward the same degree of decentralization by quite different routes, and (2) one is a division-wide strategy, while the other is limited to one plant in a large, multiplant, geographically dispersed division. The former division is Buick Motor, the latter is the Chevrolet Gear and Axle plant of the Chevrolet Motor Division.

To fully appreciate the diffusion and institutionalization process, it is important that the concepts and strategies are seen as applicable to any kind of organizational form. For example, both the Buick and Gear and Axle change/improvement processes have evolved over the last five years. Each started with different entry strategies; each has proceeded in quite unique ways; each initially involved the union at different points along the developmental continuum; each involved the hourly work force at different stages; and each has a different plan as to how it intends to evolve from where it is to what its membership believes it must become. As change/improvement strategies, both are highly successful. Both organizations are confident of what they have achieved thus far and are equally confident that they are on the right track and will accomplish their respective goals.

Some elements in the Buick story. The QWL process began in Buick in 1975. The general manager provided the initial impetus based upon his participation in a union-management QWL seminar sponsored by the GM-UAW National Quality of Work Life Committee. This meeting so impressed him that he encouraged his staff to participate in a similar seminar with the leadership of UAW Local 599, which represents the 16,000 production and maintenance workers at Buick in Flint, Michigan.

The first meeting was held in October 1975. Among other accomplishments, a joint committee was established to oversee the QWL process. After about a half dozen off-site meetings, the third of which was held at the UAW Family Education Center as guests of the union, a decision was made to provide an opportunity for the workers to become involved in some form or fashion. Since neither party was quite sure of how the process might work and how people might react to the joint invitation, they agreed upon the safe step of an open house. The voluntary participation of employees was sought in the planning, organization, and administration of a division-wide open house for Buick families and friends. The open house was so successful that it was followed over the next two years by a bond drive, blood donor campaign, hospital fund raising, and United Way of Michigan campaign.

Because the people so impressed management with their talents, their eagerness, and their desire to become more involved, the manufacturing manager began to look for a way to institutionalize the high level of involvement. As one means of doing this, a management seminar on quality control circles was held in the summer of 1977. As a result of that seminar, quality control circles were introduced into the car assembly plant. Today, about 200 circles are operational in seven different plants. All these plants are part of a 21-plant complex located on a common parcel of land in Flint, Michigan.

Throughout this period, the divisional union–management committee continued to meet on a quarterly basis. In addition, six of the plants have their own joint QWL committee. The division committee and some plant committees have participated in panel presentations at GM QWL conferences and at public forums. Because of the visibility gained through these and other media, the division has been deluged with on-site visits. Both parties attempt to honor these requests when it is practical to do so. But since this is a truly joint process, only requests from joint union-management groups are honored.

In October 1980, Buick launched another significant phase of its overall QWL strategy. It began production of a new product — transmission torque converters — in an old remodeled foundry, employing laid-off foundry workers. The plant is called Factory 81. The significance of this development is that it integrated two parallel developments underway in GM and established several new precedents.

Factory 81 is a sociotechnically designed and operating plant. The core of the operations is the use of autonomous work units. The remainder of the plant is designed to support these units. Consistent with the philosophy and goals of the plant, there are no shop rules, no time clocks, no major distinctions between hourly and salaried employees. And, indeed, the plant has most of the characteristics associated with a totally new sociotechnical system plant, such as Delco-Remy Fitzgerald. Most importantly, it was the successful existence of unique organizations such as Delco-Remy Fitzgerald that made Factory 81 possible. Had the sociotechnical systems (STS) organizational planning process and its resultant workplace systems not become institutionalized in GM, the climate and the expertise for creating a Factory 81-type organization would not have existed.

The second parallel development was what was going on elsewhere in Buick and in GM in the area of union–management cooperation, i.e., the early employee involvement programs (like the open house); the introduction and diffusion of the quality control circle concept; the existence of a division-wide union–management QWL committee; the public acclaim given Buick management and Local 599 leadership; the successful early settlement of the 1979 labor contract negotiations; and, of particular significance, the tribute paid by the corporation to the people of Buick by making that organization the sole supplier of torque converters for front-wheel-drive vehicles. All of these events provided the foundation on which a Factory 81 organization could be conceived and implemented.

The integration of these two parallel developments in the nature and form of Factory 81 attests to the wisdom that organizational change/improvement is a dynamic, idiosyncratic process governed more by practicality than ideology and, of necessity, subject to the internal controls of local union and management people. Factory 81 established a precedent in that this was the first unit of any size jointly conceived, designed, implemented, and governed by a union–management planning committee.

In the process of designing this work system, other precedents were established. In cooperation with the international union and the corporation, a single classification — quality operator — was negotiated, a pay-for-knowledge system was agreed upon, and, of even greater significance, both the local union and management people have publicly committed themselves to use Factory 81 as the "laboratory" in which to develop the process and then to share the redesign over the next five years with all of the plants at Buick. Thus, it is intended that the entire organization be recreated. It was born on the principles of an earlier century and is destined to become an organization suitable and prepared for a new century, less than two decades ahead.

Some elements in the Chevrolet Gear and Axle story. In 1976, "The Gear" was an organization on the brink of a major crisis. Its major products, technology, organizational philosophy, and structure were all "geared" to making products that were soon to become obsolete as GM vehicles shifted from rear to front wheel drive. "The Gear" was then an organization of 8,200 employees housed in seven plants, all within immediate proximity to one another. This 59-year-old complex is located in the heart of Detroit, bordered by Hamtramck, the old "Dodge Main," and all the ills that inner-city industrial complexes are heir to.

Over the course of the last five years, the top of the organization has been restructured from 14 fiefdoms into a single administrative team of six managers, each representing a broader but integrated business function. The same principle has been applied to all six plants. Each is now organized by plant teams with the same functions that are represented at the top "complex level." The functional manager at the plant level has an informal reporting relationship to his counterpart at the next higher administrative level. Part of the rationale for this reconfiguration of responsibilities was to force the day-to-day decision making down in the organization, while simultaneously freeing up the top of the organization to engage in more strategic planning. A second consideration was to create a more effective and efficient management system for administering a reduced and more dynamic organization.

As a further means of institutionalizing a team concept of management, employee involvement circles (EIC) were introduced at the bottom of the organization. By some standards, these problem-solving groups are much like those currently gaining so much publicity elsewhere in the United States. However, they also have their own unique qualities.

Comparable to what was noted in the description of Fisher Body-Fleetwood, and consistent with both the goal reflected in figure 12.2 and the overall philosophy and goals of "The Gear," the EICs (which now number about 75) represent not only problem-solving systems but decision-making bodies. One added dimension to the EICs is that they become the structural mechanism by which supervisory responsibilities are shifted downward. Over time, the EICs take on increasingly more of the administrative roles of supervision, thereby upgrading the role of the hourly worker and freeing up supervision to undertake new and more challenging responsibilities. As both groups gain greater maturity and competency, the long-term strategy is to create collateral organizations in which to move one or two levels of supervision out of the vertical chain of command.

The EICs now become the means by which new roles and responsibilities become institutionalized. Moreover, they have become the process through which the organization has been redesigned from a 59-year-old bureaucracy into a 1981 adhocracy. The administrative team, plant teams, and EICs, all of which are built on the same conceptual foundation and resemble in principle and structure Delco-Remy Fitzgerald and Buick Factory 81, are near approximations of the organization's desired end state.

The supporting mechanisms for "The Gear" transformation are comparable to those found in any successful transitional process in GM — top-level commitment, a joint union–management QWL steering committee, hours of education and training for every participating employee, changes in many traditional operating policies and practices, and a clear vision and realization that tomorrow's competitive organization must be created today.

A Flexible Reward System

It is a well-established principle of psychology that for any behavior to be effectuated it must be rewarded or reinforced. As people are required, or simply want, to adopt new ways of doing things in a work setting, conditions must exist which support or reinforce new behavior patterns. If no such reinforcement exists or, worse yet, if the behavior is negatively reinforced, the desired or newly acquired behavior will not endure. The reinforcement of desired behavior is vital to the institutionalization of change. The culture and norms of the organization must be compatible with desired or expectant behavior. If individual behavior and organizational norms are central to one another, the greatest likelihood is that the individual will adapt to the culture rather than the reverse. However, in some change situations, it is expected that an individual or a small group is capable of changing how an entire organization behaves. This is not impossible, but the probability of its occurrence is quite low. Therefore, where change strategies are being integrated, one needs to define both the behaviors that are desired and the organizational conditions that will support the behaviors. These should suggest that the two are interdependent. Organization integrity is a product and a reinforcer of human behavior. Any effective developmental effort needs to take this factor into consideration. Stated another way, human development cannot occur in the absence of organizational development, and organizational development cannot occur in the absence of human development.

Many efforts at institutionalizing organizational change fail because they do not take this factor into account. A strong tendency exists to think of rewards solely in economic terms. Therefore, when new behaviors are being manifested, which may show that some people are taking on new responsibilities, concerns are expressed that "these people are going to expect more money." That may be true, but it may not be true. The more fundamental principle is not economic equity, but human equity. Does the system, the relationship between the individual and the organization, remain in balance as judged by the individual?

Exchange theory postulates that, as long as there is a homeostatic balance between individual inputs and perceived outcome, a steady state will prevail. If either of the two — the individual or the organization — attempts to extract more than its equitable share from the other, the system's balance will be destroyed and both the input and output needs of the equation will be affected. The exchange theory also asserts that individual inputs will be governed by perceived outcomes, or rewards. If rewards are reduced, then so will the individual inputs. If one is reversed, so the theory goes, a corresponding reverse will be reflected in the other.

As one can readily infer from these theories, no single nor simple reward system is going to assure that new roles and behaviors will be normalized. Reward systems must be flexible and subject to individual preferences. Most importantly, reward systems must provide for a mixture of intrinsic and extrinsic rewards. The most common extrinsic reward is money, which can be provided in a variety of reasonably specified ways — hourly wages, piece rates, salaries, bonuses, special awards, and invested capital. Intrinsic rewards are not as amenable to determination or definition. What may be subjectively important to one individual may not be as vital to another. Some people are driven by power. Others are more stimulated by the knowledge that they have helped a fellow human by making some physical sacrifice. But generally, most people derive energy, feelings of commitment, or a strong motivational attraction from knowing that the work they do makes a difference to the organization, its performance, and its people. Strong feelings of self-worth, personal dignity, pride in accomplishment, and feelings of mastery are all intrinsic rewards.

An important distinction between intrinsic and extrinsic rewards needs to be drawn. Aside from the obvious fact that one set of rewards is external to the individual, while the other set is internal to the individual, an understanding of the sustaining nature of these two reward systems should be noted.

The primary function of all reward systems is to help create and sustain behavior. Both external and internal reward systems are effective in creating behavior. But until the "rewarding state of affairs" (a term used to include not only the content of the reward, but the context — the environment — in which the reward is "given" or extracted) becomes internalized, its sustaining power (the likelihood that the behavior will continue) will be quite low if not zero.

Intrinsic rewards, because they generally have high subjective components associated with them (if, indeed, they are not totally subjective), have a more enduring capacity. Feelings of pride can be self-nourishing, as can one's feelings of self-worth. However, subjective feelings of these or any type are dependent in part upon one's perception of the external environment. Such perceptions are thus both the source from which the initial feelings are derived and the source of their sustainment.

As one contemplates the development of reward systems, it should be apparent that ideally the system should provide for both extrinsic and intrinsic rewards. But a system of rewards that fails to take into consideration the environment in which reward systems exist will fall short of its true potential. The expression, "I wouldn't work for him for any amount of money," is a simple example of this concept.

If workplace innovations are to be successful, a sound economic base of wages and benefits must prevail. Self-regulating feelings of pride in accomplishment are difficult to experience if one experiences counterfeelings of deprivation, disunity, or disadvantage. If a sound economic floor is not sustained, it is unlikely that extrinsic feelings will be sustained.

We should be able to conclude from this reasoning that fundamental to the diffusion and institutionalization of new behavior is a reward system that supports the desired behavior in terms of both appropriate external and internal dimensions. Examples of the reward systems viewed as supportive in GM have already been noted. They include the pay-for-knowledge system, an all-merit concept of salary administration tied to appraisals of performance (including QWL performance), and a bonus system for higher executives where QWL initiatives have weighed into the actual allocation of bonus awards. Probably, at some point, a gain-sharing program will also become a reality for all employees.

A Larger Concept: An Organizational Principle and Two System-Wide Strategies

As previously described, institutionalizing new roles and new behaviors requires a number of preconditions. Intertwined with these preconditions, in the case of General Motors, is an array of corporate-wide reinforcing/supporting mechanisms. Before summarizing these mechanisms, it is important to note that these and other diffusion/institutionalizing mechanisms are guided by fundamental organizational principles. Since all systems seek to maintain a steady state, strategies must focus on producing organized change in the state of equilibrium. The energy within the organization that acts as a resisting force must be rechanneled to become a facilitating force. In order for this to be achieved, the weight and power of the driving forces must exceed the weight and power of the resisting forces. Institutionalizing new values, norms and behaviors in an established organization requires a change in basic organizational philosophy and a major shift in the organization's culture. When dealing with large or small systems, change/improvement processes must be forceful enough to cause the system to alter and redirect itself without causing so much disequilibrium that it becomes counterproductive.

Two major strategies have been employed in General Motors to accomplish this objective — critical masses and networking. The details of both of these strategies are included in the description that follows. It should simply be stated here that as more stimuli and support for change are introduced, the intent should be to bombard the system and surround its stakeholders with forces that propel them into desired and necessary directions. As an extension of the strategy of critical masses, the change/improvement processes should be bound together to form networks. The more networks that are created, the greater becomes the critical mass. Single-barreled strategies and single targets can be appropriate and effective. But if change is to be accelerated and diffused, then multibarreled, multitargeted strategies must also be employed.

As described elsewhere in this chapter, a multifaceted, four-vector strategy has been evolving in General Motors over the past decade. But these strategies alone could not and will not produce the level of change that is essential. Those strategies and, in fact, any and all improvement strategies must be embedded in a larger organizational support system. The support system in General Motors can be summarized in six major categories:

- Top level commitment
- Educational processes
- Resource commitment
- Joint union–management activities
- Organizational design/redesign
- Research and measurement

Top-Level Commitment. Organizational development efforts in General Motors have had top-level support from their early origin in the mid-1960s. It was the president of GM who was personally instrumental in launching a major project with the Institute for Social Research of the University of Michigan in 1968. Currently, periodic reviews of QWL activities are carried out with members of GM's executive committee, public policy committee (comprised exclusively of outside board members) and science advisory committee (made up of members representing major scientific disciplines and universities). In addition, a recent (August 31, 1981) update was made to the full board of directors. Aside from this role, top executives are involved in QWL off-site visits, project reviews, QWL conferences, and on-site visits. In addition, the group executives review annually the QWL survey results and related activities with the members of the executive committee and with other corporate officers.

The top executives have been involved in, and supportive of, the corporate minimum standards which have been established to guide the operating divisions and staffs in the administration of QWL processes. Among these five minimum standards is the biennial administration of the QWL survey. The other minimum standards require a top-level committee to oversee the

QWL process; a local QWL philosophy statement designed to create a vision of the future state of the organization and to serve as principles to guide local actions and decisions; the existence of an educational process to familiarize local people with QWL principles and techniques; and, lastly, qualified internal resources to assist the line organization in developing, implementing, and sustaining QWL innovations.

While it is normally not the practice in GM to involve top executives in the review and sanctioning of specific organizational development techniques, the concepts, structures, and use of employee participation groups (which are an advanced form of a QC circle) were reviewed with, approved, and supported by top corporate executives. Most of the current top-level executives have also participated in joint union–management QWL seminars. These seminars are jointly designed and provide a means by which union and company executives can explore issues of common concern and develop joint strategies for working cooperatively on their resolution. Lastly, the executives of General Motors set an example for others in the corporation as to how they believe the business should be managed. They are placing increasing importance on leadership qualities essential in managers if the corporation is to attain only the highest levels of quality of work life and organizational effectiveness.

Educational Processes. Contemporary workplace innovations are predicated on nontraditional organizational theories and practices. Accordingly, everyone at all organizational levels and functions needs to be provided with an opportunity to be exposed, through a variety of educational methods, to alternative organizational concepts, principles, structures, processes, and policies. In order to accomplish this educational objective, a variety of corporate-wide forums and media have been combined and intertwined with a complex of ideas and ideals.

As one views the vast array of workplace innovations under development or in process, it is easier to see them as bits and pieces of improved practice than as parts of a coherent and total organizational change strategy. In order to put these developments into their proper perspective, a variety of conceptual models are used in General Motors to abstract and integrate ideas. These models are designed primarily for use by line managers as a medium by which they can understand and think about workplace innovations that they themselves are engaged in, have observed elsewhere, or have heard about from others.

The major value in these and all conceptual models is that, once fully comprehended, they can help one readily move from the specific to the general. Achieving this level of broader intellectual understanding makes it far more likely that diffusion and institutionalization will occur. Transforming and shaping concepts rather than "getting stuck with someone else's packaged program" is powerful motivation for line managers and other stakeholders to gain ownership.

Consistent with this principle, over the past five years each Annual Executive QWL Conference has been designed around a conceptual model. The content of the meeting is designed to illuminate and explicate a concept or set of concepts while simultaneously educating the participants about specifics within a range of change processes. For example, the most recent QWL conference of about 275 GM managers was structured around the principal elements in a system-wide change process — goal setting, planning, implementation, monitoring, follow-up. These annual conferences, which began in 1971, involve generally from 250 to 350 top executives from GM's worldwide operations. Presentations are made by line managers to line managers. In 1980 and 1981, the UAW vice-president and director of the GM Department spoke at the conference. Several local union officials participated in the proceedings.

For the first time, in 1981, a series of seven regional conferences were held. Including those who attended both the international conference and the regional meetings, over 1,800 GM managers and about 275 union officials participated.

As a further means of diffusing the presentations from these meetings, video tapes are made and conference proceedings are published. The proceedings are distributed to everyone attending the conference. Additional copies are available for interested parties who were not attendees. The video tapes are distributed to divisions and plants to be used in connection with local seminars, off-site visits, and general training sessions. Other printed and video materials are also available for use by local units in their educational activities. For example, special video tapes on EPG's, the QWL survey process, Type Z organizations, and speeches by union leaders are widely distributed throughout the corporation.

A quarterly newsletter, *QWL Update*, is distributed to several thousand people throughout GM's international operations. The purpose of the *QWL Update* is to keep people generally informed about the QWL activities underway in GM and outside the corporation, and to feature in some detail a particular development technique (such as EPGs) or process (such as Buick's sociotechnically designed Factory 81).

In addition to these educational systems, a variety of other educational mechanisms are employed — on-site and off-site meetings of managers, supervisors, and joint union and management groups; familiarization seminars for managers alone or in partnership with union leaders; plant visits to observe workplace innovations directly; and "open houses" where locations that are swamped with requests for visits set aside a day and invite 200 to 300 union and management people from other locations to a formal presentation and an on-site visit of the plant.

While QWL specialists are involved in all of the other educational activities, regularly scheduled skill development workshops are available within the corporation administered by organizational research and development. Included are workshops on such subjects as basic consulting skills development, facilitators training, sociotechnical design, stress management, and strategic planning.

Lastly, as noted above, these support systems are bound together by various networks. They also have a common conceptual framework that serves to give the educational components internal integrity. The networks come into being as a need of the line organization to diffuse experiences, exchange and develop concepts, and provide mutual support. Examples of these networks are the following: managers of new plants, "OD/QWL heads," QWL coordinators, EPG facilitators, and QWL survey administrators.

Aside from all of these formal educational mechanisms, perhaps the most powerful learning occurs informally. A constant interchange of information exists among operating managers, union leaders, and QWL specialists. These interchanges transcend organizational boundaries, levels, geography, and tradition. These informal structures, like all informal structures, serve needs not likely to be met by any formal process. They should be encouraged and supported.

Resource Commitment. For workplace innovations to be initiated and sustained, a commitment of necessary resources is obviously required. Such commitments should rightfully be viewed as investments rather than costs. If an organization, or even a portion of it, is to be redirected, some level of investment should be expected. Of course, the level and kinds of investments will be determined by the size, complexity, and potential payoff of the change/improvement effort. Investments take many different forms, with money being only one of several kinds of commitments. Naturally, time is a vital resource — time to plan, design, implement, monitor, participate, counsel, involve, follow-up. All of these and more.

Staff resources must be committed, along with budgets to sustain staff operations. An initial phase in many change efforts involves a pilot project, frequently using outside consultations. Both the project and the advisors require financial commitments. As one begins a diffusion/institutionalization process, a full-scale training effort for large numbers of employees may be required. This calls for an investment in training time, training facilities, materials, and "floor" follow-up.

Many other kinds of resource commitments may be required. The important point is that these are investments in the future and should be treated as such. Beyond their tangible importance, they also communicate intangibly to the organization that the change effort is important and has the full support of top-level executives.

Joint Union–Management Activities. A fourth element in GM's support system is the variety of joint union–management committees now in operation. Beginning in 1973, GM and the UAW established the GM–UAW National Quality of Work Life Committee. Since that time, 74 local committees have been established. Five of these are with the International Union of Electrical Workers (IUE) and one is with a local rubber workers union in Dayton, Ohio (Local 87).

In addition to the QWL committees, GM and the UAW have established National Work Attendance and Product Quality Committees. Similar committees have also been established in some divisions and plants. These committees, especially QWL committees, perform a variety of functions. They sponsor seminars, participate in off-site meetings, develop programs such as GM's employee participation groups, participate in conferences, entertain "visiting firemen," and, generally, oversee all joint QWL activities.

Most such committees also participate in selecting and assisting union and management QWL coordinators. While the major function of these coordinators is to assist floor people, they also act as a resource to the joint committees. Most local committees also develop guidelines as a framework on which to structure their activities and to provide resources to QWL participants. For example, most guidelines stress the voluntary nature of participation and point out that QWL activities should not be used to reduce the work force, speed production, or undermine contract provisions.

As in other support systems, joint committees consist of both tangible and intangible components. The tangible components are of the kind cited above. The crucial intangible component is the committees' symbolic value. The existence of national committees conveys to local parties the legitimacy of establishing their own committees. The existence of joint committees at all levels communicates to people generally that a new, more cooperative relationship has emerged. This should signal to everyone a joint commitment to QWL both as a process and as a philosophy.

Organizational Design/Redesign

As pointed out elsewhere in this chapter, new plant designs in GM have become a kind of "living laboratory." The conscious corporate strategy is to encourage these new systems to evolve along whatever organizational dimensions are appropriate to their philosophy, goals, products, and technology. Thus, each organization is unique. And it is these unique qualities, along with some common organizational parameters, that can at times be diffused to other organizations and serve as a partial basis for the redesign of traditional organizations.

Alternative organizational structures are not limited to operating facilities. Nontraditional structures also exist on GM's engineering staff, materials management staff, and quality and reliability staff.

The engineering staff is a matrix organization structured around project centers. The activities of the nine project centers are guided by the chief engineers of the car divisions. The centers are staffed by technicians from the operating divisions and remain as members of the project team until the project is completed or their technical services are no longer required. This staff/line design is a diffusion/institutionalization model. The structure provides for the efficient integration of technical knowledge and skills and for the transfer of this technology between line and staff and staff and line. This form of line/staff relationship also assures greater relevancy of R&D activities, as judged by the joint deliberations of line and staff planners. Most importantly, this type of structure and joint responsibility increases the probability that unnecessary R&D duplication will be minimized and the transfer of new engineering products from staff to line will be maximized.

The materials management staff utilizes a kind of "parallel organization," consisting of people along a diagonal slice of purchasing, production control and logistics activities, and is structured to manage and assist in the management of all QWL-related activities.

The quality and reliability staff, a very recent organization, was established to serve as a resource to the line organization. Accordingly, its basic philosophy and structure were collaboratively designed by about 30 line and staff executives over the course of a two-and-one-half-day off-site meeting. The staff consists of only 14 individuals. Their primary function is to provide coordination between various projects and to be available to line for advice and counsel.

The structure of these staffs is important in the same sense as are the designs of nontraditional plants. They serve as examples, as models of optional ways in which work can be organized and organizations can be structured to use talent and knowledge more creatively in the pursuit of more effective workplace systems. In the broader context, the concept of collateral organizations needs to be seen as an organizational design and redesign strategy. As noted earlier, a collateral organization is a structure that operates parallel to the traditional organization. One of the major roles of the collateral organization is to integrate knowledge. Another significant role is to serve as a model for the kind of form toward which the traditional organization should be evolving.

Currently, GM has a variety of structured collateral organizations — product teams, business teams, employee participation groups, parallel organizations, and the numerous joint QWL committees at both corporate and local levels. These are all decision-making systems, structured for learning new values, norms, and behaviors as a basis for transforming large and small systems into more innovative places of work and achievement.

Research and Measurement

The bulk of the work-innovation research in General Motors is action-oriented. The intent of this philosophy is to view research as an organizational change/improvement strategy. Action research projects are designed in collaboration with line, union and management, and hourly and salaried people. These same stakeholders are also involved in the implementation and monitoring of research projects.

Based upon GM's experience, approaching research in this way accomplishes the following: (1) issues that are dealt with are those critical to operating people; (2) the action research model becomes a learning mechanism in terms of both concepts and change techniques; (3) alternative ways of assessing performance, structuring work, organizing work units, managing groups and individuals, and conceptualizing outcome variables and the integrated systems that produce them are put into operating terms and procedures; and (4) programmatic and longer-term change strategies come into better perspective so that measurement techniques become operating tools rather than academic abstractions.

Action-oriented research is a learning process. The primary objective in this form of research is to recognize that organizations are dynamic systems subject to continuous change, and that the research intervention should be designed to help guide or govern the change in directions important to the organization and its members.

From the perspective of diffusion and institutionalization, the goal is for operating people to become skillful at using action research models and strategies as a way to mobilize resources in the pursuit of common objectives. In the case of GM, after the initial involvement of line managers in an action research project, they become quite skillful in generalizing the research model to other situations. As in all QWL processes, the research process becomes the means by which other improvements occur. For example, one GM research project was designed to identify ways of improving production and quality. The task force organized to work on these interrelated issues achieved, through its collective efforts, improvements in both areas. At the same time, however, absenteeism went down, grievances were reduced, and employee attitudes were improved. While the latter improvements were not the research objectives, the task force became a galvanizing force to enhance employee commitment and create more meaningful organizational roles.

The QWL survey process in GM performs a basic, symbolic function. It conveys to all employees the importance placed on QWL by top-level executives of the corporation. Beyond that, of course, the survey provides an effective means by which employees can anonymously and confidentially express their feelings about their work, the organization, and related subjects. The survey process may frequently become the initial step in developing and launching a more comprehensive QWL process. And, finally, the survey findings can be used to monitor progress, examine statistical relationships with other measures of operating performance, and provide the basis for developing more comprehensive views as to how large, complex systems function and what strategies most effectively alter their direction and performance.

In line with other strategies discussed in this chapter, the QWL survey process creates learning systems which can be transformed readily into day-to-day operating procedures. The process that becomes institutionalized is not a survey feedback process but a formalized means by which groups can deal with here-and-now issues in a climate built on openness, candor, and mutual problem solving.

THE FUTURE OF AMERICAN ORGANIZATIONS IS IN GOOD HANDS

Based upon research in General Motors, it is clear that workplace innovations lead to improved operating performance and higher levels of quality of work life. Statistical studies of 23 assembly plants show that the GM plants with the highest QWL, as measured by a standard GM QWL questionnaire, also have better product quality, higher customer satisfaction ratings, lower absenteeism, fewer grievances, and lower labor costs. More recent analyses have shown that QWL survey findings in one year reliably predict product quality and customer satisfaction ratings the following year. This finding reaffirms earlier research in GM that shows that employee attitudes are "lead time indicators" of subsequent operating performance. Other studies conducted within GM have shown that plants that have joint union–management QWL committees also settled their 1979 contract negotiations more efficiently than did those plants that did not have joint committees.

Moreover, those plants with a cooperative union–management QWL process underway exhibit higher levels of QWL among the hourly work force than do those plants which do not have a joint process underway. (It should be pointed out that, among these same plants, the QWL survey results tend to be lower for salaried employees where there is a joint union–management QWL process underway. This finding suggests, among other things, that improvement strategies that do not involve all segments of the organization may lead to a disparate impact upon employee attitudes and, in all probability, upon their performance. These findings tend to underscore the importance of developing change strategies that have the long-term potential to be diffused throughout the organization. While it is appropriate, and frequently desirable, to start a QWL process with a limited part of the organization, the failure to diffuse the process can have a negative impact upon those who are left out. It may also have a long-term negative impact upon those involved in the initial effort because the process of diffusion not only engenders a revitalization of the attitudes and behavior of those heretofore untouched by the process, but the process of diffusion serves to renew the spirit of enthusiasm of those workers involved in the first undertaking.

As has been pointed out, diffusion and institutionalization occur in concert with one another. Through the organizational energy that is produced through the process of diffusion and institutionalization, a forward, evolutionary thrust is created. The force of this thrust helps to propel the organization from one stage of development to another.

Throughout this chapter, it has been our intent to emphasize the interconnectedness of processes with one another, outcomes with one another, and processes with outcomes. Since contemporary organizations are both dynamic and complex, only systemic principles and processes are most likely to produce both short- and long-term effects.

In the final analysis, the future state of American organizations will be based upon their convictions (the principles on which they are founded and the basis on which they operate), on the existence of organizational mechanisms that assure that these operating principles are transformed into practice, and, on the fact that workplace innovations — quality of work life — become not only the philosophy but the spirit of future organizations.

Where the process of workplace innovations will end, no one can accurately foretell. But as long as people at all levels of organizations have the opportunity and competency to help shape the nature of their work and their working lives, the future of American institutions will be in good hands.

NOTES

1. Paul S. Goodman and James W. Dean, Jr., "Institutionalization or Making Labor and Management Change Programs Work," a paper prepared for Work in America Institute, 1981.

2. Richard E. Walton, "The Diffusion of New Work Structures: Explaining Why Success Didn't Take," *Organizational Dynamics*, Winter 1975, pp. 3–22.

3. Paul S. Goodman and J.W. Dean, Jr., "Why Productivity Efforts Fail," a paper presented at the American Psychological Association Convention, Los Angeles, 1981, p. 4.

4. Ibid., p. 7.

5. For a detailed write-up of this project, see *Organizational Dynamics*, Winter 1974.

6. Robert Duncan and Jane Dutton, "Implementation of Quality of Work Life as a Response to Organizational Learning," paper presented at the annual meeting of Academy of Management, San Diego, California, October 1981.

7. W.G. Bennis and P.E. Slater, *The Temporary Society* (New York: Harper & Row, 1968).

8. Alvin Toffler, *Future Shock* (New York: Random House, 1970).

9. Peter Drucker, *The Age of Discontinuity* (New York: Harper & Row, 1969).

10. W. Warner Burke, "Organization Development and Bureaucracy in the 1980s," *Journal of Applied Behavioral Science* 16 (March 1980).

11. See figure 7.3 in chapter 7 by Richard Cherry.

Index

involvement of line, 166–69
support of, 173
training framework for, 158–60
team-based plants (General Motors)
and, 125, 133, 139, 144
Topeka work system, 264–65, 280,
284
work innovation and, 330
Management–labor agreements. *See*
Labor–management agreements
Managers
Citibank program and, 112, 117, 121
EI program and, 45, 46–47, 49, 61,
62
plant, 46, 47, 48, 52–53, 54, 55, 58
Face-to-Face program and, 25, 27,
28, 33, 39, 41–42
quality circles and, 7, 8, 9, 20
facilitators and, 12
installation strategy and, 10–11
proposal cancellation and, 18
proposal implementation and,
15–16
QWL at General Motors and plant,
90–91, 95, 97, 101
QWL strategies (General Motors)
and, 296, 304, 309, 313, 317
resistance to change and, 11
Rushton QWL and, 225, 228, 237,
242
semiautonomous work groups and,
150, 151, 153, 160–61, 178, 182
training of, 159
team-based plant, 145–46
Topeka work system, 264, 269, 271,
272, 280, 281, 283
burnout and, 277, 278
higher management and, 273
hiring and, 275, 279
WIP (HII) and, 191, 193, 194, 195,
198, 213, 216
support and, 211
Mandate of chief executive officer
(Herman Miller, Inc.), 67–71, 72, 75,
77, 86
Manual (Employe Involvement), 57
Manufacturing planning specialist (EI),
58
Marketing, Face-to-Face program and,
38
Martin Marietta quality-circle program. *See also* Quality circles
definition of, 6–7
documentation of growth of, 18–19
as educational and learning process,
8
employees and, 4, 8, 14–15, 16–18
impact of, 20
infrastructure growth and, 18
innovation and, 19
institutionalization of, 7–8
management–union agreement and,
9–10
managers and, 7, 8, 9, 10–11, 12,
15–16, 18, 20
office for, 10
organizational preparation and, 14–
17
pilot program and growth of, 5–6
as political process, 8
problems with, 8–9
production procedure (plant setting)
and, 3–4
reasons for adopting, 4–5
rule preparation and, 17–18
strategy for installing, 10–13
training and, 13
Matteis, Richard, 119, 124
Measurement
of Face-to-Face results, 35
of quality-circle results, 16–17
of semiautonomous-work-group
results, 173–76
Meck, Bob, 286
Meetings
curtailment of (Rushton QWL), 247
Face-to-Face program, 24, 33
quality-circle, 17
Methodology
QWL results analysis (Rushton),
238–39
semiautonomous-work-group analysis, 149–50
Michael, E.T., 187, 192

About the Editors and Contributors

EDITORS

ROBERT ZAGER is vice-president, Technical Assistance and Policy Studies, Work in America Institute, Inc., Scarsdale, New York. He received his B.A. from Harvard and his LL.B. from Yale Law School. Zager practiced law for five years in New Jersey, where he was actively involved in city planning, housing, and education concerns. From 1955 to 1975, he was a management consultant, in this country and the United Kingdom, dealing with management/organization development, labor relations, and manpower planning. He then served two and one-half years as a consultant to the National Center for Productivity and Quality of Working Life. His writings have appeared in newspapers and professional journals here and in the United Kingdom. He was appointed vice-president of Work in America Institute in May 1978.

MICHAEL P. ROSOW is vice-president, Education and Training Division, Work in America Institute, Inc. His present responsibilities include management of The Productivity Forum, supervision of the Institute's Studies in Productivity and direction of Work in America Institute's research and demonstration projects. Rosow received a B.A. from Windham College and a Ph.D. in applied research psychology from Hofstra University. He was involved in developmental planning and research with Daniel Yankelovich and Professor Raymond Katzell of New York University and spent three years as a project director with Daniel Yankelovich, Inc. Rosow next served as a senior study director for Booz-Allen, Hamilton, National Analyst Division, where his research interests led to the development of special concepts for electronic consumer projects and the exploration of consumer attitudes on energy conservation. He has been associated with Work in America Institute since its founding, first as consultant and then as vice-president.

CONTRIBUTORS

HOWARD C. CARLSON is executive consultant, Organizational Research and Development, General Motors Corporation. Author of articles and chapters in many professional journals and books on such topics as quality of work life, employee motivation, and identification of management potential, he has also taught courses on management philosophy and human resource utilization. He has a Ph.D. in industrial and organizational psychology from the University of Minnesota. In his work for GM, Carlson administers programs of measurement and research with the aim of achieving greater organizational effectiveness and a higher quality of work life.

RICHARD L. CHERRY is currently associate professor, Stetson University, School of Business Administration, while on a one-year leave of absence from a General Motors Corporation consultancy. He has a Ph.D. in industrial social psychology from Louisiana State University at Baton Rouge. Cherry is president/director of Consulting for Organizational Effectiveness, Inc., and was recently director of International Quality of Work Life, General Motors. In his work for General Motors, he initiated the diffusion of new plant design concepts and practices to overseas locations and aided in creating a training program for OD/QWL consultants from other countries. He has also worked extensively with the management of many new GM plants in the United States, promoting OD/QWL methods and philosophy.

CHARLES E. DWYER is director of the Management and Behavioral Science Center of the Wharton School, University of Pennsylvania. He has been active in management research, development, and consulting for the past 23 years and has participated in numerous projects dealing with productivity and the quality of work life. Dwyer received his Ph.D. from Cornell University in 1966 and has been a member of the faculty of the University of Pennsylvania since that time.

CARL F. FROST, professor of industrial/organizational psychology at Michigan State University and a consultant with Frost, Greenwood, and Associates, received his Ph.D. in clinical psychology from Clark University. He was a colleague of Joseph Scanlon, originator of the Scanlon Plan at MIT, and is a Scanlon Plan specialist in executive and organizational development. Frost has acted as consultant with Herman Miller, Inc., Donnelly Mirrors, Inc., Firestone Tire and Rubber Company, Fairchild Corporation, and Scanlon Plan Associates.

PAUL S. GOODMAN is professor of industrial administration and psychology at the Graduate School of Industrial Administration, Carnegie-Mellon University. He has also been on the faculty of the University of Chicago as well as a visiting professor at Cornell. He received his Ph.D. in organizational psychology from Cornell. Goodman's main professional interests focus on work motivation and attitudes, organizational design, productivity, and organizational effectiveness. Goodman has extensive consulting experience, and his writings appear in many professional journals and books. He has also been involved in research about human issues in the coal industry. Two of his books are *Assessing Organizational Change* and *New Perspectives on Organizational Effectiveness.*

ROBERT H. GUEST, professor emeritus of organizational behavior at the Amos Tuck School of Business Administration at Dartmouth College, has worked extensively as a business consultant, and has served on several government commissions. Guest has taught at eight colleges during his academic career and has served as lecturer and seminar leader for management education programs here and abroad. He has a Ph.D. in industrial sociology from Columbia University. He has published widely on the subject of work life and is the coauthor of *The Man on the Assembly Line,* one of the first books to outline key questions regarding the interrelation of productivity and the quality of working life.

DELMAR L. "DUTCH" LANDEN is president of D.L. Landen and Associates, a consulting company. Prior to forming his own company in 1982, Landen was associated with General Motors as director of Organizational Research and Development, a position he held for 16 of his 25 years with GM. He has a Ph.D. in organizational psychology from Ohio State University. In addition to consulting work, Landen is adjunct professor of management and psychology at Wayne State University and serves on the boards of several work-related organizations. He is also president of the Michigan Quality of Work Life Council. He currently works with his consulting company to assist union and management groups in creating cooperative relationships.

BARRY A. MACY is director and founder of the Texas Center for Productivity and Quality of Work Life and associate professor of organizational behavior, Texas Tech University. He has a Ph.D. in organizational behavior and management science from Ohio State University and is a specialist in the field of productivity, work innovation, and work design. Previously on the faculty of the University of Michigan, he has been actively involved in employee and union–management cooperative efforts to improve organizational effectiveness and enhance quality of work life. Macy has also had organizational experience with Cooper Industries and the Aluminum Company of America and held action-research assignments with Bethesda Hospital, Chrysler Corporation, Exxon, and others.

STANLEY PETERFREUND is president of Stanley Peterfreund Associates,

Inc., a consulting firm that specializes in assisting firms to develop employee participation and involvement programs. In addition, he has amassed considerable experience in developing survey techniques for identification and resolution of employee concerns. Peterfreund has an engineering degree from Brown University and an M.B.A. from the University of Michigan. He has also been associated with Dartmouth College and Columbia University, has been involved in the evaluation of many corporate management education activities, and frequently acts as a conference leader for industry and management associations.

PHILIP C. THOMPSON is program coordinator, facilitator, and trainer in the Quality Circle Program, Denver Aerospace/Michoud Division, Martin Marietta Corporation. He received a Ph.D. in sociocultural anthropology from Tulane University in 1978, and has been associated with the University of New Orleans and Tulane University Departments of Anthropology. He has several publications and lectures to his credit, including the soon-to-be-published *Quality Circles: How to Make Them Work in America.*

ERIC TRIST is professor emeritus of social systems sciences in the Wharton School, University of Pennsylvania, and professor of organizational behaviour and social ecology in the Faculty of Environmental Studies, York University, Toronto. A graduate in psychology of Cambridge University, he was a founding member and later chairman of the Tavistock Institute in London before coming to the United States in 1966. Professor Trist's early studies of work organization in the British mining industry led to the formulation of the sociotechnical system, which has become a central feature of the quality-of-working-life movement. His best-known books are *Organizational Choice* and *Towards a Social Ecology.*

ROY W. WALTERS heads the consulting firm, Roy W. Walters and Associates, Inc. Walters specializes in the redesign of work systems in organizations to help employees perform at their optimum level of ability. Before establishing his own company in 1967, Walters, a graduate of the University of Pittsburgh, was director of employment and development at AT&T. He is widely sought after as a speaker and has published extensively, including his latest publication, *Job Enrichment for Results.* Walters is also publisher of the *Behavioral Sciences Newsletter.*

RICHARD E. WALTON, professor of business administration at the Harvard Business School, had teaching and research experience at Purdue University and UCLA before joining the Harvard faculty in 1968. From 1969 to 1976 he served as the director of the Division of Research at the Harvard

Business School. He consults with industrial firms and is a member of the board of directors of the Berol Corporation. Walton, who has a Ph.D. in business administration from Harvard University, has published several books and many articles which apply the behavioral sciences to the problems of management and other spheres of action. He is an authority in conflict resolution and a leading contributor to the literature on work restructuring in industry and quality-of-work-life issues.